THE

APOCRYPHA

TRANSLATED OUT OF THE

GREEK AND LATIN TONGUES

BEING THE VERSION SET FORTH A. D. 1611

COMPARED WITH THE MOST ANCIENT AUTHORITIES AND REVISED

A. D. 1894

THE BOOK TREE
SAN DIEGO, CALIFORNIA

Revised edition of 1611 version
First published 1894
Thomas Nelson & Sons
New York

ISBN 1-58509-053-0

Cover layout & design
Lee Berube

Printed on Acid-Free Paper
in the United States of America

Published by

The Book Tree
P O Box 16476
San Diego, CA 92176
www.thebooktree.com

We provide fascinating and educational products to help awaken the public to new ideas and
information that would not be available otherwise.
Call 1 (800) 700-8733 for our *FREE BOOK TREE CATALOG*.

INTRODUCTION

The Apocryphal books were excluded from the Bible, yet consist of writings that were considered to be sacred scriptures by certain religious sects. Apocryphal literature had its origins in early Judaism and was later adopted by early Christianity. Some of these works overshadowed the canonical scriptures in both Judaism and early Christianity, despite their canonical exclusion. This is why it is important to preserve and study them.

This volume is sometimes referred to as the Apocrypha Proper, or the Apocrypha of the Old Testament as used by English-speaking Protestants. These books were generally written later than the accepted literature but bore the names (as titled) of early Hebrew authorities in order to gain better acceptance. This includes the apocalypses that were written in quick succession following the Book of Daniel. They appeared so suddenly that Jewish authorities were forced to create an official canon to separate the newer books of questionable authorship from the older.

These books were popular with the common people not because they were "banned", but because most dealt with the coming of the Messianic Kingdom. As a result, the Jewish Apocrypha became the ordinary literature of early Christianity. In fact, the writers of the New Testament were acquainted with and influenced by the apocryphal books. This is why, during the first and second centuries, most Apocryphal books were highly esteemed. After the first and second centuries, however, these books were undermined in a number of ways.

Only books accepted by the Church as being written by the apostles of Jesus were considered truly inspired. Proof of apostolic authorship consisted of universal acceptance by the Church, and nothing more. Without this stamp of approval the apocryphal books were considered invalid and heretical.

This is interesting, as research reveals that the canonical books deemed genuine were not written by the true apostles—they were simply assigned names of the apostles to make them more acceptable. This was the primary reason that the apocryphal books were discounted (they had done the same thing, but came later). No proof exists to this day to show that any book of the Bible was written by an apostle. The accepted books were, and are, no more genuine in this regard as the apocryphal literature. If interested, there are a number of books available to the reader which clearly reveal who the authors of the canonical literature were.

The real reason that these apocryphal books were excluded had to do with control. The surprising facts surrounding the formation of the canon can be found in two additional books recommended here: *A Short History of the Bible*, by Bronson C. Keeler, and *The History of the Christian Religion to the Year 200*, by Charles Waite (in limited supply). Both are currently available from The Book Tree.

In its earlier use the term "apocryphal" was used in a laudatory sense. It referred to writings that were kept secret because they contained knowledge too sacred or too profound for those not initiated. For example, the author of Ezra (contained in this collection) considered the book to be a secret work far more valuable than the canonical scriptures because of its revelations of the future. Church fathers Irenaeus and Tertullian, however, both denied that apocryphal books were part of a secret tradition.

Later, the term apocrypha applied to writings that were kept from the public by the Church. Then finally, the term became linked to books considered heretical, false and spurious.

If one accepts the original meaning of the term, then these books become more meaningful and revealing. If one accepts the later term and considers these books heretical then one will probably not consider reading this collection. It is simply a matter of choice. In fact, the original meaning of the word "heretic" was not derogatory, either. It simply means "one who chooses."

Paul Tice

THE NAMES AND ORDER

OF THE

BOOKS CALLED APOCRYPHA.

PREFACE.

THE Version of the Apocrypha which is here presented to the Reader forms the last portion of the Revision of the Authorised Version of 1611.

The present work, owing to various circumstances, has been somewhat long delayed. It will be found, however, to have been executed carefully and faithfully, though it was of necessity intrusted to small Committees formed out of the two Companies of Revisers.

The Revision of the Authorised Version of the Apocrypha was included in the arrangement between the Companies and the Representatives of the Presses of Oxford and Cambridge, and was to be proceeded with as soon as the other and greater portions of the work were concluded. No division of labour in regard to the Apocrypha was formally made between the two Companies, but as it appeared clearly desirable that there should be no unnecessary delay in the revision, there was an understanding between the Companies that the New Testament Company should commence the work as soon as the Revision of the Authorised Version of the New Testament was completed and published. For this, preparation was made by the New Testament Company as their work was drawing to its close, and in the following manner.

It was resolved (March 21, 1879) that, after the conclusion of the Revision of the Authorised Version of the New Testament, the Company should be divided into three Committees, to be called the London, Westminster, and Cambridge Committees, for the purpose of beginning the Revision of the Apocrypha.

The London Committee was to consist of the following members:— The Bishop of Gloucester and Bristol (Dr. Ellicott), the Bishop of Salisbury (Dr. Moberly), the Bishop of St. Andrews (Dr. Wordsworth), the Dean of Rochester (Dr. Scott), the Dean of Lichfield (Dr. Bickersteth), the Master of the Temple (Dr. Vaughan), Rev. Principal Angus, and Rev. Prebendary Humphry. This Committee was to take the Book of Ecclesiasticus.

The Westminster Committee was to consist of the following members:— The Archbishop of Dublin (Dr. Trench), the Dean of Westminster (Dr. Stanley), the Archdeacon of Dublin (Dr. Lee), the Archdeacon of Oxford (Dr. Palmer), Rev. Dr. Scrivener, Rev. Principal Brown, Rev. Principal Newth, and Rev. Dr. Vance Smith. This Committee was to take the First Book of Maccabees. The Books of Tobit and Judith were afterwards, by special arrangement with the Old Testament Company, undertaken by this Committee.

The Cambridge Committee was to consist of the following members:— The Bishop of Durham (Dr. Lightfoot), the Dean of Lincoln (Mr. Blakesley), Rev. Professor Hort, Rev. Professor Kennedy, Rev. Professor Westcott, Rev. Dr. Milligan, Rev. Dr. Moulton, and Rev. Dr. Roberts. This Committee was to take the Book of Wisdom and the Second Book of Maccabees.

In connexion with the foregoing resolution it was resolved at the final meeting of the Company, on Thursday, November 11, 1880:— (1) that the decisions be arrived at by simple majorities; (2) that the successive portions of the work when printed be forwarded to the members of the other two Committees. A third resolution was passed constituting the Rev. Dr. Troutbeck the General Secretary of the three Committees, and, as such, responsible for the printing of the portions of the work as they were finished; but the latter part of this resolution was modified, and the whole of the printing was carried on at the University Press, Oxford.

The London Committee, to which the Revision of the Authorised Version of the Book of Ecclesiasticus was intrusted, commenced their labours on May 11, 1881, and completed their first revision of the Version on July 20, 1882, and their second and final revision on May 25, 1883. The breaking up of the text of the Version into parallelisms was undertaken at a later period. Of the members of the Committee, two, the Bishops of Salisbury and St. Andrews, found themselves unable through age and distance from London to attend the meetings. The attendance of the remainder was such that there were rarely less than four present. Whenever the number fell below this, all debateable points were reserved for fuller meetings. Considerable attention was paid to the text; but the materials available for correcting it were but scanty. In regard to the revision of the Version, especial care was taken to preserve the general tone of the Authorised Version, and to maintain the somewhat greater freedom of rendering which characterizes the translation of the Apocrypha when compared with the translation of the Old or of the New Testament.

The Westminster Committee completed their first revision of the First Book of Maccabees on July 5, their second revision on November 3, 1881. Their first revision of the Books of Judith and Tobit was completed on July 6, their second revision on October 11, 1882. With regard to the Greek text they derived great assistance from Dr. Scrivener, but the number of places in which it was thought right to abandon readings that seemed to be represented in the Authorised Version was not large. The English Version was found to require much care. In the First Book of Maccabees, for example, a well-known peculiarity of the writer had been obliterated by the repeated introduction, with or without the use of italics, of the words 'God' and 'the Lord,' which never occur in the best Greek text. Archbishop Trench worked with the Committee until they were close to the end of the First Book of Maccabees. Dean Stanley also attended up to about the same time: Principal Brown did not take any part in the work.

Of the members of the Cambridge Committee the Bishop of Durham (Dr. Lightfoot), the Dean of Lincoln (Mr. Blakesley), and Professor Kennedy were compelled for various reasons to withdraw from the work of revision. Dr. Roberts supplied notes on various parts of the two books. Dr. Hort, Dr. Moulton and Dr. Westcott conducted the revision with this assistance at weekly meetings during term time from March 3, 1881 to the spring of 1890, when Dr. Westcott was removed to Durham. In the remainder of the work Dr. Westcott took part by correspondence. The first revision of 2 Maccabees was completed on May 20, 1885, and the final revision December 7, 1889. The first revision of Wisdom was completed between May 20, 1885 and June 20, 1888; and the second revision between November 23, 1889 and November 21, 1891. The singular difficulty and importance of the Book of Wisdom led the revisers to review the version a third time. The whole revision of the two books was substantially completed before the summer of 1892. A few questions were reserved for later decision. These were considered by Dr. Hort in the summer of that year, and, with the help of his notes, finally determined by Dr. Westcott and Dr. Moulton.

After the revision of the Old Testament had been completed the Old Testament Company (July 9, 1884) passed the following resolution : —

'That the Dean of Peterborough (Dr. Perowne), Professor Lumby, Professor Robertson Smith, Mr. Bensly, Mr. Cheyne, and the Secretary (Mr. Aldis Wright) be a Committee to translate the remaining books of the Apocrypha, and

That Dr. Field be invited to assist in the formation of the text.'

The Dean of Peterborough (Dr. Perowne), now Bishop of Worcester, and Mr. (now Professor) Cheyne, found themselves unable to take part in the work, and the Committee were deprived of the assistance of Dr. Field by his death in April, 1885.

The Books of the Apocrypha which were left for them to revise were 1 and 2 Esdras, the additions to Esther, Baruch, the Song of the Three Holy Children, the History of Susanna, Bel and the Dragon, and the Prayer of Manasses.

For the text of these portions, with the exception of 2 Esdras, they were entirely dependent upon the inadequate materials already existing, and did not therefore attempt any complete revision. But as the late Professor Bensly had reconstructed the text of the Latin version of 2 Esdras from a full collation of all the independent MSS. at present known, the Committee fully availed themselves of the results which he generously placed at their disposal. They were thus able to incorporate the missing fragment, vii. 36–105, which was edited by Professor Bensly with elaborate care, and published by the Cambridge University Press (1875), and to make use of many improved readings which he proposed to adopt in his critical edition. It is satisfactory to know that this work has been left in a sufficiently forward state to admit of its being easily completed.

In regard to the language of the Revised Version the Committee followed the general principles which were observed by the Old Testament Revision Company.

In the case of Proper Names it has not been found possible to secure uniformity of plan in the work of the four Committees. In some Books these names appear in their familiar Old Testament forms, after the Hebrew ; whilst in others, the forms of the Authorised Version are usually retained, or are but slightly altered, in accordance with the Greek. Lists of the Greek readings — or, in 2 Esdras, the Latin readings — adopted by the Committees will shortly be published.

Such is a brief account of the circumstances under which the present work was executed. The Revisers conclude with the hope and the belief that it will be found helpful to the student, and acceptable to the general reader of the Apocrypha.

January, 1895.

I. ESDRAS.

1 2 Kings
xxiii. 21 ;
2 Chr.
xxxv. 1,
&c.

1 AND ¹ Josias held the passover in Jerusalem unto his Lord, and offered the passover the fourteenth day of the 2 first month; having set the priests according to their daily courses, being arrayed in their vestments, in the 3 temple of the Lord. And he spake unto the Levites, ² the temple-servants of Israel, that they should hallow themselves unto the Lord, to set the holy ark of the Lord in the house that king Solomon the son of David had 4 built: *and said,* Ye shall no more have need to bear it upon your shoulders: now therefore serve the Lord your God, and minister unto his people Israel, and prepare you after your 5 fathers' houses and kindreds, according to the writing of David king of Israel, and according to the magnificence of Solomon his son: and standing in the holy place according to the several divisions of the families of you the Levites, who *minister* in the presence of your brethren the children 6 of Israel, offer the passover in order, and make ready the sacrifices for your brethren, and keep the passover according to the commandment of the Lord, which was given unto Mo- 7 ses. And unto the people which were present Josias gave thirty thousand lambs and kids, *and* three thousand calves: these things were given of the king's substance, according as he promised, to the people, and to the 8 priests and Levites. And Helkias, and Zacharias, and ³ Esyelus, the rulers of the temple, gave to the priests for the passover two thousand *and* six hundred sheep, *and* three hundred calves. 9 And Jeconias, and Samaias, and Nathanael his brother, and Sabias, and Ochielus, and Joram, captains over thousands, gave to the Levites for the passover five thousand sheep, *and* 10 seven hundred calves. And when these things were done, the priests and Levites, having the unleavened bread, stood in comely order accord- 11 ing to the kindreds, and according to the several divisions by fathers' houses, before the people, to offer to the Lord, as it is written in the book of Moses: and thus *did they* in the 12 morning. And they roasted the passover with fire, as appertaineth: and the sacrifices they sod in the brasen vessels and caldrons with a good sa- 13 vour: and set them before all the people: and afterward they prepared for themselves, and for the priests their 14 brethren, the sons of Aaron. For the priests offered the fat until night: and the Levites prepared for themselves, and for the priests their bre- 15 thren, the sons of Aaron. The holy singers also, the sons of Asaph, were in their order, according to the appointment of David, *to wit,* Asaph, Zacharias, and Eddinus, who ⁴ was 16 of the king's retinue. Moreover the porters were at every gate; none had need to depart from his daily course: for their brethren the Levites pre- 17 pared for them. Thus were the things that belonged to the sacrifices of the Lord accomplished in that day, in 18 holding the passover, and offering sacrifices upon the altar of the Lord, according to the commandment of 19 king Josias. So the children of Israel which were present at that time held the passover, and the feast of 20 unleavened bread seven days. And such a passover was not held in Israel since the time of the prophet Samuel. 21 Yea, all the kings of Israel held not such a passover as Josias, and the priests, and the Levites, and the Jews, held with all Israel that were present in their dwelling place at Jerusalem. 22 In the eighteenth year of the reign of 23 Josias was this passover held. And the works of Josias were upright before his Lord with a heart full of 24 godliness. Moreover the things that came to pass in his days have been written in times past, concerning those that sinned, and did wickedly against the Lord above every people and kingdom, and how they grieved him ⁵ exceedingly, so that the words of the Lord were confirmed against Israel. 25 ⁶ Now after all these acts of Josias it came to pass, that Pharaoh the king of Egypt came to raise war at Carchemish upon Euphrates: and Josias 26 went out against him. But the king of Egypt sent to him, saying, What have I to do with thee, O king of Ju- 27 dæa? I am not sent out from the Lord God against thee; for my war is upon Euphrates: and now the Lord is with me, yea, the Lord is with me hasting me forward: depart from me, 28 and be not against the Lord. Howbeit Josias did not turn back ⁷ unto his chariot, but undertook to fight with him, not regarding the words of the prophet Jeremy *spoken* by the 29 mouth of the Lord: but joined battle with him in the plain of Megiddo, and the princes came down against king

2 Thatis,
the Ne-
thinim.
See
Num.
iii. 9.

3 Jehiel,
2 Chr.
xxxv. 8.

4 An-
other
reading
is, were.

5 Or.
sensibly
Jud.
xvi. 17.

6 2 Chr.
xxxv. 20
&c.

7 An-
other
reading
is, his
chariot
from
him.

30 Josias. Then said the king unto his servants, Carry me away out of the battle; for I am very weak. And immediately his servants carried him
31 away out of the host. Then gat he up upon his second chariot; and being brought back to Jerusalem he died, and was buried in the sepulchre of
32 his fathers. And in all Jewry they mourned for Josias; and Jeremy the prophet lamented for Josias, and the chief men with the women made lamentation for him, unto this day: and this was given out for an ordinance to be done continually in all the nation of
33 Israel. These things are written in the book of the histories of the kings of Judæa, and every one of the acts that Josias did, and his glory, and his understanding in the law of the Lord, and the things that he had done before, and the things now *recited*, are reported in the book of the kings of Israel and Judah.

¹ 2 Kings xxiii. 30; 2 Chr. xxxvi. 1.
² Another reading is, *Jeco-nias*.
³ Another reading is, *Israel*.

34 ¹ And the people took ² Joachaz the son of Josias, and made him king instead of Josias his father, when he was
35 twenty and three years old. And he reigned in ³ Judah and in Jerusalem three months: and then the king of Egypt deposed him from reigning in
36 Jerusalem. And he set a tax upon the people of a hundred talents of silver
37 and one talent of gold. The king of Egypt also made king Joakim his brother king of Judæa and Jerusalem.
38 And Joakim bound the nobles: but Zarakes his brother he apprehended, and brought him up out of Egypt.

⁴ 2 Chr. xxxvi. 4, 5.

39 Five and twenty years old was ⁴ Joakim when he began to reign in Judæa and Jerusalem; and he did that which
40 was evil in the sight of the Lord. And against him Nabuchodonosor the king of Babylon came up, and bound him with a chain of brass, and carried him
41 unto Babylon. Nabuchodonosor also took of the holy vessels of the Lord, and carried them away, and set them
42 up in his own temple at Babylon. But those things that are reported of him, and of his uncleanness and impiety, are written in the chronicles of the kings.
43 And Joakim his son reigned in his stead: for when he was made king

⁵ Another reading is, *eight*.

44 he was ⁵ eighteen years old; and he reigned three months and ten days in Jerusalem; and did that which was evil before the Lord.
45 So after a year Nabuchodonosor sent and caused him to be brought unto Babylon with the holy vessels of the
46 Lord; and made Sedekias king of Judæa and Jerusalem, when he was one and twenty years old; and he reigned
47 eleven years: and he also did that which was evil in the sight of the Lord, and cared not for the words that were spoken by Jeremy the prophet from the mouth of the Lord.

48 And after that king Nabuchodonosor had made him to swear by the name of the Lord, he forswore himself, and rebelled; and hardening his neck, and his heart, he transgressed the laws of
49 the Lord, the God of Israel. Moreover the governors of the people and of the priests did many things wickedly, ⁶ and passed all the pollutions of all nations, and defiled the temple of the Lord, which was sanctified in
50 Jerusalem. And the God of their fathers sent by his messenger to call them back, because he had compassion on them and on his dwelling place.
51 But they mocked his messengers; and in the day when the Lord spake *unto them*, they scoffed at his pro-
52 phets: so far forth, that he, being wroth with his people for their great ungodliness, commanded to bring up the kings of the Chaldeans against
53 them; who slew their young men with the sword, round about their holy temple, and spared neither young man nor maid, old man nor child; but
54 he delivered all into their hands. And they took all the holy vessels of the Lord, both great and small, with ⁷ the vessels of the ark of the Lord, and the king's treasures, and carried them
55 away unto Babylon. And they burnt the house of the Lord, and brake down the walls of Jerusalem, and burnt the
56 towers thereof with fire: and as for her glorious things, they never ceased till they had brought them all to nought: and the people that were not slain with the sword he carried
57 unto Babylon: and they were servants unto him and to his children, till the Persians reigned, to fulfil the word of the Lord by the mouth of
58 Jeremy: Until the land enjoyed her sabbaths, the whole time of her desolation shall she keep sabbath, to fulfil threescore and ten years.

⁶ Another reading is, *even above all.*

⁷ Another reading is, *the arks of the Lord.*

2 In the ⁸ first year of Cyrus king of the Persians, that the word of the Lord by the mouth of Jeremy might be ac-
2 complished, the Lord stirred up the spirit of Cyrus king of the Persians, and he made proclamation through all his kingdom, and also by writing,
3 saying, Thus saith Cyrus king of the Persians; The Lord of Israel, the Most High Lord, hath made me king
4 of the whole world, and commanded me to build him a house at Jerusalem
5 that is in Judæa. If therefore there be any of you that are of his people, ⁹ let the Lord, even his Lord, be with him, and let him go up to Jerusalem that is in Judæa, and build the house of the Lord of Israel: he is the Lord
6 that dwelleth in Jerusalem. Of such therefore as dwell in divers places, let them that are in his own place help each one with gold, and with sil-
7 ver, with gifts, with horses also and

⁸ 2 Chr. xxxvi. 22, 23; Ezra i. 1, &c.

⁹ Another reading is, *let his Lord be* &c.

cattle, beside the other things which have been added by vow for the temple of the Lord which is in Jerusalem.

8 Then the chief of the families of Judah and of the tribe of Benjamin stood up; the priests also, and the Levites, and all they whose spirit the Lord had stirred to go up, to build the house for the Lord which is in

9 Jerusalem. And they that dwelt round about them helped them in all things with silver and gold, with horses and cattle, and with very many gifts that were vowed of a great number whose

10 minds were stirred up *thereto.* King Cyrus also brought forth the holy vessels of the Lord, which Nabuchodonosor had carried away from Jerusalem, and had set up in his temple of

11 idols. Now when Cyrus king of the Persians had brought them forth, he delivered them to Mithradates his

12 treasurer, and by him they were delivered to [1] Sanabassar the governor

13 of Judæa. And this was the number of them: A thousand golden cups, a thousand cups of silver, censers of silver twenty nine, vials of gold thirty, and of silver two thousand four hundred and ten, and other vessels a thousand.

14 So all the vessels of gold and of silver were brought up, even five thousand

15 four hundred threescore and nine, and were carried back by Sanabassar, together with them of the captivity, from Babylon to Jerusalem.

16 [2] But in the time of Artaxerxes king of the Persians Belemus, and Mithradates, and Tabellius, and [3] Rathumus, and Beeltethmus, and [4] Samellius the scribe, with the others that were in commission with them, dwelling in Samaria and other places, wrote unto him against them that dwelt in Judæa and Jerusalem the letter following:

17 To king Artaxerxes our lord, Thy servants, Rathumus the [5] storywriter, and Samellius the scribe, and the rest of their council, and the judges that

18 are in Cœlesyria and Phœnicia. Be it now known to our lord the king, that the Jews that are come up from you to us, being come unto Jerusalem, do build that rebellious and wicked city, and do repair the marketplaces and the walls of it, and do lay the

19 foundation of a temple. Now if this city be builded and the walls *thereof* be finished, they will not only refuse to give tribute, but will even stand up

20 against kings. And forasmuch as the things pertaining to the temple are now in hand, we think it meet not to

21 neglect such a matter, but to speak unto our lord the king, to the intent that, if it be thy pleasure, search may be made in the books of thy fathers:

22 and thou shalt find in the chronicles what is written concerning these things, and shalt understand that that

[margin notes left column:]
[1] Another reading is, *Samanassar.*

[2] Ezra iv. 7.

[3] *Rehum.*
[4] *Shimshai.*

[5] Or, *recorder*

city was rebellious, troubling both

23 kings and cities: and that the Jews were rebellious, and raised always wars therein of old time; for the which cause even this city was laid

24 waste. Wherefore now we do declare unto thee, O lord the king, that if this city be builded again, and the walls thereof set up anew, thou shalt from henceforth have no passage into Cœle-

25 syria and Phœnicia. Then the king wrote back again to Rathumus the storywriter, and Beeltethmus, and Samellius the scribe, and to the rest that were in commission, and dwelt in Samaria and Syria and Phœnicia,

26 after this manner: I have read the epistle which ye have sent unto me: therefore I commanded to make search, and it hath been found that that city of old time hath made insurrection

27 against kings; and the men were given to rebellion and war therein: and that mighty kings and fierce were in Jerusalem, who reigned and exacted tribute in Cœlesyria and Phœnicia.

28 Now therefore I have commanded to hinder those men from building the city, and heed to be taken that there be nothing done contrary to

29 this *order*; and that those wicked doings proceed no further to the an-

30 noyance of kings. Then king Artaxerxes his letters being read, Rathumus, and Samellius the scribe, and the rest that were in commission with them, removing in haste unto Jerusalem with horsemen and a multitude of people in battle array, began to hinder the builders; and the building of the temple in Jerusalem ceased until the second year of the reign of Darius king of the Persians.

3 Now king Darius made a great feast unto all his subjects, and unto all that were born in his house, and unto all the princes of Media and of Persia,

2 and to all the satraps and captains and governors that were under him, from India unto Ethiopia, in the hundred

3 twenty and seven provinces. And when they had eaten and drunken, and being satisfied were gone home, then Darius the king went into his bedchamber, and slept, and awaked out of his sleep.

4 Then the three young men of the body-guard, that kept the king's per-

5 son, spake one to another: Let every one of us say one thing which shall be strongest: and he whose sentence shall seem wiser than the others, unto him shall Darius the king give great gifts, and great honours in token of victory:

6 as, to be clothed in purple, to drink in gold, and to sleep upon gold, and a chariot with bridles of gold, and a headtire of fine linen, and a chain about

7 his neck: and he shall sit next to Darius because of his wisdom, and

8 shall be called Darius his cousin. And then they wrote every one his sentence, and set to their seals, and laid *the writing* under king Darius his pil-
9 low, and said, When the king is risen, some shall give him the writing; and of whose side the king and the three princes of Persia shall judge that his sentence is the wisest, to him shall the
10 victory be given, as it is written. The
11 first wrote, Wine is the strongest. The second wrote, The king is strongest.
12 The third wrote, Women are strongest: but above all things Truth beareth away the victory.
13 Now when the king was risen up, they took the writing, and gave it unto
14 him, and so he read it: and sending forth he called all the princes of Persia and of Media, and the satraps, and the captains, and the governors, and
15 the chief officers: and sat him down in the royal seat of judgement; and the
16 writing was read before them. And he said, Call the young men, and they shall explain their own sentences. So
17 they were called, and came in. And they said unto them, Declare unto us your mind concerning the things ye have written.

Then began the first, who had spoken
18 of the strength of wine, and said thus, O sirs, how exceeding strong is wine! it causeth all men to err that drink it:
19 it maketh the mind of the king and of the fatherless child to be all one; of the bondman and of the freeman, of
20 the poor man and of the rich: it turneth also every thought into jollity and mirth, so that a man remembereth
21 neither sorrow nor debt: and it maketh every heart rich, so that a man remembereth neither king nor satrap; and it maketh to speak all things by
22 talents: and when they are in their cups, they forget their love both to friends and brethren, and a little after
23 draw their swords: but when they awake from their wine, they remem-
24 ber not what they have done. O sirs, is not wine the strongest, seeing that it enforceth to do thus? And when he had so spoken, he held his peace.

4 Then the second, that had spoken of the strength of the king, began to say,
2 O sirs, do not men excel in strength, that bear rule over the sea and land,
3 and all things in them? But yet is the king stronger: and he is their lord, and hath dominion over them; and in whatsoever he commandeth them they
4 obey him. If he bid them make war the one against the other, they do it: and if he send them out against the enemies, they go, and overcome moun-
5 tains, walls, and towers. They slay and are slain, and transgress not the king's commandment: if they get the victory, they bring all to the king, as
6 well the spoil, as all things else. Like-

wise for those that are no soldiers, and have not to do with wars, but use husbandry, when they have reaped again that which they had sown, they bring it to the king, and compel one another
7 to pay tribute unto the king. And he is [1] but one man: if he command to kill, they kill; if he command to spare,
8 they spare; if he command to smite, they smite; if he command to make desolate, they make desolate; if he
9 command to build, they build; if he command to cut down, they cut down; if he command to plant, they plant.
10 So all his people and his armies obey him: furthermore he lieth down, he eateth and drinketh, and taketh his
11 rest: and these keep watch round about him, neither may any one depart, and do his own business, neither
12 disobey they him *in anything.* O sirs, how should not the king be strongest, seeing that in such sort he is obeyed? And he held his peace.
13 Then the third, who had spoken of women, and of truth, (this was Zoro-
14 babel) began to speak. O sirs, is not the king great, and men are many, and wine is strong? who is it then that ruleth them, or hath the lordship over
15 them? are they not women? Women have borne the king and all the people
16 that bear rule by sea and land. Even of them came they: and they nourished them up that planted the vineyards, from whence the wine cometh.
17 These also make garments for men; these bring glory unto men; and with-
18 out women cannot men be. Yea, and if men have gathered together gold and silver and every other goodly thing, [2] and see a woman which is
19 comely in favour and beauty, they let all those things go, and gape after her, and even with open mouth fix their eyes fast on her; and have all more desire unto her than unto gold or silver, or any goodly thing whatsoever.
20 A man leaveth his own father that brought him up, and his own country,
21 and cleaveth unto his wife. And with his wife he endeth his days, and remembereth neither father, nor mo-
22 ther, nor country. By this also ye must know that women have dominion over you: do ye not labour and toil, and give and bring all to women?
23 Yea, a man taketh his sword, and goeth forth to make outroads, and to rob and to steal, and to sail upon the sea
24 and upon rivers; and looketh upon a lion, and walketh in the darkness; and when he hath stolen, spoiled, and robbed, he bringeth it to his love.
25 Wherefore a man loveth his wife bet-
26 ter than father or mother. Yea, many there be that have run out of their wits for women, and become bondmen
27 for their sakes. Many also have perished, have stumbled, and sinned, for

[1] Or, one and alone

[2] Another reading is. *do they not love &c.*

28 women. And now do ye not believe me? is not the king great in his power? do not all regions fear to 29 touch him? Yet did I see him and Apame the king's concubine, the daughter of the illustrious Bartacus, sitting at the right hand of the king, 30 and taking the crown from the king's head, and setting it upon her own head; yea, she struck the king with 31 her left hand: and therewithal the king gaped and gazed upon her with open mouth: if she laughed upon him, he laughed also: but if she took any displeasure at him, he was fain to flatter, that she might be reconciled to 32 him again. O sirs, how can it be but women should be strong, seeing they do thus?

33 Then the king and the nobles looked one upon another: so he began to 34 speak concerning truth. O sirs, are not women strong? great is the earth, high is the heaven, swift is the sun in his course, for he compasseth the heavens round about, and fetcheth his course again to his own place in one 35 day. Is he not great that maketh these things? therefore great is truth, 36 and stronger than all things. All the earth calleth upon truth, and the heaven blesseth her: all works shake and tremble, but with [1] her is no un- 37 righteous thing. Wine is unrighteous, the king is unrighteous, women are unrighteous, all the children of men are unrighteous, and unrighteous are all such their works; and there is no truth in them; in their unrighteous- 38 ness also they shall perish. But truth abideth, and is strong for ever; she liveth and conquereth for evermore. 39 With her there is no accepting of persons or rewards; but she doeth the things that are just, *and refraineth* from all unrighteous and wicked things; and all men do well like of her 40 works. Neither in her judgement is any unrighteousness; and she is the strength, and the kingdom, and the power, and the majesty, of all ages. 41 Blessed be the God of truth. And with that he held his tongue. And all the people then shouted, and said, Great is truth, and strong above all things. 42 Then said the king unto him, Ask what thou wilt more than is appointed in writing, and we will give it thee, inasmuch as thou art found wisest; and thou shalt sit next me, and shalt 43 be called my cousin. Then said he unto the king, Remember thy vow, which thou didst vow to build Jerusalem, in the day when thou camest to 44 thy kingdom, and to send away all the vessels that were taken out of Jerusalem, which Cyrus set apart, when he vowed to destroy Babylon, and vowed to send them again thither. 45 Thou didst also vow to build up the

temple, which the Edomites burned when Judæa was made desolate by 46 the Chaldeans. And now, O lord the king, this is that which I require, and which I desire of thee, and this is the princely liberality that shall proceed from thee: I pray therefore that thou make good the vow, the performance whereof thou hast vowed to the King of heaven with thine own mouth.

47 Then Darius the king stood up, and kissed him, and wrote letters for him unto all the treasurers and governors and captains and satraps, that they should safely bring on their way both him, and all those that should go up 48 with him to build Jerusalem. He wrote letters also unto all the governors that were in Cœlesyria and Phœnicia, and unto them in Libanus, that they should bring cedar wood from Libanus unto Jerusalem, and that they should build the city with him. 49 Moreover he wrote for all the Jews that should go out of his realm up into Jewry, concerning their freedom, that no officer, no governor, no satrap, nor treasurer, should forcibly enter into 50 their doors; and that all the country which they occupied should be free to them without tribute; and that the Edomites should give over the villages of the Jews which then they 51 held: and that there should be yearly given twenty talents to the building of the temple, until the time that it 52 were built; and other ten talents yearly, for burnt offerings to be presented upon the altar every day, as they had a commandment to offer 53 seventeen: and that all they that should come from Babylonia to build the city should have their freedom, as well they as their posterity, and all 54 the priests that came. He wrote also *to give them* their charges, and the priests' vestments wherein they min- 55 ister; and for the Levites he wrote that their charges should be given them until the day that the house were finished, and Jerusalem builded 56 up. And he commanded to give to all that kept the city lands and wages. 57 He sent away also all the vessels from Babylon, that Cyrus had set apart; and all that Cyrus had given in commandment, the same charged he also to be done, and sent unto Jerusalem.

58 Now when this young man was gone forth, he lifted up his face to heaven toward Jerusalem, and praised the 59 King of heaven, and said, From thee cometh victory, from thee cometh wisdom, and thine is the glory, and 60 I am thy servant. Blessed art thou, who hast given me wisdom: and to thee I give thanks, O Lord of our 61 fathers. And so he took the letters, and went out, and came unto Babylon.

62 and told it all his brethren. And they praised the God of their fathers, because he had given them freedom and 63 liberty to go up, and to build Jerusalem, and the temple which is called by his name: and they feasted with instruments of music and gladness seven days.

5 After these were the chiefs of fathers' houses chosen to go up according to their tribes, with their wives and sons and daughters, with their menservants and maidservants, and their 2 cattle. And Darius sent with them a thousand horsemen, till they had brought them back to Jerusalem [1] safely, and with musical instruments, 3 tabrets and flutes. And all their brethren played, and he made them go up together with them.

4 And these are the names of the men which went up, according to their families amongst their tribes, after their 5 several divisions. The priests, the sons of Phinees, the sons of Aaron: Jesus the son of Josedek, the son of Saraias, and Joakim the son of Zorobabel, the son of Salathiel, of the house of David, of the lineage of 6 Phares, of the tribe of Judah; who spake wise sentences before Darius the king of Persia in the second year of his reign, in the month Nisan, which 7 is the first month. [2] And these are they of Jewry that came up from the captivity, where they dwelt as strangers, whom Nabuchodonosor the king of Babylon had carried away unto 8 Babylon. And they returned unto Jerusalem, and to the other parts of Jewry, every man to his own city, who came with Zorobabel, with Jesus, Nehemias, *and* [3] Zaraias, Resaias, [4] Eneneus, Mardocheus, Beelsarus, [5] Aspharasus, [6] Reelias, Roimus, *and* 9 Baana, their leaders. The number of them of the nation, and their leaders: the sons of [7] Phoros, two thousand a hundred seventy and two: the sons of [8] Saphat, four hundred seventy and 10 two: the sons of [9] Ares, seven hundred 11 fifty and six: the sons of [10] Phaath Moab, of the sons of Jesus and Joab, two thousand eight hundred and 12 twelve: the sons of Elam, a thousand two hundred fifty and four: the sons of [11] Zathui, nine hundred forty and five: the sons of [12] Chorbe, seven hundred and five: the sons of Bani, six 13 hundred forty and eight: the sons of Bebai, six hundred twenty and three: the sons of [13] Astad, [14] a thousand three 14 hundred twenty and two: the sons of Adonikam, six hundred sixty and seven: the sons of [15] Bagoi, two thousand sixty and six: the sons of [16] Adinu, 15 four hundred fifty and four: the sons of [17] Ater, of Ezekias, ninety and two: the sons of Kilan and Azetas, threescore and seven: the sons of [18] Azaru,

16 four hundred thirty and two: the sons of [19] Annis, a hundred and one: the sons of Arom: the sons of [20] Bassai, three hundred twenty and three: the sons of Arsiphurith, a hundred and 17 twelve: the sons of Baiterus, three thousand and five: the sons of [21] Bethlomon, a hundred twenty and three: 18 they of Netophas, fifty and five: they of Anathoth, a hundred fifty and eight: they of [22] Bethasmoth, forty and 19 two: they of [23] Kariathiarius, twenty and five: they of Caphira and Beroth, 20 seven hundred forty and three: the Chadiasai and Ammidioi, four hundred twenty and two: they of [24] Kirama and [25] Gabbe, six hundred twenty 21 and one: they of [26] Macalon, a hundred twenty and two: they of [27] Betolion, fifty and two: the sons of [28] Niphis, a hundred fifty and six: the sons of [29] Calamolalus and [30] Onus, seven hundred twenty and five: the sons of [31] Jerechu, [32] three hundred forty and 23 five: the sons of [33] Sanaas, three thousand three hundred and [34] thirty. 24 The priests: the sons of [35] Jeddu, the son of Jesus, among the sons of Sanasib, [36] nine hundred seventy and two: the sons of [37] Emmeruth, [38] a thousand 25 fifty and two: the sons of [39] Phassurus, a thousand two hundred forty and seven: the sons of [40] Charme, [38] a thousand 26 sand and seventeen. The Levites: the sons of Jesus, and Kadmiel, and Bannas, and Sudias, seventy and four. 27 The holy singers: the sons of Asaph, 28 a hundred [41] twenty and eight. The porters: the sons of [42] Salum, the sons of [43] Atar, the sons of Tolman, the sons of [44] Dacubi, the sons of [45] Ateta, the sons of [46] Sabi, in all a hundred 29 thirty and nine. The temple-servants: the sons of [47] Esau, the sons of [48] Asipha, the sons of Tabaoth, the sons of [49] Keras, the sons of [50] Sua, the sons of [51] Phaleas, the sons of Labana, the 30 sons of [52] Aggaba, the sons of [44] Acud, the sons of Uta, the sons of Ketab, the sons of [53] Accaba, the sons of [54] Subai, the sons of [55] Anan, the sons of [56] Ca-31 thua, the sons of [57] Geddur, the sons of [58] Jairus, the sons of [59] Daisan, the sons of [60] Noeba, the sons of Chaseba, the sons of [61] Gazera, the sons of [62] Ozias, the sons of [63] Phinoe, the sons of Asara, the sons of [64] Basthai, the sons of [65] Asana, the sons of [66] Maani, the sons of [67] Naphisi, the sons of [68] Acub, the sons of [69] Achipha, the sons of [70] Asur, the sons of Pharakim, 32 the sons of [71] Basaloth, the sons of [72] Meedda, the sons of Cutha, the sons of [73] Charea, the sons of [74] Barchus, the sons of [75] Serar, the sons of [76] Tho-

---

[1] Gr. *with peace.*

[2] Ezra ii. 1, &c.

[3] *Seraiah.*
[4] Or, *Enenis*
[5] *Mispar.*
[6] *Reelaiah.*
[7] *Parosh.*
[8] *Shephatiah.*
[9] *Arah.*
[10] *Pahathmoab.*
[11] *Zattu.*
[12] *Zaccai.*
[13] *Azgad.*
[14] According to other readings, 3622, or 3222.
[15] *Bigvai.*
[16] *Adin.*
[17] *Ater of Hezekiah.*
[18] Another reading is, *Azuru.*

[19] Another reading is, *Annius.*
[20] *Bezai.*
[21] *Bethlehem.*
[22] *Azmaveth.*
[23] *Kiriatharim,* or *Kiriathjearim.*
[24] *Ramah.*
[25] *Geba*
[26] *Michmas.*
[27] *Bethel.*
[28] *Magbish.*
[29] *Lod, Hadid.*
[30] *Ono.*
[31] *Jericho.*
[32] Another reading is, *two.*
[33] *Senaah.*
[34] Another reading is, *one.*
[35] *Jedaiah.*
[36] Another reading is, *eight.*
[37] *Immer.*
[38] Another reading is, *two hundred.*
[39] *Pashhur.*
[40] *Harim.*
[41] Another reading is, *forty.*
[42] *Shallum.*
[43] *Ater.*
[44] *Akkub.*
[45] *Hatita.*
[46] *Shobai.*
[47] *Zika.*
[48] *Hasupha.*
[49] *Keros.*
[50] *Siaha.*
[51] *Padon.*
[52] *Hagabah.*
[53] *Hagab.*
[54] *Shamlai.*
[55] *Hanan.*

[56] *Giddel.* [57] *Gahar.* [58] *Reaiah.* [59] *Rezin.* [60] *Nekoda.* [61] *Gazzam.* [62] *Uzza.* [63] *Paseah.* [64] *Besai.* [65] *Asnah.* [66] *Meunim.* [67] *Nephisim.* [68] *Bakbuk.* According to other readings, *Acum,* or *Acuph.* [69] *Hakupha.* [70] *Harhur.* [71] *Bazluth.* [72] *Mehida.* [73] *Harsha.* [74] *Barkos.* [75] *Sisera.* [76] *Temah.*

1 *Ne-ziah.* Another reading is, *Nasith.*
2 *Hasso-phereth.*
3 *Pe-ruda.*
4 *Jaalah.*
5 *Dar-kon.*
6 *Giddel.*
7 *She-phatiah.*
8 *Hat-til.*
9 *Poche-reth-haz-zebaim,* Ezra ii. 57.
10 Another reading is, *Misaias.*
11 *Tel-melah.*
12 *Tel-harsha.*
13 *Che-rub, Addan.*
14 *Dela-iah.* Another reading is, *Asan.*
15 *To-biah.* Another reading is, *Bae-nan.*
16 *Ne-koda.*
17 *Haba-iah,* or *Hoba-iah.*
18 *Hak-koz.*
19 *Bar-zillai.* Another reading is, *Phae-zeldaeus.*
20 Gr. *the manifes-tation and truth.*
21 Another reading is, *hun-dred.*

mei, the sons of [1] Nasi, the sons of 33 Atipha. The sons of the servants of Solomon : the sons of [2] Assaphioth, the sons of [3] Pharida, the sons of [4] Jeeli, the sons of [5] Lozon, the sons of [6] Isdael, the sons of [7] Saphuthi, 34 the sons of [8] Agia, the sons of [9] Pha-careth, the sons of Sabie, the sons of Sarothie, the sons of [10] Masias, the sons of Gas, the sons of Addus, the sons of Subas, the sons of Apherra, the sons of Barodis, the sons of Sa- 35 phat, the sons of Allon. All the tem-ple-servants, and the sons of the ser-vants of Solomon, were three hundred 36 seventy and two. These came up from [11] Thermeleth, and [12] Thelersas, [13] Charaathalan leading them, and 37 Allar ; and they could not shew their families, nor their stock, how they were of Israel : the sons of [14] Dalan the son of [15] Ban, the sons of [16] Neko- 38 dan, six hundred fifty and two. And of the priests, they that usurped the office of the priesthood and were not found : the sons of [17] Obdia, the sons of [18] Akkos, the sons of Jaddus, who married Augia one of the daughters of [19] Zorzelleus, and was called after 39 his name. And when the description of the kindred of these men was sought in the register, and was not found, they were removed from exe- 40 cuting the office of the priesthood : for unto them said Nehemias and Attha-rias, that they should not be partakers of the holy things, till there arose up a high priest wearing [20] Urim and 41 Thummim. So all they of Israel, from twelve years old *and upward,* beside menservants and womenser-vants, were *in number* forty and two thousand three hundred and sixty. 42 Their menservants and handmaids were seven thousand three hundred thirty and seven: the minstrels and singers, two hundred forty and five : 43 four hundred thirty and five camels, seven [21] thousand thirty and six horses, two hundred forty and five mules, five thousand five hundred twenty and five beasts of burden. 44 And certain of the chief men of their families, when they came to the tem-ple of God that is in Jerusalem, vow-ed to set up the house again in its own place according to their ability, 45 and to give into the holy treasury of the works a thousand pounds of gold, five thousand of silver, and a hundred 46 priestly vestments. And the priests and the Levites and they that were of the people dwelt in Jerusalem and the country ; the holy singers also and the porters and all Israel in their villages. 47 But when the seventh month was at hand, and when the children of Israel were every man in his own place, they came all together with one consent into the broad place before the first 48 porch which is toward the east. Then stood up Jesus the son of Josedek, and his brethren the priests, and Zoro-babel the son of Salathiel, and his brethren, and made ready the altar of 49 the God of Israel, to offer burnt sac-rifices upon it, according as it is expressly commanded in the book of 50 Moses the man of God. And certain were gathered unto them out of the other nations of the land, and they erected the altar upon its own place, because all the nations of the land were at enmity with them, and op-pressed them ; and they offered sacri-fices according to the time, and burnt offerings to the Lord both morning 51 and evening. Also they held the feast of tabernacles, as it is commanded in the law, and *offered* sacrifices daily, 52 as was meet : and after that, the con-tinual oblations, and the sacrifices of the sabbaths, and of the new moons, and of all the consecrated feasts. 53 And all they that had made any vow to God began to offer sacrifices to God from the new moon of the [22] se-venth month, although the temple of 54 God was not yet built. And they gave money unto the masons and car- 55 penters ; and meat and drink, and cars unto them of Sidon and Tyre, that they should bring cedar trees from Libanus, *and* convey them in floats to the haven of Joppa, accord-ing to the commandment which was written for them by Cyrus king of the 56 Persians. And in the second year after his coming to the temple of God at Jerusalem, in the second month, began Zorobabel the son of Salathiel, and Jesus the son of Josedek, and their brethren, and the priests the Levites, and all they that were come unto Jerusalem out of the captivity : 57 and they laid the foundation of the temple of God on the new moon of the second month, in the second year after they were come to Jewry and 58 Jerusalem. [23] And they appointed the Levites from twenty years old over the works of the Lord. Then stood up Jesus, and his sons and brethren, and Kadmiel his brother, and the sons of Jesus, Emadabun, and the sons of Joda the son of Iliadun, and their sons and brethren, all the Levites, with one accord setters forward of the business, labouring to advance the works in the house of God. So the builders builded the temple of the 59 Lord. And the priests stood arrayed in their vestments with musical in-struments and trumpets, and the Le-vites the sons of Asaph with their 60 cymbals, singing songs of thanksgiv-ing, and praising the Lord, after the 61 order of David king of Israel. And they sang aloud, praising the Lord

22 Another reading is, *first.*

23 See Ezra iii 8, 9, &c.

in songs of thanksgiving, because his
goodness and his glory are for ever in
62 all Israel. And all the people sounded
trumpets, and shouted with a loud
voice, singing songs of thanksgiving
unto the Lord for the rearing up of
63 the house of the Lord. [1] Also of the
priests the Levites, and of the heads
of their families, the ancients who
had seen the former house came to
the building of this with lamentation
64 and great weeping. But many with
trumpets and joy *shouted* with loud
65 voice, insomuch that the people heard
not the trumpets for the weeping of
the people: for the multitude sounded
marvellously, so that it was heard
afar off.
66 [2] Wherefore when the enemies of the
tribe of Judah and Benjamin heard it,
they came to know what that noise of
67 trumpets should mean. And they
perceived that they that were of the
captivity did build the temple unto
68 the Lord, the God of Israel. So they
went to Zorobabel and Jesus, and to
the chief men of the families, and said
unto them, We will build together
69 with you. For we likewise, as ye, do
obey your Lord, and do sacrifice unto
him from the days of [3] Asbasareth the
king of the Assyrians, who brought
70 us hither. Then Zorobabel and Jesus
and the chief men of the families of
Israel said unto them, It is not [4] for
you to build the house unto the Lord
71 our God. We ourselves alone will
build unto the Lord of Israel, according as Cyrus the king of the Persians
72 hath commanded us. But the heathen
of the land lying heavy upon the inhabitants of Judæa, and [5] holding
them strait, hindered their building;
73 and [6] by their secret plots, and popular persuasions and commotions, they
hindered the finishing of the building
all the time that king Cyrus lived: so
they were hindered from building for
the space of two years, until the
reign of Darius.
6 Now [7] in the second year of the reign
of Darius, Aggæus and Zacharias the
son of [8] Addo, the prophets, prophesied unto the Jews in Jewry and Jerusalem; in the name of the Lord,
the God of Israel, *prophesied they*
2 unto them. Then stood up Zorobabel
the son of Salathiel, and Jesus the
son of Josedek, and began to build
the house of the Lord at Jerusalem,
the prophets of the Lord being with
3 them, *and* helping them. [9] At the
same time came unto them [10] Sisinnes
the governor of Syria and Phœnicia,
with [11] Sathrabuzanes and his com-
4 panions, and said unto them, By
whose appointment do ye build this
house and this roof, and perform all
the other things? and who are the
builders that perform these things?

[1] Ezra iii. 12, 13.
[2] Ezra iv. 1, &c.
[3] Another reading is, *Asbacaphath.*
[4] Another reading is, *for us and you.*
[5] Or, *besieging them*
[6] Another reading is, *leading the people astray in counsel, and raising commotions.*
[7] Ezra iv. 24, and v. 1, &c.
[8] *Iddo.* Another reading is, *Eddin.*
[9] Ezra v. 3.
[10] *Tattenai.*
[11] *Shetharbozenai.*

5 Nevertheless the elders of the Jews
obtained favour, because the Lord
6 had visited the captivity; and they
were not hindered from building, until such time as communication was
made unto Darius concerning them,
and his answer signified.
7 The copy of the letter which Sisinnes,
governor of Syria and Phœnicia, and
Sathrabuzanes, with their companions, the rulers in Syria and Phœnicia, wrote and sent unto Darius; To
8 king Darius, greeting: Let all things
be known unto our lord the king, that
being come into the country of Judæa,
and entered into the city of Jerusalem, we found in the city of Jerusalem the elders of the Jews that were
9 of the captivity building a house unto
the Lord, great *and* new, of hewn and
costly stones, with timber laid in the
10 walls. And those works are done
with great speed, and the work goeth
on prosperously in their hands, and
with all glory and diligence is it ac-
11 complished. Then asked we these elders, saying, By whose commandment
build ye this house, and lay the foun-
12 dations of these works? Therefore,
to the intent that we might give knowledge unto thee by writing who were
the chief doers, we questioned them,
and we required of them the names
13 in writing of their principal men. So
they gave us this answer, We are the
servants of the Lord which made
14 heaven and earth. And as for this
house, it was builded many years ago
by a king of Israel great and strong,
15 and was finished. But when our fathers sinned against the Lord of Israel which is in heaven, and provoked
him unto wrath, he gave them over
into the hands of Nabuchodonosor
king of Babylon, king of the Chalde-
16 ans; and they pulled down the house,
and burned it, and carried away the
17 people captives unto Babylon. But
in the first year that Cyrus reigned
over the country of Babylon, king
Cyrus wrote to build up this house.
18 And the holy vessels of gold and of
silver, that Nabuchodonosor had carried away out of the house at Jerusalem, and had set up in his own temple, those Cyrus the king brought
forth again out of the temple in Babylonia, and they were delivered to Zorobabel and to [12] Sanabassarus the
19 governor, with commandment that he
should carry away [13] all these vessels,
and put them in the temple at Jerusalem; and that the temple of the
Lord should be built in its place.
20 Then Sanabassarus, being come hither, laid the foundations of the house
of the Lord which is in Jerusalem;
and from that time to this being still
a building, it is not yet fully ended.
21 Now therefore, if it seem good, O king,

[12] Another reading is, *Sabanassarus.*
[13] Another reading is, *the same.*

let search be made among the royal archives of our lord the king that are 22 in Babylon: and if it be found that the building of the house of the Lord which is in Jerusalem hath been done with the consent of king Cyrus, and it seem good unto our lord the king, let him signify unto us thereof.

23 [1] Then commanded king Darius to seek among the archives that were laid up at Babylon: and so at Ecbatana the palace, which is in the country of

Media, there was found a [2] roll wherein 24 these things were recorded. In the first year of the reign of Cyrus king Cyrus commanded to build up the house of the Lord which is in Jerusalem, where they do sacrifice with con- 25 tinual fire: whose height shall be sixty cubits, and the breadth sixty cubits, with three rows of hewn stones, and one row of new wood of that country; and the expenses thereof to be given 26 out of the house of king Cyrus: and that the holy vessels of the house of the Lord, both of gold and silver, that Nabuchodonosor took out of the house at Jerusalem, and carried away to Babylon, should be restored to the house at Jerusalem, and be set in the place 27 where they were before. And also he commanded that Sisinnes the governor of Syria and Phœnicia, and Sathrabuzanes, and their companions, and those which were appointed rulers in Syria and Phœnicia, should be careful not to meddle with the place, but suffer Zorobabel, the servant of the Lord, and governor of Judæa, and the elders of the Jews, to build that house of the 28 Lord in its place. And I also do command to have it built up whole again; and that they look diligently to help those that be of the captivity of Judæa, till the house of the Lord be finished: 29 and that out of the tribute of Cœlesyria and Phœnicia a portion be carefully given these men for the sacrifices of the Lord, that is, to Zorobabel the governor, for bullocks, and rams, and 30 lambs; and also corn, salt, wine, and oil, and that continually every year without further question, according as the priests that be in Jerusalem shall 31 signify to be daily spent: that drink offerings may be made to the Most High God for the king and for his children, and that they may pray for 32 their lives. And that commandment be given that whosoever shall transgress, yea, or neglect anything [3] herein

written, out of his own house shall a tree be taken, and he thereon be hanged, and all his goods seized for the 33 king. The Lord therefore, whose name is there called upon, utterly destroy every king and nation, that shall stretch out his hand to hinder or endamage that house of the Lord in 34 Jerusalem. I Darius the king have

ordained that according unto these things it be done with diligence. 7 Then [4] Sisinnes the governor of Cœlesyria and Phœnicia, and Sathrabuzanes, with their companions, following the commandments of king Darius, 2 did very carefully oversee the holy works, assisting the elders of the Jews 3 and rulers of the temple. And so the holy works prospered, while Aggæus and Zacharias the prophets prophe- 4 sied. And they finished these things by the commandment of the Lord, the God of Israel, and with the consent of Cyrus, Darius, and Artaxerxes, kings 5 of the Persians. And thus was [5] the house finished by the three and twentieth day of the month Adar, in the 6 sixth year of king Darius. And the children of Israel, the priests, and the Levites, and the other that were of the captivity, that were added unto them, did according to the things 7 written in the book of Moses. And to the dedication of the temple of the Lord they offered a hundred bullocks, two hundred rams, four hundred lambs; 8 and twelve he-goats for the sin of all Israel, according to the number of the twelve [6] princes of the tribes of Israel. 9 The priests also and the Levites stood arrayed in their vestments, according to their kindreds, for the services of the Lord, the God of Israel, according to the book of Moses: and the porters 10 at every gate. And the children of Israel that came out of the captivity held the passover the fourteenth day of the first month, when the priests and the Levites were 11 sanctified together, [7] and all they that were of the captivity; for they were sanctified. For the Levites were all 12 sanctified together, and they offered the passover for all them of the captivity, and for their brethren the 13 priests, and for themselves. And the children of Israel that came out of the captivity did eat, even all they that had separated themselves from the 14 abominations of the heathen of the land, and sought the Lord. And they kept the feast of unleavened bread 15 seven days, making merry before the Lord, for that he had turned the counsel of the king of Assyria toward them, to strengthen their hands in the works of the Lord, the God of Israel. 8 [8] And after these things, when Artaxerxes the king of the Persians reigned, came Esdras the son of Azaraias, the son of Zechrias, the son of Helkias, the 2 son of Salem, the son of Sadduk, the son of Ahitob, the son of Amarias, the son of Ozias, [9] the son of Memeroth, the son of Zaraias, the son of Savias, the son of Boccas, the son of Abisue, the son of Phinees, the son of Eleazar, 3 the son of Aaron the chief priest. This Esdras went up from Babylon, as be-

ing a ready scribe in the law of Moses, that was given by the God of Israel.
4 And the king did him honour: for he found grace in his sight in all his re-
5 quests. There went up with him also certain of the children of Israel, and of the priests, and Levites, and holy singers, and porters, and ¹ temple-
6 servants, unto Jerusalem, in the seventh year of the reign of Artaxerxes, in the fifth month, this was the king's seventh year; for they went from Babylon on the new moon of the first month, and came to Jerusalem, according to the prosperous journey which the Lord gave them ² for his
7 sake. For Esdras had very great skill, so that he omitted nothing of the law and commandments of the Lord, but taught all Israel the ordinances and judgements.
8 Now the commission, which was written from Artaxerxes the king, came to Esdras the priest and reader of the law of the Lord, whereof this
9 that followeth is a copy; King Artaxerxes unto Esdras the priest and reader of the law of the Lord, greet-
10 ing: Having determined to deal graciously, I have given order, that such of the nation of the Jews, and of the priests and Levites, ³ and of those within our realm, as are willing and desirous, should go with thee unto
11 Jerusalem. As many therefore as have a mind thereunto, let them depart with thee, as it hath seemed good both to me and my seven friends the
12 counsellors; that they may look unto the affairs of Judæa and Jerusalem, agreeably to that which is in the law
13 of the Lord, and carry the gifts unto the Lord of Israel to Jerusalem, which I and my friends have vowed; and that all the gold and silver that can be found in the country of Babylonia
14 for the Lord in Jerusalem, with that also which is given of the people for the temple of the Lord their God that is at Jerusalem, be collected: even the gold and silver for bullocks, rams, and lambs, and things thereunto ap-
15 pertaining; to the end that they may offer sacrifices unto the Lord upon the altar of the Lord their God, which
16 is in Jerusalem. And whatsoever thou and thy brethren are minded to do with gold and silver, that perform, according to the will of thy God.
17 And the holy vessels of the Lord, which are given thee for the use of the temple of thy God, which is in
18 Jerusalem: and whatsoever thing else thou shalt remember for the use of the temple of thy God, thou shalt give it
19 out of the king's treasury. And I king Artaxerxes have also commanded the keepers of the treasures in Syria and Phœnicia, that whatsoever Esdras the priest and reader of the law of the

Most High God shall send for, they
20 should give it him with all diligence, to the sum of a hundred talents of silver, likewise also of wheat even to a hundred ⁴ measures, and a hundred firkins of wine, and ⁵ salt in abun-
21 dance. Let all things be performed after the law of God diligently unto the Most High God, that wrath come not upon the kingdom of the king and
22 his sons. I command you also, that no tax, nor any other imposition, be laid on any of the priests, or Levites, or holy singers, or porters, or temple-servants, or any that have employment in this temple, and that no man have authority to impose anything
23 upon them. And thou, Esdras, according to the wisdom of God ordain judges and justices, that they may judge in all Syria and Phœnicia all those that know the law of thy God;
24 and those that know it not thou shalt teach. And whosoever shall transgress the law of thy God, and of the king, shall be punished diligently, whether it be by death, or other punishment, by penalty of money, or by ⁶ imprisonment.
25 Then said Esdras the scribe, Blessed be the only Lord, the God of my fathers, who hath put these things into the heart of the king, to glorify
26 his house that is in Jerusalem: and hath honoured me in the sight of the king, and his counsellors, and all his
27 friends and nobles. Therefore was I encouraged by the help of the Lord my God, and gathered together out of
28 Israel men to go up with me. And these are the chief according to their families and the several divisions thereof, that went up with me from
29 Babylon in the reign of king Artaxerxes: of the sons of Phinees, Gerson: of the sons of Ithamar, Gamael: of the sons of David, ⁷ Attus ⁸ the son of Se-
30 chenias: of the sons of Phoros, Zacharias; and with him were counted a
31 hundred and fifty men: of the sons of Phaath Moab, Eliaonias the son of ⁹ Zaraias, and with him two hundred
32 men: ¹⁰ of the sons of Zathoes, Sechenias the son of Jezelus, and with him ¹¹ three hundred men: of the sons of Adin, Obeth the son of Jonathan, and with him two hundred and fifty
33 men: of the sons of Elam, Jesias son of ¹² Gotholias, and with him seventy
34 men: of the sons of Saphatias, ¹³ Zaraias son of Michael, and with him
35 threescore and ten men: of the sons of Joab, ¹⁴ Abadias son of ¹⁵ Jezelus, and with him two hundred and twelve
36 men: ¹⁶ of the sons of Banias, Salimoth son of Josaphias, and with him a
37 hundred and threescore men: of the sons of Babi, Zacharias son of Bebai, and with him twenty and eight men:
38 of the sons of ¹⁷ Astath, Joannes son

---

¹ That is, the Nethinim.

² Some MSS. omit for his sake.

³ Another reading is, being within.

⁴ Gr. cors.

⁵ So some authorities. See Ezra vii. 22. The common reading is, other things.

⁶ Or. captivity

⁷ Hattush.

⁸ Ezra viii. 3, of the sons of Shecaniah; of the sons of Parosh.

⁹ Zerahiah.

¹⁰ Ezra viii. 5, of the sons of Shecaniah, the son of Jahaziel.

¹¹ Another reading is, two.

¹² Athaliah.

¹³ Zebadiah.

¹⁴ Obadiah.

¹⁵ Jehiel.

¹⁶ Ezra viii.10, of the sons of Shelomith, the son of Josiphiah.

¹⁷ Azgad.

of [1] Akatan, and with him a hundred
39 and ten men: of the sons of Adoni-kam, the last, and these are the names of them, Eliphalat, Jeuel, and [2] Sama-
40 ias, and with them seventy men: of the sons of [3] Bago, Uthi the son of Istalcurus, and with him seventy men.
41 And I gathered them together to the river called Theras; and there we pitched our tents three days, and
42 I surveyed them. But when I had found there none of the priests and
43 Levites, then sent I unto Eleazar, and
44 [4] Iduel, and [2] Maasmas, and Elnathan, and Samaias, and [5] Joribus, Nathan, Ennatan, Zacharias, and Mosolla-mus, principal men and men of under-
45 standing. And I bade them that they should go unto [6] Loddeus the captain, who was in the place of [7] the trea-
46 sury: and commanded them that they should speak unto Loddeus, and to his brethren, and to the treasurers in that place, to send us such men as might execute the priests' office in
47 the house of our Lord. And by the mighty hand of our Lord they brought unto us [8] men of understanding of the sons of [9] Mooli the son of Levi, the son of Israel, [10] Asebebias, and his sons, and his brethren, who were eighteen,
48 and [11] Asebias, and Annuus, and Osa-ias his brother, of the sons of Cha-nuneus, and their sons were twenty
49 men; and of the temple-servants whom David and the principal men had ap-pointed for the service of the Levites, two hundred and twenty temple-ser-vants, the catalogue of all their names
50 was shewed. And there I vowed a fast for the young men before our Lord, to desire of him a prosperous journey both for us and for our chil-dren and cattle that were with us:
51 for I was ashamed to ask of the king footmen, and horsemen, and conduct for safeguard against our adversa-
52 ries. For we had said unto the king, that the power of our Lord would be with them that seek him, to support
53 them in all ways. And again we be-sought our Lord as touching these things, and found him favourable
54 *unto us.* Then I separated twelve men of the chiefs of the priests, [12] Ese-rebias, and Assamias, and ten men
55 of their brethren with them: and I weighed them the silver, and the gold, and the holy vessels of the house of our Lord, which the king, and his counsellors, and the nobles, and all
56 Israel, had given. And when I had weighed it, I delivered unto them six hundred and fifty talents of silver, and silver vessels of a hundred talents,
57 and a hundred talents of gold, and twenty golden vessels, and twelve vessels of brass, even of fine brass,
58 glittering like gold. And I said unto them, Both ye are holy unto the Lord,

13 and the vessels are holy, and the gold and the silver are a vow unto the Lord, the Lord of our fathers.
59 Watch ye, and keep them till ye de-liver them to the chiefs of the priests and Levites, and to the principal men of the families of Israel, in Jerusalem, in the chambers of the house of our
60 Lord. So the priests and the Levites, who received the silver and the gold and the vessels which were in Jerusa-lem, brought them into the temple of the Lord.
61 And from the river Theras we de-parted the twelfth day of the first month, until we came to Jerusalem, by the mighty hand of our Lord which was upon us: and the Lord delivered us from *assault by* the way, from every enemy, and *so* we
62 came to Jerusalem. And when we had been there three days, the silver and gold was weighed and delivered in the house of our Lord on the fourth day unto [14] Marmoth the priest the
63 son of [15] Urias. And with him was Eleazar the son of Phinees, and with them were Josabdus the son of Jesus and [16] Moeth the son of Sabannus, the
64 Levites: all *was delivered them* by number and weight. And all the weight of them was written up the
65 same hour. Moreover they that were come out of the captivity offered sac-rifices unto the Lord, the God of Israel, even twelve bullocks for all
66 Israel, fourscore and sixteen rams, threescore and twelve lambs, goats
67 for a peace offering, twelve; all of them a sacrifice to the Lord. And they delivered the king's command-ments unto the king's stewards, and to the governors of Cœlesyria and Phœnicia; and they honoured the people and the temple of the Lord.
68 Now when these things were done, the principal men came unto me, and
69 said, The nation of Israel, and the princes, and the priests and the Le-vites, have not put away *from them* the strange people of the land, [17] nor the uncleannesses of the Gentiles, *to wit,* of the Canaanites, Hittites, Phere-zites, Jebusites, and the Moabites,
70 Egyptians, and Edomites. For both they and their sons have married with their daughters, and the holy seed is mixed with the strange people of the land; and from the beginning of this matter the rulers and the nobles have
71 been partakers of this iniquity. And as soon as I had heard these things, I rent my clothes, and my holy gar-ment, and plucked the hair from off my head and beard, and sat me down
72 sad and full of heaviness. So all they that were moved at the word of the Lord, the God of Israel, assembled unto me, whilst I mourned for the iniquity: but I sat still full of heavi-

73 ness until the evening sacrifice. Then rising up from the fast with my clothes and my holy garment rent, and bowing my knees, and stretching forth my 74 hands unto the Lord, I said, O Lord, I am ashamed and coufounded before 75 thy face; for our sins are multiplied above our heads, and our errors have 76 reached up unto heaven, ever since the time of our fathers; and we are in 77 great sin, even unto this day. And for our sins and our fathers' we with our brethren and our kings and our priests were given up unto the kings of the earth, to the sword, and to captivity, and for a prey with shame, unto this 78 day. And now in some measure hath mercy been shewed unto us from thee, O Lord, that there should be left us a root and a name in the place of thy 79 sanctuary; and to discover unto us a light in the house of the Lord our God, *and* to give us food in the time of our 80 servitude. Yea, when we were in bondage, we were not forsaken of our Lord; but he made us gracious before the kings of Persia, so that they gave 81 us food, and glorified the temple of our Lord, and raised up the desolate Sion, to give us a sure abiding in Jewry and 82 Jerusalem. And now, O Lord, what shall we say, having these things? for we have transgressed thy commandments, which thou gavest by the hand of thy servants the prophets, saying, 83 That the land which ye enter into to possess as a heritage, is a land polluted with the pollutions of the strangers of the land, and they have filled 84 it with their uncleanness. Therefore now shall ye not join your daughters unto their sons, neither shall ye take 85 their daughters unto your sons. Neither shall ye seek to have peace with them for ever, that ye may be strong, and eat the good things of the land, and that ye may leave it for an inheritance unto your children for evermore. 86 And all that is befallen is done unto us for our wicked works and great sins: for thou, O Lord, didst make our sins 87 light, and didst give unto us such a root: *but* we have turned back again to transgress thy law, in mingling ourselves with the uncleanness of 88 the heathen of the land. [1] Thou wast not angry with us to destroy us, till thou hadst left us neither root, seed, 89 nor name. O Lord of Israel, thou art true: for we are left a root this day. 90 Behold, now are we before thee in our iniquities, for we cannot stand any longer before thee by reason of these things. 91 [2] And as Esdras in his prayer made his confession, weeping, and lying flat upon the ground before the temple, there gathered unto him from Jerusalem a very great throng of men and women and children: for there was

great weeping among the multitude. 92 Then Jechonias the son of Jeelus, one of the sons of Israel, called out, and said, O Esdras, we have sinned against the Lord God, we have married strange women of the heathen of the 93 land, and now is all Israel [3] aloft. Let us make an oath unto the Lord herein, that we will put away all our wives, which *we have taken* of the strangers, 94 with their children, like as seemeth good unto thee, and to as many as do 95 obey the law of the Lord. Arise, and put in execution: for to thee doth this matter appertain, and we will be with 96 thee to do valiantly. So Esdras arose, and took an oath of the chief of the priests and Levites of all Israel to do after these things; and *so* they sware.

9 [4] Then Esdras rising from the court of the temple went to the chamber of 2 Jonas the son of Eliasib, and lodged there, and did eat no bread nor drink water, mourning for the great iniqui-3 ties of the multitude. And there was made proclamation in all Jewry and Jerusalem to all them that were of the captivity, that they should be 4 gathered together at Jerusalem: and that whosoever met not there within two or three days, according as the elders that bare rule appointed, their cattle should be seized to the use of the temple, and himself cast out from the multitude of them that were of the captivity. 5 And in three days were all they of the tribe of Judah and Benjamin gathered together at Jerusalem: this was the ninth month, on the twentieth day of 6 the month. And all the multitude sat together trembling in the broad place before the temple because of the pre-7 sent foul weather. So Esdras arose up, and said unto them, Ye have transgressed the law and married strange wives, *thereby* to increase the sins of 8 Israel. And now make confession and give glory unto the Lord, the God of 9 our fathers, and do his will, and separate yourselves from the heathen of the land, and from the strange women. 10 Then cried the whole multitude, and said with a loud voice, Like as thou 11 hast spoken, so will we do. But forasmuch as the multitude is great, and it is foul weather, so that we cannot stand without, and this is not a work of one day or two, seeing our sin in 12 these things is spread far: therefore let the rulers of the multitude stay, and let all them of our habitations that have strange wives come at the 13 time appointed, and with them the rulers and judges of every place, till we turn away the wrath of the Lord 14 from us for this matter. *Then* Jonathan the son of Azael and [5] Ezekias the son of Thocanus accordingly took the matter upon them: and Mosolla-

1 Or, *Wast thou not &c.*

2 Ezra x. 1.

3 Or, *exalted* Deut. xxviii. 13.

4 Ezra x. 6, &c.

5 Another reading is, *Ezias*

mus and Levis and Sabbateus were 15 assessors to them. And they that were of the captivity did according to all these things. 16 And Esdras the priest chose unto him principal men of their families, all by name: and on the new moon of the tenth month they were shut in 17 together to examine the matter. So their cause that held strange wives was brought to an end by the new 18 moon of the first month. And of the priests that were come together, and had strange wives, there were found; 19 of the sons of Jesus the son of Jose- dek, and his brethren; ¹ Mathelas, and Eleazar, and ² Joribus, and ³ Jo- 20 adanus. And they gave their hands to put away their wives, and *to offer* rams to make reconcilement for their 21 error. And of the sons of Emmer; Ananias, and Zabdeus, and ⁴ Manes, and ¹ Sameus, and ⁵ Hiereel, and ⁶ Aza- 22 rias. And of the sons of ⁷ Phaisur; Elionas, Massias, Ismael, and Nathan- 23 ael, and ⁸ Ocidelus, and ⁹ Sa.oas. And of the Levites; Jozabdus, and Semeis, and ¹⁰ Colius, who was called ¹¹ Cali- tas, and ¹² Patheus, and Judas, and 24 Jonas. Of the holy singers; ¹³ Eliasi- 25 bus, Bacchurus. Of the porters; Sal- 26 lumus, and ¹⁴ Tolbanes. Of Israel, of the sons of ¹⁵ Phoros; ¹⁶ Hiermas, and ¹⁷ Ieddias, and Melchias, and ¹⁸ Mae- lus, and Eleazar, and ¹⁹ Asibias, and 27 Banneas. Of the sons of Ela; Mat- thanias, Zacharias, and ⁵ Jezrielus, and Oabdius, and Hieremoth, and 28 ²⁰ Aedias. And of the sons of ²¹ Za- moth; ²² Eliadas, ¹³ Eliasimus, ²³ Otho- nias, Jarimoth, and ²⁴ Sabathus, and 29 ²⁵ Zardeus. Of the sons of Bebai; Jo- annes, and Ananias, and ²⁶ Jozabdus, 30 and ²⁷ Ematheis. Of the sons of ²⁸ Mani; ²⁹ Olamus, ³⁰ Mamuchus, ³¹ Je- deus, Jasubus, and ³² Jasaelus, and 31 Hieremoth. And of the sons of Addi; Naathus, and Moossias, Laccunus, and Naidus, and Matthanias, and Ses- 32 thel, Balnuus, and Manasseas. And of the sons of Annas; Elionas, and Aseas, and Melchias, and Sabbeus, 33 and Simon Chosameus. And of the sons of Asom; ³³ Maltanneus, and ³⁴ Mattathias, and ²⁴ Sabanneus, Eli- phalat, and Manasses, and Semei. 34 And of the sons of Baani; Jeremias, Momdis, Ismaerus, Juel, Mamdai, and Pedias, and Anos, Carabasion, and Enasibus, and Mamnitanemus, Elia- sis, Bannus, Eliali, Someis, Selemias, Nathanias: and of the sons of Ezora; Sesis, Ezril, Azaelus, Samatus, Zam- 35 bri, Josephus. And of the sons of Nooma; Mazitias, Zabadeas, Edos, 36 Juel, Banaias. All these had taken strange wives, and they put them 37 away with their children. And the

priests and Levites, and they that were of Israel, dwelt in Jerusalem, and in the country, on the new moon of the seventh month, and the children of Israel in their habitations. 38 ³⁵ And the whole multitude were ga- thered together with one accord into the broad place before the porch of 39 the temple toward the east: and they said unto Esdras the priest and read- er, Bring the law of Moses, that was given of the Lord, the God of Israel. 40 So Esdras the chief priest brought the law unto the whole multitude both of men and women, and to all the priests, to hear the law on the new moon of 41 the seventh month. And he read in the broad place before the porch of the temple from morning unto mid- day, before both men and women; and ³⁶ all the multitude gave heed unto 42 the law. And Esdras the priest and reader of the law stood up upon the pulpit of wood, which was made *for* 43 *that purpose.* And there stood up by him Mattathias, Sammus, Ananias, Azarias, Urias, ³⁷ Ezekias, ¹ Baalsa- 44 mus, upon the right hand: and upon his left hand, ²⁸ Phaldeus, Misael, Mel- chias, ³⁹ Lothasubus, Nabarias, Zacha- 45 rias. Then took Esdras the book of the law before the multitude, and sat honourably in the first place before 46 all. And when he opened the law, they stood all straight up. So Esdras blessed the Lord God Most High, the 47 God of hosts, Almighty. And all the people answered,· Amen; and lifting up their hands they fell to the ground, 48 and worshipped the Lord. Also Je- sus, Annus, Sarabias, Iadinus, Jacu- bus. Sabateus, ⁴⁰ Auteas, Maiannas, and Calitas, Azarias, and Jozabdus, and Ananias, Phalias, the Levites, taught the law of the Lord, ⁴¹ and read to the multitude the law of the Lord, making them withal to understand it. 49 Then said Attharates unto Esdras the chief priest and reader, and to the Levites that taught the multitude, 50 even to all, This day is holy unto the Lord; (now they all wept when they 51 heard the law:) go then, and eat the fat, and drink the sweet, and send portions to them that have nothing; 52 for the day is holy unto the Lord: and be not sorrowful; for the Lord will 53 bring you to honour. So the Levites published all things to the people, saying, This day is holy; be not sor- 54 rowful. Then went they their way, every one to eat and drink, and make merry, and to give portions to them that had nothing, and to make great 55 cheer; because they ⁴² understood the words wherein they were instructed, and for the which they had been as- sembled.

---

¹ *Maase- iah.*
² *Jarib.*
³ *Gedaliah.*

⁴ *Harim.*
⁵ *Jehiel.*
⁶ *Uzziah.*
⁷ *Pashhur.*
⁸ *Jozabad.*
⁹ *Ela- suh.*
¹⁰ *Kela- iah.*
¹¹ *Keli- ta.*
¹² *Pethahiah.*
¹³ *Elia- shib.*
¹⁴ *Telem.*
¹⁵ *Pa- rosh.*
¹⁶ *Ra- miah.*
¹⁷ *Iz- ziah.* Another reading is. *Iezias.*
¹⁸ *Mi- jamin.*
¹⁹ *Mal- chijah.*
²⁰ *Abdi.*
²¹ *Zattu.*
²² *Elio- enai.*
²³ *Mat- taniah.*
²⁴ *Za- bad.*
²⁵ *Aziza.*
²⁶ *Zab- bai.*
²⁷ *Ath- lai.*
²⁸ *Bani.*
²⁹ *Me- shullam.*
³⁰ *Mal- luch.*
³¹ *Ada- iah.*
³² *Sheal.*
³³ *Mat- tenai.*
³⁴ *Mat- tattah.*

³⁵ Neh. viii. 1.

³⁶ Another reading is, *they gave all heed.*
³⁷ *Hilkiah.*
³⁸ *Pedaiah.*
³⁹ *Hashum.*

⁴⁰ *Ho- diah.*

⁴¹ Some authorities omit *and read ... Lord.*

⁴² Or, *were inspired by*

II. ESDRAS.

1 THE second book of the prophet Esdras, the son of Saraias, the son of Azaraias, the son of Helkias, the son of Salemas, the son of Sadoc, the son 2 of Ahitob, the son of Achias, the son of Phinees, the son of Heli, the son of Amarias, the son òf Aziei, the son of Marimoth, the son of Arna, the son of Ozias, the son of Borith, the son of Abissei, the son of Phinees, the son of 3 Eleazar, the son of Aaron, of the tribe of Levi; which was captive in the land of the Medes, in the reign of Artaxerxes king of the Persians.

4 And the word of the Lord came unto 5 me, saying, Go thy way, and shew my people their sinful deeds, and their children their wickedness which they have done against me; that they may 6 tell their children's children : because the sins of their fathers are increased in them : for they have forgotten me, and have done sacrifice unto strange 7 gods. Did not I bring them out of the land of Egypt, out of the house of bondage? but they have provoked me unto wrath, and despised my counsels. 8 Shake thou then the hair of thy head, and cast all evils upon them, for they have not been obedient unto my law, 9 but it is a rebellious people. How long shall I forbear them, unto whom 10 I have done so much good? Many kings have I overthrown for their sakes; Pharaoh with his servants and 11 all his host have I smitten down. All the nations have I destroyed before them, and in the east I have scattered the people of two provinces, even of Tyre and Sidon, and have slain all 12 their adversaries. Speak thou therefore unto them, saying,

13 Thus saith the Lord, Of a truth I brought you through the sea, and where there was no path I made for you highways; I gave you Moses for a 14 leader, and Aaron for a priest. I gave you light in a pillar of fire, and great wonders have I done among you; yet have ye forgotten me, saith the Lord. 15 Thus saith the Lord Almighty, The quails were for a token to you; I gave you a camp for your safeguard, never-16 theless ye murmured there : and ye triumphed not in my name for the destruction of your enemies, but ever 17 to this day do ye yet murmur. Where are the benefits that I have done for you? when ye were hungry and thirsty in the wilderness, did ye not cry unto 18 me, saying, Why hast thou brought us into this wilderness to kill us? it

had been better for us to have served the Egyptians, than to die in this 19 wilderness. I had pity upon your mournings, and gave you manna for 20 food; ye did eat angels' bread. When ye were thirsty, did I not cleave the rock, and waters flowed out to your fill? for the heat I covered you with 21 the leaves of the trees. I divided among you fruitful lands; I cast out the Canaanites, the Pherezites, and the Philistines, before you : what shall I yet do more for you? saith the Lord. 22 Thus saith the Lord Almighty, When ye were in the wilderness, at the bitter river, being athirst, and blaspheming 23 my name, I gave you not fire for your blasphemies, but cast a tree in the water, and made the river sweet. 24 What shall I do unto thee, O Jacob? thou, Judah, wouldest not obey me : I will turn me to other nations, and unto them will I give my name, that 25 they may keep my statutes. Seeing ye have forsaken me, I also will forsake you; when ye ask me to be merciful unto you, I will have no mercy 26 upon you. Whensoever ye shall call upon me, I will not hear you : for ye have defiled your hands with blood, and your feet are swift to commit 27 manslaughter. Ye have not as it were forsaken me, but your own selves, saith the Lord. 28 Thus saith the Lord Almighty, Have I not prayed you as a father his sons, as a mother her daughters, and a nurse 29 her young babes, that ye would be my people, and I should be your God; that ye would be my children, and I should 30 be your father? I gathered you together, as a hen *gathereth* her chickens under her wings : but now, what shall I do unto you? I will cast you 31 out from my presence. When ye offer oblations unto me, I will turn my face from you : for your solemn feast days, your new moons, and your circumcisions of the flesh, have I reject-32 ed. I sent unto you my servants the prophets, whom ye have taken and slain, and torn their bodies in pieces, whose blood I will require *of your hands*, saith the Lord. 33 Thus saith the Lord Almighty, Your house is desolate, I will cast you out 34 as the wind doth stubble. And your children shall not be fruitful; for they have neglected my commandment [1] unto you, and done that which is evil be-35 fore me. Your houses will I give to a people that shall come; which not

14

having heard of me yet believe me; they to whom I have shewed no signs shall do that which I have command-
36 ed. They have seen no prophets, yet they shall call their former estate to
37 remembrance. I take to witness the grace of the people that shall come, whose little ones rejoice with gladness: and though they see me not with bodily eyes, yet in spirit they shall believe the thing that I say.
38 And now, O father, behold with glory; and see the people that come
39 from the east: unto whom I will give for leaders, Abraham, Isaac, and Jacob, Oseas, Amos, and Micheas,
40 Joel, Abdias, and Jonas, Nahum, and Abacuc, Sophonias, Aggæus, Zachary, and Malachy, which is called also the angel of the Lord.
2 Thus saith the Lord, I brought this people out of bondage, and I gave them my commandments by my servants the prophets; whom they would not hear, but set my counsels at
2 nought. The mother that bare them saith unto them, Go your way, O my children; for I am a widow and for-
3 saken. I brought you up with gladness, and with sorrow and heaviness have I lost you: for ye have sinned before the Lord God, and done that
4 which is evil before me. But what shall I now do unto you? for I am a widow and forsaken: go your way, O my children, and ask mercy of the
5 Lord. As for me, O father, I call upon thee for a witness over the mother of *these* children, because they would not
6 keep my covenant, that thou bring them to confusion, and their mother to a spoil, that there may be no offspring
7 of them. Let them be scattered abroad among the heathen, let their names be blotted out of the earth: for they have despised my [1] covenant.
8 Woe unto thee, Assur, thou that hidest the unrighteous with thee! O thou wicked nation, remember what I did unto Sodom and Gomorrah;
9 whose land lieth in clods of pitch and heaps of ashes: even so also will I do unto them that have not hearkened unto me, saith the Lord Almighty.
10 Thus saith the Lord unto Esdras, Tell my people that I will give them the kingdom of Jerusalem, which I
11 would have given unto Israel. Their glory also will I take unto me, and give these the everlasting tabernacles,
12 which I had prepared for them. They shall have the tree of life for an ointment of sweet savour; they shall
13 neither labour, nor be weary. [2] Ask, and ye shall receive: pray for few days unto you, that they may be shortened: the kingdom is already
14 prepared for you: watch. Take heaven and earth to witness, take them to witness; for I have given up the

[1] Another reading is, *sacrament,* or, *oath.*

[2] Another reading is, *Go.*

evil, and created the good: for I live, saith the Lord.
15 Mother, embrace thy children; I will bring them out with gladness like a dove; stablish their feet; for I have
16 chosen thee, saith the Lord. And those that be dead will I raise up again from their places, and bring them out of the tombs: for I [3] have
17 known my name in them. Fear not, thou mother of the children: for I have chosen thee, saith the Lord.
18 For thy help will I send my servants Esaias and Jeremy, after whose counsel I have sanctified and prepared for thee twelve trees laden with divers
19 fruits, and as many fountains flowing with milk and honey, and seven mighty mountains, whereupon there grow roses and lilies, whereby I will
20 fill thy children with joy. Do right to the widow, judge the fatherless, give to the poor, defend the orphan, clothe
21 the naked, heal the broken and the weak, laugh not a lame man to scorn, defend the maimed, and let the blind man come unto the sight of my glory.
22 Keep the old and young within thy
23 walls. Wheresoever thou findest the dead, set a sign upon them and commit them to the grave, and I will give thee the first place in my resur-
24 rection. Abide still, O my people, and take thy rest, for thy quietness shall
25 come. Nourish thy children, O thou good nurse, and stablish their feet.
26 As for the servants whom I have given thee, there shall not one of them perish; for I will require them from
27 among thy number. Be not careful overmuch: for when the day of tribulation and anguish cometh, others shall weep and be sorrowful, but thou shalt be merry and have abundance.
28 The nations shall envy thee, but tney shall be able to do nothing against
29 thee, saith the Lord. My hands shall cover thee, so that thy children see
30 not [4] hell. Be joyful, O thou mother, with thy children; for I will deliver
31 thee, saith the Lord. Remember thy children that sleep, for I shall bring them out of the secret places of the earth, and shew mercy unto them: for I am merciful, saith the Lord Al-
32 mighty. Embrace thy children until I come, and proclaim mercy unto them: for my wells run over, and my grace shall not fail.
33 I Esdras received a charge from the Lord upon the mount Horeb, that I should go unto Israel; but when I came unto them, they would none of me, and rejected the commandment
34 of the Lord. And therefore I say unto you, O ye nations, that hear and understand, look for your shepherd, he shall give you everlasting rest; for he is nigh at hand, that shall come in
35 the end of the world. Be ready to

[3] Or, *recognise*

[4] Lat. *Gehenna*

15

the rewards of the kingdom, for the
everlasting light shall shine upon you
36 for evermore. Flee the shadow of
this world, receive the joyfulness of
your glory: I call to witness my
37 saviour openly. O receive that which
is given you of the Lord, and be joyful, giving thanks unto him that hath
called you to heavenly kingdoms.
38 Arise up and stand, and behold the
number of those that be sealed in the
39 feast of the Lord; they that withdrew
them from the shadow of the world
have received glorious garments of
40 the Lord. [1] Look upon thy number,
O Sion, and make up the reckoning
of those of thine that are clothed in
white, which have fulfilled the law of
41 the Lord. The number of thy children, whom thou longedst for, is fulfilled: beseech the power of the Lord,
that thy people, which have been called from the beginning, may be hallowed.
42 I Esdras saw upon the mount Sion a
great multitude, whom I could not
number, and they all praised the Lord
43 with songs. And in the midst of them
there was a young man of a high
stature, taller than all the rest, and
upon every one of their heads he set
crowns, and was more exalted; where-
44 at I marvelled greatly. So I asked
the angel, and said, What are these,
45 my Lord? He answered and said unto
me, These be they that have put off
the mortal clothing, and put on the
immortal, and have confessed the
name of God: now are they crowned,
46 and receive palms. Then said I unto
the angel, What young man is he that
setteth crowns upon them, and giveth
47 them palms in their hands? So he
answered and said unto me, It is the
Son of God, whom they have confessed in the world. Then began I greatly to commend them that stood so
48 stiffly for the name of the Lord. Then
the angel said unto me, Go thy way,
and tell my people what manner of
things, and how great wonders of the
Lord God thou hast seen.

3 In the thirtieth year after the ruin of
the city, I Salathiel (the same is Esdras) was in Babylon, and lay troubled
upon my bed, and my thoughts came
2 up over my heart: for I saw the desolation of Sion, and the wealth of them
3 that dwelt at Babylon. And my spirit
was sore moved, so that I began to
speak words full of fear to the Most
4 High, and said, O Lord that bearest
rule, didst thou not speak at the beginning, when thou didst fashion the
earth, and that thyself alone, and
5 commandedst the [2] dust, and it [3] gave
thee Adam, a body without a soul?
yet it was the workmanship of thine
hands, and thou didst breathe into him
the breath of life, and he was made
6 living before thee. And thou leddest
him into paradise, which thy right
hand did plant, before ever the earth
7 came forward. And unto him thou
gavest thy one commandment: which
he transgressed, and immediately
thou appointedst death for him and in
his generations; and there were born
of him nations and tribes, peoples and
8 kindreds, out of number. And every
nation walked after their own will,
and did ungodly things before thee,
and despised *thy commandments*, and
9 thou didst not forbid them. Nevertheless again in process of time thou
broughtest the flood upon those that
dwelt in the world, and destroyedst
10 them. And it came to pass that the
same hap befell them; like as death
was to Adam, so was the flood to
11 these. Nevertheless one of them thou
leftest, Noah with his household, *even*
all the righteous men *that came* of
12 him. And it came to pass, that when
they that dwelt upon the earth began
to multiply, they multiplied also children, and peoples, and many nations,
and began again to be more ungodly
13 than the first. And it came to pass,
when they did wickedly before thee,
thou didst choose thee one from
among them, whose name was Abra-
14 ham; and him thou lovedst, and unto
him only thou shewedst the end of
15 the times secretly by night: and madest an everlasting covenant with him,
promising him that thou wouldest
16 never forsake his seed. And unto
him thou gavest Isaac, and unto Isaac
thou gavest Jacob and Esau. And
thou didst set apart Jacob for thyself,
but didst put by Esau: and Jacob be-
17 came a great multitude. And it came
to pass, that when thou leddest his
seed out of Egypt, thou broughtest
18 them up to the mount Sinai. Thou
bowedst the heavens also, and didst
[4] shake the earth, and movedst the
whole world, and madest the depths
to tremble, and troubledst the *course*
19 *of that* age. And thy glory went
through four gates, of fire, and of
earthquake, and of wind, and of cold;
that thou mightest give the law unto
the seed of Jacob, and the commandment unto the generation of Israel.
20 And yet tookest thou not away from
them *their* [5] wicked heart, that thy
law might bring forth fruit in them.
21 For the first Adam bearing a [5] wicked
heart transgressed, and was overcome; *and not he only*, but all they
22 also that are born of him. Thus disease was made permanent; and the
law was in the heart of the people
along with the [6] wickedness of the
root; so the good departed away, and
that which was [5] wicked abode still.
23 So the times passed away, and the

[1] Another reading is, *Take*.

[2] So the Syriac and Æthiopic.

[3] So the Syriac.

[4] So some versions. Lat. *set fast*.

[5] Or, *corrupt*

[6] Or, *corruptness*

years were brought to an end: then didst thou raise thee up a servant, 24 called David, whom thou commandedst to build a city unto thy name, and to offer oblations unto thee there- 25 in of thine own. When this was done many years, then they that inhabited 26 the city did evil, in all things doing even as Adam and all his generations had done: for they also bare a ¹ wicked 27 heart: and so thou gavest thy city over into the hands of thine enemies. 28 And I said then in mine heart, Are their deeds any better that inhabit Babylon? and hath she therefore do- 29 minion over Sion? For it came to pass when I came hither, that I saw also impieties without number, and my soul saw many evil-doers in this thirtieth year, so that my heart failed me. 30 For I have seen how thou sufferest them sinning, and hast spared the ungodly doers, and hast destroyed thy people, and hast preserved thine ene- 31 mies; and thou hast not signified unto any ² how thy way may be comprehended. Are the deeds of Babylon 32 better than those of Sion? Or is there any other nation that knoweth thee beside Israel? or what tribes have so believed thy covenants as these *tribes* 33 *of* Jacob? And yet their reward appeareth not, and their labour hath no fruit: for I have gone hither and thither through the nations, and I see that they abound *in wealth*, and think 34 not upon thy commandments. Weigh thou therefore our iniquities now in the balance, and theirs also that dwell in the world; and so shall it be found 35 which way the scale inclineth. Or when was it that they which dwell upon the earth have not sinned in thy sight? or what nation hath so kept 36 thy commandments? Thou shalt find that men *who may be reckoned* by name have kept thy precepts; but nations thou shalt not find.

4 And the angel that was sent unto me, whose name was Uriel, gave me 2 an answer, and said to me, Thy heart hath utterly failed thee in *regarding* this world, and thinkest thou to comprehend the way of the Most High? 3 Then said I, Yea, my Lord. And he answered me, and said, I am sent to shew thee three ways, and to set forth three similitudes before 4 thee: whereof if thou canst declare me one, I also will shew thee the way that thou desirest to see, and I will teach thee wherefore the heart is ¹ wicked. 5 And I said, Say on, my Lord. Then said he unto me, Go to, weigh me a weight of fire, or measure me a ³ measure of wind, or call me again the day that is past. 6 Then answered I and said, Who of the sons *of men* is able to do this,

that thou shouldest ask me of such things? 7 And he said unto me, If I had asked thee, saying, How many dwellings are there in the heart of the sea? or how many springs are there at the fountain head of the deep? or how many ³ ways are above the firmament? or which are the outgoings ⁴ of hell? or 8 which are the paths of paradise? peradventure thou wouldest say unto me, I never went down into the deep, nor as yet into hell, neither did I ever 9 climb up into heaven. Nevertheless now have I asked thee but only of the fire and wind, and of the day, things wherethrough thou hast passed, and ⁵ without which thou canst not be, and yet hast thou given me no answer of them. 10 He said moreover unto me, Thine own things, that are grown up with 11 thee, canst thou not know; how then can thy vessel comprehend the way of the Most High? and how can he that is already worn out with the corrupted world understand ⁶ incorruption? 12 ⁷ And when I heard these things I fell upon my face, and said unto him, It were better that we were not here at all, than that we should come hither and live in the midst of ungodliness, and suffer, and not know wherefore. 13 He answered me, and said, ⁸ The woods of the trees of the field went 14 forth, and took counsel together, and said, Come, let us go and make war against the sea, that it may depart away before us, and that we may 15 make us more woods. The waves of the sea also in like manner took counsel together, and said, Come, let us go up and subdue the wood of the plain, that there also we may make us 16 another country. The counsel of the wood was in vain, for the fire came 17 and consumed it: likewise also the counsel of the waves of the sea, for the sand stood up and stopped them. 18 If thou wert judge now betwixt these two, whom wouldest thou justify, or whom condemn? 19 I answered and said, It is a foolish counsel that they both have taken, for the ground is given unto the wood, and the place of the sea *is given* to bear his waves. 20 Then answered he me, and said, Thou hast given a right judgement, and why judgest thou not in thine own 21 case? For like as the ground is given unto the wood, and the sea to his waves, even so they that dwell upon the earth may understand nothing but that which is upon the earth: and he *only that dwelleth* above the heavens *may understand* the things that are above the height of the heavens. 22 Then answered I and said, I beseech thee, O Lord, ³ wherefore is the power

---

Marginal notes (left column):

¹ Or, corrupt

² So the Syriac. The Latin has *how this way may be left.*

³ After the Oriental versions.

Marginal notes (right column):

⁴ So the Syriac. The Latin omits *of hell* or *which are the paths.*

⁵ Another reading is, *from which thou canst not be separated.*

⁶ Syriac and Æthiopic, *the way of the incorruptible.*

⁷ So the Syriac and Æthiopic. The Latin is corrupt.

⁸ So the Oriental versions. The Latin is corrupt. See Judg. ix 8.

23 of understanding given unto me? For it was not my mind to be curious of the ways above, but of such things as pass by us daily; because Israel is given up as a reproach to the heathen, *and* the people whom thou hast loved is given over unto ungodly nations, and the law of our forefathers is made of none effect, and the written cove-
24 nants are nowhere *regarded*, and we pass away out of the world as grass-hoppers, and our life is as a [1] vapour, neither are we worthy to obtain mer-
25 cy. What will he then do for his name whereby we are called? Of these things have I asked.
26 Then answered he me, and said, If thou be *alive*, thou shalt see, and if thou livest [2] long, thou shalt marvel; for the world hasteth fast to pass
27 away. For it is not able to bear the things that are promised to the right-eous in the times *to come*: for this world is full of sadness and infirmi-
28 ties. For the evil [3] whereof thou askest me is sown, but the gathering
29 thereof is not yet come. If therefore that which is sown be not reaped, and if the place where the evil is sown pass not away, there cannot come the
30 field where the good is sown. For a grain of evil seed was sown in the heart of Adam from the beginning, and how much wickedness hath it brought forth unto this time! and how much shall it yet bring forth until the [4] time of threshing come!
31 Ponder now by thyself, how great fruit of wickedness a grain of evil
32 seed hath brought forth. When the ears which are without number shall be sown, how great a floor shall they fill!
33 Then I answered and said, [5] How long? and when shall these things come to pass? wherefore are our years few and evil?
34 And he answered me, and said, Thou dost not hasten more than the Most High: for thy haste is [6] for thine own self, but he that is above *hasteneth*
35 on behalf of many. Did not the souls of the righteous ask question of these things in their chambers, saying, How long [7] are we here? when cometh the fruit of the [4] threshing time of our re-
36 ward? And unto them Jeremiel the archangel gave answer, and said, Even when the number is fulfilled of them that are like unto you. For he hath weighed the world in the balance;
37 and by measure hath he measured the times, and by number hath he numbered the seasons; and he shall not [8] move nor stir them, until the said measure be fulfilled.
38 Then answered I and said, O Lord that bearest rule, yet even we all are
39 full of impiety: and for our sakes peradventure it is that the [4] threshing

time of the righteous is kept back, because of the sins of them that dwell upon the earth.
40 So he answered me, and said, Go thy way to a woman with child, and ask of her when she hath fulfilled her nine months, if her womb may keep the birth any longer within her.
41 Then said I, No, Lord, that can it not.
And he said unto me, In the grave the chambers of souls are like the
42 womb: for like as a woman that tra-vaileth maketh haste to escape the anguish of the travail: even so do these places haste to deliver those things that are committed unto them
43 from the beginning. Then shall it be shewed thee concerning those things which thou desirest to see.
44 Then answered I and said, If I have found favour in thy sight, and if it be possible, and if I be meet therefore,
45 shew me this also, whether there be more to come than is past, or whether
46 the more part is gone over us. For what is gone I know, but what is for to come I know not.
47 And he said unto me, Stand up upon the right side, and I shall expound the similitude unto thee.
48 So I stood, and saw, and, behold, a hot burning oven passed by before me: and it happened, that when the flame was gone by I looked, and, be-
49 hold, the smoke remained still. After this there passed by before me a watery cloud, and sent down much rain with a storm; and when the stormy rain was past, the drops re-mained therein still.
50 Then said he unto me, Consider with thyself; as the rain is more than the drops, and as the fire is greater than the smoke, so the quantity which is past did more exceed; but the drops and the smoke remained still.
51 Then I prayed, and said, May I live, thinkest thou, until that time? or who shall be in those days?
52 He answered me, and said, As for the tokens whereof thou askest me, I may tell thee of them in part: but as touch-ing thy life, I am not sent to shew thee;
5 for I do not know it. Nevertheless as concerning the tokens, behold, the days shall come, that they which dwell upon earth shall be taken [2] with great amazement, and the way of truth shall be hidden, and the land shall be bar-
2 ren of faith. But iniquity shall be increased above that which now thou seest, or that thou hast heard long ago.
3 And the land, that thou seest now to have rule, shall be waste and [2] untrod-
4 den, and men shall see it desolate. But if the Most High grant thee to live, thou shalt see that which is after the third *kingdom* to be troubled; and the sun shall suddenly shine forth in the night,

[1] So the chief Oriental versions. The Latin is corrupt.

[2] So the Syriac.

[3] So the Syriac and Æthi-opic.

[4] Or, thresh-ing-floor

[5] So the chief Oriental versions.

[6] So the Syriac. The Latin is corrupt.

[7] So the Syriac. The Latin has *shall I hope on this fashion?*

[8] Syr. *rest.*

¹ According to some Oriental versions, *the air.*

5 and the moon in the day: and blood shall drop out of wood, and the stone shall give his voice, and the peoples shall be troubled; and ¹ *their* goings

6 shall be changed: and he shall rule, whom they that dwell upon the earth look not for, and the fowls shall take

7 their flight away together: and the Sodomitish sea shall cast out fish, and make a noise in the night, which many have not known: but all shall hear

8 the voice thereof. There shall be chaos also in many places, and the fire shall be oft sent out, and the wild beasts shall change their places, and women shall bring forth monsters:

9 and salt waters shall be found in the sweet, and all friends shall destroy one another; then shall wit hide itself, and understanding withdraw itself

10 into its chamber; and it shall be sought of many, and shall not be found: and unrighteousness and incontinency shall be multiplied upon

11 earth. One land also shall ask another, and say, Is righteousness, is a man that doeth righteousness, gone through thee? And it shall say, No.

12 And it shall come to pass at that time that men shall hope, but shall not obtain: they shall labour, but their

13 ways shall not prosper. To shew thee such tokens I have leave; and if thou wilt pray again, and weep as now, and fast seven days, thou shalt hear yet greater things than these.

14 Then I awaked, and an extreme trembling went through my body, and my mind was troubled, so that it

15 fainted. So the angel that was come to talk with me held me, comforted

16 me, and set me up upon my feet. And in the second night it came to pass,

² The Syriac has *Psaltiel.*

that ² Phaltiel the captain of the people came unto me, saying, Where hast thou been? and why is thy counte-

17 nance sad? or knowest thou not that Israel is committed unto thee in the

18 land of their captivity? Up then, and eat some bread, and forsake us not, as the shepherd *that leaveth* his flock

19 in the hands of cruel wolves. Then said I unto him, Go thy ways from me, and come not nigh me for seven days, and then shalt thou come unto me. And he heard what I said, and went from me.

20 And so I fasted seven days, mourning and weeping, like as Uriel the an-

21 gel commanded me. And after seven days so it was, that the thoughts of my heart were very grievous unto me

22 again, and my soul recovered the spirit of understanding, and I began to speak words before the Most High

23 again, and said, O Lord that bearest rule, of all the woods of the earth, and of all the trees thereof, thou hast

24 chosen thee one vine: and of all the lands of the world thou hast chosen

thee one ³ country: and of all the flowers of the world thou hast chosen

25 thee one lily: and of all the depths of the sea thou hast filled thee one river: and of all builded cities thou hast hal-

26 lowed Sion unto thyself: and of all the fowls that are created thou hast named thee one dove: and of all the cattle that are made thou hast provided thee one

27 sheep: and among all the multitudes of peoples thou hast gotten thee one people: and unto this people, whom thou lovedst, thou gavest a law that

28 is approved of all. And now, O Lord, why hast thou given this one people over unto many, and ⁴ hast dishonoured the one root above others, and hast scattered thine only one among

29 many? And they which did gainsay thy promises have trodden them down

30 that believed thy covenants. If thou dost so much hate thy people, they should be punished with thine own hands.

31 Now when I had spoken these words, the angel that came to me the night

32 afore was sent unto me, and said unto me, Hear me, and I will instruct thee; hearken unto me, and I shall tell thee more.

33 And I said, Speak on, my Lord. Then said he unto me, Thou art sore troubled in mind for Israel's sake: lovest thou that people better than he that made them?

34 And I said, No, Lord: but of very grief have I spoken: for my reins torment me every hour, while I labour to comprehend the way of the Most High, and to seek out part of his judgement.

35 And he said unto me, Thou canst not. And I said, Wherefore, Lord, or whereunto was I born? or why was not my mother's womb then my grave, that I might not have seen the travail of Jacob, and the wearisome toil of the stock of Israel?

36 And he said unto me, Number me them that are not yet come, gather me together the drops that are scattered abroad, make me the flowers green

37 again that are withered, open me the chambers that are closed, and bring me forth the winds that in them are shut up, or shew me the image of a voice: and then I will declare to thee the travail that thou askest to see.

38 And I said, O Lord that bearest rule, who may know these things, but he that hath not his dwelling with men?

39 As for me, I am unwise: how may I then speak of these things whereof thou askest me?

40 Then said he unto me, Like as thou canst do none of these things that I have spoken of, even so canst thou not find out my judgement, or the end of the love that I have promised unto my people.

41 And I said, But, lo, O Lord, thou hast

³ After the Oriental versions. The Latin has *pit.*

⁴ After the Oriental versions. The Latin reads *hast prepared.*

made the promise unto them that be in the end: and what shall they do that have been before us, or we *that be now*, or they that shall come after us?

42 And he said unto me, I will liken my judgement unto a ring: like as there is no slackness of them that be last, even so there is no swiftness of them that be first.

43 So I answered and said, Couldest thou not make them *to be* at once that have been made, and that be now, and that are for to come; that thou mightest shew thy judgement the sooner?

44 Then answered he me, and said, The creature may not haste above the creator; neither may the world hold them at once that shall be created therein.

45 And I said, How hast thou said unto thy servant, that [1]thou wilt surely make alive at once the creature that thou hast created? [2]If therefore they shall be alive at once, and the creature shall sustain them: even so it might now also support them to be present at once.

46 And he said unto me, Ask the womb of a woman, and say unto her, If thou bringest forth ten children, why *doest thou it* at several times? pray her therefore to bring forth ten children at once.

47 And I said, She cannot: but must do it by distance of time.

48 Then said he unto me, Even so have I given the womb of the earth to those that be sown therein in their several times. For like as a young child may not bring forth, neither she that is grown old *bring forth* any more, even so have I disposed the world which I created.

50 And I asked, and said, Seeing thou hast now shewed me the way, I will speak before thee: Is our mother, of whom thou hast told me, still young? or doth she now draw nigh unto age?

51 He answered me, and said, Ask a woman that beareth children, and she

52 shall tell thee. Say unto her, Wherefore are not they whom thou hast now brought forth like those that were be-

53 fore, but less of stature? And she also shall answer thee, They that be born in the strength of youth are of one fashion, and they that are born in the time of age, when the womb faileth,

54 are otherwise. Consider therefore thou also, how that ye are less of stature than those that were before you.

55 And so are they that come after you less than ye, as *born* of the creature which now beginneth to be old, and is past the strength of youth.

56 Then said I, Lord, I beseech thee, if I have found favour in thy sight, shew thy servant by whom thou visitest thy creature.

6 And he said unto me, In the beginning, when the earth was made, before the outgoings of the world were fixed, or ever the gatherings of the winds

2 blew, before the voices of the thunder sounded and before the flashes of the lightning shone, or ever the founda-

3 tions of paradise were laid, before the fair flowers were seen, or ever the powers of the earthquake were estab-

4 lished, before the innumerable hosts of angels were gathered together, or ever the heights of the air were lifted up, before the measures of the firmament were named, or ever the foot-

5 stool of Sion [1]was established, and ere the present years were sought out, and or ever the imaginations of them that now sin were estranged, before they were sealed that have gathered

6 faith for a treasure: then did I consider these things, and they all were made through me alone, and through none other: as by me also they shall be ended, and by none other.

7 Then answered I and said, What shall be the parting asunder of the times? or when shall be the end of the first, and the beginning of it that followeth?

8 And he said unto me, From [3]Abraham unto [4]Abraham, inasmuch as Jacob and Esau were born of him, for Jacob's hand held the heel of Esau

9 from the beginning. For Esau is the end of this world, and Jacob is the

10 beginning of it that followeth. [5]The beginning of a man is his hand, and the end of a man is his heel; between the heel and the hand seek thou nought else, Esdras.

11 I answered then and said, O Lord that bearest rule, if I have found

12 favour in thy sight, I beseech thee, shew thy servant the end of thy tokens, whereof thou shewedst me part the last night.

13 So he answered and said unto me, Stand up upon thy feet, and thou shalt

14 hear a mighty sounding voice; and if the place whereon thou standest be

15 greatly moved, when it speaketh be not thou afraid: for the word is of the end, and the foundations of the earth

16 shall understand, that the speech is of them: they shall tremble and be moved: for they know that their end must be changed.

17 And it happened, that when I had heard it I stood up upon my feet, and hearkened, and, behold, there was a voice that spake, and the sound of it was like the sound of many waters.

18 And it said, Behold, the days come, and it shall be that when I draw nigh to visit them that dwell upon the

19 earth, and when I shall make inquisition of them that have done hurt unjustly with their unrighteousness, and when the affliction of Sion shall be

[1] So the Syriac.
[2] The Latin omits *If ... alive at once.*

[3] Perhaps for *Abram.*
[4] Another reading is, *Isaac.*
[5] So the Syriac, &c. The Latin is defective.

20

20 fulfilled, and when the seal shall be set upon the world that is to pass away, then will I shew these tokens: the books shall be opened before the firmament, and all shall see together:
21 and the children of a year old shall speak with their voices, the women with child shall bring forth untimely children at three or four months, and
22 they shall live, and dance. And suddenly shall the sown places appear unsown, the full storehouses shall
23 suddenly be found empty: and the trumpet shall give a sound, which when every man heareth, they shall
24 be suddenly afraid. At that time shall friends make war one against another like enemies, and the earth shall stand in fear with those that dwell therein, the springs of the fountains shall stand still, so that for three hours they shall
25 not run. And it shall be that whosoever remaineth after all these things that I have told thee of, he shall be saved, and shall see my salvation, and
26 the end of my world. And they shall see the men that have been taken up, who have not tasted death from their birth: and the heart of the inhabitants shall be changed, and turned into an-
27 other meaning. For evil shall be blotted out, and deceit shall be quenched;
28 and faith shall flourish, and corruption shall be overcome, and the truth, which hath been so long without fruit, shall be declared.
29 And when he talked with me, behold, by little and little the place whereon I
30 stood [1] rocked to and fro. And he said unto me, These things came I to
31 shew thee [2] this night. If therefore thou wilt pray yet again, and fast seven days more, I shall yet [3] tell thee great-
32 er things than these. For thy voice hath surely been heard before the Most High: for the Mighty hath seen thy righteous dealing, he hath seen aforetime also thy chastity, which thou
33 hast had ever since thy youth. And therefore hath he sent me to shew thee all these things, and to say unto thee, Be of good comfort, and fear not.
34 And be not hasty in *regard of* the former times, to think vain things, that thou mayest not hasten in the latter times.
35 And it came to pass after this, that I wept again, and fasted seven days in like manner, that I might fulfil the three weeks which he told me.
36 And in the eighth night was my heart vexed within me again, and I began
37 to speak before the Most High. For my spirit was greatly set on fire, and
38 my soul was in distress. And I said, O Lord, of a truth thou spakest at the beginning of the creation, upon the first day, and saidst thus; Let heaven and earth be made; and thy
39 word perfected the work. And then

was the spirit hovering, and darkness and silence were on every side; the sound of man's voice was not yet [4].
40 Then commandedst thou a ray of light to be brought forth of thy treasures, that then thy works might appear.
41 Upon the second day again thou madest the spirit of the firmament and commandedst it to part asunder, and to make a division betwixt the waters, that the one part might go up,
42 and the other remain beneath. Upon the third day thou didst command that the waters should be gathered together in the seventh part of the earth: six parts didst thou dry up, and keep them, to the intent that of these some being both planted and tilled might
43 serve before thee. For as soon as thy word went forth the work was
44 done. For immediately there came forth great and innumerable fruit, and manifold pleasures for the taste, and flowers of inimitable colour, and odours of most exquisite smell: and this was
45 done the third day. Upon the fourth day thou commandedst that the sun should shine, and the moon give her light, and the stars should be in their
46 order: and gavest them a charge to do service unto man, that was to
47 be made. Upon the fifth day thou saidst unto the seventh part, where the water was gathered together, that it should bring forth living creatures. fowls and fishes: and so it came to
48 pass, that the dumb water and without life brought forth living things as it was bidden, that the peoples might therefore praise thy wondrous works.
49 Then didst thou preserve two living creatures, the one thou calledst [5] Behemoth, and the other thou calledst
50 [6] Leviathan: and thou didst separate the one from the other: for the seventh part, namely, where the water was gathered together, might not hold them
51 both. Unto [5] Behemoth thou gavest one part, which was dried up on the third day, that he should dwell in the same, [5] wherein are a thousand hills:
52 but unto [6] Leviathan thou gavest the seventh part, namely, the moist; and thou hast kept them to be devoured
53 of whom thou wilt, and when. But upon the sixth day thou gavest commandment unto the earth, that it should bring forth before thee cattle,
54 beasts, and creeping things: and over these Adam, whom thou ordainedst lord over all the works that thou hast made: of him come we all, the people
55 whom thou hast chosen. All this have I spoken before thee, O Lord, because thou hast said that for our sakes thou
56 madest [7] this world. As for the other nations, which also come of Adam, thou hast said that they are nothing, and are like unto spittle: and thou hast likened the abundance of them

[1] After the Oriental versions. The Latin is corrupt.
[2] So the Syriac. The Latin is corrupt.
[3] The Latin has *tell thee by day.*

[4] The Latin adds *from thee.*

[5] Ps. l. 10.
[6] Ps. lxxiv. 14.

[7] So the Syriac. The Latin has *the firstborn world.*

21

unto a drop that falleth from a vessel.
57 And now, O Lord, behold, these nations, which are reputed as nothing,
58 be lords over us, and devour us. But we thy people, whom thou hast called thy firstborn, thy only begotten, and thy fervent lover, are given into their
59 hands. If the world now be made for our sakes, why do we not possess for an inheritance our world? how long shall this endure?

7 And when I had made an end of speaking these words, there was sent unto me the angel which had been
2 sent unto me the nights afore: and he said unto me, Up, Esdras, and hear the words that I am come to tell thee.
3 And I said, Speak on, my Lord. Then said he unto me, There is a sea set in a wide place, that it might be ¹ broad
4 and vast. But the entrance thereof shall be set in a narrow place so as to
5 be like a river; whoso then should desire to go into the sea to look upon it, or to rule it, if he went not through the narrow, how could he come into
6 the broad? Another thing also: There is a city builded and set in a plain country, and full of all good things;
7 but the entrance thereof is narrow, and is set in a dangerous place to fall, having a fire on the right hand, and on
8 the left a deep water: and there is one only path between them both, even between the fire and the water, *so small* that there could but one man go there
9 at once. If this city now be given unto a man for an inheritance, if the heir pass not the danger set before him, how shall he receive his inheritance?
10 And I said, It is so, Lord. Then said he unto me, Even so also is Israel's
11 portion. Because for their sakes I made the world: and when Adam transgressed my statutes, then was
12 decreed that now is done. Then were the entrances of this world made narrow, and sorrowful and toilsome: they are but few and evil, full of perils, and charged with great toils. For
13 ils, and charged with great toils. For the entrances of the greater world are wide and sure, and bring forth
14 fruit of immortality. If then they that live enter not these strait and vain things, they can never receive
15 those that are laid up for them. Now therefore why disquietest thou thyself, seeing thou art but a corruptible
16 man? and why art thou moved, whereas thou art but mortal? and why hast thou not considered in thy mind that which is to come, rather than
17 that which is present? Then answered I and said, O Lord that bearest rule, lo, thou hast ordained in thy law, that the righteous should inherit these things, but that the ungodly
18 should perish. The righteous therefore shall suffer strait things, and hope for wide: but they that have done

wickedly ² have suffered the strait things, and yet shall not see the wide.
19 And he said unto me, ³ Thou art not a judge above God, neither hast thou understanding above the Most High.
20 Yea, rather let many that now be perish, than that the law of God which
21 is set before them be despised. For God straitly commanded such as came, even as they came, what they should do to live, and what they should observe to avoid punishment.
22 Nevertheless they were not obedient unto him; but spake against him, and imagined for themselves vain things;
23 and framed cunning devices of wickedness; and said moreover of the Most High, that he is not; and knew not
24 his ways: but they despised his law, and denied his covenants; they have not been faithful to his statutes, and
25 have not performed his works. Therefore, Esdras, for the empty are empty things, and for the full are the full
26 things. For behold, the time shall come, and it shall be, when these tokens, of which I told thee before, shall come to pass, that the bride shall appear, even the city coming forth, and she shall be seen, that now is
27 withdrawn from the earth. And whosoever is delivered from the foresaid evils, the same shall see my wonders.
28 For my son Jesus shall be revealed with those that be with him, and shall rejoice them that remain four hundred
29 years. After these years shall my son Christ die, and all that have the breath
30 of ⁴ life. And the world shall be turned into the old silence seven days, like as in the first beginning: so that no man
31 shall remain. And after seven days the world, that yet awaketh not, shall be raised up, and that shall die that
32 is corruptible. And the earth shall restore those that are asleep in her, and so shall the dust those that dwell therein in silence, and the ⁵ secret places shall deliver those souls that
33 were committed unto them. And the Most High shall be revealed upon the seat of judgement ⁶, and compassion shall pass away, and longsuffering
34 shall be withdrawn: but judgement only shall remain, truth shall stand,
35 and faith shall wax strong: and the work shall follow, and the reward shall be shewed, and good deeds shall awake, and wicked deeds shall not
[36] sleep. ⁷ And the ⁸ pit of torment shall appear, and over against it shall be the place of rest: and the furnace of ⁹ hell shall be shewed, and over against it the paradise of delight.
[37] And then shall the Most High say to the nations that are raised from the dead, See ye and understand whom ye have denied, or whom ye have not served, or whose command-
[38] ments ye have despised. Look on

Margin notes

¹ So the chief Oriental versions. The Latin MSS. have *deep*.

² According to some authorities, *have not suffered*... *and shall not see*.

³ Another reading is, *There is no judge*... *and none that hath understanding*.

⁴ Lat. *man*.

⁵ Or, *chambers*. See ch. iv. 35.

⁶ The Syriac adds *and the end shall come*.

⁷ The passage from verse [36] to verse [105], formerly missing, has been restored to the text. See *Preface*, page ix.

⁸ So the chief Oriental versions. The Latin MSS. have *place*.

⁹ Lat. *Gehenna*.

1 So the chief Oriental versions. The Latin has *shalt thou speak.*

2 Or, *storm*

3 The Latin is here corrupt.

this side and on that: here is delight and rest, and there fire and torments. Thus ¹ shall he speak unto them in

[39] the day of judgement: This is a

[40] day that hath neither sun, nor moon, nor stars, neither cloud, nor thunder, nor lightning, neither wind, nor water, nor air, neither darkness,

[41] nor evening, nor morning, neither summer, nor spring, nor heat, nor

² winter, neither frost, nor cold, nor

[42] hail, nor rain, nor dew, neither noon, nor night, nor dawn, neither shining, nor brightness, nor light, save only the splendour of the glory of the Most High, whereby all shall see the

[43] things that are set before them: for it shall endure as it were a week of

[44] years. This is my judgement and the ordinance thereof; but to thee only have I shewed these things.

[45] And I answered, I said even then, O Lord, and I say now: Blessed are they that be now alive and keep the

[46] *statutes* ordained of thee. But as touching them for whom my prayer was made, *what shall I say?* for who is there of them that be alive that hath not sinned, and who of the sons *of men* that hath not transgressed

[47] thy covenant? And now I see, that the world to come shall bring delight to few, but torments unto many.

[48] For an evil heart hath grown up in us, which hath led us astray from these *statutes*, and hath brought us into corruption and into the ways of death. hath shewed us the paths of perdition and removed us far from life; and that, not a few only, but well nigh all that have been created.

[49] And he answered me, and said, Hearken unto me, and I will instruct thee; and I will admonish thee yet

[50] again: for this cause the Most High hath not made one world, but two.

[51] For whereas thou hast said that the just are not many, but few, and the ungodly abound, hear *the answer*

[52] thereunto. If thou have choice stones exceeding few, ³ wilt thou set for thee over against them according to their number *things of* lead and clay?

[53] And I said, Lord, how shall this be?

[54] And he said unto me, Not only this, but ask the earth, and she shall tell thee; intreat her, and she shall

[55] declare unto thee. For thou shalt say unto her, Thou bringest forth gold and silver and brass, and iron

[56] also and lead and clay: but silver is more abundant than gold, and brass than silver, and iron than brass, lead

[57] than iron, and clay than lead. Judge thou therefore which things are precious and to be desired, whatso is abundant or what is rare.

[58] And I said, O Lord that bearest rule, that which is plentiful is of less worth, for that which is more rare is more precious.

[59] And he answered me, and said, ³ Weigh within thyself the things that thou hast thought, for he that hath what is hard to get rejoiceth over

[60] him that hath what is plentiful. So also is the ³ judgement which I have promised: for I will rejoice over the few that shall be saved, inasmuch as these are they that have made my glory now to prevail, and of whom

[61] my name is now named. And I will not grieve over the multitude of them that perish; for these are they that are now like unto vapour, and are become as flame and smoke; they are set on fire and burn hotly, and are quenched.

[62] And I answered and said, O thou earth, wherefore hast thou brought forth, if the mind is made out of dust,

[63] like as all other created things? For it were better that the dust itself had been unborn, so that the mind might

[64] not have been made therefrom. But now the mind groweth with us, and by reason of this we are tormented,

[65] because we perish and know it. Let the race of men lament and the beasts of the field be glad; let all that are born lament, but let the fourfooted

[66] beasts and the cattle rejoice. For it is far better with them than with us; for they look not for judgement, neither do they know of torments or of salvation promised unto them after

[67] death. For what doth it profit us, that we shall be preserved alive, but

[68] yet be afflicted with torment? For all that are born are ³ defiled with iniquities. and are full of sins and laden with

[69] offences: and if after death we were not to come into judgement, peradventure it had been better for us.

[70] And he answered me, and said, When the Most High made the world, and Adam and all them that came of him, he first prepared the judgement and the things that pertain unto the

[71] judgement. And now understand from thine own words, for thou hast said that the mind groweth with us.

[72] They therefore that dwell upon the earth shall be tormented for this reason, that having understanding they have wrought iniquity, and receiving commandments have not kept them, and having obtained a law they dealt unfaithfully with that which they re-

[73] ceived. What then will they have to say in the judgement, or how will

[74] they answer in the last times? For how great a time hath the Most High been longsuffering with them that inhabit the world, and not for their sakes, but because of the times which he hath foreordained!

[75] And I answered and said, If I have

23

found grace in thy sight, O Lord, shew this also unto thy servant, whether after death, even now when every one of us giveth up his soul, we shall be kept in rest until those times come, in which thou shalt renew the creation, or whether we shall be tormented forthwith.

[76] And he answered me, and said, I will shew thee this also; but join not thyself with them that are scorners, nor number thyself with them [77] that are tormented. For thou hast a treasure of *good* works laid up with the Most High, but it shall not be shewed thee until the last times. [78] For concerning death the teaching is: When the determinate sentence hath gone forth from the Most High that a man should die, as the spirit leaveth the body to return again to him who gave it, it adoreth the glory [79] of the Most High first of all. And if it be one of those that have been scorners and have not kept the way of the Most High, and that have despised his law, and that hate them that [80] fear ¹ God, these spirits shall not enter into habitations, but shall wander and be in torments forthwith, ever grieving and sad, in seven ways. [81] The first way, because they have despised the law of the Most High. [82] The second way, because they cannot now make a good returning that [83] they may live. The third way, they shall see the reward laid up for them that have believed the covenants of [84] the Most High. The fourth way, they shall consider the torment laid up for themselves in the last days. [85] The fifth way, they shall see the dwelling places of the others guarded [86] by angels, with great quietness. The sixth way, they shall see ² how forthwith some of them shall pass into [87] torment. The seventh way, which is ³ more grievous than all the aforesaid ways, because they shall pine away in confusion and be consumed with ⁴ shame, and shall be withered up by fears, seeing the glory of the Most High before whom they have sinned whilst living, and before whom they shall be judged in the last times. [88] Now this is the order of those who have kept the ways of the Most High, when they shall be separated from the [89] corruptible vessel. In the time ⁴ that they dwelt therein they painfully served the Most High, and were in jeopardy every hour, that they might keep the law of the lawgiver perfectly. [90] Wherefore this is the teaching concerning them: [91] First of all they shall see with great joy the glory of him who taketh them up, for they shall [92] have rest in seven orders. The first order, because they have striven with great labour to overcome the evil

thought which was fashioned together with them, that it might not lead them astray from life into death. [93] The second order, because they see the perplexity in which the souls of the ungodly wander, and the punish- [94] ment that awaiteth them. The third order, they see the witness which he that fashioned them beareth concerning them, that while they lived they kept the law which was given [95] them in trust. The fourth order, they understand the rest which, being gathered in their chambers, they now enjoy with great quietness, guarded by angels, and the glory that awaiteth [96] them in the last days. The fifth order, they rejoice, *seeing* how they have now escaped from that which is corruptible, and how they shall inherit that which is to come, while they see moreover the straitness and the ⁴ painfulness from which they have been delivered, and the large room which they shall receive with joy and immor- [97] tality. The sixth order, when it is shewed unto them how their face shall shine as the sun, and how they shall be made like unto the light of the stars, being henceforth incorruptible. [98] The seventh order, which is greater than all the aforesaid orders, because they shall rejoice with confidence, and because they shall be bold without confusion, and shall be glad without fear, for they hasten to behold the face of him whom in their lifetime they served, and from whom they shall receive *their* reward in glory. [99] This is the order of the souls of the just, as from henceforth ⁴ is announced unto them, *and* aforesaid are the ways of torture which they that would not give heed shall suffer from hence- [100] forth. And I answered and said, Shall time therefore be given unto the souls after they are separated from the bodies, that they may see that whereof thou hast spoken unto me? [101] And he said, Their freedom shall be for seven days, that for seven days they may see the things whereof thou hast been told, and afterwards they shall be gathered together in their [102] habitations. And I answered and said, If I have found favour in thy sight, shew further unto me thy servant whether in the day of judgement the just will be able to intercede for the ungodly or to intreat the Most [103] High for them, whether fathers for children, or children for parents, or brethren for brethren, or kinsfolk for their next of kin, or ⁵ friends for them [104] that are most dear. And he answered me, and said, Since thou hast found favour in my sight, I will shew thee this also: The day of judgement is ⁶ a day of decision, and displayeth unto all the seal of truth; even as now

Margin notes (left):
¹ Another reading is, *him.*

² The passage is corrupt.
³ Lat. *greater.*

⁴ The Latin is here corrupt.

Margin notes (right):
⁵ So the Oriental versions

⁶ The Latin has *a bold* day

a father sendeth not his son, or a son
his father, or a master his slave, or a
[1] friend him that is most dear, that in
his stead he may [2] be sick, or sleep, or
[105] eat, or be healed: so never shall
any one pray for another [3] in that day,
neither shall one lay a burden on another, for then shall all bear every
one his own righteousness or unrighteousness.
36 And I answered and said, How do
we now find that first Abraham prayed for the people of Sodom, and Moses
[106] for the fathers that sinned in the wil-
[107] 37 derness: and Joshua after him for
[108] 38 Israel in the days of [4] Achar: and
Samuel [5] in the days of Saul; and
David for the plague: and Solomon
for them that *should worship* in the
[109] 39 sanctuary: and Elijah for those that
received rain; and for the dead, that
[110] 40 he might live: and Hezekiah for the
people in the days of Sennacherib:
[111] 41 and many for many? If therefore
now, when corruption is grown up,
and unrighteousness increased, the
righteous have prayed for the ungodly,
wherefore shall it not be so then also?
42 He answered me, and said, This pre-
[112] sent world is not the end; the full
glory abideth [6] not therein: therefore
have they who were able prayed for
43 the weak. But the day of judgement
[113] shall be the end of this time, [6] and the
beginning of the immortality for to
come, wherein corruption is passed
[114] 44 away, intemperance is at an end, in-
fidelity is cut off, but righteousness
is grown, and truth is sprung up.
[115] 45 Then shall no man be able to have
mercy on him that is cast in judgement, nor to thrust down him that
hath gotten the victory.
[116] 46 I answered then and said, This is my
first and last saying, that it had been
better that the earth had not [7] given
thee Adam: or else, when it had given
him, to have restrained him from sin-
[117] 47 ning. For what profit is it for all
that are in this present time to live in
heaviness, and after death to look for
[118] 48 punishment? O thou Adam, what
hast thou done? for though it was
thou that sinned, the evil is not fallen
on thee alone, but upon all of us that
[119] 49 come of thee. For what profit is it
unto us, if there be promised us an
immortal time, whereas we have done
[120] 50 the works that bring death? And
that there is promised us an everlasting hope, whereas ourselves most
[121] 51 miserably are become vain? And
that there are reserved habitations of
health and safety, whereas we have
[122] 52 lived wickedly? And that the glory
of the Most High shall defend them
which have led a pure life, whereas
we have walked in the most wicked
[123] 53 ways of all? And that there shall be
shewed a paradise, whose fruit endureth without decay, wherein is abundance and healing, but we shall not
54 enter into it, for we have walked in [124]
55 unpleasant places? And that the [125]
faces of them which have used absti-
nence shall shine above the stars,
whereas our faces shall be blacker
56 than darkness? For while we lived [126]
and committed iniquity, we considered
not what we should have to suffer
after death.
57 Then he answered and said, This is [127]
the [8] condition of the battle, which
man that is born upon the earth shall
58 fight; that, if he be overcome, he shall [128]
suffer as thou hast said: but if he get
the victory, he shall receive the thing
59 that I say. For this is the way where- [129]
of Moses spake unto the people while
he lived, saying, [9] Choose thee life,
60 that thou mayest live. Nevertheless [130]
they believed not him, nor yet the
prophets after him, no, nor me which
61 have spoken unto them; so that there [131]
shall not be such heaviness in their
destruction, as there shall be joy over
them that are persuaded to salvation.
62 I answered then and said, I know, [132]
Lord, that the Most High is now
called merciful, in that he hath mercy
upon them which are not yet come
63 into the world; and compassionate, [133]
in that he hath compassion upon
64 those that turn to his law; and long- [134]
suffering, for that he long suffereth
those that have sinned, as his crea-
65 tures; and bountiful, for that he is [135]
ready to give rather than to exact;
66 and of great mercy, for that he mul- [136]
tiplieth more and more mercies to
them that are present, and that are
past, and also to them which are to
67 come; (for if he multiplied not *his* [137]
mercies, the world would not continue
68 with them that dwell therein;) and [138]
one that forgiveth, for if he did not
forgive of his goodness, that they
which have committed iniquities
might be eased of them, the ten thou-
sandth part of men would not remain
69 living; and a judge, *for* if he did not [139]
pardon them that were created by
his word, and blot out the multitude
70 of [10] offences, there would peradven- [140]
ture be very few left in an innumerable multitude.
8 And he answered me, and said, The
Most High hath made this world for
many, but the world to come for few.
2 I will tell thee now a similitude, Esdras; As when thou askest the earth,
it shall say unto thee, that it giveth
very much mould whereof earthen
vessels are made, and little dust that
gold cometh of: even so is the course
3 of the present world. There be many
created, but few shall be saved.
4 And I answered and said, Swallow
down understanding then, O my soul,

1 So the Oriental versions.
2 The Latin has *understand*.
3 So the Syriac. The Latin omits *in that day . . . another*.
4 That is, *Achan*. See Josh. vii. 1.
5 So the Syriac and other versions. The Latin omits *in the days of Saul*.
6 Omitted in the Latin.
7 See ch. iii. 5.
8 Or, *intent*
9 Deut. xxx. 19.
10 Lat. *contempts*.

5 and let *my heart* devour wisdom. For thou [1]art come hither without thy will, and departest when thou would-
6 est not: for there is given thee no longer space than only to live a short time. O Lord, that art over us, suffer thy servant, that we may pray before thee, and give us seed unto our heart, and culture to our understanding, that there may come fruit of it, whereby every one shall live that is corrupt,

who beareth the [2]likeness of a man.
7 For thou art alone, and we all one workmanship of thine hands, like as
8 thou hast said. Forasmuch as thou quickenest the body that is fashioned now in the womb, and givest it members, thy creature is preserved in fire and water, and nine months doth thy workmanship endure thy creature
9 which is created in her. But that which keepeth and that which is kept

shall both be kept [3]by thy keeping: and when the womb giveth up again
10 that which hath grown in it, thou hast commanded that out of the parts of the body, that is to say, out of the breasts, be given milk, which is the
11 fruit of the breasts, that the thing which is fashioned may be nourished for a time, and afterwards thou shalt
12 order it in thy mercy. Yea, thou hast brought it up in thy righteousness, and nurtured it in thy law, and
13 corrected it with thy judgement. And thou shalt mortify it as thy creature,
14 and quicken it as thy work. If therefore thou shalt [1]lightly and suddenly destroy him which with so great labour was fashioned by thy commandment, to what purpose was he made?
15 Now therefore I will speak; touching man in general, thou knowest best; but touching thy people *will I speak*,
16 for whose sake I am sorry; and for thine inheritance, for whose cause I mourn; and for Israel, for whom I am heavy; and for the seed of Jacob,
17 for whose sake I am troubled; therefore will I begin to pray before thee for myself and for them: for I see the falls of us that dwell in the land;
18 but I have heard the swiftness of the
19 judgement which is to come. Therefore hear my voice, and understand my saying, and I will speak before thee.

The beginning of the words of Esdras, before he was taken up. And he said,

20 O Lord, thou that [4]abidest for ever, whose eyes are exalted, and whose
21 chambers are in the air; whose throne is inestimable; whose glory may not be comprehended; before whom the hosts of angels stand with trembling,
22 [5]at whose bidding they are changed to wind and fire; whose word is sure, and sayings constant; whose ordinance is strong, and commandment

23 fearful; whose look drieth up the depths, and whose indignation maketh the mountains to melt away, and
24 whose truth beareth witness: hear, O Lord, the prayer of thy servant, and give ear to the petition of thy handy-
25 work; attend unto my words, for so long as I live I will speak, and so long as I have understanding I will answer.
26 O look not upon the sins of thy people; but on them that have served thee in
27 truth. Regard not the doings of them that deal wickedly, but of them that have kept thy covenants in affliction.
28 Think not upon those that have walked feignedly before thee; but remember them which have willingly known
29 thy fear. Let it not be thy will to destroy them which have lived like cattle; but look upon them that have
30 [6]clearly taught thy law. Take thou no indignation at them which are deemed worse than beasts; but love them that have alway put their trust
31 in thy glory. For we and our fathers have [7]passed our lives in [8]ways that bring death: but thou because of us
32 sinners [9]art called merciful. For if thou hast a desire to have mercy upon us, then shalt thou be called merciful, to us, namely, that have no works of
33 righteousness. For the just, which have many *good* works laid up with thee, shall for their own deeds receive
34 reward. For what is man, that thou shouldest take displeasure at him? or what is a corruptible race, that thou
35 shouldest be so bitter toward it? For in truth there is no man among them that be born, but he hath dealt wickedly; and among them [10]that have lived there is none which hath not
36 done amiss. For in this, O Lord, thy righteousness and thy goodness shall be declared, if thou be merciful unto them which have no store of good works.
37 Then answered he me, and said, Some things hast thou spoken aright, and according unto thy words so shall
38 it come to pass. For indeed I will not think on the fashioning of them which have sinned, or their death, their judgement, or their destruction:
39 but I will rejoice over the framing of the righteous, their pilgrimage also, and the salvation, and the reward, that
40 they shall have. Like therefore as I
41 have spoken, so shall it be. For as the husbandman soweth much seed upon the ground, and planteth many trees, and yet not all that is sown shall [11]come up in due season, neither shall all that is planted take root: even so they that are sown in the world shall not all be saved.
42 I answered then and said, If I have found favour, let me speak before
43 thee. Forasmuch as the husbandman's seed, if it come not up, seeing

that it hath not received thy rain in due season, or if it be corrupted through too much rain, [1] so perish-
44 eth; likewise man, which is formed with thy hands, and is called thine own image, because he is made like *unto thee*, for whose sake thou hast formed all things, even him hast thou made like unto the husbandman's
45 seed. Be not wroth with us, but spare thy people, and have mercy upon thine inheritance; for thou hast mercy upon thine own creation.
46 Then answered he me, and said, Things present are for them that now be, and things to come for such as
47 shall be hereafter. For thou comest far short that thou shouldest be able to love my creature more than I. But thou hast brought thyself full nigh unto the unrighteous. *Let this* never
48 *be.* Yet in this shalt thou be admi-
49 rable before the Most High; in that thou hast humbled thyself, as it becometh thee, and hast not judged thyself *worthy to be* among the righteous,
50 so as to be much glorified. For many grievous miseries shall befall them that in the last times dwell in the world, because they have walked in
51 great pride. But understand thou for thyself, and of such as be like thee
52 seek out the glory. For unto you is paradise opened, the tree of life is planted, the time to come is prepared, plenteousness is made ready, a city is builded, and rest is [2]allowed, goodness is perfected, wisdom being perfect
53 aforehand. The root *of evil* is sealed up from you, weakness is done away from you, and [3] [death] is hidden; hell and corruption are fled into forgetful-
54 ness: sorrows are passed away, and in the end is shewed the treasure of
55 immortality. Therefore ask thou no more questions concerning the multi-
56 tude of them that perish. For when they had received liberty, they despised the Most High, thought scorn of his law, and forsook his ways.
57 Moreover they have trodden down his
58 righteous, and said in their heart, that there is no God; yea, and that know-
59 ing they must die. For as the things aforesaid shall receive you, so thirst and pain which are prepared *shall receive* them: for the Most High willed not that men should come to nought:
60 but they which be created have themselves defiled the name of him that made them, and were unthankful unto
61 him which prepared life for them. And therefore is my judgement now at
62 hand, which I have not shewed unto all men, but unto thee, and a few like thee.
63 Then answered I and said, Behold, O Lord, now hast thou shewed me the multitude of the wonders, which thou wilt do in the last times: but

at what time, thou hast not shewed me.
9 And he answered me, and said, Measure thou diligently within thyself: and when thou seest that a certain part of the signs are past, which have
2 been told thee beforehand, then shalt thou understand, that it is the very time, wherein the Most High will visit the world which was made by him.
3 And when there shall be seen in the world earthquakes, disquietude of peoples, devices of nations, wavering
4 of leaders, disquietude of princes, then shalt thou understand, that the Most High spake of these things from the days that were aforetime from the
5 beginning. For like as of all that is made in the world, the beginning [4] is
6 evident, and the end manifest; so also are the times of the Most High: the beginnings are manifest in wonders and mighty works, and the end in
7 effects and signs. And every one that shall be saved, and shall be able to escape by his works, or by faith,
8 whereby he hath believed, shall be preserved from the said perils, and shall see my salvation in my land, and within my borders, which I have sanc-
9 tified for me from the beginning. Then shall they be amazed, which now have abused my ways: and they that have cast them away despitefully shall
10 dwell in torments. For as many as in their life have received benefits, and
11 yet have not known me; and as many as have scorned my law, while they had yet liberty, and, when as yet place of repentance was open unto them,
12 understood not, but despised [5]*it*; the same must know [5]*it* after death by
13 torment. And therefore be thou no longer curious how the ungodly shall be punished; but inquire how the righteous shall be saved, [6]they whose the world is, and for whom the world [6]*was created.*
14
15 And I answered and said, I have said before, and now do speak, and will speak it also hereafter, that there be more of them which perish, than
16 of them which shall be saved: like as a wave is greater than a drop.
17 And he answered me, saying, Like as the field is, so is also the seed; and as the flowers be, such are the colours also; and such as the work is, such also is the [7] judgement *thereon*; and as is the husbandman, so is his threshing-floor also. For there was a time in
18 the world, even then when I was preparing for them that now live, before the world was made for them to dwell in; and then no man spake against
19 me, for [8] there was not any: but now they which are created in this world that is prepared, both [8] with a table that faileth not, and a law which is unsearchable, are corrupted in their

20 manners. So I considered my world, and, lo, it was destroyed, and my earth, and, lo, it was in peril, because of the
21 devices that were come into it. And I saw, and spared them, but not greatly, and saved me a grape out of a cluster, and a plant out of [1] a great forest.
22 Let the multitude perish then, which was born in vain; and let my grape be saved, and my plant; for with great labour have I made them per-
23 fect. Nevertheless if thou wilt cease yet seven days more, (howbeit thou
24 shalt not fast in them, but shalt go into a field of flowers, where no house is builded, and eat only of the flowers of the field; and thou shalt taste no flesh, and shalt drink no wine, but
25 *shalt eat* flowers only;) and pray unto the Most High continually, then will I come and talk with thee.
26 So I went my way, like as he commanded me, into the field which is called [2] Ardat; and there I sat among the flowers, and did eat of the herbs of the field, and the meat of the same
27 satisfied me. And it came to pass after seven days that I lay upon the grass, and my heart was vexed again,
28 like as before: and my mouth was opened, and I began to speak before
29 the Most High, and said, O Lord, thou didst shew thyself among us, unto our fathers in the wilderness, when they went forth out of Egypt, and when they came into the wilderness, where no man treadeth and that bear-
30 eth no fruit; and thou didst say, Hear me, thou Israel; and mark my words,
31 O seed of Jacob. For, behold, I sow my law in you, and it shall bring forth fruit in you, and ye shall be glorified
32 in it for ever. But our fathers, which received the law, kept it not, and observed not the statutes: and the fruit of the law did not perish, neither could
33 it, for it was thine; yet they that received it perished, because they kept not the thing that was sown in them.
34 And, lo, it is a custom, that when the ground hath received seed, or the sea a ship, or any vessel meat or drink, and when it cometh to pass that that
35 which is sown, or that which is launched, or the things which have been received, should come to an end, these come to an end, but the receptacles remain: yet with us it hath not hap-
36 pened so. For we that have received the law shall perish by sin, and our
37 heart also which received it. Notwithstanding the law perisheth not, but remaineth in its honour.
38 And when I spake these things in my heart, I looked about me with mine eyes, and upon the right side I saw a woman, and, behold, she mourned and wept with a loud voice, and was much grieved in mind, and her clothes were rent, and she had ashes

39 upon her head. Then let I my thoughts go wherein I was occupied,
40 and turned me unto her, and said unto her, Wherefore weepest thou? and why art thou grieved in thy mind?
41 And she said unto me, Let me alone, my lord, that I may bewail myself, and add unto my sorrow, for I am sore vexed in my mind, and brought very low.
42 And I said unto her, What aileth
43 thee? tell me. She said unto me, I thy servant was barren, and had no child, though I had a husband thirty years.
44 And every hour and every day these thirty years did I make my prayer to
45 the Most High day and night. And it came to pass after thirty years that God heard me thine handmaid, and looked upon my low estate, and considered my trouble, and gave me a son: and I rejoiced in him greatly, I and my husband, and all my [3] neighbours: and we gave great honour
46 unto the Mighty. And I nourished
47 him with great travail. So when he grew up, and I came to take him a
10 wife, I made a feast day. And it so came to pass, that when my son was entered into his wedding chamber, he
2 fell down, and died. Then we all overthrew the lights. and all my [3] neighbours rose up to comfort me: and I remained quiet unto the second
3 day at night. And it came to pass, when they had all left off to comfort me, to the end I might be quiet, then rose I up by night, and fled, and came hither into this field, as thou seest.
4 And I do now purpose not to return into the city, but here to stay, and neither to eat nor drink, but continually to mourn and to fast until I die.
5 Then left I the meditations wherein I was, and answered her in anger,
6 and said, Thou foolish woman above all other, seest thou not our mourning, and what hath happened unto us?
7 how that Sion the mother of us all is full of sorrow, and much humbled.
8 [4] It is right now to mourn very sore, seeing we all mourn, and to be sorrowful, seeing we are all in sorrow, but
9 thou sorrowest for one son. For ask the earth, and she shall tell thee, that it is she which ought to mourn for so
10 many that grow upon her. For out of her all had their beginnings, and others shall come; and, behold, they walk almost all into destruction, and the multitude of them is utterly rooted
11 out. Who then should make more mourning, [5] she, that hath lost so great a multitude, or thou, which art
12 grieved but for one? But if thou sayest unto me, My lamentation is not like the earth's, for I have lost the fruit of my womb, which I brought forth with pains, and bare with sor-
13 rows: but *it is with* the earth after

[1] So the Syriac and other versions. The Latin has *great tribes.*

[2] The Syriac and Æthiopic have *Arphad.*

[3] Lat. *townsmen.*

[4] See the Oriental versions. The Latin is corrupt.

[5] So the Syriac.

the manner of the earth; the multitude present in it is gone, as it came:
14 then say I unto thee, Like as thou hast brought forth with sorrow; even so the earth also hath given her fruit, namely, man, ever since the beginning
15 unto him that made her. Now therefore keep thy sorrow to thyself, and bear with a good courage the adversi-
16 ties which have befallen thee. For if thou shalt acknowledge the decree of God to be just, thou shalt both receive thy son in time, and shalt be
17 praised among women. Go thy way then into the city to thine husband.
18 And she said unto me, That will I not do: I will not go into the city, but here will I die.
19 So I proceeded to speak further un-
20 to her, and said, Do not so, but suffer thyself to be prevailed on by reason of the adversities of Sion; and be comforted by reason of the sorrow of
21 Jerusalem. For thou seest that our sanctuary is laid waste, our altar broken down, our temple destroyed;
22 our psaltery is brought low, our song is put to silence, our rejoicing is at an end; the light of our candlestick is put out, the ark of our covenant is spoiled, our holy things are defiled, and the name that is called upon us is profaned; our freemen are despitefully treated, our priests are burnt, our Levites are gone into captivity, our virgins are defiled, and our wives ravished; our righteous men carried away, our little ones betrayed, our young men are brought into bondage, and our strong men are become weak;
23 and, what is more than all, the seal of Sion — for she hath now lost the seal of her honour, and is delivered into
24 the hands of them that hate us. Thou therefore shake off thy great heaviness, and put away from thee the multitude of sorrows, that the Mighty may be merciful unto thee again, and the Most High may give thee rest, even ease from thy travails.
25 And it came to pass, while I was talking with her, behold, her face upon a sudden shined exceedingly, and her countenance glistered like lightning, so that I was sore afraid
26 [1] of her, and mused what this might be; and, behold, suddenly she made a great cry very fearful; so that the
27 earth shook at the noise. And I looked, and, behold, the woman appeared unto me no more, but there was a city builded, and a place shewed itself from large foundations: then was I afraid, and cried with a loud
28 voice, and said, Where is Uriel the angel, who came unto me at the first? for he hath caused me to fall into this great trance, and mine end is turned into corruption, and my prayer to re-
29 buke. And as I was speaking these

1 The Syriac has to draw near unto her, and my heart was greatly astonied, and when I mused &c.

words, behold, the angel who had come unto me at the first came unto
30 me, and he looked upon me: and, lo, I lay as one that had been dead, and mine understanding was taken from me; and he took me by the right hand, and comforted me, and set me
31 upon my feet, and said unto me, What aileth thee? and why art thou so disquieted? and why is thine understanding troubled, and the thoughts
32 of thine heart? And I said, Because thou hast forsaken me: yet I did according to thy words, and went into the field, and, lo, I have seen, and yet see, that which I am not able to ex-
33 press. And he said unto me, Stand up like a man, and I will advise thee.
34 Then said I, Speak on, my Lord; only forsake me not, lest I die frustrate
35 of my hope. For I have seen that I knew not, and hear that I do not
36 know. Or is my sense deceived, or
37 my soul in a dream? Now therefore I beseech thee to shew thy servant concerning this trance.
38 And he answered me, and said, Hear me, and I shall inform thee, and tell thee concerning the things whereof thou art afraid: for the Most High hath revealed many secret things un-
39 to thee. He hath seen that thy way is right: for that thou sorrowest continually for thy people, and makest
40 great lamentation for Sion. This therefore is the meaning of the vision.
41 The woman which appeared unto thee a little while ago, whom thou sawest mourning, and begannest to
42 comfort her: but now seest thou the likeness of the woman no more, but there appeared unto thee a city in
43 building: and whereas she told thee of the death of her son, this is the so-
44 lution: This woman, whom thou sawest, is [2] Sion, [2] whom thou now seest
45 as a city builded; and whereas she said unto thee, that she hath been thirty years barren, it is, because there were three [2] thousand years in the world wherein there was no offer-
46 ing as yet offered in her. And it came to pass after three [2] thousand years that Solomon builded the city, and offered offerings: then it was that the
47 barren bare a son. And whereas she told thee that she nourished him with travail: that was the dwelling
48 in Jerusalem. And whereas she said unto thee, My son coming into his marriage chamber died, and that misfortune befell her: this was the destruction that came to Jerusalem.
49 And, behold, thou sawest her likeness, how she mourned for her son, and thou begannest to comfort her for what hath befallen her; [3] these
50 were the things to be opened unto thee. For now the Most High, seeing that thou art grieved unfeignedly,

2 So the Syriac and other versions. The Latin is incorrect.

3 Omitted in the Oriental versions.

and sufferest from thy whole heart for her, hath shewed thee the brightness of her glory, and the comeliness 51 of her beauty: and therefore I bade thee remain in the field where no 52 house was builded: for I knew that the Most High would shew this unto 53 thee. Therefore I commanded thee to come into the field, where no foun- 54 dation of any building was. For in the place wherein the city of the Most High was to be builded, the work of 55 no man's building could stand. Therefore fear thou not, nor let thine heart be affrighted, but go thy way in, and see the beauty and greatness of the building, as much as thine eyes be 56 able to see: and then shalt thou hear as much as thine ears may compre- 57 hend. For thou art blessed above many, and with the Most High art 58 called by name, like as but few. But to-morrow at night thou shalt remain 59 here; and so shall the Most High shew thee those visions in dreams, of what the Most High will do unto them that dwell upon earth in the last days. So I slept that night and another, like as he commanded me.

11 And it came to pass the second night that I saw a dream, and, behold, there came up from the sea an eagle, which had twelve feathered wings, and three 2 heads. And I saw, and, behold, she spread her wings over all the earth, and all the winds of heaven blew on her, [1] and the clouds were gathered 3 together against her. And I beheld, and out of her wings there grew *other* wings over against them; and they 4 became little wings and small. But her heads were at rest: the head in the midst was greater than the other 5 heads, yet rested it with them. Moreover I beheld, and, lo, the eagle flew with her wings, to reign over the earth, and over them that dwell therein. 6 And I beheld how that all things under heaven were subject unto her, and no man spake against her, no, not 7 one creature upon earth. And I beheld, and, lo, the eagle rose upon her talons, and uttered her voice to her 8 wings, saying, Watch not all at once: sleep every one in his own place, and 9 watch by course: but let the heads be 10 preserved for the last. And I beheld, and, lo, the voice went not out of her heads, but from the midst of her body. 11 And I numbered [2] her wings that were over against the other, and, behold, 12 there were eight of them. And I beheld, and, lo, on the right side there arose one wing, and reigned over all 13 the earth; and so it was, that when it reigned, the end of it came, and it appeared not, so that the place thereof appeared no more: and the next following rose up, and reigned, and it 14 bare rule a great time; and it hap-

pened, that when it reigned, the end of it came also, so that it appeared no 15 more, like as the first. And, lo, there 16 came a voice unto it, and said, Hear thou that hast borne rule over the earth all this time: this I proclaim unto thee, before thou shalt appear 17 no more, There shall none after thee attain unto thy time, neither unto the 18 half thereof. Then arose the third, and had the rule as the others before, 19 and it also appeared no more. So went it with all the wings one after another, as that every one bare rule, 20 and then appeared no more. And I beheld, and, lo, in process of time the [3] wings that followed were set up upon the [4] right side, that they might rule also; and some of them ruled, but 21 within a while they appeared no more: 22 some also of them were set up, but ruled not. After this I beheld, and, lo, 23 the twelve wings appeared no more, nor two of the little wings: and there was no more left upon the eagle's body, but the three heads that rested, 24 and six little wings. And I beheld, and, lo, two little wings divided themselves from the six, and remained under the head that was upon the right 25 side: but four remained in their place. And I beheld, and, lo, these [3] under wings thought to set up themselves, 26 and to have the rule. And I beheld, and, lo, there was one set up, but within a while it appeared no more. 27 A second also, and it was sooner away 28 than the first. And I beheld, and, lo, the two that remained thought also in 29 themselves to reign: and while they so thought, behold, there awaked one of the heads that were at rest, *namely,* it that was in the midst; for that was greater than the two *other* heads. 30 And I beheld how that it joined the 31 two *other* heads with it. And, behold, the head was turned with them that were with it. and did eat up the two [3] under wings that thought to have 32 reigned. But this head held the whole earth in possession, and bare rule over those that dwell therein with much oppression; and it had the governance of the world more than all 33 the wings that had been. And after this I beheld, and, lo, the head also that was in the midst suddenly appeared no more, like as the wings. 34 But there remained the two heads, which also in like sort reigned over the earth, and over those that dwell 35 therein. And I beheld, and, lo, the head upon the right side devoured that that was upon the left side. 36 Then I heard a voice, which said unto me, Look before thee, and con- 37 sider the thing that thou seest. And I beheld, and, lo, as it were a lion roused out of the wood roaring: and I heard how that he sent out a man's

Marginal notes:

[1] So the chief Oriental versions. The Latin has only *and were gathered together.*

[2] The Syriac has *her little wings, and, &c.*

[3] The Syriac has *little wings.*

[4] The Æthiopic has *left.*

voice unto the eagle, and spake, say-
38 ing, Hear thou, I will talk with thee,
and the Most High shall say unto
39 thee, Art not thou it that remainest
of the four beasts, whom I made to
reign in my world, that the end of
my times might come through them?
40 And the fourth came, and overcame
all the beasts that were past, and held
the world in governance with great
trembling, and the whole compass of
the earth with grievous oppression;
and so long time dwelt he upon the
41 earth with deceit. And thou hast
judged the earth, but not with truth.
42 For thou hast afflicted the meek, thou
hast hurt the peaceable, thou hast
hated them that speak truth, thou
hast loved liars, and destroyed the
dwellings of them that brought forth
fruit, and hast cast down the walls of
43 such as did thee no harm. Therefore
is thy insolent dealing come up unto
the Most High, and thy pride unto the
44 Mighty. The Most High also hath
looked upon his times, and, behold,
they are ended, and his ages are ful-
45 filled. And therefore appear no more,
thou eagle, nor thy horrible wings,
nor thy evil little wings, nor thy cruel
heads, nor thy hurtful talons, nor all
46 thy vain body: that all the earth may
be refreshed, and be eased, being delivered from thy violence, and that
she may hope for the judgement and
mercy of him that made her.

12 And it came to pass, whiles the lion
spake these words unto the eagle, I
2 beheld, and, lo, the head that remained appeared no more, and ¹ the two
wings which went over unto it arose
and set themselves up to reign, and
their kingdom was small, and full of
3 uproar. And I beheld, and, lo, they
appeared no more, and the whole body
of the eagle was burnt, so that the
earth was in great fear: then awaked
I by reason of great ecstasy of mind,
and from great fear, and said unto
4 my spirit, Lo, this hast thou done unto
me, in that thou searchest out the
5 ways of the Most High. Lo, I am
yet weary in my mind, and very weak
in my spirit; nor is there the least
strength in me, for the great fear
wherewith I was affrighted this night.
6 Therefore will I now beseech the
Most High, that he will strengthen
7 me unto the end. And I said, O Lord
that bearest rule, if I have found favour in thy sight, and if I am justified
with thee above many others, and if
my prayer indeed be come up before
8 thy face: strengthen me then, and
shew me thy servant the interpretation and plain meaning of this fearful
vision, that thou mayest perfectly
9 comfort my soul. For thou hast
judged me worthy to shew me the end
of time and the last times.

10 And he said unto me, This is the interpretation of this vision which thou
11 sawest: The eagle, whom thou sawest
come up from the sea, is the fourth
kingdom which appeared in vision to
12 thy brother Daniel. But it was not expounded unto him, as I now expound
it unto thee or have expounded it.
13 Behold, the days come, that there shall
rise up a kingdom upon earth, and it
shall be feared above all the kingdoms
14 that were before it. In the same shall
twelve kings reign, one after another:
15 whereof the second shall begin to
reign, and shall have a longer time
16 than *any of* the twelve. This is the
interpretation of the twelve wings,
17 which thou sawest. And whereas
thou heardest a voice which spake,
not going out from the heads, but
from the midst of the body thereof,
18 this is the interpretation: That ²after
the time of that kingdom there shall
arise no small contentions, and it shall
stand in peril of falling: nevertheless
it shall not then fall, but shall be re-
19 stored again to its first estate. And
whereas thou sawest the eight under
wings sticking to her wings, this is
20 the interpretation: That in it there
shall arise eight kings, whose times
shall be but small, and their years
21 shall be swift. And two of them shall perish,
when the middle time approacheth:
four shall be kept for a while until
the time of the ending thereof shall
22 approach: but two shall be kept unto
the end. And whereas thou sawest
three heads resting, this is the inter-
23 pretation: In the last days thereof
shall the Most High raise up three
³ kingdoms, and renew many things
therein, and they shall bear rule over
24 the earth, and over those that dwell
therein, with much oppression, above
all those that were before them:
therefore are they called the heads
25 of the eagle. For these are they
that shall accomplish her wickedness,
and that shall finish her last end.
26 And whereas thou sawest that the
great head appeared no more, *it sig-
nifieth* that one of them shall die
upon his bed, and yet with pain.
27 But for the two that remained, the
28 sword shall devour them. For the
sword of the one shall devour him that
was with him: but he also shall fall
29 by the sword in the last days. And
whereas thou sawest two under wings
passing ⁴ over unto the head that is
on the right side, this is the interpre-
30 tation: These are they, whom the
Most High hath kept unto his end:
this is the small kingdom and full of
31 trouble, as thou sawest. And the lion,
whom thou sawest rising up out of
the wood, and roaring, and speaking
to the eagle, and rebuking her for her
unrighteousness, and all her words

32 which thou hast heard; this is the anointed one, whom the Most High hath kept unto the end [1] [of days, who shall spring up out of the seed of David, and he shall come and speak] unto them and reprove them for their wickedness and their unrighteousness, and shall [2] heap up before them their contemptuous deal-
33 ings. For at the first he shall set them alive in his judgement, and when he hath reproved them, he shall de-
34 stroy them. For the rest of my people shall he deliver with mercy, those that have been preserved throughout my borders, and he shall make them joyful until the coming of the end, even the day of judgement, whereof I have spoken unto thee from the beginning.
35 This is the dream that thou sawest, and this is the interpretation thereof:
36 and thou only hast been meet to know
37 this secret of the Most High. Therefore write all these things that thou hast seen in a book, and put them in
38 a secret place: and thou shalt teach them to the wise of thy people, whose hearts thou knowest are able to com-
39 prehend and keep these secrets. But wait thou here thyself yet seven days more, that there may be shewed unto thee whatsoever it pleaseth the Most High to shew thee. And he departed from me.
40 And it came to pass, when all the people [3] saw that the seven days were past, and I not come again into the city, they gathered them all together, from the least unto the greatest, and came unto me, and spake to me, say-
41 ing, What have we offended thee? and what evil have we done against thee, that thou hast utterly forsaken us,
42 and sittest in this place? For of all the prophets thou only art left us, as a cluster of the vintage, and as a lamp in a dark place, and as a haven for a
43 ship saved from the tempest. Are not the evils which are come to us suffi-
44 cient? If thou shalt forsake us, how much better had it been for us, if we also had been consumed in the burn-
45 ing of Sion! For we are not better than they that died there. And they wept with a loud voice. And I an-
46 swered them, and said, Be of good comfort, O Israel; and be not sorrow-
47 ful, thou house of Jacob: for the Most High hath you in remembrance, and the Mighty hath not forgotten you
48 [4] for ever. As for me, I have not forsaken you, neither am I departed from you: but am come into this place, to pray for the desolation of Sion, and that I might seek mercy for the low estate of your sanctuary.
49 And now go your way every man to his own house, and after these days
50 will I come unto you. So the people went their way into the city, like as I

51 said unto them: but I sat in the field seven days, as *the angel* commanded me; and in those days I did eat only of the flowers of the field, and had my meat of the herbs.
13 And it came to pass after seven days,
2 I dreamed a dream by night: and, lo, there arose a wind from the sea, that
3 it moved all the waves thereof. And I beheld, and, lo, [1] [this wind caused to come up from the midst of the sea as it were the likeness of a man, and I beheld, and, lo,] that man [5] flew with the clouds of heaven: and when he turned his countenance to look, all things trembled that were seen under
4 him. And whensoever the voice went out of his mouth, all they burned that heard his voice, like as the [6] wax melt-
5 eth when it feeleth the fire. And after this I beheld, and, lo, there was gathered together a multitude of men, out of number, from the four winds of heaven, to make war against the man
6 that came out of the sea. And I beheld, and, lo, he graved himself a great mountain, and flew up upon it.
7 But I sought to see the region or place whereout the mountain was graven,
8 and I could not. And after this I beheld, and, lo, all they which were gathered together to fight against him were sore afraid, and yet durst fight.
9 And, lo, as he saw the assault of the multitude that came, he neither lifted up his hand, nor held spear, nor any
10 instrument of war: but only I saw how that he sent out of his mouth as it had been a flood of fire, and out of his lips a flaming breath, and out of his tongue he cast forth sparks [7] of
11 the storm. And these were all mingled together; the flood of fire, the flaming breath, and the great storm; and fell upon the assault of the multitude which was prepared to fight, and burned them up every one, so that upon a sudden of an innumerable multitude nothing was to be perceived, but only dust of ashes and smell of smoke: when I saw this I
12 was amazed. Afterward I beheld the same man come down from the mountain, and call unto him another multi-
13 tude which was peaceable. And there came [8] much people unto him, whereof some were glad, some were sorry, some of them were bound, and other some brought of them that were offered: then through great fear I
14 awaked, and prayed unto the Most High, and said, Thou hast shewed thy servant these wonders from the beginning, and hast counted me worthy that thou shouldest receive
15 my prayer: and now shew me moreover the interpretation of this dream.
16 For as I conceive in mine understanding, woe unto them that shall be left in those days! and much more

1 The words in brackets are added from the Syriac.
2 The Syriac has *set in order.* See Ps. 1. 21.

3 So the Syriac. The Latin has *heard.*

4 So the Syriac.

5 So the Syriac. The Latin has *grew strong.*

6 So the Syriac and other Oriental versions.

7 So the Syriac and Arabic.

8 Lat. *the faces of many people.*

17 woe unto them that are not left! for they that were not left shall be in
18 heaviness, understanding the things that are laid up in the latter days, but
19 not attaining unto them. But woe unto them also that are left, for this cause; for they shall see great perils and many necessities, like as these dreams
20 declare. Yet is it [1] better for one to be in peril and to come into [2] these things, than to pass away as a cloud out of the world, and not to see the things that [2] shall happen in the last days.

And he answered unto me, and said,
21 The interpretation of the vision shall I tell thee, and I will also open unto thee the things whereof thou hast
22 made mention. Whereas thou hast spoken of them that are left behind,
23 this is the interpretation: He that shall [2] endure the peril in that time shall keep them that be fallen into danger, even such as have works, and
24 faith toward the Almighty. Know therefore, that they which be left behind are more blessed than they that
25 be dead. These are the interpretations of the vision: Whereas thou sawest a man coming up from the midst
26 of the sea, the same is he whom the Most High hath kept a great season, which by his own self shall deliver his creature: and he shall order them
27 that are left behind. And whereas thou sawest, that out of his mouth there came wind, and fire, and storm;
28 and whereas he held neither spear, nor any instrument of war, but destroyed the assault of that multitude which came to fight against him; this
29 is the interpretation: Behold, the days come, when the Most High will begin to deliver them that are upon the
30 earth. And there shall come astonishment of mind upon them that dwell on
31 the earth. And one shall think to war against another, city against city, place against place, people against people, and kingdom against kingdom.
32 And it shall be, when these things shall come to pass, and the signs shall happen which I shewed thee before, then shall my Son be revealed, whom
33 thou sawest as a man ascending. And it shall be, when all the nations hear his voice, every man shall leave his own land and the battle they have one
34 against another. And an innumerable multitude shall be gathered together, as thou sawest, desiring to come, and
35 to fight against him. But he shall stand upon the top of the mount Sion.
36 And Sion shall come, and shall be shewed to all men, being prepared and builded, like as thou sawest the
37 mountain graven without hands. And this my Son shall rebuke the nations which are come for their wickedness, with plagues that are like unto a tem-

[1] Lat. easier.
[2] So the Syriac.

38 pest; and shall taunt them to their face with their evil thoughts, and the torments wherewith they shall be tormented, which are likened unto a flame: and he shall destroy them without labour by the law, which is liken-
39 ed unto fire. And whereas thou sawest that he gathered unto him another
40 multitude that was peaceable; these are the ten tribes, which were led away out of their own land in the time of Osea the king, whom Salmanasar the king of the Assyrians led away captive, and he carried them beyond the River, and they were carried into
41 another land. But they took this counsel among themselves, that they would leave the multitude of the heathen, and go forth into a further country, where never mankind dwelt,
42 that they might there keep their statutes, which they had not kept in
43 their own land. And they entered by the narrow passages of the river
44 Euphrates. For the Most High then wrought signs for them, and stayed the springs of the River, till they were
45 passed over. For through that country there was a great way to go, namely, of a year and a half: and the same
46 region is called [3] Arzareth. Then dwelt they there until the latter time; and now when they begin to come
47 again, the Most High stayeth the springs of the River again, that they may go through: therefore sawest thou the multitude gathered together
48 with peace. But those that be left behind of thy people are they that are
49 found within my holy border. It shall be therefore when he shall destroy the multitude of the nations that are gathered together, he shall defend the
50 people that remain. And then shall he shew them very many wonders.
51 Then said I, O Lord that bearest rule, shew me this: wherefore I have seen the man coming up from the midst of
52 the sea. And he said unto me, Like as one can neither seek out nor know what is in the deep of the sea, even so can no man upon earth see my Son, or those that be with him, but in the
53 time of [4] his day. This is the interpretation of the dream which thou sawest, and for this thou only art en-
54 lightened herein. For thou hast forsaken thine own ways, and applied thy diligence unto mine, and hast sought
55 out my law. Thy life hast thou ordered in wisdom, and hast called un-
56 derstanding thy mother. And therefore have I shewed thee this; for there is a reward laid up with the Most High: and it shall be, after other three days I will speak other things unto thee, and declare unto thee
57 mighty and wondrous things. Then went I forth and passed into the field, giving praise and thanks greatly unto

[3] That is, another land. See Deut. xxix. 28.

[4] So the Oriental versions. The Latin omits his.

the Most High because of his wonders,
58 which he did from time to time; and
because he governeth the time, and
such things as fall in their seasons.
And there I sat three days.

14 And it came to pass upon the third
day, I sat under an oak, and, behold,
there came a voice out of a bush over
against me, and said, Esdras, Esdras.
2 And I said, Here am I, Lord. And I
3 stood up upon my feet. Then said he
unto me, In the bush I did manifestly
reveal myself, and talked with Moses,
when my people were in bondage in
4 Egypt: and I sent him, and [1] he led
my people out of Egypt; and I brought
him up to the mount of Sinai, where
5 I held him by me for many days; and
told him many wondrous things, and
shewed him the secrets of the times,
and the end of the seasons; and com-
6 manded him, saying, These words
shalt thou publish openly, and these
7 shalt thou hide. And now I say unto
8 thee, Lay up in thy heart the signs
that I have shewed, and the dreams
that thou hast seen, and the interpre-
9 tations which thou hast heard: for
thou shalt be taken away from men,
and from henceforth thou shalt remain with my Son, and with such as
be like thee, until the times be ended.
10 For the world hath lost its youth, and
11 the times begin to wax old. [2] For the
world is divided into twelve parts, and
ten parts of it are gone already, [3] even
12 the half of the tenth part: and there
remain of it two parts after the middle
13 of the tenth part. Now therefore set
thine house in order, and reprove thy
people, comfort the lowly among
them, [4] and instruct such of them as
be wise, and now renounce the life
14 that is corruptible, and let go from
thee the mortal thoughts, cast away from
thee the burdens of man, put off now
15 thy weak nature, and lay aside the
thoughts that are most grievous unto
thee, and haste thee to remove from
16 these times. For yet worse evils than
those which thou hast seen happen
17 shall be done hereafter. For look,
how much the world shall be weaker
through age, so much the more shall
18 evils increase upon them that dwell
therein. For the truth shall withdraw
itself further off, and leasing be hard
at hand: for now hasteth [5] the eagle
to come, which thou sawest in vision.
19 Then answered I and said, [6] I will
20 speak before thee, O Lord. Behold, I
will go, as thou hast commanded me,
and reprove the people that now be:
but they that shall be born afterward,
who shall admonish them? for the
world is set in darkness, and they that
21 dwell therein are without light. For
thy law is burnt, therefore no man
knoweth the things that are done of
thee, or the works that shall be done.

22 But if I have found favour before thee,
send the Holy Spirit into me, and I
shall write all that hath been done in
the world since the beginning, even
the things that were written in thy
law, that men may be able to find the
path, and that they which would live
23 in the latter days may live. And he
answered me and said. Go thy way,
gather the people together, and say
unto them, that they seek thee not
24 for forty days. But look thou prepare
thee many tablets, and take with thee
Sarea, Dabria, Selemia, Ethanus, and
Asiel, these five, which are ready to
25 write swiftly; and come hither, and I
shall light a lamp of understanding in
thine heart, which shall not be put out,
till the things be ended which thou
26 shalt write. And when thou hast
done, some things shalt thou publish
openly, and some things shalt thou
deliver in secret to the wise: to-morrow this hour shalt thou begin to write.
27 Then went I forth, as he commanded
me, and gathered all the people to-
28 gether, and said, Hear these words,
29 O Israel. Our fathers at the beginning were strangers in Egypt, and
30 they were delivered from thence, and
received the law of life, which they
kept not, which ye also have trans-
31 gressed after them. Then was [7] the
land, even the land of Sion, given you
for a possession: but ye yourselves,
and your fathers, have done unrighteousness, and have not kept the ways
which the Most High commanded
32 you. And forasmuch as he is a righteous judge, he took from you for a
while the thing that he had given you.
33 And now ye are here, and your bre-
34 thren are among you. Therefore if so
be that ye will rule over your own understanding, and instruct your hearts,
ye shall be kept alive, and after death
35 ye shall obtain mercy. For after death
shall the judgement come, when we
shall live again: and then shall the
names of the righteous be manifest,
and the works of the ungodly shall be
36 declared. Let no man therefore come
unto me now, nor seek after me these
37 forty days. So I took the five men, as
he commanded me, and we went forth
into the field, and remained there.
38 And it came to pass on the morrow
that, lo, a voice called me, saying, Esdras, open thy mouth, and drink that I
39 give thee to drink. Then opened I my
mouth, and, and, behold, there was reached
unto me a full cup, which was full
as it were with water, but the colour
40 of it was like fire. And I took it,
and drank: and when I had drunk of
it, my heart uttered understanding,
and wisdom grew in my breast, for
41 my spirit retained its memory: and
my mouth was opened, and shut no
42 more. The Most High gave under-

---

[1] Another reading is, I.

[2] Verses 11, 12 are omitted in the Syriac. The Æthiopic has For the world is divided into ten parts, and is come unto the tenth: and half of the tenth remaineth. Now &c.

[3] Lat. and.

[4] The Latin alone omits and . . . wise.

[5] So the Oriental versions.

[6] The Latin omits I will speak.

[7] Another reading is, a land in the land of Sion

standing unto the five men, and they wrote by course the things that were told them, in [1] characters which they knew not, and they sat forty days: now they wrote in the day-time, and
43 at night they ate bread. As for me, I spake in the day, and by night I
44 held not my tongue. So in forty days were written [2] fourscore and fourteen
45 books. And it came to pass, when the forty days were fulfilled, that the Most High spake unto me, saying, The first that thou hast written publish openly, and let the worthy and un-
46 worthy read it: but keep the seventy last, that thou mayest deliver them to such as be wise among thy people:
47 for in them is the spring of understanding, the fountain of wisdom, and
48 the stream of knowledge. And I did so.

15 Behold, speak thou in the ears of my people the words of prophecy, which I will put in thy mouth, saith the
2 Lord: and cause thou them to be written in paper: for they are faithful
3 and true. Fear not their imaginations against thee, let not the unbelief of them that speak against thee trouble
4 thee. For all the unbelievers shall die in their unbelief.
5 Behold, saith the Lord, I bring evils upon the whole earth; sword and famine, and death and destruction.
6 For wickedness hath prevailed over every land, and their hurtful works
7 are come to the full. Therefore saith
8 the Lord, I will hold my peace no more as touching their wickedness, which they profanely commit, neither will I suffer them in these things, which they wickedly practise: behold, the innocent and righteous blood cri-eth unto me, and the souls of the right-
9 eous cry out continually. I will surely avenge them, saith the Lord, and will receive unto me all the innocent blood
10 from among them. Behold, my people is led as a flock to the slaughter: I will not suffer them now to dwell in
11 the land of Egypt: but I will bring them out with a mighty hand and with a high arm, and will smite Egypt with plagues, as aforetime, and will
12 destroy all the land thereof. Let Egypt mourn, and the foundations thereof, for the plague of the chastisement and the punishment that God
13 shall bring upon it. Let the husbandmen that till the ground mourn: for their seeds shall fail and their trees shall be laid waste through the blast-
14 ing and hail, and a terrible star. Woe to the world and them that dwell
15 therein! for the sword and their destruction draweth nigh, and nation shall rise up against nation to battle
16 with weapons in their hands. For there shall be sedition among men; and waxing strong one against an-

other, they shall not regard their king nor the chief of their great ones, in
17 their might. For a man shall desire to go into a city, and shall not be able.
18 For because of their pride the cities shall be troubled, the houses shall be destroyed, and men shall be afraid.
19 A man shall have no pity upon his neighbour, but shall make an assault on their houses with the sword, and spoil their goods, because of the lack of bread, and for great tribulation.
20 Behold, saith God, I call together all the kings of the earth, to stir up them that are from the rising of the sun, from the south, from the east, and Libanus; to turn themselves one against another, and repay the things
21 that they have done to them. Like as they do yet this day unto my chosen, so will I do also, and recompense in their bosom. Thus saith the Lord
22 God: My right hand shall not spare the sinners, and my sword shall not cease over them that shed innocent
23 blood upon the earth. And a fire is gone forth from his wrath, and hath consumed the foundations of the earth, and the sinners, like the straw
24 that is kindled. Woe to them that sin, and keep not my commandments!
25 saith the Lord. I will not spare them: go your way, ye rebellious children,
26 defile not my sanctuary. For the Lord knoweth all them that trespass against him, therefore hath he delivered them unto death and destruction.
27 For now are the evils come upon the whole earth, and ye shall remain in them: for God shall not deliver you, because ye have sinned against him.
28 Behold, a vision horrible, and the appearance thereof from the east!
29 And the nations of the dragons of Arabia shall come out with many chariots, and from the day that they set forth the hissing of them is carried over the earth, so that all they which shall hear them may fear also and
30 tremble. Also the Carmonians raging in wrath shall go forth as the wild boars of the wood, and with great power shall they come, and join battle with them, and shall waste a portion of the land of the Assyrians with their
31 teeth. And then shall the dragons have the upper hand, remembering their [3] nature; and if they shall turn themselves, conspiring together in
32 great power to persecute them, then these shall be troubled, and keep silence through their power, and shall
33 turn and flee. And from the land of the Assyrians shall the lier in wait besiege them, and consume one of them, and upon their host shall be fear and trembling, and sedition against their
34 kings. Behold, clouds from the east and from the north unto the south,

and they are very horrible to look
35 upon, full of wrath and storm. They
shall dash one against another, and

they shall pour out a plentiful ¹ storm
upon the earth, even their own star;
and there shall be blood from the
36 sword unto the horse's belly, and to
the thigh of man, and to the camel's
37 hough. And there shall be fearfulness and great trembling upon earth:
and they that see that wrath shall be
afraid, and trembling shall take hold
38 upon them. And after this shall there
be stirred up great storms from the
south, and from the north, and an-
39 other part from the west. And strong
winds shall arise from the east, and
shall shut it up, even the cloud which
he raised in wrath; and the star that
was to cause destruction by the east
wind shall be violently driven toward
40 the south and west. And great clouds
and mighty and full of wrath shall be
lifted up, and the star, that they may
destroy all the earth, and them that
dwell therein; and they shall pour
out over every high and eminent one
41 a terrible star, fire, and hail, and
flying swords, and many waters, that
all plains may be full, and all rivers,
with the abundance of those waters.
42 And they shall break down the cities
and walls, mountains and hills, trees
of the wood, and grass of the mea-
43 dows, and their corn. And they shall
go on stedfastly unto Babylon, and
44 destroy her. They shall come unto
her, and compass her about; the star
and all wrath shall they pour out
upon her: then shall the dust and
smoke go up unto the heaven, and all
they that be about her shall bewail
45 her. And they that remain shall do
service unto them that have put her
in fear.
46 And thou, Asia, that art partaker in
the beauty of Babylon, and in the
47 glory of her person: woe unto thee,
thou wretch, because thou hast made
thyself like unto her; thou hast
decked thy daughters in whoredom,
that they might please and glory in
thy lovers, which have alway desired
thee to commit whoredom withal!
48 Thou hast followed her that is hateful in all her works and inventions:
49 therefore saith God, I will send evils
upon thee; widowhood, poverty, famine, sword, and pestilence, to waste
thy houses unto destruction and
50 death. And the glory of thy power
shall be dried up as a flower, when
the heat shall arise that is sent over
51 thee. Thou shalt be weakened as a
poor woman with stripes, and as one
chastised with wounds, so that thy
mighty ones and thy lovers thou shalt
52 not be able to receive. Would I with
jealousy have so proceeded against
53 thee, saith the Lord, if thou hadst not

always slain my chosen, exalting the
stroke of thine hands, and saying
over their ² dead, when thou wast

54 drunken, Set forth the beauty of thy
55 countenance? The reward of a harlot shall be in thy bosom, therefore
56 shalt thou receive recompense. Like
as thou shalt do unto my chosen,
saith the Lord, even so shall God do
unto thee, and shall deliver thee into
57 mischief. And thy children shall die
of hunger, and thou shalt fall by the
sword: and thy cities shall be broken
down, and all thine shall perish by
58 the sword in the field. And they that
be in the mountains shall die of hunger, and eat their own flesh, and
drink their own blood, for very hunger of bread, and thirst of water.
59 Thou unhappy above all shalt come
60 and shalt again receive evils. And in
the passage they shall rush on the
³ idle city, and shall destroy some por-

tion of thy land, and mar part of thy
glory, and shall return again to Baby-
61 lon that was destroyed. And thou
shalt be cast down by them as stubble,
and they shall be unto thee as fire;
62 and shall devour thee, and thy cities,
thy land, and thy mountains; all thy
woods and thy fruitful trees shall
63 they burn up with fire. They shall
carry thy children away captive, and
shall spoil thy wealth, and mar the
glory of thy face.

16 Woe unto thee, Babylon, and Asia!
woe unto thee, Egypt, and Syria!
2 Gird up yourselves with sackcloth and
garments of hair, and bewail your
children, and lament; for your de-
3 struction is at hand. A sword is sent
upon you, and who is he that may turn
4 it back? A fire is sent upon you, and
5 who is he that may quench it? Evils
are sent upon you, and who is he that
6 may drive them away? May one drive
away a hungry lion in the wood? or
may one quench the fire in stubble,
when it hath once begun to burn?
7 May one turn again the arrow that is
8 shot of a strong archer? The Lord
God sendeth the evils, and who shall
9 drive them away? A fire shall go forth
from his wrath, and who is he that
10 may quench it? He shall cast lightning, and who shall not fear? he shall
thunder, and who shall not tremble?
11 The Lord shall threaten, and who
shall not be utterly broken in pieces
12 at his presence? The earth quaketh,
and the foundations thereof; the sea
ariseth up with waves from the deep,
and the waves of it shall be troubled,
and the fishes thereof also, at the
presence of the Lord, and before the
13 glory of his power: for strong is his
right hand that bendeth the bow, his
arrows that he shooteth are sharp,
and shall not miss, when they begin
to be shot into the ends of the world.

14 Behold, the evils are sent forth, and shall not return again, until they come
15 upon the earth. The fire is kindled, and shall not be put out, till it consume the foundations of the earth.
16 Like as an arrow which is shot of a mighty archer returneth not backward, even so the evils that are sent forth upon earth shall not return
17 again. Woe is me! woe is me! who will deliver me in those days?
18 The beginning of sorrows, and *there shall be* great mournings; the beginning of famine, and many shall perish; the beginning of wars, and the powers shall stand in fear; the beginning of evils, and all shall tremble! what shall they do in *all* this when the evils shall
19 come? Behold, famine and plague, tribulation and anguish! they are sent
20 as scourges for amendment. But for all these things they shall not turn them from their wickedness, nor be
21 alway mindful of the scourges. Behold, victuals shall be so good cheap upon earth, that they shall think themselves to be in good case, and even then shall evils grow upon earth, sword, famine, and great confusion.
22 For many of them that dwell upon earth shall perish of famine; and the other, that escape the famine, shall
23 the sword destroy. And the dead shall be cast out as dung, and there shall be no man to comfort them: for the earth shall be left desolate, and the cities thereof shall be cast down.
24 There shall be no husbandman left to
25 till the earth, and to sow it. The trees shall give fruit, and who shall gather
26 them? The grapes shall ripen, and who shall tread them? for in *all* places there shall be a great forsak-
27 ing: for one man shall desire to see
28 another, or to hear his voice. For of a city there shall be ten left, and two of the field, which have hidden themselves in the thick groves, and in the
29 clefts of the rocks. As in an orchard of olives upon every tree there be
30 left three or four olives, or as when a vineyard is gathered there be some clusters left by them that diligently
31 seek through the vineyard; even so in those days there shall be three or four left by them that search their
32 houses with the sword. And the earth shall be left desolate, and the fields thereof shall be for [1] briers, and her ways and all her paths shall bring forth thorns, because no sheep shall
33 pass therethrough. The virgins shall mourn, having no bridegrooms; the women shall mourn, having no husbands; their daughters shall mourn,
34 having no helpers. In the wars shall their bridegrooms be destroyed, and their husbands shall perish of famine.
35 Hear now these things, and understand them, ye servants of the Lord.

36 Behold, the word of the Lord, receive it: disbelieve not the things whereof
37 the Lord speaketh. Behold, the evils
38 draw nigh, and are not slack. Like as a woman with child in the ninth month, when the hour of her delivery draweth near, within two or three hours doleful pains compass her womb, and when the child cometh forth from the womb, there shall be no tarrying for
39 a moment: even so shall not the evils be slack to come upon the earth, and the world shall groan, and sorrows
40 shall take hold of it on every side. O my people, hear my word: make you ready to the battle, and in those evils be even as pilgrims upon the earth.
41 He that selleth, let him be as he that fleeth away: and he that buyeth, as
42 one that will lose: he that occupieth merchandise, as he that hath no profit by it: and he that buildeth, as he
43 that shall not dwell therein: he that soweth, as if he should not reap: so also he that pruneth *the vines*, as he
44 that shall not gather the grapes: they that marry, as they that shall get no children; and they that marry not, as
45 the widowed. Inasmuch as they that
46 labour labour in vain; for strangers shall reap their fruits, and spoil their goods, overthrow their houses, and take their children captive, for in captivity and famine shall they beget
47 their children: and they that traffick traffick to become a spoil: the more they deck their cities, their houses, their possessions, and their own per-
48 sons, the more will I hate them for
49 their sins, saith the Lord. Like as a right honest and virtuous woman
50 hateth a harlot, so shall righteousness hate iniquity, when she decketh herself, and shall accuse her to her face, when he cometh that shall defend him that diligently searcheth out every sin upon earth.
51 Therefore be ye not like thereunto,
52 nor to the works thereof. For yet a little while, and iniquity shall be taken away out of the earth, and righteous-
53 ness shall reign over us. Let not the sinner say that he hath not sinned: for he shall burn coals of fire upon his head, which saith, I have not sinned
54 before God and his glory. Behold, the Lord knoweth all the works of men, their imaginations, their thoughts,
55 and their hearts. Who said, Let the earth be made; and it was made: Let the heaven be made; and it was made.
56 And at his word were the stars established, and he knoweth the number of
57 the stars. Who searcheth the deep, and the treasures thereof; he hath measured the sea, and what it con-
58 taineth. Who hath shut the sea in the midst of the waters, and with his word hath he hanged the earth upon
59 the waters. Who spreadeth out the

[1] See Is. vii. 23.

heaven like a vault; upon the waters
60 hath he founded it. Who hath made in the desert springs of water, and pools upon the tops of the mountains, to send forth rivers from the height to
61 water the earth. Who framed man, and put a heart in the midst of the body, and gave him breath, life, and
62 understanding, yea, the spirit of God Almighty. He who made all things, and searcheth out hidden things in
63 hidden places, surely he knoweth your imagination, and what ye think in your hearts. Woe to them that sin, and would fain hide their sin!
64 Forasmuch as the Lord will exactly search out all your works, and he will
65 put you all to shame. And when your sins are brought forth before men, ye shall be ashamed, and your own iniquities shall stand as your
66 accusers in that day. What will ye do? or how will ye hide your sins be-
67 fore God and his angels? Behold, God is the judge, fear him: leave off from your sins, and forget your iniquities, to meddle no more with them for ever: so shall God lead you forth, and deliver you from all tribulation.
68 For, behold, the burning wrath of a great multitude is kindled over you, and they shall take away certain of

you, and feed you with that which is
69 slain unto idols. And they that consent unto them shall be had in derision and in reproach, and be trodden
70 under foot of them. For there shall be [1] in divers places, and in the next cities, a great insurrection upon those
71 that fear the Lord. They shall be like mad men, sparing none, but spoiling and destroying them that still fear the
72 Lord. For they shall waste and take away their goods, and cast them out
73 of their houses. Then shall be manifest the trial of mine elect; even as the gold that is tried in the fire.
74 Hear, O ye mine elect, saith the Lord: behold, the days of tribulation are at hand, and I will deliver you from
75 them. Be ye not afraid, neither doubt;
76 for God is your guide: and ye who keep my commandments and precepts, saith the Lord God, let not your
77 sins weigh you down, and let not your iniquities lift up themselves. Woe unto them that are fast bound with their sins, and covered with their iniquities, like as a field is fast bound with bushes, and the path thereof covered with thorns, that no man
78 may travel through! [2] It is even shut off, and given up to be consumed of fire.

[1] The Latin is uncertain.

[2] Or, *They are every one shut out, &c.*

TOBIT.

1 THE book of the words of Tobit, the son of Tobiel, the son of Ananiel, the son of Aduel, the son of Gabael, of the seed of Asiel, of the tribe of Naphtali;
2 who in the days of [1] Enemessar king of the Assyrians was carried away captive out of Thisbe, which is on the right hand of Kedesh Naphtali in Galilee above Asher.
3 I Tobit walked in the ways of truth and righteousness all the days of my life, and I did many almsdeeds to my brethren and my nation, who went with me into the land of the Assyri-
4 ans, to Nineveh. And when I was in mine own country, in the land of Israel, while I was yet young, all the tribe of Naphtali my father fell away from the house of Jerusalem, which was chosen out of all the tribes of Israel, that all the tribes should sacrifice *there,* and the temple of the habitation of the Most High was hallowed and built *therein* for all ages.
5 And all the tribes which fell away together sacrificed to the heifer Baal, and so did the house of Naphtali my
6 father. And I alone went often to

Jerusalem at the feasts, as it hath been ordained unto all Israel by an everlasting decree, having the first-fruits and the tenths of mine increase, and that which was first shorn; and I gave them at the altar to the priests
7 the sons of Aaron. The tenth part of all mine increase I gave to the sons of Levi, who ministered at Jerusalem: and the second tenth part I sold away, and went, and spent it each year at
8 Jerusalem: and the third I gave unto them to whom it was meet, as Deborah my father's mother had commanded me, because I was left an orphan by
9 my father. And when I became a man, I took to wife Anna of the seed of our own family, and of her I
10 begat Tobias. And when I was carried away captive to Nineveh, all my brethren and those that were of my kindred did eat of the bread of the
11 Gentiles: but I kept myself from eat-
12 ing, because I remembered God with
13 all my soul. And the Most High gave me grace and [2] favour in the sight of Enemessar, and I was his purveyor.
14 And I went into Media, and left in

[1] That is, *Shalmaneser.* Compare 2 Kings xvii. 3, 23.

[2] Gr. *beauty*

trust with Gabael, the brother of Gabrias, at Rages of Media, ten talents of silver.

15 And when Enemessar was dead, Sennacherib his son reigned in his stead; and [1] in his time the highways were troubled, and I could no more 16 go into Media. And in the days of Enemessar I did many almsdeeds to 17 my brethren: I gave my bread to the hungry, and my garments to the naked: and if I saw any of my race dead, and cast forth [2] on the wall of 18 Nineveh, I buried him. And if Sennacherib the king slew any, when he came fleeing from Judæa, I buried them privily; for in his wrath he slew many; and the bodies were sought for by the king, and were not found. 19 But one of the Ninevites went and shewed to the king concerning me, how that I buried them, and hid myself; and when I knew that I was sought for to be put to death, I with- 20 drew myself for fear. And all my goods were forcibly taken away, and there was nothing left unto me, save my wife Anna and my son Tobias. 21 And there passed not five and fifty days, before two of his sons slew him, and they fled into the mountains of Ararat. And [3] Sarchedonus his son reigned in his stead; and he appointed over all the accounts of his kingdom, and over all his affairs, Achiacharus 22 my brother Anael's son. And Achiacharus made request for me, and I came to Nineveh. Now Achiacharus was cupbearer, and keeper of the signet, and steward, and overseer of the accounts: and Sarchedonus appointed him next unto himself: but he was my brother's son.

2 Now when I was come home again, and my wife Anna was restored unto me, and my son Tobias, in the feast of Pentecost, which is the holy feast of the seven weeks, there was a good dinner prepared me, and I sat down 2 to eat. And I saw abundance of meat, and I said to my son, Go and bring what poor man soever thou shalt find of our brethren, who is mindful of the Lord; and, lo, I tarry for thee. 3 And he came, and said, Father, one of our race is strangled, and is cast out 4 in the marketplace. And before I had tasted aught, I sprang up, and took him up into a chamber until the sun 5 was set. And I returned, and washed myself, and ate my bread in heavi- 6 ness, and remembered the prophecy of Amos, as he said,

　[4] Your feasts shall be turned into mourning,
　And all your mirth into lamentation.

7 And I wept: and when the sun was set, I went and made a grave, and bu- 8 ried him. And my neighbours mock-

ed me, and said, He is no longer afraid to be put to death for this matter: and yet he fled away: and, lo, he buri- 9 eth the dead again. And the same night I returned from burying him, and slept by the wall of my courtyard, being polluted; and my face was un- 10 covered: and I knew not that there were sparrows in the wall; and, mine eyes being open, the sparrows muted warm dung into mine eyes, and white films came in mine eyes; and I went to the physicians, and they helped me not: but Achiacharus did nourish me, [5] until I went into Elymais. 11 And my wife Anna did spin in the 12 women's chambers, and did send the work back to the owners. And they on their part paid her wages, and gave 13 her also besides a kid. But when it came to my house, it began to cry, and I said unto her, From whence is this kid? is it stolen? render it to the owners; for it is not lawful to eat 14 anything that is stolen. But she said, It hath been given me for a gift more than the wages. And I did not believe her, and I bade her render it to the owners; and I was abashed at her. But she answered and said unto me, Where are thine alms and thy righteous deeds? behold, [6] thou and all thy works are known.

3 And I was grieved and wept, and prayed in sorrow, saying, 2 O Lord, thou art righteous, and all thy works and all thy ways are mercy 3 and truth, and thou judgest true and righteous judgement for ever. Remember me, and look on me; take not vengeance on me for my sins and mine ignorances, and *the sins* of my fathers, which sinned before thee: 4 for they disobeyed thy commandments; and thou gavest us for a spoil, and for captivity, and for death, and for a proverb of reproach to all the nations among whom we are dispers- 5 ed. And now many are thy judgements, true are they; that thou shouldest deal with me according to my sins and *the sins* of my fathers: because we did not keep thy commandments, for we walked not in truth before 6 thee. And now deal with me according to that which is pleasing in thy sight, command my spirit to be taken from me, that I may be released, and become earth: for it is profitable for me to die rather than to live, because I have heard false reproaches, and there is much sorrow in me: command that I be now released from my distress, and go to the everlasting place: turn not thy face away from me. 7 The same day it happened unto Sarah the daughter of Raguel in Ecbatana of Media, that she also was reproached by her father's maidser-

---

Margin notes:

[1] Gr. *his highways were troubled.*

[2] Some ancient authorities read *behind.*

[3] That is, *Esarhaddon,* and so in ver. 22.

[4] Amos viii. 10.

[5] Some authorities read *until he went.*

[6] Gr. *all things are known with thee.*

¹ Gr.
demon.

² Gr.
Hades.

³ Gr. *if.*

8 vants; because that she had been given to seven husbands, and Asmodæus the evil ¹ spirit slew them, before they had lain with her. And they said unto her, Dost thou not know that thou stranglest thy husbands? thou hast had already seven husbands, and thou hast had no profit of any one 9 of them. Wherefore dost thou scourge us? if they be dead, go thy ways with them; let us never see of thee either 10 son or daughter. When she heard these things, she was grieved exceedingly, so that she thought to have hanged herself: and she said, I am the only daughter of my father; if I do this, it shall be a reproach unto him, and I shall bring down his old age 11 with sorrow to ² the grave. And she prayed by the window, and said, Blessed art thou, O Lord my God, and blessed is thy holy and honourable name for ever: let all thy works praise 12 thee for ever. And now, Lord, I have set mine eyes and my face toward 13 thee: command that I be released from the earth, and that I no more 14 hear reproach. Thou knowest, Lord, that I am pure from all sin with man, 15 and that I never polluted my name, nor the name of my father, in the land of my captivity: I am the only daughter of my father, and he hath no child that shall be his heir, nor brother near him, nor son belonging to him, that I should keep myself for a wife unto him: seven husbands of mine are dead already; why should I live? And if it pleaseth thee not to slay me, command some regard to be had of me, and pity taken of me, and that I hear no more reproach.

16 And the prayer of both was heard before the glory of the great *God.* 17 Raphael also was sent to heal them both, to scale away the white films from Tobit's eyes, and to give Sarah the daughter of Raguel for a wife to Tobias the son of Tobit; and to bind Asmodæus the evil ¹ spirit; because it belonged to Tobias that he should inherit her. The selfsame time did Tobit return and enter into his house, and Sarah the daughter of Raguel came down from her upper chamber.

4 In that day Tobit remembered concerning the money which he had left in trust with Gabael in Rages of Me-2 dia, and he said in himself, I have asked for death; why do I not call my son Tobias, that I may shew to him 3 *of the money* before I die? And he called him, and said,

My child, ³ when I die, bury me: and despise not thy mother; honour her all the days of thy life, and do that which is pleasing unto her, and grieve her 4 not. Remember, my child, that she hath seen many dangers for thee, *when thou wast* in her womb. When she is

dead, bury her by me in one grave. 5 My child, be mindful of the Lord our God all thy days, and let not thy will be set to sin and to transgress his commandments: do righteousness all the days of thy life, and follow not the 6 ways of unrighteousness. For if thou doest the truth, thy doings shall prosperously succeed to thee, and to all 7 them that do righteousness. Give alms of thy substance; and when thou givest alms, let not thine eye be envious: turn not away thy face from any poor man, and the face of God shall 8 not be turned away from thee. As thy substance is, give alms of it according to thine abundance: if thou have little, be not afraid to give alms according to 9 that little: for thou layest up a good treasure for thyself against the day 10 of necessity: because alms delivereth from death, and suffereth not to come 11 into darkness. Alms is a good gift in the sight of the Most High for all that 12 give it. Beware, my child, of all whoredom, and take first a wife of the seed of thy fathers, and take not a strange wife, which is not of thy father's tribe: for we are the sons of the prophets. Noah, Abraham, Isaac, Jacob, our fathers of old time, remember, my child, that they all took wives of their brethren, and were blessed in their children, and their seed shall inherit the 13 land. And now, my child, love thy brethren, and scorn not in thy heart thy brethren, and the sons and the daughters of thy people, to take a wife of them: for in scornfulness is destruction and much trouble, and in naughtiness is decay and great want: for naughtiness is the mother of famine. 14 Let not the wages of any man, which shall work for thee, tarry with thee, but render it unto him out of hand: and if thou serve God, recompense shall be made unto thee. Take heed to thyself, my child, in all thy works, and be discreet in all thy behaviour. 15 And what thou thyself hatest, do to no man. Drink not wine unto drunkenness, and let not drunkenness go 16 with thee on thy way. Give of thy bread to the hungry, and of thy garments to them that are naked: of all thine abundance give alms; and let not thine eye be envious when thou 17 givest alms. Pour out thy bread on the ⁴ burial of the just, and give no-18 thing to sinners. Ask counsel of every man that is wise, and despise not any 19 counsel that is profitable. And bless the Lord thy God at all times, and ask of him that thy ways may be made straight, and that all thy paths and counsels may prosper: for every nation hath not counsel; but the Lord himself giveth all good things, and humbleth whom he will, as he will. And now, my child, remember my

⁴ Or *tomb.*

commandments, and let them not be
20 blotted out of thy mind. And now I
shew thee of the ten talents of silver,
which I left in trust with Gabael the
son of Gabrias at Rages of Media.
21 And fear not, my child, because we
are made poor: thou hast much
wealth, if thou fear God, and depart
from all sin, and do that which is
pleasing in his sight.

5 And Tobias answered and said unto
him, Father, I will do all things, what-
2 soever thou hast commanded me: but
how shall I be able to receive the
3 money, seeing I know him not? And
he gave him the handwriting, and
said unto him, Seek thee a man which
shall go with thee, and I will give
him wages, whiles I yet live: and go
4 and receive the money. And he went
to seek a man, and found Raphael
5 which was an angel; and he knew it
not; and he said unto him, Can I go
with thee to Rages of Media? and
6 knowest thou the places well? And
the angel said unto him, I will go with
thee, and I know the way well: and I
have lodged with our brother Gabael.
7 And Tobias said unto him, Wait for
8 me, and I will tell my father. And
he said unto him, Go, and tarry not.
And he went in and said to his father,
Behold, I have found one which will
go with me. But he said, Call him
unto me, that I may know of what
tribe he is, and whether he be a trusty
man to go with thee.
9 And he called him, and he came in,
10 and they saluted one another. And
Tobit said unto him, Brother, of what
tribe and of what family art thou?
11 Shew me. And he said unto him,
Seekest thou a tribe and a family, or
a hired man which shall go with thy
son? And Tobit said unto him, I
would know, brother, thy kindred and
12 thy name. And he said, I am Azarias,
the son of Ananias the great, of thy
13 brethren. And he said unto him, Welcome, brother; and be not angry with
me, because I sought to know thy
tribe and family: and thou art my
brother, of an honest and good lineage: for I knew Ananias and Jathan,
the sons of Shemaiah the great, when
we went together to Jerusalem to
worship, and offered the firstborn,
and the tenths of our increase; and
they went not astray in the error of
our brethren: my brother, thou art
14 of a great stock. But tell me, what
wages shall I give thee? a drachma
a day, and those things that be neces-
15 sary for thee, as unto my son? And
moreover, if ye return safe and sound,
I will add something to thy wages.
16 And so they consented. And he said
to Tobias, Prepare thyself for the journey, and God prosper you. And his
son prepared what was needful for

the journey, and his father said unto
him, Go thou with this man; but God,
which dwelleth in heaven, shall prosper your journey; and may his angel
go with you. And they both went
forth to depart, and the young man's
dog with them.
17 But Anna his mother wept, and said
to Tobit, Why hast thou sent away
our child? is he not the staff of our
hand, in going in and out before us?
18 Be not greedy to add money to money:
but let it be as refuse in respect of
19 our child. For as the Lord hath given
20 us to live, so doth it suffice us. And
Tobit said to her, Take no care, my
sister; he shall return safe and sound,
21 and thine eyes shall see him. For a
good angel shall go with him, and his
journey shall be prospered, and he
22 shall return safe and sound. And she
made an end of weeping.

6 Now as they went on their journey,
they came at eventide to the river
2 Tigris, and they lodged there. But
the young man went down to wash
himself, and a fish leaped out of the
river, and would have swallowed up
3 the young man. But the angel said
unto him, Take hold on the fish. And
the young man caught hold of the fish,
4 and cast it up on the land. And the
angel said unto him, Cut the fish open,
and take the heart and the liver and
5 the gall, and put them up safely. And
the young man did as the angel commanded him; but they roasted the
fish, and ate it. And they both went
on their way, till they drew near to
6 Ecbatana. And the young man said
to the angel, Brother Azarias, to what
use is the heart and the liver and the
7 gall of the fish? And he said unto him,
Touching the heart and the liver, if a
[1] devil or an evil spirit trouble any,
we must make a smoke thereof before
the man or the woman, and the party
8 shall be no more vexed. But as for
the gall, it is good to anoint a man
that hath white films in his eyes, and
he shall be healed.
9 But when they drew nigh unto Rages,
10 the angel said to the young man,
Brother, to-day we shall lodge with
Raguel, and he is thy kinsman; and
he hath an only daughter, named Sarah. I will speak for her, that she
11 should be given thee for a wife. For
to thee doth the inheritance of her
appertain, and thou only art of her
12 kindred: and the maid is fair and
wise. And now hear me, and I will
speak to her father; and when we
return from Rages we will celebrate
the marriage: for I know that Raguel
may in no wise marry her to another
according to the law of Moses, or else
he shall be liable to death, because it
appertaineth unto thee to take the
inheritance, rather than any other.

1 Gr.
δειμος

13 Then the young man said unto the angel, Brother Azarias, I have heard that this maid hath been given to seven men, and that they all perished 14 in the bride-chamber. And now I am the only son of my father, and I am afraid, lest I go in and die, even as those before me: for a [1] devil loveth her, which hurteth no man, but those which come unto her: and now I fear lest I die, and bring my father's and my mother's life to the grave with sorrow because of me: and they have 15 no other son to bury them. But the angel said unto him, Dost thou not remember the words which thy father commanded thee, that thou shouldest take a wife of thine own kindred? and now hear me, brother; for she shall be thy wife; and make thou no reck-   oning of the devil; for this night shall 16 she be given thee to wife. And [2] when thou shalt come into the bride-chamber, thou shalt take the ashes of incense, and shalt lay upon them some of the heart and liver of the fish, and 17 shalt make a smoke *therewith*: and the devil shall smell it, and flee away, and never come again any more. But when thou goest nigh unto her, rise up both of you, and cry to God which is merciful, and he shall save you, and have mercy on you. Fear not, for she was prepared for thee from the beginning; and thou shalt save her, and she shall go with thee. And I suppose that thou shalt have children of her. And when Tobias heard these things, he loved her, and his soul clave to her exceedingly.

7 And they came to Ecbatana, and arrived at the house of Raguel. But Sarah met them; and she saluted them, and they her; and she brought 2 them into the house. And he said to Edna his wife, How like is the young 3 man to Tobit my cousin. And Raguel asked them, From whence are ye, brethren? And they said unto him, We are of the sons of Naphtali, which 4 are captives in Nineveh. And he said unto them, Know ye Tobit our brother? But they said, We know him. And he said unto them, Is he in good 5 health? But they said, He is both alive, and in good health: and Tobias 6 said, He is my father. And Raguel sprang up, and kissed him, and wept, 7 and blessed him, and said unto him, Thou art the son of an honest and good man. And when he had heard that Tobit had lost his sight, he was 8 grieved, and wept; and Edna his wife and Sarah his daughter wept. And they received them gladly; and they killed a ram of the flock, and set store of meat before them. But Tobias said to Raphael, Brother Azarias, speak of those things of which thou didst talk in the way, and let the

9 matter be finished. And he communicated the thing to Raguel: and Raguel said to Tobias, Eat and drink, 10 and make merry: for it appertaineth unto thee to take my child. Howbeit 11 I will shew thee the truth. I have given my child to seven men, and whensoever they came in unto her, they died in the night. But for the present be merry. And Tobias said, I will taste nothing here, until ye make covenant and enter into cove- 12 nant with me. And Raguel said, Take her to thyself from henceforth according to the manner: thou art her brother, and she is thine: but the merciful God shall give all good suc- 13 cess to you. And he called his daughter Sarah, and took her by the hand, and gave her to be wife to Tobias, and said, Behold, take her to thyself after the law of Moses, and lead her away to thy father. And he blessed 14 them; and he called Edna his wife, . and took a book, and wrote an instru- 15 ment, and sealed it. And they began to eat.

16 And Raguel called his wife Edna, and said unto her, Sister, prepare the other chamber, and bring her in 17 thither. And she did as he bade her, and brought her in thither: and she wept, and she received the tears of 18 her daughter, and said unto her, Be of good comfort, my child; the Lord of heaven and earth give thee [3] favour for this thy sorrow: be of good comfort, my daughter.

8 And when they had finished their supper, they brought Tobias in unto 2 her. But as he went, he remembered the words of Raphael, and took the ashes of the incense, and put the heart and the liver of the fish thereupon, 3 and made a smoke *therewith*. But when the [4] devil smelled the smell, he fled into the uppermost parts of Egypt, 4 and the angel bound him. But after they were both shut in together, Tobias rose up from the bed, and said, Sister, arise, and let us pray that the 5 Lord may have mercy on us. And Tobias began to say, Blessed art thou, O God of our fathers, and blessed is thy holy and glorious name for ever; let the heavens bless thee, and all thy 6 creatures. Thou madest Adam, and gavest him Eve his wife for a helper and a stay: of them came the seed of men: thou didst say, It is not good that the man should be alone; let us make him a helper like unto him. 7 And now, O Lord, I take not this my sister for lust, but in truth: command that I may find mercy and grow old 8 with her. And she said with him, 9 Amen. And they slept both that night. And Raguel arose, and went and 10 digged a grave, saying, Lest he also 11 should die. And Raguel came into

Side notes (left column):
[1] Gr. *demon*, and so in ver. 15, 17.

[2] Gr. *if*.

Side notes (right column):
[3] Many ancient authorities read *joy*.

[4] Gr. *demon*.

12 his house, and said to Edna his wife, Send one of the maidservants, and let them see whether he be alive: but if 13 not, that we may bury him, and no man know it. So the maidservant 14 opened the door, and went in, and found them both sleeping, and came forth, and told them that he was alive. 15 And Raguel blessed God, saying, Blessed art thou, O God, with all pure and holy blessing; and let thy saints bless thee, and all thy creatures; and let all thine angels and thine elect 16 bless thee for ever. Blessed art thou, because thou hast made me glad; and it hath not befallen me as I suspected; but thou hast dealt with us according 17 to thy great mercy. Blessed art thou, because thou hast had mercy on two that were the only begotten children of their parents: shew them mercy, O Lord; accomplish their life in health with gladness and mercy. 18 But he commanded his servants to 19 fill the grave. And he kept the wedding feast for them fourteen days. 20 And before the days of the wedding feast were finished, Raguel sware unto him, that he should not depart till the fourteen days of the wedding feast 21 were fulfilled; and that then he should take the half of his goods, and go in safety to his father; and the rest, *said he*, when I and my wife shall die.

9 And Tobias called Raphael, and said 2 unto him, Brother Azarias, take with thee a servant, and two camels, and go to Rages of Media to Gabael, and receive the money for me, and bring 3 him to the wedding feast: because Raguel hath sworn that I shall not 4 depart; and my father counteth the days; and if I tarry long, he will be 5 sorely grieved. And Raphael went on his way, and lodged with Gabael, and gave him the handwriting: but he brought forth the bags with their seals, 6 and gave them to him. And they rose up early in the morning together, and came to the wedding feast: and Tobias blessed his wife.

10 And Tobit his father made his count every day: and when the days of the journey were expired, and they came 2 not, he said, [1] Is he perchance detained? or is Gabael perchance dead, and there is no man to give him the 3 money? And he was sorely grieved. 4 But his wife said unto him. The child hath perished, seeing he tarrieth long; and she began to bewail him, and said, 5 [2] I care for nothing, my child, since I have let thee go, the light of mine eyes. 6 And Tobit saith unto her, Hold thy peace, take no care; he is in good 7 health. And she said unto him, Hold thy peace, deceive me not; my child hath perished. And she went out every day into the way by which they went, and did eat no bread in the day-

time, and ceased not whole nights to bewail her son Tobias, until the fourteen days of the wedding feast were expired, which Raguel had sworn that he should spend there.

But Tobias said unto Raguel, Send me away, for my father and my mother 8 look no more to see me. But his father in law said unto him, Abide with me, and I will send to thy father, and they shall declare unto him how things 9 go with thee. And Tobias saith, No; 10 but send me away to my father. But Raguel arose, and gave him Sarah his wife, and half his goods, servants and 11 cattle and money; and he blessed them, and sent them away, saying, The God of heaven shall prosper you, my chil- 12 dren, before I die. And he said to his daughter, Honour thy father and thy mother in law; they are now thy parents; let me hear a good report of thee. And he kissed her. And Edna said to Tobias, The Lord of heaven restore thee, dear brother, and grant to me that I may see thy children of my daughter Sarah, that I may rejoice before the Lord: and, behold, I commit my daughter unto thee in special trust: vex her not.

11 After these things Tobias also went his way, blessing God because he had prospered his journey; and he blessed Raguel and Edna his wife. And he went on his way till they drew near 2 unto Nineveh. And Raphael said to Tobias, Knowest thou not, brother, 3 how thou didst leave thy father? Let us run forward before thy wife, and 4 prepare the house. But take in thy hand the gall of the fish. And they went their way, and the dog went after 5 them. And Anna sat looking about 6 toward the way for her son. And she espied him coming, and said to his father, Behold, thy son cometh, and 7 the man that went with him. And Raphael said, I know, Tobias, that 8 thy father will open his eyes. Do thou therefore anoint his eyes with the gall, and being pricked therewith, he shall rub, and shall make the white films to fall away, and he shall see thee.

9 And Anna ran unto him, and fell upon the neck of her son, and said unto him, I have seen thee, my child; from henceforth I will die. And they wept both. 10 And Tobit went forth toward the door, and stumbled: but his son ran unto 11 him, and took hold of his father: and he strake the gall on his father's eyes, saying, Be of good cheer, my father. 12 But when his eyes began to smart, 13 he rubbed them; and the white films scaled away from the corners of his eyes; and he saw his son, and fell up- 14 on his neck. And he wept, and said, Blessed art thou, O God, and blessed is thy name for ever, and blessed are

[1] Many ancient authorities read *Are they perchance put to shame?*

[2] Some authorities read *Woe is me.*

15 all thy holy angels; for thou didst scourge, and didst have mercy on me: behold, I see my son Tobias. And his son went in rejoicing, and told his father the great things that had happened to him in Media.
16 And Tobit went out to meet his daughter in law at the gate of Nineveh, rejoicing, and blessing God: and they which saw him go marvelled, because he had received his sight. And
17 Tobit gave thanks before them, because God had shewed mercy on him. And when Tobit came near to Sarah his daughter in law, he blessed her, saying, Welcome, daughter: blessed is God which hath brought thee unto us, and *blessed are* thy father and thy mother. And there was joy to all his brethren which were at Nineveh.
18 And Achiacharus, and Nasbas his
19 brother's son, came: and Tobias' wedding feast was kept seven days with great gladness.
12 And Tobit called his son Tobias, and said unto him, See, my child, that the man which went with thee have his wages, and thou must give him more.
2 And he said unto him, Father, it is no harm to me to give him the half of those things which I have brought:
3 for he hath led me for thee in safety, and he cured my wife, and brought my money, and likewise cured thee.
4 And the old man said, It is due unto
5 him. And he called the angel, and said unto him, Take the half of all
6 that ye have brought. Then he called them both privily, and said unto them,
Bless God, and give him thanks, and magnify him, and give him thanks in the sight of all that live, for the things which he hath done with you. It is good to bless God and exalt his name, shewing forth with honour the works of God; and be not slack to give him
7 thanks. It is good to keep close the secret of a king, but to reveal gloriously the works of God. Do good,
8 and evil shall not find you. Good is prayer with fasting and alms and righteousness. A little with righteousness is better than much with unrighteousness. It is better to give
9 alms than to lay up gold: alms doth deliver from death, and it shall purge away all sin. They that do alms and righteousness shall be filled with life;
10 but they that sin are enemies to their
11 own life. Surely I will keep close nothing from you. I have said, It is good to keep close the secret of a king, but to reveal gloriously the
12 works of God. And now, when thou didst pray, and Sarah thy daughter in law, I did bring the memorial of your prayer before the Holy One: and when thou didst bury the dead,
13 I was with thee likewise. And when thou didst not delay to rise up, and leave thy dinner, that thou mightest go and cover the dead, thy good deed was not hid from me: but I was with
14 thee. And now God did send me to heal thee and Sarah thy daughter in
15 law. I am Raphael, one of the seven holy angels, which present the prayers of the saints, and go in before the glory of the Holy One.
16 And they were both troubled, and fell upon their faces; for they were afraid.
17 And he said unto them, Be not afraid, ye shall have peace; but bless God
18 for ever. For not of any favour of mine, but by the will of your God I came; wherefore bless him for ever.
19 All these days did I appear unto you;
20 and I did neither eat nor drink, but ye saw a vision. And now give God thanks: because I ascend to him that sent me: and write in a book all the
21 things which have been done. And they rose up, and saw him no more.
22 And they confessed the great and wonderful works of God, and how the angel of the Lord had appeared unto them.
13 And Tobit wrote a prayer for rejoicing, and said,
Blessed is God that liveth for ever,
And *blessed is* his kingdom.
2 For he scourgeth, and sheweth mercy:
He leadeth down to [1] the grave, and bringeth up again:
And there is none that shall escape his hand.
3 Give thanks unto him before the Gentiles, ye children of Israel:
For he hath scattered us among them.
4 There declare his greatness,
And extol him before all the living:
Because he is our Lord,
And God is our Father for ever.
5 And he will scourge us for our iniquities, and will again shew mercy.
And will gather us out of all the nations among whom ye are scattered.
6 If ye turn to him with your whole heart and with your whole soul,
To do truth before him,
Then will he turn unto you,
And will not hide his face from you.
And see what he will do with you,
And give him thanks with your whole mouth,
And bless the Lord of righteousness,
And exalt the everlasting King.
I in the land of my captivity give him thanks,
And shew his strength and majesty to a nation of sinners.
Turn, ye sinners, and do righteousness before him:

[1] Gr. *Hades*

Who can tell if he will accept you and have mercy on you?

7 I exalt my God,
And my soul *doth exalt* the King of heaven,
And it shall rejoice in his greatness.

8 Let all men speak, and let them give him thanks in Jerusalem.

9 O Jerusalem, the holy city,
He will scourge thee for the works of thy sons,
And will again have mercy on the sons of the righteous.

10 Give thanks to the Lord with goodness,
And bless the everlasting King,
That his tabernacle may be builded in thee again with joy,
And that he may make glad in thee those that are captives,
And love in thee for ever those that are miserable.

11 Many nations shall come from far to the name of the Lord God
With gifts in their hands, even gifts to the King of heaven;
Generations of generations shall praise thee,
And sing songs of rejoicing.

12 Cursed are all they that hate thee;
Blessed shall be all they that love thee for ever.

13 Rejoice and be exceeding glad for the sons of the righteous:
For they shall be gathered together and shall bless the Lord of the righteous.

14 O blessed are they that love thee;
They shall rejoice for thy peace:
Blessed are all they that sorrowed for all thy scourges:
Because they shall rejoice for thee,
When they have seen all thy glory;
And they shall be made glad for ever.

15 Let my soul bless God the great King.

16 For Jerusalem shall be builded with sapphires and emeralds and precious stones;
Thy walls and towers and battlements with pure gold.

17 And the streets of Jerusalem shall be paved with beryl and carbuncle and stones of Ophir.

18 And all her streets shall say, Hallelujah, and give praise,
Saying, Blessed is God, which hath exalted *thee* for ever.

14 And Tobit made an end of giving
2 thanks. And he was eight and fifty years old when he lost his sight; and after eight years he received it again: and he gave alms, and he feared the Lord God more and more, and gave thanks unto him.
3 Now he grew very old; and he called his son, and the six sons of his son, and said unto him,
My child, take thy sons: behold, I am grown old, and am ready to depart
4 out of this life. Go into Media, my

child, for I surely believe all the things which Jonah the prophet spake of Nineveh, that it shall be overthrown, but in Media there shall rather be peace for a season; and that our brethren shall be scattered in the earth from the good land; and Jerusalem shall be desolate, and the house of God in it shall be burned up, and shall
5 be desolate for a time; and God shall again have mercy on them, and bring them back into the land, and they shall build the house, but not like to the former *house*, until the times of that age be fulfilled; and afterward they shall return from the places of their captivity, and build up Jerusalem with honour, and the house of God shall be built in it for ever with a glorious building, even as the prophets
6 spake concerning it. And all the nations shall turn to fear the Lord God
7 truly, and shall bury their idols. And all the nations shall bless the Lord, and his people shall give thanks unto God, and the Lord shall exalt his people; and all they that love the Lord God in truth and righteousness shall rejoice, shewing mercy to our
8 brethren. And now, my child, depart from Nineveh, because those things which the prophet Jonah spake shall
9 surely come to pass. But keep thou the law and the ordinances, and shew thyself merciful and righteous, that
10 it may be well with thee. And bury me decently, and thy mother with me; and dwell ye no longer at Nineveh. See, my child, what Aman did to Achiacharus that nourished him, how out of light he brought him into darkness, and all the recompense that he made him: and Achiacharus was saved, but the other had his recompense, and he went down into darkness. Manasses gave alms, and escaped the snare of death which he set for him: but Aman fell into the
11 snare, and perished. And now, my children, consider what alms doeth, and how righteousness doth deliver.
And while he was saying these things, he gave up the ghost in the bed; but he was a hundred and eight and fifty years old; and he buried him
12 magnificently. And when Anna died, he buried her with his father. But Tobias departed with his wife and his sons to Ecbatana unto Raguel his fa-
13 ther in law, and he grew old in honour, and he buried his father and mother in law magnificently, and he inherited their substance, and his father Tobit's.
14 And he died at Ecbatana of Media, being a hundred and seven and twenty
15 years old. And before he died he heard of the destruction of Nineveh, which Nebuchadnezzar and Ahasuerus took captive; and before his death he rejoiced over Nineveh.

JUDITH.

1 In the twelfth year of the reign of Nebuchadnezzar, who reigned over the Assyrians in Nineveh, the great city; in the days of Arphaxad, who reigned over the Medes in Ecbatana, 2 and built at Ecbatana and round about it walls of hewn stones three cubits broad and six cubits long, and made the height of the wall seventy cubits, and the breadth thereof fifty cubits; 3 and set the towers thereof at the gates thereof, a hundred cubits *high*, and the breadth thereof in the foundation 4 threescore cubits; and made the gates thereof, even gates that were raised to the height of seventy cubits, and the breadth of them forty cubits, for the going forth of his mighty hosts, and the setting in array of his footmen: 5 even in those days king Nebuchadnezzar made war with king Arphaxad in the great plain: this plain is in the 6 borders of Ragau. And there came to meet him all that dwelt in the hill country, and all that dwelt by Euphrates, and Tigris, and Hydaspes, and in the plain of Arioch the king of the Elymæans; and many nations of the sons of Chelod assembled themselves to the battle. 7 And Nebuchadnezzar king of the Assyrians sent unto all that dwelt in Persia, and to all that dwelt westward, to those that dwelt in Cilicia and Damascus and Libanus and Antilibanus, and to all that dwelt over against the 8 sea coast, and to those among the nations that were of Carmel and Gilead, and to the higher Galilee and the great 9 plain of Esdraelon, and to all that were in Samaria and the cities thereof, and beyond Jordan unto Jerusalem, and Betane, and Chellus, and Kadesh, and the river of Egypt, and Tahpanhes, and Rameses, and all the land of 10 Goshen, until thou comest above Tanis and Memphis, and to all that dwelt in Egypt, until thou comest to the bor-11 ders of Ethiopia. And all they that dwelt in all the land made light of the commandment of Nebuchadnezzar king of the Assyrians, and went not with him to the war; for they were not afraid of him, but he was before them as one man; and they turned away his messengers from their presence without effect, and with disgrace. 12 And Nebuchadnezzar was exceeding wroth with all this land, and he sware by his throne and kingdom, that he would surely be avenged upon all the coasts of Cilicia and Damascus and Syria, that he would slay with his sword all the inhabitants of the land of Moab, and the children of Ammon, and all Judæa, and all that were in Egypt, until thou comest to the bor-13 ders of the two seas. And he set the battle in array with his host against king Arphaxad in the seventeenth year; and he prevailed in his battle, and turned to flight all the host of Arphaxad, and all his horse, and all 14 his chariots; and he became master of his cities, and he came even unto Ecbatana, and took the towers, and spoiled the streets thereof, and turned 15 the beauty thereof into shame. And he took Arphaxad in the mountains of Ragau, and smote him through with his darts, and destroyed him utterly, 16 unto this day. And he returned with them to Nineveh, he and all his company of sundry nations, an exceeding great multitude of men of war, and there he took his ease and banqueted, he and his host, a hundred and twenty days.

2 And in the eighteenth year, the two and twentieth day of the first month, there was talk in the house of Nebuchadnezzar king of the Assyrians, that he should be avenged on all the 2 land, even as he spake. And he called together all his servants, and all his great men, and communicated with them his secret counsel, and concluded the afflicting of all the land out of his 3 own mouth. And they decreed to destroy all flesh which followed not the 4 word of his mouth. And it came to pass, when he had ended his counsel, Nebuchadnezzar king of the Assyrians called Holofernes the chief captain of his host, which was next after himself, and said unto him, 5 Thus saith the great king, the lord of all the earth, Behold, thou shalt go forth from my presence, and take with thee men that trust in their strength, unto a hundred and twenty thousand footmen; and the number of horses with their riders twelve thousand: 6 and thou shalt go forth against all the west country, because they disobeyed 7 the commandment of my mouth. And thou shalt declare unto them, that they prepare earth and water; because I will go forth in my wrath against them, and will cover the whole face of the earth with the feet of my host, and I will give them for a spoil unto them: 8 and their slain shall fill their valleys

and brooks, and the river shall be filled
9 with their dead, till it overflow: and
I will lead them captives to the ut-
10 most parts of all the earth. But thou
shalt go forth, and take beforehand
for me all their coasts; and [1]if they
shall yield themselves unto thee, then
shalt thou reserve them for me till the
11 day of their reproof. But as for them
that are disobedient, thine eye shall
not spare; but thou shalt give them up
to be slain and to be spoiled in all thy
12 land. For as I live, and by the power
of my kingdom, I have spoken, and I
13 will do this with my hand. And thou,
moreover, shalt not transgress aught
of the commandments of thy lord, but
thou shalt surely accomplish them, as
I have commanded thee, and thou
shalt not defer to do them.
14 And Holofernes went forth from the
presence of his lord, and called all the
governors and the captains and offi-
15 cers of the host of Asshur; and he
numbered chosen men for the battle,
as his lord had commanded him, unto
a hundred and twenty thousand, and
twelve thousand archers on horse-
16 back; and he ranged them, as a great
17 multitude is ordered for the war. And
he took camels and asses and mules
for their baggage, an exceeding great
multitude; and sheep and oxen and
goats without number for their pro-
18 vision; and great store of victual for
every man, and exceeding much gold
and silver out of the king's house.
19 And he went forth, he and all his host,
on their journey, to go before king
Nebuchadnezzar, and to cover all the
face of the earth westward with their
chariots and horsemen and chosen
20 footmen. And a great company of
sundry nations went forth with them
like locusts, and like the sand of the
earth: for they could not be numbered
by reason of their multitude.
21 And they departed out of Nineveh
three days' journey toward the plain
of Bectileth, and encamped from Bectileth near the mountain which is at
the left hand of the upper Cilicia.
22 And he took all his host, his footmen
and horsemen and chariots, and went
away from thence into the hill coun-
23 try, and destroyed Put and Lud, and
spoiled all the children of Rasses, and
the children of Ishmael, which were
over against the wilderness to the
south of the land of the Chellians.
24 And he went over Euphrates, and
went through Mesopotamia, and
brake down all the high cities that
were upon the river Arbonai, until
25 thou comest to the sea. And he
took possession of the borders of
Cilicia, and slew all that resisted him,
and came unto the borders of Japheth,
which were toward the south, over
26 against Arabia. And he compassed

about all the children of Midian, and
set on fire their tents, and spoiled
27 their sheepcotes. And he went down
into the plain of Damascus in the
days of wheat harvest, and set on fire
all their fields, and utterly destroyed
their flocks and herds, and spoiled
their cities, and laid their plains
waste, and smote all their young men
with the edge of the sword.
28 And the fear and the dread of him
fell upon them that dwelt on the sea
coast, upon them that were in Sidon
and Tyre, and them that dwelt in Sur
and Ocina, and all that dwelt in Jem-
naan; and they that dwelt in Azotus
and Ascalon feared him exceedingly.
3 And they sent unto him messengers
2 with words of peace, saying, Behold,
we the servants of Nebuchadnezzar
the great king lie before thee: use us
3 as it is pleasing in thy sight. Behold,
our dwellings, and all our country,
and all our fields of wheat, and our
flocks and herds, and all the sheepcotes of our tents, lie before thy face:
4 use them as it may please thee. Behold, even our cities and they that
dwell in them are thy servants: come
and deal with them as it is good in
5 thine eyes. And the men came to
Holofernes, and declared unto him
according to these words.
6 And he came down toward the sea
coast, he and his host, and set garrisons in the high cities, and took out
7 of them chosen men for allies. And
they received him, they and all the
country round about them, with gar-
8 lands and dances and timbrels. And
he cast down all their borders, and cut
down their groves: and it had been
given unto him to destroy all the gods
of the land, that all the nations should
worship Nebuchadnezzar only, and
that all their tongues and their tribes
9 should call upon him as god. And he
came towards Esdraelon nigh unto
Dotæa, which is over against the
10 great ridge of Judæa. And he encamped between Geba and Scythopolis, and he was there a whole month,
that he might gather together all the
baggage of his host.
4 And the children of Israel that dwelt
in Judæa heard all that Holofernes
the chief captain of Nebuchadnezzar
king of the Assyrians had done to the
nations, and after what manner he
had spoiled all their temples, and
2 destroyed them utterly. And they
were exceedingly afraid before him,
and were troubled for Jerusalem, and
for the temple of the Lord their God:
3 because they were newly come up
from the captivity, and all the people
of Judæa were lately gathered together; and the vessels, and the altar,
and the house, were sanctified after
the profanation.

[1] Gr.
they
shall
yield
. . . and
thou
shalt re-
serve.

4 And they sent into every coast of Samaria, and to Konæ, and to Beth-horon, and Belmaim, and Jericho, and to Choba, and Æsora, and to the 5 valley of Salem; and they possessed themselves beforehand of all the tops of the high mountains, and fortified the villages that were in them, and laid up victual for the provision of war: for their fields were newly reap-6 ed. And Joakim the high priest, which was in those days at Jerusalem, wrote to them that dwelt in Bethulia, and Betomesthaim, which is over against Esdraelon toward the plain 7 that is nigh unto Dothaim, charging them to seize upon the ascents of the hill country; because by them was the entrance into Judæa, and it was easy to stop them from approaching, inasmuch as the approach was nar-row, *with space* for two men at the 8 most. And the children of Israel did as Joakim the high priest had com-manded them, and the senate of all the people of Israel, which dwelt at Jerusalem.

9 And every man of Israel cried to God with great earnestness, and with great earnestness did they humble their 10 souls. They, and their wives, and their babes, and their cattle, and every sojourner and hireling and ser-vant bought with their money, put 11 sackcloth upon their loins. And every man and woman of Israel, and the little children, and the inhabitants of Jerusalem, fell before the temple, and cast ashes upon their heads, and spread out their sackcloth before the Lord; and they put sackcloth about 12 the altar: and they cried to the God of Israel earnestly with one consent, that he would not give their babes for a prey, and their wives for a spoil, and the cities of their inheritance to destruction, and the sanctuary to pro-fanation and reproach, for the nations 13 to rejoice at. And the Lord heard their voice, and looked upon their affliction: and the people continued fasting many days in all Judæa and Jerusalem before the sanctuary of 14 the Lord Almighty. And Joakim the high priest, and all the priests that stood before the Lord, and they that ministered unto the Lord, had their loins girt about with sackcloth, and offered the continual burnt offering, and the vows and the free gifts of the 15 people; and they had ashes on their mitres: and they cried unto the Lord with all their power, that he would look upon all the house of Israel for good.

5 And it was told Holofernes, the chief captain of the host of Asshur, that the children of Israel had prepared for war, and had shut up the passages of the hill country, and had fortified all the tops of the high hills, and had laid 2 impediments in the plains: and he was exceeding wroth, and he called all the princes of Moab, and the cap-tains of Ammon, and all the governors 3 of the sea coast, and he said unto them, Tell me now, ye sons of Canaan, who is this people, that dwelleth in the hill country, and what are the cit-ies that they inhabit, and what is the multitude of their host, and wherein is their power and their strength, and what king is set over them, to be the 4 leader of their army; and why have they turned their backs, that they should not come and meet me, more than all that dwell in the west.

5 And Achior, the leader of all the children of Ammon, said unto him, Let my lord now hear a word from the mouth of thy servant, and I will tell thee the truth concerning this people, which dwelleth in this hill country, nigh unto the place where thou dwellest: and there shall no lie come out of the mouth of thy servant. 6 This people are descended of the Chal-7 deans: and they sojourned heretofore in Mesopotamia, because they were not minded to follow the gods of their fathers, which were in the land of the 8 Chaldeans. And they departed from the way of their parents, and wor-shipped the God of heaven, the God whom they knew: and they cast them out from the face of their gods, and they fled into Mesopotamia, and so-9 journed there many days. And their God commanded them to depart from the place where they sojourned, and to go into the land of Canaan: and they dwelt there, and were increased with gold and silver, and with exceed-10 ing much cattle. And they went down into Egypt, for a famine covered all the land of Canaan; and there they sojourned, until they were grown up; and they became there a great multi-tude, so that one could not number 11 their nation. And the king of Egypt rose up against them, and dealt sub-tilly with them, [1] and brought them low, making them to labour in brick, 12 and made them slaves. And they cried unto their God, and he smote all the land of Egypt with incurable plagues: and the Egyptians cast them 13 out of their sight. And God dried up 14 the Red sea before them, and brought them into the way of Sinai, and Ka-desh-Barnea, and they cast out all 15 that dwelt in the wilderness. And they dwelt in the land of the Amorites, and they destroyed by their strength all them of Heshbon, and passing over Jordan they possessed all the 16 hill country. And they cast out be-fore them the Canaanite, the Periz-zite, the Jebusite, and the Shechemite, and all the Girgashites, and they

[1] Some authori-ties read *and he brought them low with clay and brick, &c*

dwelt in that country many days.
17 And whilst they sinned not before their God, they prospered, because God that hateth iniquity was with
18 them. But when they departed from the way which he appointed them, they were destroyed in many battles very sore, and were led captives into a land that was not theirs, and the temple of their God was cast to the ground, and their cities were taken
19 by their adversaries. And now they are returned to their God, and are come up from the dispersion where they were dispersed, and have possessed Jerusalem, where their sanctuary is, and are seated in the hill
20 country: for it was desolate. And now, my lord and master, if there is any error in this people, and they sin against their God, we will consider what this thing is wherein they stumble, and we will go up and overcome
21 them. But if there is no lawlessness in their nation, let my lord now pass by, lest their Lord defend them, and their God be for them, and we shall be a reproach before all the earth.
22 And it came to pass, when Achior had finished speaking these words, all the people that compassed the tent and stood round about it murmured; and the great men of Holofernes, and all that dwelt by the sea side, and in Moab, spake that he should kill him.
23 For, *said they*, we will not be afraid of the children of Israel: for, lo, it is a people that hath no power nor might
24 to make the battle strong. Wherefore now we will go up, and they shall be a prey to be devoured of all thine army, lord Holofernes.

6 And when the tumult of the men that were about the council was ceased, Holofernes the chief captain of the host of Asshur said unto Achior and to all the children of [1] Moab before all the people of the aliens,
2 And who art thou, Achior, and the hirelings of [1] Ephraim, that thou hast prophesied among us as to-day, and hast said, that we should not make war with the race of Israel, because their God will defend them? And
3 who is God but Nebuchadnezzar? He shall send forth his might, and shall destroy them from the face of the earth, and their God shall not deliver them: but we his servants shall smite them as one man; and they shall not
4 sustain the might of our horses. For with them we shall burn them up, and their mountains shall be drunken with their blood, and their plains shall be filled with their dead bodies, and their footsteps shall not stand before us, but they shall surely perish, saith king Nebuchadnezzar, lord of all the earth: for he said, The words that [2] I have spoken shall not be in vain.

5 But thou, Achior, hireling of Ammon, which hast spoken these words in the day of thine iniquity, shalt see my face no more from this day, until I shall be avenged of the race of those
6 that came out of Egypt. And then shall the sword of mine army, and the multitude of them that serve me, pass through thy sides, and thou shalt fall among their slain, when I shall return.
7 And my servants shall bring thee back into the hill country, and shall set thee in one of the cities of the ascents:
8 and thou shalt not perish, till thou
9 be destroyed with them. And if thou hopest in thy heart that they shall not be taken, let not thy countenance fall. I have spoken it, and none of my words shall fall to the ground.
10 And Holofernes commanded his servants, that waited in his tent, to take Achior, and bring him back to Bethulia, and deliver him into the hands
11 of the children of Israel. And his servants took him, and brought him out of the camp into the plain, and they removed from the midst of the plain country into the hill country, and came unto the fountains that
12 were under Bethulia. And when the men of the city saw them on the top of the hill, they took up their weapons, and went out of the city against them to the top of the hill: and every man that used a sling kept them from coming up, and cast stones against
13 them. And they gat them privily under the hill, and bound Achior, and cast him down, and left him at the foot of the hill, and went away unto
14 their lord. But the children of Israel descended from their city, and came upon him, and loosed him, and led him away into Bethulia, and presented him to the rulers of their city;
15 which were in those days Ozias the son of Micah, of the tribe of Simeon, and Chabris the son of Gothoniel, and
16 Charmis the son of Melchiel. And they called together all the elders of the city; and all their young men ran together, and their women, to the assembly; and they set Achior in the midst of all their people. And Ozias
17 asked him of that which had happened: and he answered and declared unto them the words of the council of Holofernes, and all the words that he had spoken in the midst of the princes of the children of Asshur, and all the great words that Holofernes had spoken against the house of Israel.
18 And the people fell down and wor-
19 shipped God, and cried, saying, O Lord God of heaven, behold their arrogance, and pity the low estate of our race, and look upon the face of those that are sanctified unto thee this
20 day. And they comforted Achior, and
21 praised him exceedingly. And Ozias

took him out of the assembly into his house, and made a feast to the elders; and they called on the God of Israel for help all that night.

7 But the next day Holofernes gave command to all his army, and to all his people which were come to be his allies, that they should remove their camp toward Bethulia, and take aforehand the ascents of the hill country, and make war against the children

2 of Israel. And every mighty man of them removed that day, and the host of their men of war was a hundred and seventy thousand footmen, and twelve thousand horsemen, beside the baggage, and the men that were afoot among them, an exceeding great mul-

3 titude. And they encamped in the valley near unto Bethulia, by the fountain, and they spread themselves in breadth over Dothaim even to Belmaim, and in length from Bethulia unto Cyamon, which is over against Esdraelon.

4 But the children of Israel, when they saw the multitude of them, were troubled exceedingly, and said every one to his neighbour, Now shall these men lick up the face of all the earth; and neither the high mountains, nor the valleys, nor the hills, shall be able

5 to bear their weight. And every man took up his weapons of war, and when they had kindled fires upon their towers, they remained and watched all that night.

6 But on the second day Holofernes led out all his horse in the sight of the children of Israel which were in Beth-

7 ulia, and viewed the ascents to their city, and searched out the fountains of the waters, and seized upon them, and set garrisons of men of war over them, and himself departed to his people.

8 And there came unto him all the rulers of the children of Esau, and all the leaders of the people of Moab, and the captains of the sea coast, and said,

9 Let our lord now hear a word, that there be not an overthrow in thy host.

10 For this people of the children of Israel do not trust in their spears, but in the height of the mountains wherein they dwell, for it is not easy to come up to the tops of their mountains.

11 And now, my lord, fight not against them as men fight who join battle, and there shall not so much as one man

12 of thy people perish. Remain in thy camp, and keep safe every man of thy host, and let thy servants get possession of the fountain of water, which issueth forth of the foot of the moun-

13 tain: because all the inhabitants of Bethulia have their water thence; and thirst shall kill them, and they shall give up their city: and we and our people will go up to the tops of the mountains that are near, and will

encamp upon them, to watch that not

14 one man go out of the city. And they shall be consumed with famine, they and their wives and their children, and before the sword come against them they shall be laid low in the

15 streets where they dwell. And thou shalt render them an evil reward; because they rebelled, and met not thy face in peace.

16 And their words were pleasing in the sight of Holofernes and in the sight of all his servants; and he appointed to

17 do as they had spoken. And the army of the children of Ammon removed, and with them five thousand of the children of Asshur, and they encamped in the valley, and seized upon the waters and the fountains of the waters

18 of the children of Israel. And the children of Esau went up with the children of Ammon, and encamped in the hill country over against Dothaim: and they sent some of them toward the south, and toward the east, over against Ekrebel, which is near unto Chusi, that is upon the brook Mochmur; and the rest of the army of the Assyrians encamped in the plain, and covered all the face of the land; and their tents and baggage were pitched upon it in a great crowd, and they were an exceeding great multitude.

19 And the children of Israel cried unto the Lord their God, for their spirit fainted; for all their enemies had compassed them round about, and there was no way to escape out from among

20 them. And all the army of Asshur remained about them, their footmen and their chariots and their horsemen, four and thirty days; and all their vessels of water failed all the inhabi-

21 tants of Bethulia. And the cisterns were emptied, and they had not water to drink their fill for one day: for they

22 gave them drink by measure. And their young children were out of heart, and the women and the young men fainted for thirst, and they fell down in the streets of the city, and in the passages of the gates, and there was

23 no longer any strength in them. And all the people were gathered together against Ozias, and against the rulers of the city, the young men and the women and the children, and cried with a loud voice, and said before all the elders,

24 God be judge between you and us: because ye have done us great wrong, in that ye have not spoken words of peace with the children of Asshur.

25 And now we have no helper: but God hath sold us into their hands, that we should be laid low before them with

26 thirst and great destruction. And now call them unto you, and deliver up the whole city for a prey to the people of Holofernes, and to all his

27 host. For it is better for us to be made a spoil unto them: for we shall be servants, and our souls shall live, and we shall not see the death of our babes before our eyes, and our wives and our children fainting in death.

28 We take to witness against you the heaven and the earth, and our God and the Lord of our fathers, which punisheth us according to our sins and the sins of our fathers, that he do not according as we have said this day.

29 And there was great weeping of all with one consent in the midst of the assembly; and they cried unto the

30 Lord God with a loud voice. And Ozias said to them, Brethren, be of good courage, let us yet endure five days, in the which space the Lord our God shall turn his mercy toward us;

31 for he will not forsake us utterly. But if these days pass, and there come no help unto us, I will do according to

32 your words. And he dispersed the people, every man to his own camp; and they went away unto the walls and towers of their city; and he sent the women and children into their houses: and they were brought very low in the city.

8 And in those days Judith heard thereof, the daughter of Merari, the son of Ox, the son of Joseph, the son of Oziel, the son of Elkiah, the son of Ananias, the son of Gideon, the son of Raphaim, the son of Ahitub, the son of Elihu, the son of Eliab, the son of Nathanael, the son of Salamiel, the son of Salasadai, the son of Israel.

2 And her husband was Manasses, of her tribe and of her family, and he died in the days of barley harvest.

3 For he stood over them that bound sheaves in the field, and the heat came upon his head, and he fell on his bed, and died in his city Bethulia: and they buried him with his fathers in the field which is between Dothaim and

4 Balamon. And Judith was a widow in her house three years and four

5 months. And she made her a tent upon the roof of her house, and put on sackcloth upon her loins; and the garments of her widowhood were

6 upon her. And she fasted all the days of her widowhood, save the eves of the sabbaths, and the sabbaths, and the eves of the new moons, and the new moons, and the feasts and joyful days of the house of Israel.

7 And she was of a goodly countenance, and exceeding beautiful to behold: and her husband Manasses had left her gold, and silver, and menservants, and maidservants, and cattle, and lands; and she remained upon them.

8 And there was none that gave her an evil word; for she feared God exceedingly.

9 And she heard the evil words of the people against the governor, because they fainted for lack of water; and Judith heard all the words that Ozias spake unto them, how he sware to them that he would deliver the city unto the Assyrians after five days.

10 And she sent her maid, that was over all things that she had, to call Ozias and Chabris and Charmis, the elders

11 of her city. And they came unto her, and she said unto them,

Hear me now, O ye rulers of the inhabitants of Bethulia: for your word that ye have spoken before the people this day is not right, and ye have set the oath which ye have pronounced between God and you, and have promised to deliver the city to our enemies, unless within these days the

12 Lord turn to help you. And now who are ye that have tempted God this day, and stand instead of God among

13 the children of men? And now try the Lord Almighty, and ye shall never

14 know anything. For ye shall not find the depth of the heart of man, and ye shall not perceive the things that he thinketh: and how shall ye search out God, which hath made all these things, and know his mind, and comprehend his purpose? Nay, my brethren, provoke not the Lord our God

15 to anger. For if he be not minded to help us within these five days, he hath power to defend us in such time as he will, or to destroy us before the face

16 of our enemies. But do not ye pledge the counsels of the Lord our God: for God is not as man, that he should be threatened; neither as the son of man, that he should be turned by in-

17 treaty. Wherefore let us wait for the salvation that cometh from him, and call upon him to help us, and he will

18 hear our voice, if it please him. For there arose none in our age, neither is there any of us to-day, tribe, or kindred, or family, or city, which worship gods made with hands, as it was

19 in the former days; for the which cause our fathers were given to the sword, and for a spoil, and fell with

20 a great fall before our enemies. But we know none other god beside him, wherefore we hope that he will not

21 despise us, nor any of our race. For if we be taken so, all Judæa shall sit upon the ground, and our sanctuary shall be spoiled; and of our blood shall he require the profanation there-

22 of. And the slaughter of our brethren, and the captivity of the land, and the desolation of our inheritance, shall he turn upon our heads among the Gentiles, wheresoever we shall be in bondage; and we shall be an offence and a reproach before them that take us

23 for a possession. For our bondage shall not be ordered to favour: but

the Lord our God shall turn it to dis-
24 honour. And now, brethren, let us
shew an example to our brethren, because their soul hangeth upon us, and
the sanctuary and the house and the
25 altar rest upon us. Besides all this
let us give thanks to the Lord our
God, which trieth us, even as he did
26 our fathers also. Remember all the
things which he did to Abraham, and
all the things in which he tried Isaac,
and all the things which happened to
Jacob in Mesopotamia of Syria, when
he kept the sheep of Laban his mo-
27 ther's brother. For he hath not tried
us in the fire, as he did them, to search
out their hearts, neither hath he taken
vengeance on us; but the Lord doth
scourge them that come near unto
him, to admonish them.
28 And Ozias said to her, All that thou
hast spoken hast thou spoken with a
good heart, and there is none that
29 shall gainsay thy words. For this is
not the first day wherein thy wisdom
is manifested; but from the beginning
of thy days all the people have known
thine understanding, because the dis-
30 position of thy heart is good. But
the people were exceeding thirsty,
and compelled us to do as we spake
to them, and to bring an oath upon
ourselves, which we will not break.
31 And now pray thou for us, because
thou art a godly woman, and the Lord
shall send us rain to fill our cisterns,
32 and we shall faint no more. And
Judith said unto them, Hear me, and
I will do a thing, which shall go down
to all generations among the children
33 of our race. Ye shall stand at the
gate this night, and I will go forth
with my maid: and, within the days
after which ye said that ye would deliver the city to our enemies, the Lord
34 shall visit Israel by my hand. But ye
shall not inquire of mine act: for I
will not declare it unto you, till the
35 things be finished that I do. And
Ozias and the rulers said unto her,
Go in peace, and the Lord God be before thee, to take vengeance on our
36 enemies. And they returned from the
tent, and went to their stations.
9 But Judith fell upon her face, and
put ashes upon her head, and uncovered the sackcloth wherewith she was
clothed; and the incense of that evening was now being offered at Jerusalem in the house of God, and Judith
cried unto the Lord with a loud voice,
and said,
2 O Lord God of my father Simeon, into whose hand thou gavest a sword
to take vengeance of the strangers,
who loosened the girdle of a virgin to
defile her, and uncovered the thigh to
her shame, and profaned the womb to
her reproach; for thou saidst, It shall
3 not be so; and they did so: wherefore

thou gavest their rulers to be slain,
and their bed, [1] which was ashamed
for her that was deceived, to be dyed
in blood, and smotest the servants
with their lords, and the lords upon
4 their thrones; and gavest their wives
for a prey, and their daughters to be
captives, and all their spoils to be
divided among thy dear children;
which were moved with zeal for thee,
and abhorred the pollution of their
blood, and called upon thee for aid:
O God, O my God, hear me also that
5 am a widow. For thou wroughtest
the things that were before those
things, and those things, and such as
ensued after; and thou didst devise
the things which are now, and the
things which are to come: and the
things which thou didst devise came
6 to pass; yea, the things which thou
didst determine stood before thee,
and said, Lo, we are here: for all thy
ways are prepared, and thy judgement
7 is with foreknowledge. For, behold,
the Assyrians are multiplied in their
power; they are exalted with horse
and rider; they have gloried in the
[2] strength of their footmen; they have
trusted in shield and spear and bow
and sling; and they know not that
thou art the Lord that breaketh the
8 battles: the Lord is thy name. Dash
thou down their strength in thy power,
and bring down their force in thy
wrath: for they have purposed to
profane thy sanctuary, and to defile
the tabernacle where thy glorious
name resteth, and to cast down with
the sword the horn of thine altar.
9 Look upon their pride, and send thy
wrath upon their heads: give into my
hand, which am a widow, the might
10 that I have conceived. Smite by the
deceit of my lips the servant with the
prince, and the prince with his servant: break down their stateliness
11 by the hand of a woman. For thy
power standeth not in multitude, nor
thy might in strong men: but thou
art a God of the afflicted, thou art a
helper of the [3] oppressed, an upholder
of the weak, a protector of the forlorn,
a saviour of them that are without
12 hope. Yea, yea, God of my father,
and God of the inheritance of Israel,
Lord of the heavens and of the earth,
Creator of the waters, King [4] of every
13 creature, hear thou my prayer: and
make my speech and deceit to be
their wound and stripe, who have
purposed hard things against thy
covenant, and thy hallowed house,
and the top of Sion, and the house of
14 the possession of thy children. And
make every nation and tribe of thine
to know that thou art God, the God
of all power and might, and that there
is none other that protecteth the race
of Israel but thou.

[1] Some authorities read *which was ashamed for their deceit that they wrought.*

[2] Gr. *arm.*

[3] Gr. *fewer.*

[4] Gr. *of all thy creation*

10 And it came to pass, when she had ceased to cry unto the God of Israel, and had made an end of all these 2 words, that she rose up where she had fallen down, and called her maid, and went down into the house, in the which she was wont to abide on the sabbath days and on her feast days, 3 and pulled off the sackcloth which she had put on, and put off the garments of her widowhood, and washed her body all over with water, and anointed herself with rich ointment, and braided the hair of her head, and put a tire upon it, and put on her garments of gladness, wherewith she was wont to be clad in the days of the life of Ma- 4 nasses her husband. And she took sandals for her feet, and put her chains about her, and her bracelets, and her rings, and her earrings, and all her ornaments, and decked herself bravely, to beguile the eyes of all men that 5 should see her. And she gave her maid a leathern bottle of wine, and a cruse of oil, and filled a bag with parched corn and lumps of figs and ¹ fine bread; and she packed all her vessels together, and laid them upon her.

6 And they went forth to the gate of the city of Bethulia, and found standing thereby Ozias, and the elders of 7 the city, Chabris and Charmis. But when they saw her, that her countenance was altered, and her apparel was changed, they wondered at her beauty very exceedingly, and said unto 8 her, The God of our fathers give thee favour, and accomplish thy purposes to the glory of the children of Israel, and to the exaltation of Jerusalem. 9 And she worshipped God, and said unto them, Command that they open unto me the gate of the city, and I will go forth to accomplish the things whereof ye spake with me. And they commanded the young men to open 10 unto her, as she had spoken : and they did so.

And Judith went out, she, and her handmaid with her; and the men of the city looked after her, until she was gone down the mountain, until she had passed the valley, and they could 11 see her no more. And they went straight onward in the valley : and the 12 watch of the Assyrians met her ; and they took her, and asked her, Of what people art thou ? and whence comest thou ? and whither goest thou ? And she said, I am a daughter of the Hebrews, and I flee away from their presence ; because they are about to 13 be given you to be consumed : and I am coming into the presence of Holofernes the chief captain of your host, to declare words of truth ; and I will shew before him a way, whereby he shall go, and win all the hill country,

and there shall not be lacking of his 14 men one person, nor one life. Now when the men heard her words, and considered her countenance, the beauty thereof was exceeding marvellous in their eyes, and they said unto her, 15 Thou hast saved thy life, in that thou hast hasted to come down to the presence of our lord : and now come to his tent, and some of us shall conduct thee, until they shall deliver thee into 16 his hands. But ² when thou standest before him, be not afraid in thine heart, but declare unto him according to thy words ; and he shall entreat 17 thee well. And they chose out of them a hundred men, and appointed them to accompany her and her maid ; and they brought them to the tent of Holofernes.

18 And there was a concourse throughout all the camp, for her coming was noised among the tents ; and they came and compassed her about, as she stood without the tent of Holofernes, 19 until they told him of her. And they marvelled at her beauty, and marvelled at the children of Israel because of her, and each one said to his neighbour, Who shall despise this people, that have among them such women ? for it is not good that one man of them be left, seeing that, if they are let go, they shall be able to 20 deceive the whole earth. And they that lay near Holofernes, and all his servants, went forth and brought her 21 into the tent. And Holofernes was resting upon his bed under the canopy, which was woven with purple and gold and emeralds and precious 22 stones. And they told him of her ; and he came forth into the space before his tent, with silver lamps going 23 before him. But when Judith was come before him and his servants, they all marvelled at the beauty of her countenance ; and she fell down upon her face, and did reverence unto him : and his servants raised her up.

11 And Holofernes said unto her, Woman, be of good comfort, fear not in thy heart : for I never hurt any that hath chosen to serve Nebuchadnezzar, 2 the king of all the earth. And now, if thy people that dwelleth in the hill country had not set light by me, I would not have lifted up my spear against them : but they have done 3 these things to themselves. And now tell me wherefore thou didst flee from them, and camest unto us : for thou art come to save thyself ; be of good comfort, thou shalt live this night, and 4 hereafter : for there is none that shall wrong thee, but all shall entreat thee well, as is done unto the servants of 5 king Nebuchadnezzar my lord. And Judith said unto him, Receive the words of thy servant, and

let thy handmaid speak in thy presence, and I will declare no lie unto
6 my lord this night. And if thou shalt follow the words of thy handmaid, God shall bring the thing to pass perfectly with thee; and my lord shall
7 not fail of his purposes. As Nebuchadnezzar king of all the earth liveth, and as his power liveth, who hath sent thee for the preservation of every living thing, not only do men serve him by thee, but also the beasts of the field and the cattle and the birds of the heaven shall live through thy strength, in the time of Nebuchad-
8 nezzar and of all his house. For we have heard of thy wisdom and the subtil devices of thy soul, and it hath been reported in all the earth, that thou only art brave in all the kingdom, and mighty in knowledge, and won-
9 derful in feats of war. And now as concerning the matter, which Achior did speak in thy council, we have heard his words: for the men of Bethulia saved him, and he declared unto them all that he had spoken before
10 thee. Wherefore, O lord and master, neglect not his word; but lay it up in thy heart, for it is true: for our race shall not be punished, neither shall the sword prevail against them, ex-
11 cept they sin against their God. And now, that my lord be not defeated and frustrate of his purpose, and that death may fall upon them, their sin hath overtaken them, wherewith they shall provoke their God to anger, whensoever they shall do wickedness.
12 Since their victuals failed them, and all their water was scant, they took counsel to lay hands upon their cattle, and determined to consume all those things, which God charged them by his laws that they should not eat:
13 and they are resolved to spend the firstfruits of the corn, and the tenths of the wine and the oil, which they had sanctified, and reserved for the priests that stand before the face of our God in Jerusalem; the which things it is not fitting for any of the people so much as to touch with their hands.
14 And they have sent some to Jerusalem, because they also that dwell there have done this thing, to bring
15 them a licence from the senate. And it shall be, when one shall bring them word, and they shall do it, they shall be given thee to be destroyed the
16 same day. Wherefore I thy servant, knowing all this, fled away from their presence; and God sent me to work things with thee, whereat all the earth shall be astonished, even as many as
17 shall hear it. For thy servant is religious, and serveth the God of heaven day and night: and now, my lord, I will abide with thee, and thy servant will go forth by night into the valley,

and I will pray unto God, and he shall tell me when they have com-
18 mitted their sins: and I will come and shew it also unto thee; and thou shalt go forth with all thy host, and there shall be none of them that shall
19 resist thee. And I will lead thee through the midst of Judæa, until thou comest over against Jerusalem; and I will set thy seat in the midst thereof; and thou shalt drive them as sheep that have no shepherd, and a dog shall not so much as open his mouth before thee: for these things were told me according to my foreknowledge, and were declared unto me, and I was sent to tell thee.
20 And her words were pleasing in the sight of Holofernes and of all his servants; and they marvelled at her wis-
21 dom, and said, There is not such a woman from one end of the earth to the other, for beauty of face, and wis-
22 dom of words. And Holofernes said unto her, God did well to send thee before the people, that might should be in our hands, and destruction among them that lightly regarded my
23 lord. And now thou art beautiful in thy countenance, and witty in thy words: for if thou shalt do as thou hast spoken, thy God shall be my God, and thou shalt dwell in the house of king Nebuchadnezzar, and shalt be renowned through the whole earth.

12 And he commanded to bring her in where his silver vessels were set, and bade that they should prepare for her of his own meats, and that she should
2 drink of his own wine. And Judith said, I will not eat thereof, lest there be an occasion of stumbling: but provision shall be made for me of the
3 things that are come with me. And Holofernes said unto her, But if the things that be with thee should fail, whence shall we be able to give thee the like? for there is none of thy race
4 with us. And Judith said unto him, As thy soul liveth, my lord, thy servant shall not spend those things that be with me, until the Lord work by my hand the things that he hath de-
5 termined. And the servants of Holofernes brought her into the tent, and she slept till midnight, and she rose
6 up toward the morning watch, and sent to Holofernes, saying, Let my lord now command that they suffer thy servant to go forth unto prayer.
7 And Holofernes commanded his guards that they should not stay her: and she abode in the camp three days, and went out every night into the valley of Bethulia, and washed herself at the fountain of water in the camp.
8 And when she came up, she besought the Lord God of Israel to direct her way to the raising up of the children

9 of his people. And she came in clean, and remained in the tent, until she took her meat toward evening.

10 And it came to pass on the fourth day, Holofernes made a feast to his own servants only, and called none of

11 the officers to the banquet. And he said to Bagoas the eunuch, who had charge over all that he had, Go now, and persuade this Hebrew woman which is with thee, that she come unto us, and eat and drink with us.

12 For, lo, it is a shame for our person, if we shall let such a woman go, not having had her company; for if we draw her not unto us, she shall laugh us to

13 scorn. And Bagoas went from the presence of Holofernes, and came in to her, and said, Let not this fair damsel fear to come to my lord, and to be honoured in his presence, and to drink wine and be merry with us, and to be made this day as one of the daughters of the children of Asshur, which wait

14 in the house of Nebuchadnezzar. And Judith said unto him, And who am I, that I should gainsay my lord? for whatsoever shall be pleasing in his eyes I will do speedily, and this shall be my joy unto the day of my death.

15 And she arose, and decked herself with her apparel and all her woman's attire; and her servant went and laid fleeces on the ground for her over against Holofernes, which she had received of Bagoas for her daily use, that she might sit and eat upon them.

16 And Judith came in and sat down, and Holofernes' heart was ravished with her, and his soul was moved, and he desired exceedingly her company: and he was watching for a time to deceive her, from the day that he had seen her.

17 And Holofernes said unto her, Drink

18 now, and be merry with us. And Judith said, I will drink now, my lord, because my life is magnified in me this day more than all the days since I was

19 born. And she took and ate and drank before him what her servant had pre-

20 pared. And Holofernes took great delight in her, and drank exceeding much wine, more than he had drunk at any time in one day since he was born.

13 But when the evening was come, his servants made haste to depart, and Bagoas shut the tent without, and dismissed them that waited from the presence of his lord; and they went away to their beds: for they were all weary,

2 because the feast had been long. But Judith was left alone in the tent, and Holofernes lying along upon his bed:

3 for he was overflown with wine. And Judith had said to her servant that she should stand without her bedchamber, and wait for her coming forth, as she did daily: for she said she would go forth to her prayer; and she spake to

Bagoas according to the same words.

4 And all went away from her presence, and none was left in the bedchamber, neither small nor great. And Judith, standing by his bed, said in her heart, O Lord God of all power, look in this hour upon the works of my hands for

5 the exaltation of Jerusalem. For now is the time to help thine inheritance, and to do the thing that I have purposed to the destruction of the enemies which are risen up against us.

6 And she came to the rail of the bed, which was at Holofernes' head, and took down his scimitar from thence;

7 and she drew near unto the bed, and took hold of the hair of his head, and said, Strengthen me, O Lord God of

8 Israel, this day. And she smote twice upon his neck with all her might, and

9 took away his head from him, and tumbled his body down from the bed, and took down the canopy from the pillars; and after a little while she went forth, and gave Holofernes' head

10 to her maid; and she put it in her bag of victuals: and they twain went forth together unto prayer, according to their custom: and they passed through the camp, and compassed that valley, and went up to the mountain of Bethulia, and came to the gates thereof.

11 And Judith said afar off to the watchmen at the gates, Open, open now the gate: God is with us, even our God, to shew his power yet in Israel, and his might against the enemy, as he hath

12 done even this day. And it came to pass, when the men of her city heard her voice, they made haste to go down to the gate of their city, and they called together the elders of the city.

13 And they ran all together, both small and great, for it was strange unto them that she was come: and they opened the gate, and received them, making a fire to give light, and com-

14 passed them round about. And she said to them with a loud voice, Praise God, praise him: praise God, who hath not taken away his mercy from the house of Israel, but hath destroyed our

15 enemies by my hand this night. And she took forth the head out of the bag, and shewed it, and said unto them, Behold, the head of Holofernes, the chief captain of the host of Asshur, and behold, the canopy, wherein he did lie in his drunkenness; and the Lord smote him by the hand of a woman.

16 And as the Lord liveth, who preserved me in my way that I went, my countenance deceived him to his destruction, and he did not commit sin with me,

17 to defile and shame me. And all the people were exceedingly amazed, and bowed themselves, and worshipped God, and said with one accord, Blessed art thou, O our God, which hast this day brought to nought the enemies of

18 thy people. And Ozias said unto her, Blessed art thou, daughter, in the sight of the Most High God, above all the women upon the earth; and blessed is the Lord God, who created the heavens and the earth, who directed thee to the smiting of the head of the 19 prince of our enemies. For thy hope shall not depart from the heart of men that remember the strength of 20 God for ever. And God turn these things to thee for a perpetual praise, to visit thee with good things, because thou didst not spare thy life by reason of the affliction of our race, but didst avenge our fall, walking a straight way before our God. And all the people said, So be it, so be it.

14 And Judith said unto them, Hear me now, my brethren, and take this head, and hang it upon the battlement 2 of your wall. And it shall be, so soon as the morning shall appear, and the sun shall come forth upon the earth, ye shall take up every one his weapons of war, and go forth every valiant man of you out of the city, and ye shall set a captain over them, as though ye would go down to the plain toward the watch of the children of Asshur; and 3 ye shall not go down. And these shall take up their panoplies, and shall go into their camp, and rouse up the captains of the host of Asshur, and they shall run together to the tent of Holofernes, and they shall not find him: and fear shall fall upon them, and 4 they shall flee before your face. And ye, and all that inhabit every coast of Israel, shall pursue them, and over-5 throw them as they go. But before ye do these things, call me Achior the Ammonite, that he may see and know him that despised the house of Israel, and that sent him to us, as it were to death.

6 And they called Achior out of the house of Ozias; but when he came, and saw the head of Holofernes in a man's hand in the assembly of the people, he fell upon his face, and his spirit 7 failed. But when [1] they had recovered him, he fell at Judith's feet, and did reverence unto her, and said, Blessed art thou in every tent of Judah, and in every nation, which hearing thy name 8 shall be troubled. And now tell me all the things that thou hast done in these days. And Judith declared unto him in the midst of the people all the things that she had done, from the day that she went forth until the time 9 that she spake unto them. But when she left off speaking, the people shouted with a loud voice, and made a joy-10 ful noise in their city. But when Achior saw all the things that the God of Israel had done, he believed in God exceedingly, and circumcised the flesh of his foreskin, and was joined

[1] Many authorities read *he had recovered himself.*

unto the house of Israel, unto this day.

11 But as soon as the morning arose, they hanged the head of Holofernes upon the wall, and every man took up his weapons, and they went forth by bands unto the ascents of the moun-12 tain. But when the children of Asshur saw them, they sent hither and thither to their leaders; but they went to their captains and tribunes, 13 and to every one of their rulers. And they came to Holofernes' tent, and said to him that was over all that he had, Waken now our lord: for the slaves have been bold to come down against us to battle, that they may 14 be utterly destroyed. And Bagoas went in, and knocked at the outer door of the tent; for he supposed that he was sleeping with Judith. 15 But when none hearkened to him, he opened it, and went into the bedchamber, and found him cast upon the threshold dead, and his head had been 16 taken from him. And he cried with a loud voice, with weeping and groaning and a mighty cry, and rent his gar-17 ments. And he entered into the tent where Judith lodged: and he found her not, and he leaped out to the peo-18 ple, and cried aloud, The slaves have dealt treacherously: one woman of the Hebrews hath brought shame upon the house of king Nebuchadnezzar; for, behold, Holofernes *lieth* upon the ground, and his head is not 19 on him. But when the rulers of the host of Asshur heard the words, they rent their coats, and their soul was troubled exceedingly, and there was a cry and an exceeding great noise in the midst of the camp.

15 And when they that were in the tents heard, they were amazed at the 2 thing that was come to pass. And trembling and fear fell upon them, and no man durst abide any more in the sight of his neighbour, but rushing out with one accord, they fled into every way of the plain and of the hill country. 3 And they that had encamped in the hill country round about Bethulia fled away. And then the children of Israel, every one that was a warrior among 4 them, rushed out upon them. And Ozias sent to Betomasthaim, and Bebai, and Chobai, and Chola, and to every coast of Israel, such as should tell concerning the things that had been accomplished, and that all should rush forth upon their enemies to destroy 5 them. But when the children of Israel heard, they all fell upon them with one accord, and smote them unto Chobai: yea, and in like manner also they of Jerusalem and of all the hill country came (for men had told them what things were come to pass in the camp of their enemies), and they that were

in Gilead and in Galilee fell upon their flank with a great slaughter, until they were past Damascus and the 6 borders thereof. But the residue, that dwelt at Bethulia, fell upon the camp of Asshur, and spoiled them, 7 and were enriched exceedingly. But the children of Israel returned from the slaughter, and gat possession of that which remained; and the villages and the cities, that were in the hill country and in the plain country, took many spoils: for there was an exceeding great store.

8 And Joakim the high priest, and the senate of the children of Israel that dwelt in Jerusalem, came to behold the good things which the Lord had shewed to Israel, and to see Judith, 9 and to salute her. But when they came unto her, they all blessed her with one accord, and said unto her, Thou art the exaltation of Jerusalem, thou art the great glory of Israel, thou art the great rejoicing of our 10 race: thou hast done all these things by thy hand: thou hast done with Israel the things that are good, and God is pleased therewith: blessed be thou with the Almighty Lord for evermore. And all the people said, 11 So be it. And the people spoiled the camp for the space of thirty days: and they gave unto Judith Holofernes' tent. and all his silver cups, and his beds, and his vessels, and all his furniture: and she took them, and placed them on her mule, and made ready her wagons, and heaped them thereon. 12 And all the women of Israel ran together to see her; and they blessed her, and made a dance among them for her; and she took ¹ branches in her hand, and gave to the women 13 that were with her. And they made themselves garlands of olive, she and they that were with her, and she went before all the people in the dance, leading all the women: and all the men of Israel followed in their armour with garlands, and with songs 16 in their mouths. And Judith began to sing this thanksgiving in all Israel, and all the people sang with loud 2 voices this song of praise. And Judith said,

Begin unto my God with timbrels,
Sing unto my Lord with cymbals:
Tune unto him psalm and praise:
Exalt him, and call upon his name.
3 For the Lord is the God that breaketh the battles:
For in his armies in the midst of the people
He delivered me out of the hand of them that persecuted me.
4 Asshur came out of the mountains from the north,
He came with ten thousands of his host,

¹ Compare
2 Macc. x. 7.

The multitude whereof stopped the torrents,
And their horsemen covered the hills.
5 He said that he would burn up my borders,
And kill my young men with the sword,
And throw my sucking children to the ground,
And give mine infants for a prey,
And make my virgins a spoil.
6 The Almighty Lord brought them to nought by the hand of a woman.
7 For their mighty one did not fall by young men,
Neither did sons of the Titans smite him,
Nor did high giants set upon him:
But Judith the daughter of Merari made him weak with the beauty of her countenance.
8 For she put off the apparel of her widowhood
For the exaltation of those that were distressed in Israel.
She anointed her face with ointment,
And bound her hair in a tire,
And took a linen garment to deceive him.
9 Her sandal ravished his eye,
And her beauty took his soul prisoner:
The scimitar passed through his neck.
10 The Persians quaked at her daring,
And the Medes were daunted at her boldness.
11 Then my lowly ones shouted aloud,
And my weak ones were terrified and crouched for fear:
They lifted up their voice, and they were turned to flight.
12 The sons of damsels pierced them through,
And wounded them as runagates' children;
They perished by the battle of my Lord.
13 I will sing unto my God a new song:
O Lord, thou art great and glorious,
Marvellous in strength, invincible.
14 Let all thy creation serve thee:
For thou spakest, and they were made,
Thou didst send forth thy spirit, and it builded them,
And there is none that shall resist thy voice.
15 For the mountains shall be moved from their foundations with the waters,
And the rocks shall melt as wax at thy presence:
But thou art yet merciful to them that fear thee.
16 For all sacrifice is little for a sweet savour,

And all the fat is very little for a
whole burnt offering to thee:
But he that feareth the Lord is
great continually.

17 Woe to the nations that rise up
against my race:
The Lord Almighty will take vengeance of them in the day of judgement,
To put fire and worms in their flesh;
And they shall weep and feel their
pain for ever.

18 Now when they came to Jerusalem,
they worshipped God; and when the
people were purified, they offered
their whole burnt offerings, and their
freewill offerings, and their gifts.

19 And Judith dedicated all the stuff
of Holofernes, which the people had
given her, and gave the canopy, which
she had taken for herself out of his
bedchamber, for a gift unto the Lord.

20 And the people continued feasting in
Jerusalem before the sanctuary for
the space of three months, and Judith

21 remained with them. But after these
days every one departed to his own
inheritance, and Judith went away to
Bethulia, and remained in her own
possession, and was honourable in
her time in all the land. And many

22 desired her, and no man knew her all
the days of her life, from the day that
Manasses her husband died and was

23 gathered to his people. And she increased in greatness exceedingly; and
she waxed old in her husband's house,
unto a hundred and five years, and let
her maid go free: and she died in Bethulia; and they buried her in the cave

24 of her husband Manasses. And the
house of Israel mourned for her seven
days: and she distributed her goods
before she died to all them that were
nearest of kin to Manasses her husband, and to them that were nearest

25 of her own kindred. And there was
none that made the children of Israel
any more afraid in the days of Judith, nor a long time after her death.

THE REST OF THE CHAPTERS

OF THE

BOOK OF ESTHER,

WHICH ARE FOUND NEITHER IN THE HEBREW, NOR IN THE CHALDEE.

PART OF THE TENTH CHAPTER AFTER THE GREEK.

10 Then Mardocheus said, These things
5 are of God. For I remember the
dream [1] which I saw concerning these
6 matters, and nothing thereof hath
failed. As for the little fountain that
became a river, and there was light,
and the sun, and much water, the
7 river is Esther, whom the king mar-
8 ried, and made queen: and the two
dragons are I and Aman: and the
9 nations *are those* that were assembled
to destroy the name of the Jews: and
my nation, this is Israel, which cried
to God, and were saved: for the Lord
hath saved his people, and the Lord
hath delivered us from all these evils,
and God hath wrought signs and great
wonders, which have not been done
10 among the nations. Therefore hath
he made two lots, one for the people
of God, and another for all the nations.
11 And these two lots came at the hour,
and time, and day of judgement, be-
12 fore God among all the nations. So
God remembered his people, and jus-
13 tified his inheritance. Therefore these
days shall be unto them in the month
Adar, the fourteenth and fifteenth day

of the month, with an assembly, and
joy, and with gladness before God,
throughout the generations for ever
among his people Israel.

11 In the fourth year of the reign of
Ptolemy and Cleopatra, Dositheus,
who said he was a priest and Levite,
and Ptolemy his son, brought the epistle of Phrurai *here* set forth, which
they said was the same, and that
Lysimachus the son of Ptolemy, that
was in Jerusalem, had interpreted it.

2 [2] In the second year of the reign of
Artaxerxes the great, in the first day
of the month Nisan, Mardocheus the
son of Jairus, the son of Semeias,
the son of Kiseus, of the tribe of
3 Benjamin, had a dream; who was a
Jew, and dwelt in the city of Susa,
a great man, being a servitor in the
4 king's court; and he was of the captivity, which Nabuchodonosor the
king of Babylon carried from Jerusalem with Jechonias king of Judæa; and
5 this was his dream: Behold, [3] noise
and tumult, thunderings and earthquake, *and* uproar upon the earth:
6 and, behold, two great dragons came
forth, both of them ready to fight,
7 and their cry was great. And at their

Side notes:

[1] See ch. xi. 5-11.

[2] The beginning of the first chapter after the Greek.

[3] Another reading is, *a noise of a tumult.*

cry all nations were ready to battle, that they might fight against the 8 righteous nation. And, lo, a day of darkness and gloominess, tribulation and anguish, affliction and great up-9 roar upon the earth. And the whole righteous nation was troubled, fearing [1] the evils that should befall them, 10 and were ready to perish. Then they cried unto God, and upon their cry, as it were from a little fountain, there came a great river, *even* much water. 11 The light and the sun rose up, and the lowly were exalted, and devoured 12 the glorious. Now when Mardocheus, who had seen this dream, and what God had determined to do, was awake, he bare it in mind, and until night by all means was desirous to know it.

12 And Mardocheus took his rest in the court with Gabatha and Tharra, the two eunuchs of the king, that were 2 keepers of the court. And he heard their communings, and searched out their purposes, and learned that they were about to lay hands upon Artax-erxes the king; and he certified the 3 king of them. Then the king exam-ined the two eunuchs, and after that they had confessed it, they were led 4 to execution. And the king wrote these things for a memorial; Mardo-cheus also wrote concerning these 5 things. So the king commanded Mar-docheus to serve in the court, and 6 for this he gave him gifts. Howbeit Aman the son of Amadathus, a Bu-gean, who was in great honour with the king, sought to molest Mardo-cheus and his people because of the two eunuchs of the king.

13 [2] Now this is the copy of the letter: The great king Artaxerxes writeth these things to the princes of a hun-dred and seven and twenty provinces from India unto Ethiopia, and to the governors that are set under them. 2 After that I became lord over many nations, and had dominion over the whole world, not lifted up with pre-sumption of my authority, but carry-ing myself alway with equity and mildness, I purposed to settle my sub-jects continually in a quiet life, and making my kingdom peaceable, and open for passage to the utmost coasts, to renew peace, which is desired of 3 all men. Now when I asked my coun-sellors how this might be brought to pass, Aman, that excelled in wisdom among us, and was approved for his constant good will and stedfast fidel-ity, and had the honour of the second 4 place in the kingdom, declared unto us, that in all nations throughout the world there was scattered a certain malignant people, that had laws con-trary to all nations, and continually set aside the commandments of kings, so as the uniting of our kingdoms,

honourably intended by us, cannot 5 go forward. Seeing then we under-stand that this nation is alone con-tinually in opposition unto all men, following perversely a life which is strange to *our* laws, and evil affected to our state, working all the mischief they can, that our kingdom may not 6 be firmly stablished: therefore have we commanded, that they that are signified in writing unto you by Aman, who is ordained over the affairs, and is a second father unto us, shall all, with their wives and children, be ut-terly destroyed by the sword of their enemies, without all mercy and pity, the fourteenth day of the twelfth month Adar of this present year: 7 that they, who of old and now also are malicious, may in one day with violence go down to [3] the grave, and so ever hereafter cause our affairs to be well settled, and without trouble.

8 [4] Then *Mardocheus* made his prayer unto the Lord, calling to remembrance 9 all the works of the Lord, and said, O Lord, Lord, thou King Almighty: for the whole world is in thy power, and if it be thy will to save Israel, there is no man that can gainsay thee: 10 for thou hast made heaven and earth, and all the wondrous things that are 11 beneath the heaven; and thou art Lord of all, and there is no man that can resist thee, which art the Lord. 12 Thou knowest all things, and thou knowest, Lord, that it was neither in contempt nor pride, nor for any desire of glory, that I did not bow down to 13 proud Aman. For I could have been content with good will for the salva-tion of Israel to kiss the soles of his 14 feet. But I did this, that I might not prefer the glory of man above the glory of God: neither will I bow down unto any but to thee, which art my Lord, neither will I do it in pride. 15 And now, O Lord, thou God *and* King, the God of Abraham, spare thy peo-ple: for their eyes are upon us to bring us to nought, and they desire to destroy the heritage, that hath 16 been thine from the beginning. De-spise not thy portion, which thou didst redeem out of the land of Egypt for 17 thine own self. Hear my prayer, and be merciful unto thine inheritance: and turn our mourning into feasting, that we may live, O Lord, and sing praises to thy name: and destroy not the mouth of them that praise thee, O Lord.

18 And all Israel cried out mightily, because their death was before their 14 eyes. Queen Esther also, being seiz-ed *as it were* with the agony of death, 2 resorted unto the Lord: and laid away her glorious apparel, and put on the garments of anguish and mourn-ing: and instead of the most excellent

Marginal notes:

[1] Gr. *their own evils.*

[2] Part of the third chapter after the Greek, following Esth. iii. 13.

[3] Gr. *Hades.*

[4] Part of the fourth and fifth chapters after the Greek, follow-ing Esth. iv. 17.

ointments, she covered her head with ashes and dung, and she humbled her body greatly, and all the places of the ornaments of her joy she covered with 3 her tangled hair. And she prayed unto the Lord, the God of Israel, saying, O my Lord, thou only art our King: help me that am desolate and have no other 4 helper but thee: for my danger is in 5 mine hand. From my youth up I have heard in the tribe of my family, that thou, O Lord, tookest Israel from among all the nations, and our fathers from all their progenitors, for a perpetual inheritance, and didst perform for them whatsoever thou didst pro-6 mise. And now we have sinned before thee, and thou hast given us into the 7 hands of our enemies, because we glorified their gods: O Lord, thou art 8 righteous. Nevertheless it satisfieth them not, that we are in bitter captivity: but they have stricken hands with 9 their idols, that they will abolish the thing that thou with thy mouth hast ordained, and destroy thine inheritance, and stop the mouth of them that praise thee, and quench the glory of 10 thy house, and thine altar, and open the mouths of the heathen to set forth the virtues of [1] idols, and that a fleshly 11 king shall be magnified for ever. O Lord, give not thy sceptre unto them that be nothing, and let them not laugh at our fall; but turn their device upon themselves, and make him an example, that hath begun this against us. 12 Remember, O Lord, make thyself known in the time of our affliction, and give me boldness, O King of the gods, 13 and holder of all dominion. Give me eloquent speech in my mouth before the lion: and turn his heart to hate him that fighteth against us, that there may be an end of him, and of them that 14 are likeminded with him: but deliver us with thine hand, and help me that am desolate and have no other *helper* 15 but thee, O Lord. Thou hast knowledge of all things; and thou knowest that I hate the glory of the wicked, and abhor the bed of the uncircum-16 cised, and of every alien. Thou knowest my necessity: that I abhor the sign of my high estate, which is upon mine head in the days wherein I shew myself. I abhor it as a menstruous rag, and I wear it not when I am pri-17 vate by myself. And thine handmaid hath not eaten at Aman's table, neither have I honoured the king's feast, nor drunk the wine of the drink offer-18 ings. Neither had thine handmaid any joy since the day that I was brought hither to this present, but in thee, O 19 Lord, thou God of Abraham. O God, that art mighty above all, hear the voice of the forlorn, and deliver us out of the hands of the mischievous, and deliver me out of my fear.

[1] Gr. *vain things.*

15 And upon the third day, when she had ended her prayer, she laid away her garments of service, and put on 2 her glorious apparel. And being majestically adorned, after she had called upon the all-seeing God and saviour, 3 she took her two maids with her: and upon the one she leaned, as carrying 4 herself delicately; and the other followed, bearing up her train. And she 5 lowed, bearing up her train. And she was ruddy through the perfection of her beauty, and her countenance was cheerful *and* right amiable: but her 6 heart was in anguish for fear. Then having passed through all the doors, she stood before the king, who sat upon his royal throne, and was clothed with all his robes of majesty, all *glittering* with gold and precious stones; 7 and he was very dreadful. Then lifting up his countenance that was flushed with glory, he looked *upon her* in fierce anger: and the queen fell down, and turned pale, and fainted, and she bowed herself upon the head of the 8 maid that went before. Then God changed the spirit of the king into mildness, who in an agony leaped from his throne, and took her in his arms, till she came to herself again, and 9 comforted her with soothing words, and said unto her, Esther, what is the 10 matter? I am thy brother, be of good cheer: thou shalt not die, for [2] our commandment is for our subjects: 11 come near. So he held up his golden 12 sceptre, and laid it upon her neck, and embraced her, and said, Speak unto 13 me. Then said she unto him, I saw thee, my lord, as an angel of God, and my heart was troubled for fear of thy 14 glory. For wonderful art thou, my lord, and thy countenance is full of 15 grace. And as she was speaking, she 16 fell down for faintness. Then the king was troubled, and all his servants comforted her.[3]

16 [4] The great king Artaxerxes unto the governors of countries in a hundred and seven and twenty provinces from India unto Ethiopia, and unto them that are well affected to our state, 2 greeting. Many, the more often they are honoured with the great bounty of their benefactors, the more proud they 3 are waxen, and endeavour to hurt not our subjects only, but not being able to bear abundance, do take in hand to practise also against those that do 4 them good: and take not only thankfulness away from among men, but also lifted up with the boastful words of them that were never good, they think to escape the evil-hating justice of God, who alway seeth all things. 5 Oftentimes also fair speech of those that are put in trust to manage their friends' affairs, hath caused many that are in authority to be partakers of innocent blood, and hath enwrapped

[2] Or, *the commandment is as well thine as mine* Gr. *our commandment is common.*

[3] Here follows Esth. v. 3.
[4] Part of the eighth chapter after the Greek, following Esth. viii. 13.

6 them in remediless calamities: beguiling with the false deceit of their lewd 7 disposition the innocent good will of princes. Now ye may see this, as we have declared, not so much by more ancient histories, as ye may, if ye search what hath been wickedly done of late through the pestilent behaviour of them that are unworthily placed in 8 authority. And we must take care for the time to come, to render our kingdom quiet and peaceable for all men, 9 both by changing our purposes, and always judging things that come before our eyes with more equal proceed-10 ing. For Aman, a Macedonian, the son of Amadathus, an alien in truth from the Persian blood, and far distant from our goodness, being as a guest received 11 of us, had so far forth obtained the favour that we shew toward every nation, as that he was called our father, and was continually honoured of all men, as the next person unto the royal throne. 12 But he, not bearing his high estate, went about to deprive us of our king-13 dom and our life; having by manifold and cunning deceits sought *of us* the destruction, as well of Mardocheus, who saved our life, and continually procured our good, as also of Esther the blameless partaker of our kingdom, 14 together with their whole nation. For by these means he thought, finding us destitute *of friends*, to have translated the kingdom of the Persians to the 15 Macedonians. But we find that the Jews, whom this most ungracious wretch hath delivered to utter de-struction, are no evil-doers, but live 16 by most just laws : and that they be children of the most high and most mighty living God, who hath ordered the kingdom both unto us and to our progenitors in the most excellent man-17 ner. Wherefore ye shall do well not to put in execution the letters sent un-to you by Aman the son of Amadathus. 18 For he, that was the worker of these things, is hanged at the gates of Susa with all his family : God, who ruleth all things, speedily rendering vengeance to him according to his deserts. 19 Therefore ye shall publish openly the copy of this letter in all places, and let the Jews live after their own laws, 20 and ye shall aid them, that even the same day, being the thirteenth day of the twelfth month Adar, they may defend themselves against those who set upon them in the time of their 21 affliction. For Almighty God hath made this day to be a joy unto them, instead of the destruction of the 22 chosen people. And ye shall therefore among your commemorative feasts keep it a high day with all feasting : 23 that both now and hereafter there may be safety to us, and the well affected Persians; but to those which do conspire against us a memorial of destruc-24 tion. Therefore every city or country whatsoever, which shall not do according to these things, shall be utterly destroyed without mercy with [1] fire and sword ; it shall be made not only unpassable for men, but also most hateful to wild beasts and fowls for ever.

[1] Gr. *spear and fire.*

THE
WISDOM OF SOLOMON.

1 LOVE righteousness, ye that be judges of the earth,
Think ye of the Lord [1] with a good mind,
And in singleness of heart seek ye him;
2 Because he is found of them that tempt him not,
And is manifested to them that do not distrust him.
3 For crooked thoughts separate from God;
And the *supreme* Power, when it is brought to the proof, [2] putteth to confusion the foolish :
4 Because wisdom will not enter into a soul that deviseth evil,
Nor dwell in a body that is held in pledge by sin.

5 For a holy spirit of discipline will flee deceit,
And will start away from thoughts that are without understanding,
And will be [3] put to confusion when unrighteousness hath come in.
6 For [4] wisdom is a spirit that loveth man,
And she will not hold a [5] blasphemer guiltless for his lips;
Because God beareth witness of his reins,
And is a true overseer of his heart,
And a hearer of his tongue :
7 Because the spirit of the Lord hath filled [6] the world,
And that which holdeth all things together hath knowledge of *every* voice.

[1] Gr. *in goodness.*

[2] Gr. *convicteth.*

[3] Gr. *convicted.*

[4] Some authorities read *the spirit of wisdom is loving to man.*

[5] Or, *reviler*

[6] Gr. *the inhabited earth.*

8 Therefore no man that uttereth unrighteous things shall be unseen;
  [1] Neither shall Justice, when it convicteth, pass him by.
9 For in *the midst of* his counsels the
ungodly shall be searched out;
And the sound of his words shall come
unto the Lord
To bring to conviction his lawless
deeds:
10 Because *there is* an ear of jealousy
that listeneth to all things,
And the noise of murmurings is not
hid.
11 Beware then of unprofitable murmuring,
And refrain your tongue from back-
biting;
Because no secret utterance shall go
on its way void,
And a mouth that belieth destroyeth
a soul.
12 Court not death in the error of your
life;
Neither draw upon yourselves destruction by the works of your hands:
13 Because God made not death;
Neither delighteth he when the living
perish:
14 For he created all things that they
might have being:
And [2] the generative powers of the
world *are* healthsome,
And there is no poison of destruction
in them:
Nor hath Hades [3] royal dominion upon earth,
15 For righteousness is immortal:
16 But ungodly men by their hands and
their words called [4] death unto
them:
Deeming him a friend they [5] consumed
away,
And they made a covenant with him,
Because they are worthy to be of his
portion.

2 For they said [6] within themselves,
reasoning not aright,
Short and sorrowful is our life;
And there is no healing when a man
cometh to his end,
And none was ever known that [7] gave
release from Hades:
2 Because by mere chance were we
born,
And hereafter we shall be as though
we had never been:
Because the breath in our nostrils is
smoke,
And [8] while our heart beateth reason
is a spark,
3 Which being extinguished, the body
shall be turned into ashes,
And the spirit shall be dispersed as
thin air;
4 And our name shall be forgotten in
time,
And no man shall remember our
works;

And our life shall pass away as the
traces of a cloud,
And shall be scattered as is a mist,
When it is chased by the beams of the
sun,
And [9] overcome by the heat thereof.
5 For our allotted time is the passing of
a shadow,
And [10] our end retreateth not;
Because it is fast sealed, and none
[11] turneth it back.
6 Come therefore and let us enjoy the
good things [12] that *now* are;
And let us use the creation [13] with all
our soul [14] as youth's *possession.*
7 Let us fill ourselves with costly wine
and perfumes;
And let no flower of [15] spring pass us
by:
8 Let us crown ourselves with rose-
buds, before they be withered:
9 Let none of us go without his share
in our proud revelry':
Everywhere let us leave tokens of
our mirth:
Because this is our portion, and our
lot is this.
10 Let us oppress the righteous poor;
Let us not spare the widow,
Nor reverence the hairs of the old
man gray for length of years.
11 But let our strength be *to us* a law of
righteousness;
For that which is weak is [16] found to
be of no service.
12 But let us lie in wait for the righteous
man,
Because he is of disservice to us,
And is contrary to our works,
And upbraideth us with sins against
[17] the law,
And layeth to our charge sins against
our discipline.
13 He professeth to have knowledge of
God,
And nameth himself [18] servant of the
Lord.
14 He became to us a reproof of our
thoughts.
15 He is grievous unto us even to behold,
Because his life is unlike other men's,
And his paths are of strange fashion.
16 We were accounted of him as base
metal,
And he abstaineth from our ways as
from uncleannesses.
The latter end of the righteous he
calleth happy;
And he vaunteth that God is his father.
17 Let us see if his words be true,
And let us try what shall befall in the
ending of his *life.*
18 For if the righteous man is God's son,
he will uphold him,
And he will deliver him out of the
hand of his adversaries.
19 With outrage and torture let us put
him to the test,
That we may learn his gentleness,

Left margin notes:

[1] Some authorities read *Nor indeed.*

[2] Or, all the races of creatures in the world
[3] Or, a royal house
[4] Or, Hades Gr. him.
[5] Or, were consumed with love of him

[6] Or, among

[7] Or, returned out of Hades

[8] Or, reason is a spark kindled by the beating of our heart

Right margin notes:

[9] Gr. weighed down.
[10] Or, there is no putting back of our end
[11] Or, cometh again
[12] Or, that are
[13] Gr. earnestly.
[14] Some authorities read even as our youth.
[15] Some authorities read air.

[16] Gr. convicted.

[17] Or, law

[18] Or, child

And may prove his patience under wrong.

20 Let us condemn him to a shameful death;

For [1] he shall be visited according to his words.

21 Thus reasoned they, and they were led astray;

For their [2] wickedness blinded them,

22 And they knew not the mysteries of God,

Neither hoped they for wages of holiness,

Nor did they judge *that there is a* prize for blameless souls.

23 Because God created man for incorruption,

And made him an image of his own [3] proper being;

24 But by the envy of the devil death entered into the world,

And they that are of his portion make trial thereof.

3 But the souls of the righteous are in the hand of God,

And no torment shall touch them.

2 In the eyes of the foolish they seemed to have died;

And their departure was accounted *to be their* hurt,

3 And their journeying away from us *to be their* ruin :

But they are in peace.

4 For even if in the sight of men they be punished,

Their hope is full of immortality ;

5 And having borne a little chastening, they shall receive great good;

Because God made trial of them, and found them worthy of himself.

6 As gold in the furnace he proved them,

And as a whole burnt offering he accepted them.

7 And in the time of their visitation they shall shine forth,

And as sparks among stubble they shall run to and fro.

8 They shall judge nations, and have dominion over peoples ;

And the Lord shall reign over them for evermore.

9 They that trust on him shall understand truth,

And [4] the faithful shall abide with him in love ;

Because grace and mercy are to his chosen.

10 But the ungodly shall be requited even as they reasoned,

They which lightly regarded [5] the righteous *man*, and revolted from the Lord;

11 (For he that setteth at nought wisdom and discipline is miserable ;)

And void is their hope and their toils unprofitable,

And useless are their works :

12 Their wives are foolish, and wicked are their children ;

13 Accursed is their begetting.

Because happy is the barren that is undefiled,

She who hath not conceived in transgression ;

She shall have fruit when *God* visiteth souls.

14 And *happy is* the eunuch which hath wrought no lawless deed with his hands,

Nor imagined wicked things against the Lord ;

For there shall be given him for his faithfulness [6] a peculiar favour,

And a lot in the sanctuary of the Lord more delightsome *than wife or children.*

15 For good labours have fruit of great renown ;

And the root of understanding cannot fail.

16 But children of adulterers shall not come to maturity,

And the seed of an unlawful bed shall vanish away.

17 For if they live long, they shall be held in no account,

And at the last their old age shall be without honour.

18 And if they die quickly, they [7] shall have no hope,

Nor in the day of decision *shall they have* consolation.

19 For [8] the end of an unrighteous generation is alway grievous.

4 Better *than this* is childlessness with virtue ;

For in the memory [9] of virtue is immortality :

Because it is recognised both before God and before men.

2 When it is present, *men* imitate it;

And they long after it when it is departed :

And [10] throughout all time it marcheth crowned in triumph,

Victorious in the strife for the prizes that are undefiled.

3 But the multiplying brood of the ungodly shall be of no profit,

And [11] with bastard [12] slips they shall not strike deep root,

Nor shall they establish a sure hold.

4 For even if these [13] put forth boughs and flourish for a season,

Yet, standing unsure, they shall be shaken by the wind,

And by the violence of winds they shall be rooted out.

5 *Their* branches shall be broken off before they come to maturity,

And their fruit *shall be* useless,

Never ripe to eat, and fit for nothing.

6 For children unlawfully begotten are witnesses of wickedness

Against parents when *God* searcheth them out.

---

[1] Gr. *there shall be a visitation of him out of his words.*

[2] Or. *malice*

[3] Some authorities read *everlastingness.*

[4] Or, *they that are faithful through love shall abide with him*

[5] Or, *that which is righteous*

[6] Or, *the grace of God's chosen* Gr. *a chosen grace.*

[7] Some authorities read *have.*

[8] Gr. *the ends ... are grievous.*

[9] Gr. *of it.*

[10] Gr. *in the age.*

[11] Gr. *from.*

[12] Or, *offshoots*

[13] Gr. *in boughs flourish*

7 But a righteous man, though he die
before his time, shall be at rest.

8 (For honourable old age is not that
which standeth in length of time,
Nor is its measure given by number
of years :

9 But understanding is gray hairs unto
men,
And an unspotted life is ripe old age.)

10 Being found well-pleasing unto God
he was beloved *of him*,
And while living among sinners he
was translated :

11 He was caught away, lest [1] wickedness should change his understanding,
Or guile deceive his soul.

12 (For the bewitching of naughtiness
bedimmeth the things which are
good,
And the giddy whirl of desire perverteth an innocent mind.)

13 Being made perfect in a little while,
he fulfilled long [2] years ;

14 For his soul was pleasing unto the
Lord :
Therefore [3] hasted he out of the midst
of wickedness.

15 But as for the peoples, seeing and
understanding not,
Neither laying [4] this to heart,
That grace and mercy are with his
chosen,
And that [5] he visiteth his holy ones : —

16 But a righteous man that is dead
shall condemn the ungodly that are
living,
And youth that is quickly perfected
the many years of an unrighteous
man's old age ;

17 For *the ungodly* shall see a wise
man's end,
And shall not understand what the
Lord purposed concerning him,
And for what he safely kept him : —

18 They shall see, and they shall despise ;
But them the Lord shall laugh to
scorn.
And after this they shall become a
dishonoured carcase,
And [6] a reproach among the dead for
ever :

19 Because he shall dash them speechless to the ground,
And shall shake them from the foundations,
And they shall [7] lie utterly waste, and
they shall be in anguish,
And their memory shall perish.

20 They shall come, [8] when their sins are
reckoned up, with coward fear ;
And their lawless deeds shall convict
them to their face.

5 Then shall the righteous man stand
in great boldness
Before the face of them that afflicted
him,

And them that make his labours of no
account.

2 When they see [9] *it*, they shall be
troubled with terrible fear,
And shall be amazed at the marvel of
God's salvation.

3 They shall say [10] within themselves
repenting,
And for distress of spirit shall they
groan,
This was he whom aforetime we had
in derision,
And *made* a parable of [11] reproach :

4 We fools accounted his life madness,
And his end without honour :

5 How was he numbered among sons
of God ?
And *how* is his lot among saints ?

6 Verily we went astray from the way
of truth,
And the light of righteousness shined
not for us,
And the sun rose not for us.

7 We [12] took our fill of the paths of lawlessness and destruction,
And we journeyed through trackless
deserts,
But the way of the Lord we knew
not.

8 What did our arrogancy profit us ?
And what good have riches [13] and
vaunting brought us ?

9 Those things all passed away as a
shadow,
And as a message that runneth by :

10 As a ship passing through the billowy
water,
Whereof, when it is gone by, there is
no trace to be found,
Neither pathway of its keel in the
billows :

11 Or as when a bird flieth through the
air,
No token of *her* passage is found,
But the light air, lashed with the
stroke of her pinions,
And rent asunder [14] with the violent
rush of the moving wings, is passed
through,
And afterwards no sign of *her* coming
is found therein :

12 Or as when an arrow is shot at a
mark,
The air disparted closeth up again
immediately,
So that men know not where it passed
through :

13 So we also, as soon as we were born,
[15] ceased to be ;
And of virtue we had no sign to shew,
But in our wickedness we were utterly consumed.

14 Because the hope of the ungodly man
is as chaff carried by the wind,
And [16] as [17] foam vanishing before a
tempest ;
And is scattered as smoke *is scattered*
by the wind,
And passeth by as the remembrance
of a guest that tarrieth but a day.

Marginal notes:

[1] Or, *malice*

[2] Gr. *times.*

[3] Or, *he hastened him away*

[4] Gr. *such a thing as this.*

[5] Gr. his *visitation is with.*

[6] Or, *be for outrage*

[7] Or, *be a perpetual desolation*

[8] Or, *when they reckon up their sins*

[9] Or, *him*

[10] Or, *among*

[11] Or, *reproach, we fools : we accounted*

[12] See Prov. xiv. 14.

[13] Gr. *with.*

[14] Or, *with the violent rush, is passed through by the motion of her wings*

[15] Gr. *failed.*

[16] Gr. *as foam chased to thinness :* or, *as thin foam chased.*

[17] Most Greek authorities read *hoar frost :* some authorities, perhaps rightly, *a spider's web.*

15 But the righteous live for ever,
And in the Lord is their reward,
And the care for them with the Most
High.
16 Therefore shall they receive the
crown of royal dignity
And the diadem of beauty from the
Lord's hand;
Because with his right hand shall he
cover them,
And with his arm shall he shield
them.
17 He shall take his jealousy as complete
armour,
And shall make the *whole* creation
his weapons [1] for vengeance on *his*
enemies:

1 Or, to repel his enemies

18 He shall put on righteousness as a
breastplate,
And shall array himself with judgement unfeigned as with a helmet;
19 He shall take holiness as an invincible shield,
20 And he shall sharpen stern wrath for
a sword:
And the world shall go forth with him
to fight against *his* insensate *foes*.
21 Shafts of lightning shall fly with true
aim,
And from the clouds, as from a well
drawn bow, shall they leap to the
mark.
22 And *as* from an engine of war shall be
hurled hailstones full of wrath;
The water of the sea shall be angered
against them,
And rivers shall sternly overwhelm
them;
23 A mighty blast shall encounter them,
And as a tempest shall it winnow
them away:
And *so* shall lawlessness make all the
land desolate,
And their evil-doing shall overturn the
thrones of princes.

6 Hear therefore, ye kings, and understand;
Learn, ye judges of the ends of the
earth:
2 Give ear, ye that have dominion over
much people,
And make your boast [2] in multitudes
of nations.

2 Or, in the multitudes of your nations

3 Because your dominion was given
you from the Lord,
And your sovereignty from the Most
High;
Who shall search out your works,
And shall make inquisition of your
counsels:
4 Because being officers of his kingdom
ye did not judge aright,
Neither kept ye [3] law, nor walked
after the counsel of God.

3 Or, the law

5 Awfully and swiftly shall he come
upon you;
Because a stern judgement befalleth
them that be in high place:

6 For the man of low estate may be
pardoned in mercy,
But mighty men shall be [4] searched
out mightily.

4 Gr. put to the test.

7 For the Sovereign Lord of all will not
refrain himself for any *man's* person,
Neither will he reverence greatness;
Because it is he that made *both* small
and great,
And alike he taketh thought for
all;
8 But [5] strict is the scrutiny that cometh
upon the powerful.

5 Gr. strong.

9 Unto you therefore, O princes, are my
words,
That ye may learn wisdom and [6] fall
not from the right way.

6 Gr. fall not aside.

10 For they that have kept holily the
things that are holy shall *themselves*
be [7] hallowed;
And they that have been taught them
shall find what to answer;

7 Or, accounted holy

11 Set your desire therefore on my
words;
Long for *them*, and ye shall be [8] trained by *their* discipline.

8 Gr. disciplined.

12 Wisdom is radiant and fadeth not
away;
And easily is she beheld of them that
love her,
And found of them that seek her.
13 She forestalleth them that desire *to
know her*, making herself first
known.
14 He that riseth up early to *seek* her
shall have no toil,
For he shall find her sitting at his
gates.
15 For to think upon her is perfectness
of understanding,
And he that watcheth for her sake
shall quickly be free from care.
16 Because she goeth about, herself seeking them that are worthy of her,
And in their paths she appeareth unto
them graciously,
And in every purpose she meeteth
them.
17 For [9] her [10] true beginning is desire of
discipline;
And the care for discipline is love *of
her*;

9 Or, her beginning is the true desire
10 Or, truest.

18 And love *of her* is observance of her
laws;
And to give heed to *her* laws con-
firmeth incorruption;
19 And incorruption [11] bringeth near unto
God;

11 Gr. maketh to be near.

20 So then desire of wisdom promoteth
to a kingdom.
21 If therefore ye delight in thrones and
sceptres, ye princes of peoples,
Honour wisdom, that ye may reign
for ever.
22 But what wisdom is, and how she
came into being, I will declare,
And I will not hide mysteries from
you;

But I will trace *her* out [1]from the beginning of creation,
And bring the knowledge of her into clear light,
And I will not pass by the truth;

23 Neither indeed will I take [2]pining envy for my companion in the way,
Because [3]envy shall have no fellowship with wisdom.

24 But a multitude of wise men is salvation to the world,
And an understanding king is tranquillity to *his* people.

25 Wherefore be disciplined by my words, and *thereby* shall ye profit.

7 I myself also am [4]mortal, like to all,
And am sprung from one born of the earth, *the man* first formed,

2 And in the womb of a mother was I moulded into flesh in the time of ten months,
Being compacted in blood of the seed of man and pleasure that came with sleep.

3 And I also, when I was born, drew in the common air,
And fell upon the [5]kindred earth,
Uttering, like all, for my first voice, the selfsame wail:

4 In swaddling clothes was I nursed, and [6]with *watchful* cares.

5 For no king had any other first beginning;

6 But all men have one entrance into life, and a like departure.

7 For this cause I prayed, and understanding was given me:
I called upon *God*, and there came to me a spirit of wisdom.

8 I preferred her before sceptres and thrones,
And riches I esteemed nothing in comparison of her.

9 Neither did I liken to her any priceless gem,
Because all the gold *of the earth* in her presence is a little sand,
And silver shall be accounted as clay before her.

10 Above health and comeliness I loved her,
And I chose to have her rather than light,
Because her bright shining is never laid to sleep.

11 But with her there came to me all good things together,
And in her hands innumerable riches:

12 And I rejoiced over *them* all because wisdom leadeth them;
Though I knew not that she was the [7]mother of them.

13 As I learned without guile, I impart without grudging;
I do not hide her riches.

14 For she is unto men a treasure that faileth not,
And they that use it [8]obtain friendship with God,

Commended *to him* [9]by the gifts which they through discipline present *to him.*

15 But to me may God give to speak [10]with judgement,
And to conceive thoughts worthy of what [11]hath been given *me*;
Because himself is one that guideth even wisdom and that correcteth the wise.

16 For in his hand are both we and our words;
All understanding, and *all* acquaintance with divers crafts.

17 For himself gave me an unerring knowledge of the things that are,
To know the constitution of the world, and the operation of the elements;

18 The beginning and end and middle of times,
The alternations of the solstices and the changes of seasons,

19 The circuits of years and the [12]positions of stars;

20 The natures of living creatures and the ragings of wild beasts,
The violences of [13]winds and the thoughts of men,
The diversities of plants and the virtues of roots:

21 All things that are either secret or manifest I learned,

22 For she that is the artificer of all things taught me, *even* wisdom.

For there is in her a spirit quick of understanding, holy,
[14]Alone in kind, manifold,
Subtil, freely moving,
Clear in utterance, unpolluted,
Distinct, unharmed,
Loving what is good, keen, unhindered,

23 Beneficent, loving toward man,
Stedfast, sure, free from care,
All-powerful, all-surveying,
And penetrating through all spirits
That are quick of understanding, pure, most subtil:

24 For wisdom is more mobile than any motion;
Yea, she pervadeth and penetrateth all things by reason of her pureness.

25 For she is a [15]breath of the power of God,
And a clear effluence of the glory of the Almighty;
Therefore can nothing defiled find entrance into her.

26 For she is an effulgence from everlasting light,
And an unspotted mirror of the working of God,
And an image of his goodness.

27 And she, being one, hath power to do all things;
And remaining in herself, reneweth all things:

Margin notes:

[1] Or, *from her first beginning*

[2] Gr. *wasted.*

[3] Gr. *this.*

[4] Many authorities read *a mortal man.*

[5] Gr. *of like qualities.*

[6] Gr. *in.*

[7] Some authorities read *first origin.*

[8] Gr. *prepare for themselves.*

[9] Gr. *for the sake of the presents that come of discipline.*

[10] Or, *according to his mind* Or, *according to my mind*

[11] Some authorities read *is said.*

[12] Or, *constellations*

[13] Or, *spirits*

[14] Gr. *Sole-born.*

[15] Gr. *vapour*

1 Gr.
every
arrange-
ment of
stars.

2 Gr.
to this.

3 Or,
reacheth
from end
onward
unto end
mightily
4 Or,
unto
good use

5 Some
authori-
ties read
deviseth
for him.

6 The
Greek
text of
this
clause is
perhaps
corrupt.
7 Gr. she.
8 Gr. Her
labours
are.

9 Some
authori-
ties read
how to
divine
the
things
of old
and the
things
to come.
10 Gr.
conjec-
tureth.
11 Or,
hold
counsel
with me
for good
things,
and . . .
against
cares
and
grief
12 Or,
exhort
Or,
advise

And from generation to generation
passing into holy souls
She maketh *men* friends of God and
prophets.
28 For nothing doth God love save him
that dwelleth with wisdom.
29 For she is fairer than the sun,
And above ¹all the constellations of
the stars:
Being compared with light, she is
found *to be* before it;
30 For ²to the light *of day* succeedeth
night,
But against wisdom evil doth not
prevail;

8 But she ³reacheth from one end *of*
the world to the other with full
strength,
And ordereth all things ⁴graciously.

2 Her I loved and sought out from my
youth,
And I sought to take her for my
bride,
And I became enamoured of her
beauty.
3 She glorifieth *her* noble birth in that
it is given her to live with God,
And the Sovereign Lord of all loved
her.
4 For she is initiated into the knowledge of God,
And she ⁵chooseth out *for him* his
works.
5 But if riches are a desired possession
in life,
What is richer than wisdom, which
worketh all things?
6 ⁶And if understanding worketh,
Who more than ⁷wisdom is an artificer of the things that are?
7 And if a man loveth righteousness,
⁸The fruits of wisdom's labour are
virtues,
For she teacheth soberness and understanding, righteousness and courage;
And there is nothing in life for men
more profitable than these.
8 And if a man longeth even for much
experience,
She knoweth ⁹the things of old, and
¹⁰divineth the things to come:
She understandeth subtilties of
speeches and interpretations of
dark sayings:
She foreseeth signs and wonders, and
the issues of seasons and times.
9 I determined therefore to take her
unto me to live with me,
Knowing that she is one who would
¹¹give me good *thoughts* for counsel,
And ¹²encourage me in cares and
grief.
10 Because of her I shall have glory
among multitudes,
And honour in the sight of elders,
though I be young.
11 I shall be found of a quick conceit
when I give judgement,

And in the presence of ¹³princes I
shall be admired.
12 When I am silent, they shall wait for
me;
And when I open my lips, they shall
give heed unto me;
And if I continue speaking, they shall
lay their hand upon their mouth.
13 Because of her I shall have immortality,
And leave behind an eternal memory
to them that come after me.
14 I shall govern peoples,
And nations shall be subjected to
me.
15 Dread princes shall fear me when
they hear *of me*:
Among *my* ¹⁴people I shall shew
myself a good *ruler*, and in war
courageous.
16 When I am come into my house, I
shall find rest with her;
For converse with her hath no bitterness,
And to live with her hath no pain, but
gladness and joy.
17 When I considered these things in
myself,
And took thought in my heart how
that in kinship unto wisdom is immortality,
18 And in her friendship is good delight,
And in the labours of her hands is
wealth that faileth not,
And in ¹⁵assiduous communing with
her is understanding,
And great renown in having fellowship with her words,
I went about seeking how to take her
unto myself.
19 Now I was ¹⁶a child of parts, and a
good soul fell to my lot;
20 Nay rather, being good, I came into a
body undefiled.
21 But perceiving that I could not otherwise ¹⁷possess *wisdom* except God
gave *her* me
(Yea and to know ¹⁸by whom the
grace is given, this *too* came of understanding),
I pleaded with the Lord and besought
him,
And with my whole heart I said,

9 O God of the fathers, and ¹⁹Lord who
keepest thy mercy,
Who madest all things ²⁰by thy word;
2 And by thy wisdom thou formedst
man,
That he should have dominion over
the creatures that were made by
thee,
3 And rule the world in holiness and
righteousness,
And execute judgement in uprightness of soul;
4 Give me wisdom, her that sitteth by
thee on thy ²¹throne;
And reject me not from among thy
²²servants:

13 Or,
mighty
men

14 Gr.
multi-
tude.

15 Gr.
practice
of com-
munion.

16 Or, a
goodly
child

17 This
is the
probable
sense:
the
Greek
text is
perhaps
defec-
tive.
18 Gr. of
whom
is the
grace.
19 Gr.
Lord
of thy
mercy.
Compare
2 Sam.
vii. 15;
Ps.
lxxxix.
49.
20 Gr. in.

21 Gr.
thrones.
22 Or,
children

5 Because I am thy bondman and the
son of thy handmaid,
A man weak and short-lived,
And of small power to understand
judgement and laws.

6 For even if a man be perfect among
the sons of men,
Yet if the wisdom that cometh from
thee be not with him, he shall be
held in no account.

7 Thou didst choose me before *my brethren* to be king of thy people,
And to do judgement for thy sons and
daughters.

8 Thou gavest command to build a sanctuary in thy holy mountain,
And [1] an altar in the city of thy [2] habitation,
A copy of the holy tabernacle which
thou preparedst aforehand from the
beginning.

9 And with thee is wisdom, which
knoweth thy works,
And was present when thou wast
making the world,
And which understandeth what is
pleasing in thine eyes,
And what is right [3] according to thy
commandments.

10 Send her forth out of the holy heavens,
And from the throne of thy glory bid
her come,
That being present with me she may
toil *with me*,
And *that* I may learn what is well-
pleasing before thee.

11 For she knoweth all things and hath
understanding *thereof*,
And in my doings she shall guide me
in *ways of* soberness,
And she shall guard me in her glory.

12 And *so* shall my works be acceptable,
And I shall judge thy people righteously,
And I shall be worthy of my father's
[4] throne.

13 For what man shall know the counsel
of God?
Or who shall conceive what the Lord
willeth?

14 For the thoughts of mortals are
[5] timorous,
And our devices are prone to fail.

15 For a corruptible body weigheth
down the soul,
And the earthy frame lieth heavy on
a mind that [6] is full of cares.

16 And hardly do we [7] divine the things
that are on earth,
And the things that are close at hand
we find with labour;
But the things that are in the heavens
who *ever yet* traced out?

17 And who *ever* gained knowledge of
thy counsel, except thou [8] gavest
wisdom,
And sentest thy holy spirit [9] from on
high?

18 And it was thus that the ways of

them which are on earth were corrected,
And men were taught the things that
are pleasing unto thee;
And through wisdom were they saved.

10 [10] Wisdom guarded to the end the
first formed father of the world, that
was created alone,
And delivered him out of his own
transgression,

2 And gave him strength to get dominion over all things.

3 But when an unrighteous man fell
away from her in his anger,
He perished himself in the rage
wherewith he slew his brother.

4 And when for his cause the earth was
drowning with a flood,
Wisdom again saved it,
Guiding the righteous man's course
by a poor piece of wood.

5 Moreover, when nations consenting
together in wickedness had been
confounded,
[10] Wisdom knew the righteous man,
and preserved him blameless unto
God,
And kept him strong when his heart
yearned toward his child.

6 While the ungodly were perishing,
[10] wisdom delivered a righteous
man,
When he fled from the fire that descended out of heaven on [11] Penta-
polis.

7 To whose wickedness a smoking
waste still witnesseth,
And plants bearing fair fruit that
cometh not to ripeness;
Yea and a [12] disbelieving soul hath a
memorial *there*, a pillar of salt *still*
standing.

8 For having passed wisdom by,
Not only were they disabled from
recognising the things which are
good,
But they also left behind them [13] for
human life a monument of their
folly;
To the end that [14] where they [15] went
astray they might fail even to be
unseen:

9 But wisdom delivered out of troubles
those that waited on her.

10 When a righteous man was a fugitive
from a brother's wrath, [10] wisdom
guided him in straight paths;
She shewed him God's kingdom, and
gave him knowledge of holy things;
She prospered him in his toils, and
multiplied the fruits of his labour;

Left margin notes:
[1] Or, *a place of sacrifice*
[2] Gr. *tabernacting.*
[3] Gr. *in.*
[4] Gr. *thrones.*
[5] The Greek text here is perhaps corrupt.
[6] Or, *museth upon many things*
[7] Gr. *conjecture.*
[8] Or, *hadst given ...and sent*
[9] Gr. *from the highest.*

Right margin notes:
[10] Gr. *She.*
[11] That is, *the region of the five cities.*
[12] Or, *distrustful*
[13] Or, *by their life*
[14] Gr. *wherein.*
[15] Gr. *stumbled*

11 When in their covetousness *men* dealt hardly with him,
She stood by him and made him rich;
12 She guarded him from enemies,
And from those that lay in wait she kept him safe,
And over his sore conflict she watched as judge,
That he might know that godliness is more powerful than [1] all.

13 When a righteous man was sold, [2] wisdom forsook him not,
But [3] from sin she delivered him;
She went down with him into a dungeon,
14 And in bonds she left him not,
Till she brought him the sceptre of a kingdom,
And authority over those that dealt tyrannously with him;
She shewed them also to be false that had mockingly accused him,
And gave him eternal glory.

15 [4] Wisdom delivered a holy people and a blameless seed from a nation of oppressors.
16 She entered into the soul of a servant of the Lord,
And withstood terrible kings in wonders and signs.
17 She rendered unto holy men a reward of their toils,
She guided them along a marvellous way,
And became unto them a covering in the day-time,
And a flame of stars through the night.
18 She brought them over the Red sea,
And led them through much water;
19 But their enemies she drowned,
And out of the bottom of the deep she cast them up.
20 Therefore the righteous spoiled the ungodly;
And they sang praise to thy holy name, O Lord,
And extolled with one accord thy hand that fought for them:
21 Because wisdom opened the mouth of the dumb,
And made the tongues of babes to speak clearly.

11 She prospered their works in the hand of a holy prophet.

2 They journeyed through a desert without inhabitant,
And in trackless regions they pitched their tents.
3 They withstood enemies, and [5] repelled foes.
4 They thirsted, and they called upon thee,
And there was given them water out of [6] the [7] flinty rock,
And healing of their thirst out of the hard stone.
5 For by what things their foes were punished,
By these they in their need were benefited.
6 [8] When *the enemy* were troubled with clotted blood instead of a river's ever-flowing fountain,
7 To rebuke the decree for the slaying of babes,
Thou gavest them abundant water beyond all hope,
8 Having shewn *them* by [9] the thirst which they had suffered how thou didst punish the adversaries.
9 For when they were tried, albeit but in mercy chastened,
They learned how the ungodly were tormented, being judged with wrath:
10 For these, as a father, admonishing them, thou didst prove;
But those, as a stern king, condemning them, thou didst search out.
11 Yea and whether they were far off *from the righteous* or near *them,* they were alike distressed;
12 For a double grief took hold on them,
And a groaning at the remembrance of things past.
13 For when they heard that through their own punishments the others [10] had been benefited,
They felt *the presence of* the Lord;
14 For him who long before was [11] cast forth and exposed they left off mocking:
In the last issue of what came to pass [12] they marvelled,
Having thirsted in another manner than the righteous.
15 But in requital of the senseless imaginings of their unrighteousness,
Wherein they were led astray to worship irrational reptiles and wretched vermin,
Thou didst send upon them a multitude of irrational creatures for vengeance;
16 That they might learn, that by what things a man sinneth, by these he is punished.
17 For thine all-powerful hand,
That created the world out of formless matter,
Lacked not means to send upon them a multitude of bears, or fierce lions,
18 Or [13] new-created wild beasts, full of rage, *of* unknown *kind,*
Either breathing out a blast of fiery breath,
Or blowing forth *from their nostrils* noisome smoke,
Or flashing dreadful sparkles from their eyes;
19 Which had power not only to consume them by their [14] violence,
But to destroy them even by the terror of their sight.

Side notes:

[1] Gr. *every one.*
[2] Gr. *she.*
[3] Or, *from the sin of his brethren ... into a pit*
[4] Gr. *She.*
[5] Or, *took vengeance on foes*
[6] Or, *the steep rock*
[7] See Deut. viii. 15: Ps. cxiv. 8.
[8] The text of this verse is perhaps corrupt.
[9] Gr. *the then thirst.*
[10] Some authorities read *were being.*
[11] Some authorities read *cast forth in hatred they.*
[12] Or, *they marvelled at him*
[13] Some authorities read *unknown wild beasts, full of new-created rage.*
[14] Gr. *harmfulness.*

20 Yea and without these might they have fallen by a single breath,
Being pursued by Justice, and scattered abroad by the breath of thy power.
But by measure and number and weight thou didst order all things.

21 For to be greatly strong is thine at all times;
And the might of thine arm who shall withstand?

22 Because the whole world before thee is as [1] a grain [2] in a balance,
And as a drop of dew that at morning cometh down upon the earth.

23 But thou hast mercy on all men, because thou hast power to do all things,
And thou overlookest the sins of men to the end they may repent.

24 For thou lovest all things that are,
And abhorrest none of the things which thou didst make;
For never wouldest thou have formed anything if thou didst hate it.

25 And how would anything have endured, except thou hadst willed it?
Or that which was not called by thee, *how would* it have been preserved?

26 But thou sparest all things, because they are thine,
O Sovereign Lord, thou lover of *men's* [3] lives;

12 For thine incorruptible spirit is in all things.

2 Wherefore thou convictest by little and little them that [4] fall from the right way,
And, putting them in remembrance by the *very* things wherein they sin, dost thou admonish them,
That escaping from their wickedness they may believe on thee, O Lord.

3 For verily the old inhabitants of thy holy land,
4 Hating *them* because they practised detestable works of enchantments and unholy rites
5 ([5] Merciless slaughters of children,
And sacrificial banquets of men's flesh and of blood),
6 Confederates in an impious fellowship,
And murderers of their own helpless babes,
It was thy counsel to destroy by the hands of our fathers;
7 That the land which in thy sight is most precious of all *lands*
Might receive a worthy colony of God's [6] servants.
8 Nevertheless even these thou didst spare as *being* men,
And thou sentest [7] hornets as forerunners of thy host,

To cause them to perish by little and little;
9 Not that thou wast unable to subdue the ungodly under the hand of the righteous in battle,
Or by terrible beasts or by *one* stern word to make away with them at once;
10 But judging them by little and little thou gavest them a place of repentance,
Not being ignorant that their nature by birth was evil, and their wickedness inborn,
And that their manner of thought would in no wise ever be changed,
11 For they were a seed accursed from the beginning:
Neither was it through fear of any that thou didst leave them *then* unpunished for their sins.

12 For who shall say, What hast thou done?
Or who shall withstand thy judgement?
And who shall accuse thee for the perishing of nations which thou didst make?
Or who shall come and stand before thee as an avenger for unrighteous men?
13 For neither is there any God beside thee that careth for all,
That thou mightest shew *unto him* that thou didst not judge unrighteously:
14 Neither shall king or prince be able to look thee in the face *to plead* for those whom thou hast punished.
15 But being righteous thou rulest all things righteously,
Deeming it a thing alien from thy power
To condemn one that doth not himself deserve to be punished.
16 For thy strength is the beginning of righteousness,
And thy sovereignty over all maketh thee to forbear all.
17 For when men believe not that thou art perfect in power, thou shewest thy strength,
[8] And [9] in dealing with them that know *it* thou puttest their boldness to confusion.
18 But thou, being sovereign over *thy* strength, judgest in gentleness,
And with great forbearance dost thou govern us;
For the power is thine whensoever thou hast the will.

19 But thou didst teach thy people by such works as these,
How that the righteous must be a lover of men;

[1] Gr. *that which just turneth.*
[2] Gr. *from.*

[3] Or, *souls*

[4] Gr. *fall aside.*

[5] The words rendered *slaughters* and *impious* in verses 5 and 6 differ but slightly from the readings of the Greek text, which here yield no sense.
[6] Or, *children*
[7] Or, *wasps*

[8] The Greek text here is perhaps corrupt.
[9] Or, *in them*

And thou didst make thy sons to be of
good hope,
Because thou givest repentance when
men have sinned.
20 For if on them that were enemies of
thy [1] servants and due to death
Thou didst take vengeance with so
great heedfulness and indulgence,
Giving them times and place whereby
they might escape from their wickedness;
21 With how great carefulness didst thou
judge thy sons,
To whose fathers thou gavest oaths
and covenants of good promises!
22 While therefore thou dost chasten us,
thou scourgest our enemies ten
thousand times more,
To the intent that we may ponder thy
goodness when we judge,
And when we are judged may look
for mercy.
23 Wherefore also the unrighteous that
lived in folly of life
Thou didst torment through their own
abominations.
24 For verily they went astray very far
[2] in the ways of error,
Taking as gods those [3] animals which
even among their enemies were held
in dishonour,
Deceived like foolish babes.
25 Therefore, as unto unreasoning children, thou didst send thy judgement
to mock them.
26 But they that would not be admon-
ished [4] by a mocking correction as
of children
Shall have experience of a judgement
worthy of God.
27 For through the sufferings whereat
they were indignant,
Being punished in these creatures
which they supposed to be gods,
They saw, and recognised as the true
God him whom before they [5] refused
to know:
Wherefore also the last end of condemnation came upon them.

13 For verily all men by nature [6] *were*
but vain who had no perception of
God,
And from the good things that are
seen they gained not power to know
him that is,
Neither by giving heed to the works
did they recognise the artificer;
2 But either fire, or wind, or swift air,
Or [7] circling stars, or raging water, or
[8] luminaries of heaven,
They thought to be gods that rule the
world.
3 And if it was through delight in their
beauty that they took them to be
gods,
Let them know how much better than
these is their Sovereign Lord;
For the first author of beauty created
them:

1 Or, *children*
2 Or, *even beyond*
3 Gr. *living creatures*: and so elsewhere in this book.
4 Or, *by a correction, which was as children's play* Gr. *by childplay of correction.*
5 Or, *denied that they knew*
6 Or, *are*
7 Gr. *circle of stars.*
8 Or, *luminaries of heaven, rulers of the world, they thought to be gods*

4 But if it was through astonishment at
their power and [9] influence,
Let them understand from them how
much more powerful is he that
formed them;
5 For from the [10] greatness of the beauty
[11] even of created things
[12] In like proportion [13] does man form
the image of their first maker.
6 But yet for these [14] men there is but
small blame,
For they too peradventure do *but* go
astray
While they are seeking God and
desiring to find him.
7 For [15] living among his works they
make diligent search,
And they [16] yield themselves up to
sight, because the things that they
look upon are beautiful.
8 But again even they are not to be
excused.
9 For if they had power to know so
much,
That they should be able to explore
[17] the course *of things*,
How is it that they did not sooner find
the Sovereign Lord of these *his*
works?

10 But miserable [6] *were* they, and [18] in
dead things [6] *were* their hopes,
Who called them gods which are
works of men's hands,
Gold and silver, wrought with careful
art, and likenesses of animals,
Or a useless stone, the work of an
ancient hand.
11 Yea and if some [19] woodcutter, having
sawn down a [20] tree that is easily
moved,
Skilfully strippeth away all its bark,
And fashioning it in comely form maketh a vessel useful for the service of
life;
12 And burning the refuse of his handywork to dress his food, eateth his fill;
13 And taking the very refuse thereof
which served to no use,
A crooked piece of wood and full of
knots,
Carveth it with the diligence of his
idleness,
And shapeth it by the skill of his
[21] indolence:
[22] *Then* he giveth it the semblance of
the image of a man,
14 Or maketh it like some paltry animal,
Smearing it with vermilion, and with
[23] paint colouring it red,
And smearing over every stain that is
therein;
15 And having made for it a chamber
worthy of it,
He setteth it in a wall, making it fast
with iron.
16 While then he taketh thought for it
that it may not fall down,
Knowing that it is unable to help
itself;

9 Gr. *efficacy.*
10 Some authorities read *greatness and beauty of.*
11 Some authorities omit *even.*
12 Or, *Correspondently*
13 Gr. *is the first maker of them beheld.*
14 Or, *things*
15 Or, *being occupied with*
16 Or, *trust their sight that the things*
17 Or, *life* Or, *the world* Gr. *the age.*
18 Or, *amongst*
19 Gr. *carpenter* who is a *woodcutter.*
20 Gr. *plant.* The Greek word, slightly changed, would mean *trunk.*
21 Or, *leisure*
22 Or, And
23 Gr. *rouge.*

(For verily it is an image, and hath need of help;)

17 When he maketh his prayer concerning goods and his marriage and children,

He is not ashamed to speak to that which hath no life;

18 Yea for health he calleth upon that which is weak,

And for life he beseecheth that which is dead,

And for aid he supplicateth that which hath least experience,

And for a *good* journey that which cannot so much as move a step,

19 And for gaining and ¹ getting and good success of his hands

He asketh ability of that which with its hands is most unable.

14 Again, one preparing to sail, and about to journey over raging waves,

Calleth upon a piece of wood more rotten than the vessel that carrieth him;

2 For that *vessel* the hunger for gains devised,

And an artificer, *even* wisdom, built it;

3 And thy providence, O Father, guideth it along,

Because even in the sea thou gavest a way,

And in the waves a sure path,

4 Shewing that thou canst save out of every *danger*,

That *so* even without art a man may put to sea;

5 And it is thy will that the works of thy wisdom should not be idle;

Therefore also do men intrust their lives to a little piece of wood,

And passing through the surge ² on a raft are brought safe *to land*.

6 For ³ in the old time also, when proud giants were perishing,

The hope of the world, taking refuge on a raft,

Left to ⁴ the race of men a seed of generations *to come*,

Thy hand guiding the helm.

7 For blessed ⁵ hath been wood through which cometh righteousness:

8 But the *idol* made with hands is accursed, itself and he that made it;

Because his was the working, and the corruptible thing was named a god:

9 For both the ungodly doer and his ungodliness are alike hateful to God;

10 For verily the deed shall be punished together with him that committed it.

11 Therefore also ⁶ among the idols of the nations shall there be a visitation,

Because, though formed of things which God created, they were made an abomination,

And stumblingblocks to the souls of men,

And a snare to the feet of the foolish.

12 For the devising of idols was the beginning of fornication,

And the invention of them the corruption of life:

13 For neither were they from the beginning, neither shall they be for ever;

14 For by the vaingloriousness of men they entered into the world,

And therefore was a speedy end devised for them.

15 For a father worn with untimely grief,

Making an image of the child quickly taken away,

Now honoured him as a god which was then a dead man,

And delivered to those that were under him mysteries and solemn rites.

16 Afterward the ungodly custom, in process of time grown strong, was kept as a law,

And by the commandments of princes the graven images received worship.

17 And when men could not honour them in presence because they dwelt far off,

Imagining the likeness from afar,

They made a visible image of the king whom they honoured,

That by their zeal they might flatter the absent as if present.

18 But unto a yet higher pitch was worship raised even by them that knew *him* not,

Urged forward by the ambition of the artificer:

19 For he, wishing peradventure to please one in authority,

Used his art to force the likeness toward a greater beauty;

20 And the multitude, allured by reason of the grace of his handywork,

Now accounted as an object of devotion him that a little before was honoured as a man.

21 And this became ⁷ a hidden danger unto life,

Because men, in bondage either to calamity or to tyranny,

Invested stones and stocks with the incommunicable Name.

22 Afterward it was not enough for them to go astray as touching the knowledge of God;

But also, while they live ⁸ in ⁹ sore conflict through ignorance *of him*,

That multitude of evils they call peace.

23 For either slaughtering children in solemn rites, or celebrating secret mysteries,

Or holding frantic revels of strange ordinances,

24 No longer do they ¹⁰ guard either life or purity of marriage,

---

¹ Or, *handy-work*

² Gr. *by.*

³ The Greek text here is perhaps corrupt.
⁴ Or, *future time* Gr. *age.*
⁵ Or, *is*

⁶ Or, *upon* Gr. *in.*

⁷ Gr. *an ambush.*

⁸ Or, *for*
⁹ Gr. *a great war of ignorance.*

¹⁰ Or, *keep unstained either life or marriage*

But one brings upon another either
death by treachery, or anguish by
adulterate offspring.

25 And all things confusedly are filled
with blood and murder, theft and
deceit,

Corruption, faithlessness, tumult, per-
26 jury, [1] turmoil,

Ingratitude for benefits *received*,

Defiling of souls, confusion of [2] sex,

Disorder in marriage, adultery and
wantonness.

27 For the worship of [3] those [4] nameless
idols

Is a beginning and cause and end of
every evil.

28 For *their worshippers* either make
merry unto madness, or prophesy
lies,

Or live unrighteously, or lightly for-
swear themselves.

29 For putting their trust in lifeless
idols,

When they have sworn a wicked
oath, they expect not to suffer
harm.

30 But for both *sins* shall the just doom
pursue them,

Because they had evil thoughts of
God by giving heed to idols,

And swore unrighteously in deceit
through contempt for holiness.

31 For it is not the power of them by
whom men swear,

But it is [5] that Justice which hath regard to them that sin,

That visiteth always the transgression of the unrighteous.

15 But thou, our God, art gracious and
true,

Longsuffering, and in mercy ordering
all things.

2 For even if we sin, we are thine,
knowing thy dominion;

But we shall not sin, knowing that we
have been accounted thine:

3 For to be acquainted with thee is
[6] perfect righteousness,

And to know thy dominion is the root
of immortality.

4 For neither were we led astray by any
evil device of men's art,

Nor yet by painters' fruitless labour,

A form stained with varied colours;

5 The sight whereof leadeth fools into
[7] lust:

Their desire is for the breathless form
of a dead image.

6 Lovers of evil things, and worthy of
such hopes *as these*,

Are both they that do, and they that
desire, and they that worship.

7 For a potter, kneading soft earth,

Laboriously mouldeth each several
vessel for our service:

Nay, out of the same clay doth he
fashion

Both the vessels that minister to clean
uses, and those of a contrary sort,

All in like manner;

But what shall be the use of each *vessel* of either sort,

The [8] craftsman *himself* is the judge.

8 And also, labouring to an evil end, he
mouldeth a vain god out of the same
clay,

He who, having but a little before
been made of earth,

After a short space goeth his way *to
the earth* out of which he was taken,

When he is required to render back
the [9] soul which was lent him.

9 Howbeit he hath anxious care,

Not because his powers must fail,

Nor because his span of life is short;

But he matcheth himself against goldsmiths and [10] silversmiths,

And he imitateth moulders in [11] brass,

And esteemeth it glory that he mouldeth counterfeits.

10 His heart is ashes,

And his hope of less value than earth,

And his life of less honour than clay:

11 Because he was ignorant of him that
moulded him,

And of him that inspired into him
[12] an active [9] soul,

And breathed into him a vital spirit:

12 But [13] he accounted our *very* life to be
a [14] plaything,

And our [15] lifetime a gainful [16] fair;

For, saith he, one must get gain
whence one can, though it be by
evil.

13 For this man beyond all others knoweth that he sinneth,

Out of earthy matter making brittle
vessels and graven images.

14 But most foolish [17] *were* they all, and
[18] of feebler soul than a babe,

The enemies of thy people, who op-
pressed them;

15 Because they even accounted all the
idols of the nations *to be* gods;

Which have neither the use of eyes
for seeing,

Nor nostrils for drawing breath,

Nor ears to hear,

Nor fingers for handling,

And their feet are helpless for walking.

16 For a man made them,

And one whose own spirit is borrow-
ed moulded them;

For no one hath power, *being* a man,
to mould a god like unto himself,

17 But, being mortal, he maketh a dead
thing by the work of lawless hands;

For he is better than the objects of
his worship,

[19] Forasmuch as he indeed had life,
but they never.

18 Yea, and the creatures that are most
hateful do they worship,

[20] For, being compared as to want of
sense, these are worse than all
others;

Margin notes (left column):

[1] Or, *trou-bling of the good, forget-fulness of favours*

[2] Or, *kind*

[3] Or, *idols that may not be named* See Ex. xxiii. 13; Ps. xvi. 4; Hos. ii. 17.

[4] See ver. 21.

[5] Gr. *the Justice of them that sin.*

[6] Gr. *entire.*

[7] Some authori-ties read *re-proach.*

Margin notes (right column):

[8] Gr. *worker in clay.*

[9] Or, *life*

[10] Gr. *silver-founders*

[11] Or, *copper*

[12] Gr. *a soul that moveth to acti-vity.*

[13] Some authori-ties read *they ac-counted.*

[14] Or, *sport*

[15] Or, *way of life*

[16] Or, *keeping of festival*

[17] Or, *are*

[18] Gr. *more wretched than the soul of a babe.* The Greek text here is perhaps corrupt.

[19] Most authori-ties read *Of which, he indeed.*

[20] The Greek text here is perhaps corrupt.

19 Neither, as seen beside *other* creatures, are they beautiful, so that one should desire them,
But they have escaped both the praise of God and his blessing.

16 For this cause were *these men* worthily punished through *creatures* like *those which they worship*,
And tormented through a multitude of vermin.

2 Instead of which punishment, thou, bestowing benefits on thy people,
Preparedst quails for food,
Food of [1] rare taste, to *satisfy* the desire of *their* appetite ;

3 To the end that [2] thine enemies, desiring food,
Might for the hideousness of the *creatures* sent among them
Loathe even the necessary appetite ;
But these, *thy people*, having for a short space suffered want,
Might even partake of *food of* [1] rare taste.

4 For it was needful that upon those should come inexorable want in their tyrannous dealing,
But that to these it should only be shewed how their enemies were tormented.

5 For even when terrible raging of wild beasts came upon [3] thy people,
And they were perishing by the bites of crooked serpents,
Thy wrath continued not to the uttermost ;

6 But for admonition were they troubled for a short space,
Having a token of salvation,
To put them in remembrance of the commandment of thy law :

7 For he that turned toward it was not saved because of that which was beheld,
But because of thee, the Saviour of all.

8 Yea, and in this didst thou persuade our enemies,
That thou art he that delivereth out of every evil.

9 For them verily the bites of locusts and flies did slay,
And there was not found a healing for their life,
Because they were worthy to be punished by such *as these*;

10 But thy sons not the very teeth of venomous dragons overcame,
For thy mercy passed by where they were, and healed them.

11 For they were [4] bitten, to put them in remembrance of thine oracles ;
And were quickly saved, lest, falling into deep forgetfulness,
They should become [5] unable to be [6] roused by thy beneficence :

12 For of a truth it was neither herb nor mollifying plaister that cured them,
But thy word, O Lord, which healeth all things ;

13 For thou hast authority over life and death,
And thou leadest down to the gates of Hades, and leadest up again.

14 But though a man *may* slay by his [7] wickedness,
Yet the spirit that is gone forth he turneth not again,
Neither giveth release to the soul that *Hades* hath received.

15 But thy hand it is not possible to escape ;

16 For ungodly men, [8] refusing to know thee, were scourged in the strength of thine arm,
Pursued with strange rains and hails and showers inexorable,
And utterly consumed with fire ;

17 For, what was most marvellous *of all*,
In the water which quencheth all things the fire wrought yet more mightily ;
For the world fighteth for the righteous.

18 For at one time the flame lost its fierceness,
That it might not burn up the creatures sent against the ungodly,
But that *these* themselves as they looked might [9] see that they were chased through the judgement of God :

19 And at another time even in the midst of water it burneth above the power of fire,
That it may destroy the [10] fruits of an unrighteous land.

20 Instead whereof thou gavest thy people angels' food to eat,
And bread ready *for their use* didst thou provide for them from heaven without *their* toil,
Bread having the virtue of every pleasant savour,
And agreeing to every taste ;

21 For [11] thy [12] nature manifested thy sweetness toward *thy* children ;
While *that bread*, ministering to the desire of the eater,
Tempered itself according to every man's choice.

22 But snow and ice endured fire, and melted not,
That *men* might know that fire was destroying the fruits of the enemies,
Burning in the hail and flashing in the rains ;

23 And [13] that this *element* again, in order that righteous men may be nourished,
Hath even forgotten its own power.

24 For the creation, ministering to thee its maker,
Straineth its force against the unrighteous, for punishment,
And slackeneth it in behalf of them that trust in thee, for beneficence.

25 Therefore at that time also, converting itself into all forms,

---

1 Gr. *strange*.
2 Gr. *those*.
3 Gr. *them*.
4 Gr. *pricked*.
5 Some authorities read *bereft of help from thy beneficence*.
6 Gr. *distracted*, or, *drawn away*. The meaning is somewhat obscure.
7 Or, *malice*
8 Or, *denying that they knew thee*
9 Some authorities read *know*.
10 Gr. *products*.
11 Some authorities read *the substance thereof*.
12 Or, *creation* Gr. *substance*.
13 Some authorities omit *that*.

It ministered to thine all-nourishing bounty,

According to the desire of them that [1] made supplication;

26 That thy sons, whom thou lovedst, O Lord, might learn

That it is not the [2] growth of *the earth's* fruits that nourisheth a man,

But that thy word preserveth them that trust thee.

27 For that which was not marred by fire,

When it was simply warmed by a faint sunbeam melted away;

28 That it might be known that *we* must rise before the sun to give thee thanks,

And must plead with thee at the dawning of the light:

29 For the hope of the unthankful shall melt as the winter's hoar frost,

And shall flow away as water that hath no use.

17 For great are thy judgements, and hard to [3] interpret;

Therefore souls undisciplined went astray.

2 For when lawless men had supposed that they held a holy nation in their power,

They *themselves*, prisoners of darkness, and bound in the fetters of a long night,

Close kept beneath their roofs,

Lay exiled from the eternal providence.

3 For while they thought that they were unseen in *their* secret sins,

They were [4] sundered one from another by a dark curtain of forgetfulness,

Stricken with terrible awe, and sore troubled by spectral forms.

4 For neither did [5] the dark recesses that held them guard them from fears,

But sounds [6] rushing down rang around them,

And phantoms appeared, cheerless with unsmiling faces.

5 And no force of fire prevailed to give *them* light,

Neither were the brightest flames of the stars strong enough to illumine that gloomy night:

6 But only there appeared to them the glimmering of a fire self-kindled, full of fear;

And in terror they deemed the things which they saw

To be worse than that sight, on which they could not gaze.

7 [7] And they lay *helpless*, made the sport of magic art,

And a shameful rebuke of their vaunts of understanding:

8 For they that promised to drive away terrors and troublings from a sick soul,

These were *themselves* sick with a ludicrous fearfulness:

9 For even if no troublous thing affrighted them,

Yet, scared with the creepings of vermin and hissings of serpents, they

10 perished [8] for very trembling,

Refusing even to look on the air, which could on no side be escaped.

11 [9] For wickedness, condemned by a witness within, is a coward thing,

And, being pressed hard by conscience, always [10] forecasteth the worst *lot*:

12 For fear is nothing else but a surrender of the succours which reason offereth;

13 And from within *the heart* the expectation *of them* being less

Maketh of greater account the ignorance of the cause that bringeth the torment.

14 But they, all through the night which was powerless indeed,

And which came upon them out of the recesses of powerless Hades,

All sleeping the same sleep,

15 Now were haunted by monstrous apparitions,

And now were paralysed by their soul's surrendering;

For fear sudden and unlooked for [11] came upon them.

16 So then *every man*, whosoever it might be, sinking down [12] in his place,

Was kept in ward shut up in that prison which was barred not with iron:

17 For whether he were a husbandman, or a shepherd,

Or a labourer whose toils were in the wilderness,

He was overtaken, and endured that inevitable necessity,

For with one chain of darkness were they all bound.

18 Whether there were a whistling wind,

Or a melodious noise of birds among the spreading branches,

Or a measured fall of water running violently,

19 Or a harsh crashing of rocks hurled down,

Or the swift course of animals bounding along unseen,

Or the voice of wild beasts harshly roaring,

Or an echo rebounding from [13] the hollows of the mountains,

All these things paralysed them with terror.

20 For the whole world *beside* was enlightened with clear light,

And was occupied with unhindered works;

21 While over them alone was spread a heavy night,

An image of the darkness that should afterward receive them;

Marginal notes (left column):

[1] Or, *had need*

[2] Gr. *generations*.

[2] Or, *set forth*

[4] Gr. *scattered by.*

[5] Gr. *the recess.*

[6] Some authorities read *troubling them sore.*

[7] Some authorities read *And the mockeries of magic art lay low, and shameful was the rebuke &c.*

Marginal notes (right column):

[8] Or, *trembling, and refusing to*

[9] This is the probable sense: the Greek text is perhaps slightly corrupt.

[10] Most authorities read *hath added.*

[11] Some authorities read *was poured upon them.*

[12] Gr. *there.*

[13] Or, *a hollow*

But yet heavier than darkness were they unto themselves.

18 But for thy holy ones there was great light;

And *the Egyptians*, hearing their voice but seeing not their form,

Counted it a happy thing that they too had suffered,

2 Yet for that they do not hurt them *now*, though wronged *by them* before, they are thankful;

And because they had been at variance *with them*, they made supplication *to them*.

3 Whereas thou didst provide *for thy people* a burning pillar of fire,

To be a guide for *their* unknown journey,

And withal a [1]kindly sun for *their* [2]proud exile.

4 For well did [3]the Egyptians deserve to be deprived of light and imprisoned by darkness,

They who had kept in close ward thy sons,

Through whom the incorruptible light of the law was to be given to [4]the race of men.

5 After they had taken counsel to slay the babes of the holy ones,

And when a single child had been cast forth and saved [5]to convict *them of their sin*,

Thou tookest away from them their multitude of children,

And destroyedst all *their host* together in a mighty flood.

6 Of that night were our fathers made aware beforehand,

That, having sure knowledge, they might be cheered by the oaths which they had trusted:

7 *So* by thy people was expected salvation of the righteous and destruction of the enemies;

8 For as thou didst take vengeance on the adversaries,

[6]By the same means, calling us unto thyself, thou didst glorify us.

9 For holy children [7]of good men offered sacrifice in secret,

And with one consent they took upon themselves the covenant of the [8]divine law,

That [9]they would partake alike in the same good things and the same perils;

The fathers already leading the sacred songs of praise.

10 But there sounded back in discord the cry of the enemies,

[10]And a piteous voice of lamentation for children was borne abroad.

11 And servant along with master punished with a like just doom,

And commoner suffering the same as king,

12 Yea, all *the people* together, under one form of death,

Had *with them* corpses without number;

For the living were not sufficient even to bury them,

Since at a single [11]stroke their [12]nobler offspring was consumed.

13 For while they were disbelieving all things by reason of the enchantments,

Upon the destruction of the firstborn they confessed the people to be God's son.

14 For while peaceful silence enwrapped all things,

And night in her own swiftness was in mid course,

15 Thine all-powerful word leaped from heaven out of [13]the royal [14]throne,

A stern warrior, into the midst of the [15]doomed land,

16 Bearing as a sharp sword thine unfeigned commandment;

And standing it filled all things with death;

And while it touched the heaven it trode upon the earth.

17 Then forthwith apparitions in dreams terribly troubled them,

And fears came upon them unlooked for:

18 And *each*, one thrown here half dead, another there,

Made manifest wherefore he was dying:

19 For the dreams, perturbing them, did foreshew this,

That they might not perish without knowing why they were afflicted.

20 But it [16]befell the righteous also to make trial of death,

And a multitude were stricken in the wilderness:

Howbeit the wrath endured not for long.

21 For a blameless man hasted to be their champion:

Bringing the weapon of his own ministry,

Even prayer and the propitiation of incense,

He withstood the indignation, and set an end to the calamity,

Shewing that he was thy servant.

22 And he overcame the [17]anger,

Not by strength of body, not by efficacy of weapons;

But [18]by word did he subdue [19]the minister of punishment,

By bringing to remembrance oaths and covenants made with the fathers.

23 For when the dead were already fallen in heaps one upon another,

Standing between he stopped the *advancing* wrath,

And [20]cut off the way to the living.

24 For upon *his* long *high-priestly* robe was the whole world,

And the glories of the fathers *were*

Left margin notes:

[1] Gr. *unharmful.*
[2] Or, *aspiring*
[3] Gr. *they.*
[4] Or, *future time* Gr. *the age.*
[5] Or, *to be to them a rebuke*
[6] Gr. *By this.*
[7] Or. *of blessing* Gr. *of good men, or, of good things.*
[8] Gr. *law of divineness.*
[9] Some authorities read *the saints would partake ...perils; already leading the fathers' songs of praise.*
[10] Some authorities read *And was piteously borne abroad in lamentation for children.*

Right margin notes:

[11] Gr. *turn of the scale.*
[12] Or, *more cherished*
[13] Or, *thy*
[14] Gr. *thrones.*
[15] Or, *destroying*
[16] Gr. *touched.*
[17] The word rendered *anger* differs only by the transposition of two letters from the reading of the Greek text, which here yields no sense.
[18] Or, *to a word did he subject*
[19] Gr. *him who was punishing.*
[20] Gr. *cleft asunder.*

upon the graving of the four rows of [1] precious stones,

And thy majesty *was* upon the diadem of his head.

25 To these the destroyer gave place, and these [2] *the people* feared;

For it was enough only to make trial of the wrath.

19 But upon the ungodly there came unto the end indignation without mercy;

For their future also *God* foreknew,

2 How that, having changed their minds to *let thy people* go,

And having speeded them eagerly on their way,

They would repent themselves and pursue them.

3 For while they were yet in the midst of their mourning,

And making lamentation at the graves of the dead,

They drew upon themselves another counsel of folly,

And pursued as fugitives those whom with intreaties they had cast out.

4 For [3] the doom which they deserved was drawing them [4] unto this end,

And it made them forget the things that had befallen them,

That they might fill up the punishment which was yet wanting to their torments,

5 And that thy people might [5] journey on by a marvellous road,

But they *themselves* might find a strange death.

6 For the whole creation, *each part* in its several kind, was fashioned again anew,

Ministering to *thy* several commandments,

That thy [6] servants might be guarded free from hurt.

7 *Then* was beheld the cloud that shadowed the camp,

And dry land rising up out of what before was water,

Out of the Red sea an unhindered highway,

And a grassy plain out of the violent surge;

8 [7] By which they passed over with all their hosts,

These that were covered with thy hand,

Having beheld strange marvels.

9 For like horses they roamed at large,

And they skipped about like lambs,

Praising thee, O Lord, who wast their deliverer.

10 For they still remembered the things that came to pass in the time of their sojourning,

How that instead of [8] bearing [9] cattle the land brought forth [10] lice,

And instead of [11] fish the river cast up a multitude of frogs.

11 But afterwards they saw also a new [12] race of birds,

When, led on by desire, they asked for luxurious dainties;

12 For, to solace them, there came up for them quails from the sea.

13 And upon the sinners came the punishments

Not without the tokens that were given [13] beforehand by the force of the thunders;

For justly did they suffer through their own wickednesses,

For [14] grievous indeed was the hatred which they practised toward guests.

14 [15] For whereas the *men of Sodom* received not [16] the strangers when they came among *them*;

[17] The Egyptians made slaves of guests who were their benefactors.

15 And not only so, *but God* shall [18] visit [19] the men of Sodom after another sort,

Since they received as enemies them that were aliens;

16 Whereas these *first* welcomed with feastings,

And then afflicted with dreadful toils,

Them that had already shared *with them* in the same rights.

17 And moreover they were stricken with loss of sight

(Even as were those *others* at the righteous man's doors),

When, being compassed about with yawning darkness,

They sought every one the passage through his own door.

18 For as the notes of a psaltery vary the character of the rhythm,

Even so *did* the elements, changing their order one with another,

Continuing always *the same, each* in its *several* sound:

As may clearly be [20] divined from the sight of the things that are come to pass.

19 For creatures of the dry land were turned into creatures of the waters,

And creatures that swim trode *now* upon the earth:

20 Fire kept the mastery of its own power in *the midst of* water,

And water forgat its quenching nature:

21 Contrariwise, flames wasted not the flesh of perishable creatures that walked among them;

Neither [21] melted they the [22] ice-like grains of ambrosial food, that were *of nature* apt to melt.

22 For in all things, O Lord, thou didst magnify thy people,

And thou didst glorify them and not lightly regard them;

Standing by their side in every time and place.

Margin notes (left):

1 Gr. stone.

2 Some authorities read *he feared.*

3 Or, *their desert by necessity was*

4 Some authorities read *unto this at last.*

5 Some authorities read *make trial of.*

6 Or, *children*

7 Or, *Through*

8 Or, *birth of cattle*

9 Gr. *living creatures.*

10 Or, *sand flies*

11 Gr. *creatures of the waters.*

Margin notes (right):

12 Or, *production* Gr. *generation.*

13 Some authorities omit *beforehand.*

14 Or, *yet more grievous was*

15 The Greek text of this and the following verse is perhaps corrupt.

16 Gr. *them who knew them not.*

17 Gr. *These.*

18 Or, *visit them . . . sort; since the men of Sodom received . . . aliens*

19 Gr. *them.*

20 Gr. *conjectured.*

21 The Greek authorities read *could be melted.* The Latin seems to have preserved the original Greek text.

22 Gr. *ice-like kind.*

THE WISDOM OF JESUS THE SON OF SIRACH,

OR

ECCLESIASTICUS.

The Prologue of the Wisdom of Jesus the Son of Sirach.

WHEREAS many and great things have been delivered unto us by the law and the prophets, and by the others that have followed in their steps, for the which things we must give Israel the praise of instruction and wisdom; and since not only the readers must needs become skilful themselves, but also they that love learning must be able to profit them which are without, both by speaking and writing; my grandfather Jesus, having much given himself to the reading of the law, and the prophets, and the other books of our fathers, and having gained great familiarity therein, was drawn on also himself to write somewhat pertaining to instruction and wisdom; in order that those who love learning, and are addicted to these things, might make progress much more by living according to the law. Ye are intreated therefore to read with favour and attention, and to pardon us, if in any parts of what we have laboured to interpret, we may seem to fail in some of the phrases. For things originally spoken in Hebrew have not the same force in them, when they are translated into another tongue: and not only these, but the law itself, and the prophecies, and the rest of the books, have no small difference, when they are spoken in their original language. For having come into Egypt in the eight and thirtieth year of Euergetes the king, and having continued there some time, I found [1] a copy affording no small instruction. I thought it therefore most necessary for me to apply some diligence and travail to interpret this book; applying indeed much watchfulness and skill in that space of time to bring the book to an end, and set it forth for them also, who in the land of their sojourning are desirous to learn, fashioning their manners beforehand, so as to live according to the law.

1 Or, a like work The word is of very doubtful meaning.

1 ALL wisdom *cometh* from the Lord,
And is with him for ever.
2 The sand of the seas, and the drops of rain,
And the days of eternity, who shall number?
3 The height of the heaven, and the breadth of the earth,
And the deep, and wisdom, who shall search *them* out?
4 Wisdom hath been created before all things,
And the understanding of prudence from everlasting.[2]

2 Verses 5 and 7 are omitted by the best authorities.

6 To whom hath the root of wisdom been revealed?
And who hath known her shrewd counsels?[2]
8 There is one wise, greatly to be feared,
The Lord sitting upon his throne:
9 He created her,
And saw, and numbered her,
And poured her out upon all his works.
10 *She is* with all flesh according to his gift;
And he gave her freely to them that love him.
11 The fear of the Lord is glory, and exultation,
And gladness, and a crown of rejoicing.
12 The fear of the Lord shall delight the heart,
And shall give gladness, and joy, and length of days.
13 Whoso feareth the Lord, it shall go well with him at the last,
And in the day of his death he shall be blessed.
14 To fear the Lord is the beginning of wisdom;
And it was created together with the faithful in the womb.
15 With men she [3] laid an eternal foundation;
And with their seed shall she be had in trust.

3 Gr. nested.

16 To fear the Lord is the fulness of wisdom;
And she satiateth men with her fruits.
17 She shall fill all her house with desirable things,
And her garners with her produce.
18 The fear of the Lord is the crown of wisdom,
Making peace and [4] perfect health to flourish.[5]
19 He both saw and numbered her;
He rained down skill and knowledge of understanding,
And exalted the honour of them that hold her fast.

4 Gr. health of cure.
5 The remainder of this verse is omitted by the best authorities.

78

20 To fear the Lord is the root of wisdom;
And her branches are length of days.[1]

22 Unjust wrath can never be justified;
For the sway of his wrath is his downfall.

23 A man that is longsuffering will [2]bear [3]for a season,
And afterward gladness shall spring up unto him;

24 He will hide his words [3]for a season,
And the lips of many shall tell forth his understanding.

25 A parable of knowledge is in the treasures of wisdom;
But godliness is an abomination to a sinner.

26 If thou desire wisdom, keep the commandments,
And the Lord shall give her unto thee freely:

27 For the fear of the Lord is wisdom and instruction;
And in faith and meekness is his good pleasure.

28 Disobey not the fear of the Lord [4];
And come not unto him with a double heart.

29 Be not a hypocrite in the mouths of men;
And take good heed to thy lips.

30 Exalt not thyself, lest thou fall,
And bring dishonour upon thy soul;
And so the Lord shall reveal thy secrets,
And shall cast thee down in the midst of the congregation;
Because thou camest not unto the fear of the Lord,
And thy heart was full of deceit.

2 My son, if thou comest to serve the Lord,
Prepare thy soul for temptation.

2 Set thy heart aright, and constantly endure,
And make not haste in time of calamity.

3 Cleave unto him, and depart not,
That thou mayest be increased at thy latter end.

4 Accept whatsoever is brought upon thee,
And be longsuffering [5]when thou passest into humiliation.

5 For gold is tried in the fire,
And acceptable men in the furnace of humiliation.

6 Put thy trust in him, and he will help thee:
Order thy ways aright, and set thy hope on him.

7 Ye that fear the Lord, wait for his mercy;
And turn not aside, lest ye fall.

8 Ye that fear the Lord, put your trust in him;
And your reward shall not fail.

9 Ye that fear the Lord, hope for good things,
And for eternal gladness and mercy.

10 Look at the generations of old, and see:
Who did ever put his trust in the Lord, and was ashamed?
Or who did abide in his fear, and was forsaken?
Or who did call upon him, and he despised him?

11 For the Lord is full of compassion and mercy;
And he forgiveth sins, and saveth in time of affliction.

12 Woe unto fearful hearts, and to faint hands,
And to the sinner that goeth two ways!

13 Woe unto the faint heart! for it believeth not;
Therefore shall it not be defended.

14 Woe unto you that have lost your patience!
And what will ye do when the Lord shall visit you?

15 They that fear the Lord will not disobey his words;
And they that love him will keep his ways.

16 They that fear the Lord will seek his good pleasure;
And they that love him shall be filled with the law.

17 They that fear the Lord will prepare their hearts,
And will humble their souls in his
18 sight, saying,
We will fall into the hands of the Lord,
And not into the hands of men:
For as his majesty is,
So also is his mercy.

3 Hear me your father, O my children,
And do thereafter, that ye may be saved.

2 For the Lord hath given the father glory as touching the children,
And hath confirmed the judgement of the mother as touching the sons.

3 He that honoureth his father shall make atonement for sins:

4 And he that giveth glory to his mother is as one that layeth up treasure.

5 Whoso honoureth his father shall have joy of his children;
And in the day of his prayer he shall be heard.

6 He that giveth glory to his father shall have length of days;
And he that hearkeneth unto the Lord shall bring rest unto his mother.

7 [6]And will do service under his parents, as unto masters.

8 In deed and word honour thy father,
That a blessing may come upon thee from him.

79

9 For the blessing of the father establisheth the houses of children;
But the curse of the mother rooteth out the foundations.

10 Glorify not thyself in the dishonour of thy father;
For thy father's dishonour is no glory unto thee.

11 For the glory of a man is from the honour of his father;
And a mother in dishonour is a reproach to her children.

12 My son, help thy father in his old age;
And grieve him not as long as he liveth.

13 And if he fail in understanding, have patience with him;
And dishonour him not *while thou art* in thy full strength.

14 For the relieving of thy father shall not be forgotten:
And instead of sins it shall be added to build thee up.

15 In the day of thine affliction it shall remember thee;
As fair weather upon ice,
So shall thy sins also melt away.

16 He that forsaketh his father is as a blasphemer;
And he that provoketh his mother is cursed of the Lord.

17 My son, go on with thy business in meekness;
So shalt thou be beloved of an acceptable man.

18 The greater thou art, humble thyself the more,
And thou shalt find favour before the Lord.[1]

20 For great is the potency of the Lord,
And he is glorified of them that are lowly.

21 Seek not things that are too hard for thee,
And search not out things that are above thy strength.

22 The things that have been commanded thee, think thereupon;
For thou hast no need of the things that are secret.

23 Be not over busy in thy superfluous works:
For more things are shewed unto thee than men can understand.

24 For the conceit of many hath led them astray;
And evil surmising hath caused their judgement to slip.[2]

26 A stubborn heart shall fare ill at the last;
And he that loveth danger shall perish therein.

27 A stubborn heart shall be laden with troubles;
And the sinner shall heap sin upon [3] sin.

28 The calamity of the proud is no healing;
For a plant of wickedness hath taken root in him.

29 The heart of the prudent will understand a parable;
And the ear of a listener is the desire of a wise man.

30 Water will quench a flaming fire;
And almsgiving will make atonement for sins.

31 He that requiteth good turns is mindful of that which cometh afterward;
And in the time of his falling he shall find a support.

4 My son, deprive not the poor of his living,
And make not the needy eyes to wait long.

2 Make not a hungry soul sorrowful;
Neither provoke a man in his distress.

3 To a heart that is provoked add not more trouble;
And defer not to give to him that is in need.

4 Reject not a suppliant in his affliction;
And turn not away thy face from a poor man.

5 Turn not away thine eye from one that asketh *of thee*,
And give none occasion to a man to curse thee:

6 For if he curse thee in the bitterness of his soul,
He that made him will hear his supplication.

7 Get thyself the love of the congregation;
And to a great man bow thy head.

8 Incline thine ear to a poor man,
And answer him with peaceable words in meekness.

9 Deliver him that is wronged from the hand of him that wrongeth him;
And be not fainthearted in giving judgement.

10 Be as a father unto the fatherless,
And instead of a husband unto their mother:
So shalt thou be as a son of the Most High,
And he shall love thee more than thy mother doth.

11 Wisdom exalteth her sons,
And taketh hold of them that seek her.

12 He that loveth her loveth life;
And they that seek her early shall be filled with gladness.

13 He that holdeth her fast shall inherit glory;
And where [4] he entereth, the Lord will bless.

14 They that do her service shall minister to the Holy One;

[1] Verse 19 is omitted by the best authorities.

[2] Most authorities omit verse 25, and transpose the lines in verse 26.

[3] Gr. *sins.*

[4] Or, *she*

And them that love her the Lord doth love.

15 He that giveth ear unto her shall judge the nations;
And he that giveth heed unto her shall dwell securely.

16 If he trust her, he shall inherit her;
And his generations shall have her in possession.

17 For at the first she will walk with him in crooked ways,
And will bring fear and dread upon him,
And torment him with her discipline,
Until she may trust his soul, and try him by her judgements:

18 Then will she return again the straight way unto him,
And will gladden him, and reveal to him her secrets.

19 If he go astray, she will forsake him,
And give him over [1] to his fall.

20 Observe the opportunity, and beware of [2] evil;
And be not ashamed concerning thy soul.

21 For there is a shame that bringeth sin;
And there is a shame *that is* glory and grace.

22 Accept not the person *of any* against thy soul;
And [3] reverence no man unto thy falling.

23 Refrain not speech, [4] when it tendeth to safety;
[5] And hide not thy wisdom for the sake of fair-seeming.

24 For by speech wisdom shall be known;
And instruction by the word of the tongue.

25 Speak not against the truth;
And be abashed for thine ignorance.

26 Be not ashamed to make confession of thy sins;
And force not the current of the river.

27 Lay not thyself down for a fool to tread upon;
And accept not the person of one that is mighty.

28 Strive for the truth unto death, and the Lord God shall fight for thee.

29 Be not [6] hasty in thy tongue,
And in thy deeds slack and remiss.

30 Be not as a lion in thy house,
Nor fanciful among thy servants.

31 Let not thine hand be stretched out to receive, and [7] closed when thou shouldest repay.

5 Set not thy heart upon thy goods;
And say not, They are sufficient for me.

2 Follow not thine own mind and thy strength,
To walk in the desires of thy heart;

3 And say not, Who shall have dominion over me?

For the Lord will surely take vengeance on thee.

4 Say not, I sinned, and what happened unto me?
For the Lord is longsuffering.[8]

5 Concerning atonement, be not without fear,
To add sin upon sins:

6 And say not, His compassion is great;
He will be pacified for the multitude of my sins:
For mercy and wrath are with him,
And his indignation will rest upon sinners.

7 Make no tarrying to turn to the Lord;
And put not off from day to day:
For suddenly shall the wrath of the Lord come forth;[9]
And thou shalt perish in the time of vengeance.

8 Set not thine heart upon unrighteous gains:
For thou shalt profit nothing in the day of calamity.

9 Winnow not with every wind,
And walk not in every path:
Thus doeth the sinner that hath a double tongue.

10 Be stedfast in thy understanding;
And let thy word be one.

11 Be swift to hear;[10]
And with patience make thine answer.

12 If thou hast understanding, answer thy neighbour;
And if not, let thy hand be upon thy mouth.

13 Glory and dishonour is in talk:
And the tongue of a man is his fall.

14 Be not called a whisperer;
And lie not in wait with thy tongue:
For upon the thief there is shame,
And an evil condemnation upon him that hath a double tongue.

15 In a great matter and in a small, be not ignorant;

6 And instead of a friend become not an enemy;
For an evil name shall inherit shame and reproach:
Even so shall the sinner that hath a double tongue.

2 Exalt not thyself in the counsel of thy soul;
That thy soul be not torn in pieces as a bull:

3 Thou shalt eat up thy leaves, and destroy thy fruits,
And leave thyself as a dry tree.

4 A wicked soul shall destroy him that hath gotten it,
And shall make him [11] a laughing-stock to his enemies.

5 [12] Sweet words will multiply [13] a man's friends;

---

[1] Gr. *to the hands of his fall.*
[2] Or, *an evil man*
[3] Or, *be not abashed*
[4] Gr. *in an occasion of safety.*
[5] Most authorities omit this line.
[6] Some authorities read *rough.*
[7] Or, *drawn back*

[8] The remainder of this verse is omitted by the best authorities.

[9] A line of this verse is here omitted by the best authorities.

[10] The remainder of this line is omitted by the best authorities.

[11] Or, *a rejoicing*
[12] Gr. *A sweet throat.*
[13] Gr. *his.*

81

And a fair-speaking tongue will multiply courtesies.

6 Let those that are at peace with thee be many;
But thy counsellors one of a thousand.

7 If thou wouldest get thee a friend, get him [1] by proving,
And be not in haste to trust him.

8 For there is a friend *that is so* for his own occasion;
And he will not continue in the day of thy affliction.

9 And there is a friend that turneth to enmity;
And he will discover strife to thy reproach.

10 And there is a friend that is a companion at the table;
And he will not continue in the day of thy affliction.

11 And in thy prosperity he will be as thyself,
And will be bold over thy servants:

12 If thou shalt be brought low, he will be against thee,
And will hide himself from thy face.

13 Separate thyself from thine enemies;
And beware of thy friends.

14 A faithful friend is a strong [2] defence;
And he that hath found him hath found a treasure.

15 There is nothing that can be taken in exchange for a faithful friend;
And his excellency is beyond [3] price.

16 A faithful friend is a medicine of life;
And they that fear the Lord shall find him.

17 He that feareth the Lord directeth his friendship aright;
For as he is, so is his neighbour also.

18 My son, gather instruction from thy youth up:
And even unto hoar hairs thou shalt find wisdom.

19 Come unto her as one that ploweth and soweth,
And wait for her good fruits;
For thy toil shall be little in the tillage of her,
And thou shalt eat of her fruits right soon.

20 How exceeding harsh is she to the unlearned!
And he that is without understanding will not abide in her.

21 As a mighty stone of trial shall she rest upon him;
And he will not delay to cast her from him.

22 For wisdom is according to her name;
and she is not manifest unto many.

23 Give ear, my son, and accept my judgement,
And refuse not my counsel,

24 And bring thy feet into her fetters,
And thy neck into her chain.

25 Put thy shoulder under her, and bear her,
And be not grieved with her bonds.

26 Come unto her with all thy soul,
And keep her ways with thy whole power.

27 Search, and seek, and she shall be made known unto thee;
And when thou hast got hold of her, let her not go.

28 For at the last thou shalt find her rest;
And [4] she shall be turned for thee into gladness.

29 And her fetters shall be to thee for a covering of strength,
And her chains for a robe of glory.

30 For there is a golden ornament upon her,
And her bands are [5] a riband of blue.

31 Thou shalt put her on *as* a robe of glory,
And shalt array thee with her *as* a crown of rejoicing.

32 My son, if thou wilt, thou shalt be instructed;
And if thou wilt yield thy soul, thou shalt be [6] prudent.

33 If thou love to hear, thou shalt receive;
And if thou incline thine ear, thou shalt be wise.

34 Stand thou in the multitude of the elders;
And whoso is wise, cleave thou unto him.

35 Be willing to listen to every godly discourse;
And let not the proverbs of understanding escape thee.

36 If thou seest a man of understanding, get thee betimes unto him,
And let thy foot wear out the steps of his doors.

37 Let thy mind dwell upon the ordinances of the Lord,
And meditate continually in his commandments:
He shall establish thine heart,
And thy desire of wisdom shall be given unto thee.

7 Do no evil, so shall no evil overtake thee.

2 Depart from wrong, and it shall turn aside from thee.

3 My son, sow not upon the furrows of unrighteousness,
And thou shalt not reap them sevenfold.

4 Seek not of the Lord preeminence,
Neither of the king the seat of honour.

5 Justify not thyself in the presence of the Lord;
And display not thy wisdom before the king.

6 Seek not to be a judge,

Margin notes:
[1] Or, *in the time of trial*
[2] Or, *covert*
[3] Gr. *weight.*
[4] Or, *it*
[5] Num. xv. 38.
[6] Or, *shrewd*

Lest thou be not able to take away iniquities;
Lest haply thou fear the person of a mighty man,
And lay a stumblingblock in the way of thy uprightness.

7 Sin not against the multitude of the city,
And cast not thyself down in the crowd.

8 Bind not up sin twice;
For in one *sin* thou shalt not be unpunished.

9 Say not, He will look upon the multitude of my gifts,
And when I offer to the Most High God, he will accept [1] it.

10 Be not fainthearted in thy prayer;
And neglect not to give alms.

11 Laugh not a man to scorn when he is in the bitterness of his soul;
For there is one who humbleth and exalteth.

12 [2] Devise not a lie against thy brother;
Neither do the like to a friend.

13 Love not to make any manner of lie;
For the custom thereof is not for good.

14 Prate not in the multitude of elders;
And repeat not thy words in thy prayer.

15 Hate not laborious work;
Neither husbandry, which the Most High hath [3] ordained.

16 Number not thyself among the multitude of sinners:
Remember that wrath will not tarry.

17 Humble thy soul greatly;
For the punishment of the ungodly man is fire and the worm.

18 Change not a friend for a thing indifferent;
Neither a true brother for the gold of Ophir.

19 Forgo not a wise and good wife;
For her grace is above gold.

20 Entreat not evil a servant that worketh truly,
Nor a hireling that giveth *thee* his [4] life.

21 Let thy soul love a wise servant;
Defraud him not of liberty.

22 Hast thou cattle? have an eye to them;
And if they are profitable to thee, let them stay by thee.

23 Hast thou children? correct them,
And bow down their neck from their youth.

24 Hast thou daughters? give heed to their body,
And make not thy face cheerful toward them.

25 Give thy daughter in marriage, and thou shalt have accomplished a great matter:

And give her to a man of understanding.

26 Hast thou a wife after thy mind? cast her not out:
[5] But trust not thyself to one that is [6] hateful.

27 Give glory to thy father with thy whole heart;
And forget not the pangs of thy mother.

28 Remember that of them thou wast born:
And what wilt thou recompense them for the things that they have done for thee?

29 Fear the Lord with all thy soul;
And reverence his priests.

30 With all thy strength love him that made thee;
And forsake not his ministers.

31 Fear the Lord, and glorify the priest;
And give him his portion, even as it is commanded thee;
The firstfruits, and the trespass offering, and the gift of the shoulders,
And the sacrifice of sanctification, and the firstfruits of holy things.

32 Also to the poor man stretch out thy hand,
That thy blessing may be perfected.

33 A gift hath grace in the sight of every man living;
And for a dead man keep not back grace.

34 Be not wanting to them that weep;
And mourn with them that mourn.

35 Be not slow to visit a sick man;
For by such things thou shalt gain love.

36 In all thy [7] matters remember thy last end,
And thou shalt never do amiss.

8 Contend not with a mighty man,
Lest haply thou fall into his hands.

2 Strive not with a rich man, lest haply he overweigh thee:
For gold hath destroyed many,
And turned aside the hearts of kings.

3 Contend not with a man that is full of tongue,
And heap not wood upon his fire.

4 Jest not with a rude man,
Lest thine ancestors be dishonoured.

5 Reproach not a man when he turneth from sin:
Remember that we are all worthy of punishment.

6 Dishonour not a man in his old age;
For some of us also are waxing old.

7 Rejoice not over one that is dead:
Remember that we die all.

8 Neglect not the discourse of the wise,
And be conversant with their proverbs;

[1] Or, *them*

[2] Gr. *Plow not.*

[3] Gr. *created.*

[4] Or, *soul*

[5] Many authorities omit this line.

[6] Or, *hated*

[7] Or, *words*

For of them thou shalt learn instruction,
And how to minister to great men.

9 Miss not the discourse of the aged;
For they also learned of their fathers:
Because from them thou shalt learn understanding,
And to give answer in time of need.

10 Kindle not the coals of a sinner,
Lest thou be burned with the [1] flame of his fire.

11 Rise not up from the presence of an insolent man,
Lest he lie in wait as an ambush for thy mouth.

12 Lend not to a man that is mightier than thyself;
And if thou lend, be as one that hath lost.

13 Be not surety above thy power:
And if thou be surety, take thought as one that will have to pay.

14 Go not to law with a judge;
For according to his honour will they give judgement for him.

15 Go not in the way with a rash man,
Lest he be aggrieved with thee;
For he will do according to his own will,
And thou shalt perish with his folly.

16 Fight not with a wrathful man,
And travel not with him through the desert:
For blood is as nothing in his sight;
And where there is no help, he will overthrow thee.

17 Take not counsel with a fool;
For he will not be able to conceal the matter.

18 Do no secret thing before a stranger;
For thou knowest not what [2] he will bring forth.

19 Open not thine heart to every man;
And let him not return thee a favour.

9 Be not jealous over the wife of thy bosom,
And teach her not an evil lesson against thyself.

2 Give not thy soul unto a woman,
That she should set her foot upon thy strength.

3 Go not to meet a woman that playeth the harlot,
Lest haply thou fall into her snares.

4 Use not the company of a woman that is a singer,
Lest haply thou be caught by her attempts.

5 Gaze not on a maid, lest haply thou be trapped in her penalties.

6 Give not thy soul unto harlots,
That thou lose not thine inheritance.

7 Look not round about thee in the streets of the city,
Neither wander thou in the solitary places thereof.

8 Turn away thine eye from a comely woman,
And gaze not on another's beauty:
By the beauty of a woman many have been led astray;
And herewith love is kindled as a fire.

9 Sit not at all with a woman that hath a husband; [3]
And revel not with her at the wine;
Lest haply thy soul turn aside unto her,
And with thy spirit thou slide into destruction.

10 Forsake not an old friend;
For the new is not comparable to him:
As new wine, *so* is a new friend;
If it become old, thou shalt drink it with gladness.

11 Envy not the glory of a sinner;
For thou knowest not what shall be his overthrow.

12 Delight not in the delights of the ungodly:
Remember they shall not go unpunished unto [4] the grave.

13 Keep thee far from the man that hath [5] power to kill,
And thou shalt have no suspicion of the fear of death:
And if thou come unto him, commit no fault,
Lest he take away thy life:
Know surely that thou goest about in the midst of snares,
And walkest upon the battlements of a city.

14 As well as thou canst, guess at thy neighbours;
And take counsel with the wise.

15 Let thy converse be with men of understanding;
And let all thy discourse be in the law of the Most High.

16 Let just men be the companions of thy board;
And let thy glorying be in the fear of the Lord.

17 For the hand of the artificers a work shall be commended:
And he that ruleth the people *shall be counted* wise for his speech.

18 A man full of tongue is dangerous in his city;
And he that is headlong in his speech shall be hated.

10 A wise judge will instruct his people;
And the government of a man of understanding shall be well ordered.

2 As is the judge of his people, so are his ministers;
And as is the ruler of the city, *such are* all they that dwell therein.

3 An uninstructed king will destroy his people;

Side notes:

[1] Gr. *fire of his flame.*

[2] Or, *it*

[3] A line of this verse is here omitted by the best authorities.

[4] Gr. *Hades.*

[5] Or, *authority*

And a city will be established through the understanding of the powerful.

4 In the hand of the Lord is the authority of the earth;
And in due time he will raise up over it one that is profitable.

5 In the hand of the Lord is the prosperity of a man;
And upon the person of the scribe shall he lay his honour.

6 Be not wroth with thy neighbour for every wrong;
And do nothing by works of violence.

7 Pride is hateful before the Lord and *before* men;
And in the judgement of both will unrighteousness err.

8 Sovereignty is transferred from nation to nation,
Because of iniquities, and deeds of violence, and greed of money.

9 [1] Why is earth and ashes proud? [2]
Because in *his* life he hath cast away his bowels.

10 *It is* a long disease; the physician mocketh:
And *he is* a king to-day, and to-morrow he shall die.

11 For when a man is dead,
He shall inherit creeping things, and beasts, and worms.

12 *It is* the beginning of pride when a man departeth from the Lord;
And his heart is departed from him that made him.

13 For the beginning of pride is sin;
And he that keepeth it will pour forth abomination.
For this cause the Lord brought upon them strange calamities,
And overthrew them utterly.

14 The Lord cast down the thrones of rulers,
And set the meek in their stead.

15 The Lord plucked up the roots of nations,
And planted the lowly in their stead.

16 The Lord overthrew the lands of nations,
And destroyed them unto the foundations of the earth.

17 He took some of them away, and destroyed them,
And made their memorial to cease from the earth.

18 Pride hath not been created for men,
Nor wrathful anger for the offspring of women.

19 [3] What manner of seed hath honour? the seed of man.
What manner of seed hath honour? they that fear the Lord.
What manner of seed hath no honour? the seed of man.
What manner of seed hath no honour? they that transgress the commandments.

20 In the midst of brethren he that ruleth them hath honour;
And in the eyes of the Lord they that fear him. [4]

22 The rich man, and the honourable, and the poor,
Their glorying is the fear of the Lord.

23 It is not right to dishonour a poor man that hath understanding;
And it is not fitting to glorify a man that is a sinner.

24 The great man, and the judge, and the mighty man, shall be glorified;
And there is not one of them greater than he that feareth the Lord.

25 Free men shall minister unto a wise servant;
And a man that hath knowledge will not murmur *thereat*.

26 Be not over wise in doing thy work;
And glorify not thyself in the time of thy distress.

27 [5] Better is he that laboureth, and aboundeth in all things,
Than he that glorifieth himself, and lacketh bread.

28 My son, glorify thy soul in meekness,
And give it honour according to the worthiness thereof.

29 Who will justify him that sinneth against his own soul?
And who will glorify him that dishonoureth his own life?

30 A poor man is glorified for his knowledge;
And a rich man is glorified for his riches.

31 But he that is glorified in poverty, how much more in riches?
And he that is inglorious in riches, how much more in poverty?

11 The wisdom of the lowly shall lift up his head,
And make him to sit in the midst of great men.

2 Commend not a man for his beauty;
And abhor not a man for his outward appearance.

3 The bee is little among such as fly;
And her fruit is the chief of sweetmeats.

4 Glory not in the putting on of raiment,
And exalt not thyself in the day of honour;
For the works of the Lord are wonderful,
And his works are hidden among men.

5 Many [6] kings have sat down upon the ground;
And one that was never thought of hath worn a diadem.

6 Many mighty men have been greatly disgraced;
And men of renown have been delivered into other men's hands.

---

[1] The text here is uncertain.
[2] Two lines of this verse are here omitted by the best authorities.
[3] The MSS. here greatly differ. The rendering represents the most probable text.
[4] Verse 21 is omitted by the best authorities
[5] The Greek text of this verse is uncertain
[6] Gr. *tyrants*.

7 Blame not before thou hast examined :
Understand first, and then rebuke.
8 Answer not before thou hast heard ;
And interrupt not in the midst of speech.
9 Strive not in a matter that concerneth thee not ;
And where sinners judge, sit not thou with them.

10 My son, be not busy about many matters :
For if thou meddle much, thou shalt not be unpunished ;
And if thou pursue, thou shalt not overtake ;
And thou shalt not escape by fleeing.
11 There is one that toileth, and labour-eth, and maketh haste,
And is so much the more behind.
12 There is one that is sluggish, and hath need of help,
Lacking in strength, and that abound-eth in poverty ;
And the eyes of the Lord looked upon him for good,
And he set him up from his low estate,
13 And lifted up his head ;
And many marvelled at him.

14 Good things and evil, life and death,
Poverty and riches, are from the Lord.[1]

17 The gift of the Lord remaineth with the godly,
And his good pleasure shall prosper for ever.
18 There is that waxeth rich by his wariness and pinching,
And this is the portion of his reward :
19 When he saith, I have found rest,
And now will I eat of my goods ;
Yet he knoweth not what time shall pass,
And he shall leave them to others, and die.
20 Be stedfast in thy covenant, and be conversant therein,
And wax old in thy work.

21 Marvel not at the works of a sinner ;
But trust the Lord, and abide in thy labour :
For it is an easy thing in the sight of the Lord swiftly on the sudden to make a poor man rich.
22 The blessing of the Lord is in the reward of the godly ;
And in an hour that cometh swiftly he maketh his blessing to flour-ish.
23 Say not, What use is there of me ?
And what from henceforth shall my good things be ?
24 Say not, I have sufficient,
And from henceforth what harm shall happen unto me ?

25 In the day of good things there is a forgetfulness of evil things ;
And in the day of evil things a man will not remember things that are good.
26 For it is an easy thing in the sight of the Lord
To reward a man in the day of death according to his ways.
27 The affliction of an hour causeth for-getfulness of delight ;
And in the last end of a man is the revelation of his deeds.
28 Call no man blessed before his death ;
And a man shall be known in his children.

29 Bring not every man into thine house ;
For many are the plots of the deceit-ful man.
30 As a decoy partridge in a cage, so is the heart of a proud man ;
And as one that is a spy, he looketh upon thy falling.
31 For he lieth in wait to turn things that are good into evil ;
And in things that are praiseworthy he will lay blame.
32 From a spark of fire a heap of many coals is kindled ;
And a sinful man lieth in wait for blood.
33 Take heed of an evil-doer, for he contriveth wicked things ;
Lest haply he bring upon thee blame for ever.
34 Receive a stranger into thine house, and he will distract thee with brawls,
And estrange thee from thine own.

12 If thou do good, know to whom thou doest it ;
And thy good deeds shall have thanks.
2 Do good to a godly man, and thou shalt find a recompense ;
And if not from him, yet from the Most High.
3 There shall no good come to him that continueth to do evil,
Nor to him that giveth no alms.
4 Give to the godly man,
And help not the sinner.
5 Do good to one that is lowly,
And give not to an ungodly man :
Keep back his bread, and give it not to him,
Lest he overmaster thee thereby :
For thou shalt receive twice as much evil
For all the good thou shalt have done unto him.
6 For the Most High also hateth sin-ners,
And will repay vengeance unto the ungodly.[2]
7 Give to the good man,
And help not the sinner.

1 Or, *pun-ished*

8 A man's friend will not be [1] fully tried in prosperity;
And his enemy will not be hidden in adversity.
9 In a man's prosperity his enemies are grieved;
And in his adversity even his friend will be separated *from him*.
10 Never trust thine enemy:
For like as the brass rusteth, so is his wickedness.
11 Though he humble himself, and go crouching,
Yet take good heed, and beware of him,
And thou shalt be unto him as one that hath wiped a mirror,
And thou shalt know that [2] he hath not utterly rusted it.
12 Set him not by thee,
Lest he overthrow thee and stand in thy place;
Let him not sit on thy right hand,
Lest he seek to take thy seat,
And at the last thou acknowledge my words,
And be pricked with my sayings.
13 Who will pity a charmer that is bitten with a serpent,
Or any that come nigh wild beasts?
14 Even so *who will pity* him that goeth to a sinner,
And is mingled with him in his sins?
15 For a while he will abide with thee,
And if thou give way, he will not hold out.
16 And the enemy will speak sweetly with his lips,
And in his heart take counsel how to overthrow thee into a pit:
The enemy will weep with his eyes,
And if he find opportunity, he will not be satiated with blood.
17 If adversity meet thee, thou shalt find him there before thee;
And as though he would help thee, he will trip up thy heel.
18 He will shake his head, and clap his hands,
And whisper much, and change his countenance.

13 He that toucheth pitch shall be defiled;
And he that hath fellowship with a proud man shall become like unto him.
2 Take not up a burden above thy strength;
And have no fellowship with one that is mightier and richer than thyself.
What fellowship shall the earthen pot have with the kettle?
This shall smite, and that shall be dashed in pieces.
3 The rich man doeth a wrong, and he threateneth withal:
The poor is wronged, and he shall intreat withal.

2 Or, *it hath not utterly rusted him*

4 If thou be profitable, he will make merchandise of thee;
And if thou be in want, he will forsake thee.
5 If thou have substance, he will live with thee;
And he will make thee bare, and will not be sorry.
6 Hath he had need of thee? then he will deceive thee,
And smile upon thee, and give thee hope:
He will speak thee fair, and say, What needest thou?
7 And he will shame thee by his meats,
Until he have made thee bare twice or thrice,
And at the last he will laugh thee to scorn:
Afterward will he see thee, and will forsake thee,
And shake his head at thee.
8 Beware that thou be not deceived, and brought low in thy mirth.
9 If a mighty man invite thee, be retiring,
And so much the more will he invite thee.
10 Press not upon him, lest thou be thrust back;
And stand not far off, lest thou be forgotten.
11 Affect not to speak with him as an equal,
And believe not his many words:
For with much talk will he try thee,
And in a smiling manner will search thee out.
12 He that keepeth not to himself words spoken is unmerciful;
And he will not spare to hurt and to bind.
13 Keep *them* to thyself, and take earnest heed,
For thou walkest [3] in peril of thy falling.[4]

15 Every living creature loveth his like,
And every man *loveth* his neighbour.
16 All flesh consorteth according to kind,
And a man will cleave to his like.
17 What fellowship shall the wolf have with the lamb?
So *is* the sinner unto the godly.
18 What peace is there between the hyena and the dog?
And what peace between the rich man and the poor?
19 Wild asses are the prey of lions in the wilderness;
So poor men are pasture for the rich.
20 Lowliness is an abomination to a proud man:
So a poor man is an abomination to the rich.
21 A rich man when he is shaken is held up of his friends;
But one of low degree being down is thrust away also by his friends.

3 Gr. *along with.*
4 The remainder of verse 13, and verse 14, are omitted by the best authorities

¹ Or, *secrets, and*

22 When a rich man is fallen, there are many helpers;
He speaketh ¹ things not to be spoken, and men justify him:
A man of low degree falleth, and men rebuke him withal;
He uttereth wisdom, and no place is allowed him.
23 A rich man speaketh, and all keep silence;
And what he saith they extol to the clouds:
A poor man speaketh, and they say, Who is this?
And if he stumble, they will help to overthrow him.

24 Riches are good that have no sin;
And poverty is evil in the mouth of the ungodly.
25 The heart of a man changeth his countenance,

² The remainder of this verse is omitted by the best authorities.

Whether it be for good or for evil.²
26 A cheerful countenance is a token of a heart that is in prosperity;
And the finding out of parables is a weariness of thinking.
14 Blessed is the man that hath not slipped with his mouth,
And is not pricked with sorrow for sins.
2 Blessed is he whose soul doth not condemn him,
And who is not fallen from his hope.

3 Riches are not comely for a niggard;
And what should an envious man do with money?
4 He that gathereth *by taking* from his own soul gathereth for others;
And others shall revel in his goods.
5 He that is evil to himself, to whom will he be good?
And he shall not rejoice in his possessions.
6 There is none more evil than he that envieth himself;
And this is a recompense of his wickedness.
7 Even if he doeth good, he doeth it in forgetfulness;
And at the last he sheweth forth his wickedness.
8 Evil is he that envieth with his eye,
Turning away the face, and despising the souls *of men*.
9 A covetous man's eye is not satisfied with his portion;
And wicked injustice drieth up his soul.
10 An evil eye is grudging of bread,
And he is miserly at his table.

11 My son, according as thou hast, do well unto thyself,
And bring offerings unto the Lord worthily.
12 Remember that death will not tarry,

³ Gr. *Hades.*

And that the covenant of ³ the grave is not shewed unto thee.

13 Do well unto thy friend before thou die;
And according to thy ability stretch out *thy hand* and give to him.
14 Defraud not *thyself* of a good day;
And let not the portion of a good desire pass thee by.
15 Shalt thou not leave thy labours unto another?
And thy toils to be divided by lot?
16 Give, and take, and beguile thy soul;
For there is no seeking of luxury in ³ the grave.
17 All flesh waxeth old as a garment;
For the covenant from the beginning is, Thou shalt die the death.
18 As of the leaves flourishing on a thick tree,
Some it sheddeth, and some it maketh to grow;
So also of the generations of flesh and blood,
One cometh to an end, and another is born.
19 Every work rotteth and falleth away,
And the worker thereof shall depart with it.

20 Blessed is the man that shall ⁴ meditate in wisdom,
And that shall discourse by his understanding.
21 He that considereth her ways in his heart
Shall also have knowledge in her secrets.
22 Go forth after her as one that tracketh,
And lie in wait in her ways.
23 He that prieth in at her windows
Shall also hearken at her doors.
24 He that lodgeth close to her house
Shall also fasten a nail in her walls.
25 He shall pitch his tent nigh at hand to her,
And shall lodge in a lodging where good things are.
26 He shall set his children under her shelter,
And shall rest under her branches.
27 By her he shall be covered from heat,
And shall lodge in her glory.
15 He that feareth the Lord will do this;
And he that hath possession of the law shall obtain her.
2 And as a mother shall she meet him,
And receive him as a wife married in her virginity.
3 With bread of understanding shall she feed him,
And give him water of wisdom to drink.
4 He shall be stayed upon her, and shall not be moved;
And shall rely upon her, and shall not be confounded.
5 And she shall exalt him above his neighbours;
And in the midst of the congregation shall she open his mouth.

⁴ Most authorities read *come to an end.*

6 He shall inherit joy, and a crown of gladness,
And an everlasting name.
7 Foolish men shall not obtain her;
And sinners shall not see her.
8 She is far from pride;
And liars shall not remember her.
9 Praise is not comely in the mouth of a sinner;
For it was not sent him from the Lord.
10 For praise shall be spoken in wisdom;
And the Lord will prosper it.

11 Say not thou, It is through the Lord that I fell away;
For thou shalt not do the things that he hateth.
12 Say not thou, It is he that caused me to err;
For he hath no need of a sinful man.
13 The Lord hateth every abomination;
And they that fear him love it not.
14 He himself made man from the beginning.
And left him in the hand of his own counsel.
15 If thou wilt, thou shalt keep the commandments;
And to perform faithfulness is of *thine own* good pleasure.
16 He hath set fire and water before thee:
Thou shalt stretch forth thy hand unto whichsoever thou wilt.
17 Before man is life and death;
And whichsoever he liketh, it shall be given him.
18 For great is the wisdom of the Lord:
He is mighty in power, and beholdeth all things;
19 And his eyes are upon them that fear him;
And he will take knowledge of every work of man.
20 He hath not commanded any man to be ungodly;
And he hath not given any man licence to sin.

16 Desire not a multitude of unprofitable children,
Neither delight in ungodly sons.
2 If they multiply, delight not in them,
Except the fear of the Lord be with them.
3 Trust not thou in their life,
Neither rely on their condition:
For one is better than a thousand;
And to die childless than to have ungodly children.
4 For from one that hath understanding shall a city be peopled;
But a race of wicked men shall be made desolate.
5 Many such things have I seen with mine eyes;
And mine ear hath heard mightier things than these.

6 In the congregation of sinners shall a fire be kindled;
And in a disobedient nation wrath is kindled.
7 He was not pacified toward the giants of old time,
Who revolted in their strength.
8 He spared not those with whom Lot sojourned,
Whom he abhorred for their pride.
9 He pitied not the people of perdition,
Who were taken away in their sins.
10 And in like manner the six hundred thousand footmen,
Who were gathered together in the hardness of their hearts.
11 Even if there be one stiffnecked person,
It is marvel if he shall be unpunished:
For mercy and wrath are with him;
He is mighty to forgive, and he poureth out wrath.
12 As his mercy is great, so is his correction also:
He judgeth a man according to his works.
13 The sinner shall not escape with *his* plunder;
And the patience of the godly shall not be frustrate.
14 He will make room for every work of mercy;
Each man shall find according to his works.[1]

17 Say not thou, I shall be hidden from the Lord;
And who shall remember me from on high?
I shall not be known among so many people:
For what is my soul in a boundless creation?
18 Behold, the heaven, and the heaven of heavens,
The deep, and the earth, shall be moved when he shall visit.
19 The mountains and the foundations of the earth together
Are shaken with trembling, when he looketh upon them.
20 And no heart shall think upon these things:
And who shall conceive his ways?
21 And *there is* a tempest which no man shall see;
Yea, the more part of his works are [2] hid.
22 Who shall declare the works of *his* righteousness?
Or who shall endure them?
For his covenant is afar off.[3]
23 He that is wanting in [4] understanding thinketh upon these things;
And an unwise and erring man thinketh follies.
24 My son, hearken unto me, and learn knowledge,

[1] Verses 15 and 16 are omitted by the best authorities

[2] Gr. *among hidden things.*
[3] The remainder of this verse is omitted by the best authorities
[4] Gr. *heart.*

And give heed to my words with thy heart.

25 I will shew forth instruction by weight,
And declare knowledge exactly.

26 In the judgement of the Lord are his works from the beginning;
And from the making of them he disposed the parts thereof.

27 He garnished his works for ever,
And the beginnings of them unto their generations:
They neither hunger, nor are weary,
And they cease not from their works.

28 No one thrusteth aside his neighbour;
And they shall never disobey his word.

29 After this also the Lord looked upon the earth,
And filled it with his blessings.

30 [1] [2] All manner of living things covered the face thereof;
And into it is their return.

17 The Lord created man of the earth,
And turned him back unto it again.

2 He gave them days by number, and a set time,
And gave them authority over the things that are thereon.

3 He endued them with strength proper to them;
And made them according to his own image.

4 He put the fear of [3] man upon all flesh,
And *gave him* to have dominion over beasts and fowls.[4]

6 Counsel, and tongue, and eyes,
Ears, and heart, gave he them to understand withal.

7 He filled them with the knowledge of wisdom,
And shewed them good and evil.

8 He set his eye upon their hearts,
To shew them the majesty of his works.[5]

10 And they shall praise the name of *his* holiness,
[6] That they may declare the majesty of his works.

11 He added unto them knowledge,
And gave them a law of life for a heritage.

12 He made an everlasting covenant with them,
And shewed them his judgements.

13 Their eyes saw the majesty of *his* glory;
And their ear heard the glory of [7] his voice.

14 And he said unto them, Beware of all unrighteousness;
And he gave them commandment, each man concerning his neighbour.

15 Their ways are ever before him;
They shall not be hid from his eyes.[8]

17 [9] For every nation he appointed a ruler;
And Israel is the Lord's portion.[8]

19 All their works are as the sun before him;
And his eyes are continually upon their ways.

20 Their iniquities are not hid from him;
And all their sins are before the Lord.[8]

22 With him the alms of a man is as a signet;
And he will keep the bounty of a man as the apple of the eye.[10]

23 Afterwards he will rise up and recompense them,
And render their recompense upon their head.

24 Howbeit unto them that repent he granteth a return;
And he comforteth them that are losing patience.

25 Return unto the Lord, and forsake sins:
Make thy prayer before *his* face, and lessen the offence.

26 Turn again to the Most High, and turn away from iniquity;[11]
And greatly hate the abominable thing.

27 Who shall give praise to the Most High in [12] the grave,
Instead of them which live and return thanks?

28 Thanksgiving perisheth from the dead, as from one that is not:
He that is in life and health shall praise the Lord.

29 How great is the mercy of the Lord,
And his forgiveness unto them that turn unto him!

30 For all things cannot be in men,
Because the son of man is not immortal.

31 What is brighter than the sun? yet this faileth:
And an evil man will think on flesh and blood.

32 He looketh upon the power of the height of heaven:
And all men are earth and ashes.

18 He that liveth for ever created all things in common.

2 The Lord alone shall be justified.[13]

4 To none hath he given power to declare his works:
And who shall trace out his mighty deeds?

5 Who shall number the strength of his majesty?
And who shall also tell out his mercies?

6 As for the wondrous works of the Lord, it is not possible to take from them nor add to them,
Neither is it possible to track them out.

7 When a man hath finished, then he is but at the beginning;
And when he ceaseth, then shall he be in perplexity.

8 What is man, and whereto serveth he?

[1] The Greek text of this line is uncertain.
[2] Gr. *The soul of every living thing.*
[3] Gr. *him.*
[4] Verse 5 is omitted by the best authorities.
[5] Verse 9 is omitted by the best authorities.
[6] This line is added by the best authorities.
[7] Some ancient authorities read *their.*
[8] Verses 16, 18, and 21 are omitted by the best authorities.
[9] The preceding part of this verse is omitted by the best authorities.
[10] The remainder of this verse is omitted by the best authorities.
[11] A line is here omitted by the best authorities.
[12] Gr. *Hades.*
[13] The remainder of verse 2, and verse 3, are omitted by the best authorities.

What is his good, and what is his evil?

9 The number of man's days at the most are a hundred years.

10 As a drop of water from the sea, and a pebble from the sand;
So are a few years in the day of eternity.

11 For this cause the Lord was long-suffering over them,
And poured out his mercy upon them.

12 He saw and perceived their end, that it is evil;
Therefore he multiplied his forgiveness.

13 The mercy of a man is upon his neighbour;
But the mercy of the Lord is upon all flesh;
Reproving, and chastening, and teaching,
And bringing again, as a shepherd doth his flock.

14 He hath mercy on them that accept chastening,
And that diligently seek after his judgements.

15 My son, to thy good deeds add no blemish;
And no grief of words in any of thy giving.

16 Shall not the dew assuage the scorching heat?
So is a word better than a gift.

17 Lo, is not a word better than a gift?
And both are with a gracious man.

18 A fool will upbraid ungraciously;
And the gift of an envious man consumeth the eyes.

19 Learn before thou speak;
And have a care of thy health or ever thou be sick.

20 Before judgement examine thyself;
And in the hour of visitation thou shalt find forgiveness.

21 Humble thyself before thou be sick;
And in the time of sins shew repentance.

22 Let nothing hinder thee to pay thy vow in due time;
And wait not until death to be justified.

23 Before thou makest a vow, prepare thyself;
And be not as a man that tempteth the Lord.

24 Think upon the wrath *that shall be* in the days of the end,
And the time of vengeance, when he turneth away his face.

25 In the days of fulness remember the time of hunger,
And poverty and want in the days of wealth.

26 From morning until evening the time changeth;
And all things are speedy before the Lord.

27 A wise man will fear in everything;
And in days of sinning he will beware of offence.[1]

28 Every man of understanding knoweth wisdom;
And he will give thanks unto him that found her.

29 They that were of understanding in sayings became also wise themselves,
And poured forth apt proverbs.

30 Go not after thy lusts;
And refrain thyself from thine appetites.

31 If thou give fully to thy soul the delight of her desire,
She will make thee [2] the laughing-stock of thine enemies.

32 Make not merry in much luxury;
Neither be tied to the expense thereof.

33 Be not made a beggar by banqueting upon borrowing,
When thou hast nothing in thy purse.[1]

19 A workman that is a drunkard shall not become rich:
He that despiseth small things shall fall by little and little.

2 Wine and women will make men of understanding to fall away:
And he that cleaveth to harlots will be the more reckless.

3 Moths and worms shall have him to heritage;
And a reckless soul shall be taken away.

4 He that is hasty to trust is light-minded;
And he that sinneth shall offend against his own soul.

5 He that maketh merry in his heart shall be condemned:[1]

6 [3] And he that hateth talk hath the less wickedness.

7 Never repeat what is told thee,
And thou shalt fare never the worse.

8 Whether it be of friend or foe, tell it not;
And unless it is a sin to thee, reveal it not.

9 For he hath heard thee, and observed thee,
And when the time cometh he will hate thee.

10 Hast thou heard a word? let it die with thee:
Be of good courage, it will not burst thee.

11 A fool will travail in pain with a word,
As a woman in labour with a child.

12 As an arrow that sticketh in the [4] flesh of the thigh,
So is a word in a fool's belly.

13 Reprove a friend; it may be he did it not:

[1] The remainder of this verse is omitted by the best authorities.

[2] Or, *a rejoicing to*

[3] The preceding part of this verse is omitted by the best authorities.

[4] Gr. *thigh of flesh.*

And if he did something, that he may do it no more.

14 Reprove thy neighbour; it may be he said it not:

And if he hath said it, that he may not say it again.

15 Reprove a friend; for many times there is slander:

And trust not every word.

16 There is one that slippeth, and not from the heart:

And who is he that hath not sinned with his tongue?

17 Reprove thy neighbour before thou threaten him;

And give place to the law of the Most High.[1]

20 All wisdom is the fear of the Lord;

And in all wisdom is the doing of the law.[2]

22 And the knowledge of wickedness is not wisdom;

And the prudence of sinners is not counsel.

23 There is a wickedness, and the same is abomination;

And there is a fool wanting in wisdom.

24 Better is one that hath small understanding, and feareth,

Than one that hath much prudence, and transgresseth the law.

25 There is an exquisite subtilty, and the same is unjust;

And there is one that perverteth favour [3] to gain a judgement.[4]

26 There is one that doeth wickedly, that hangeth down his head with mourning;

But inwardly he is full of deceit,

27 Bowing down his face, and making as if he were deaf of one ear:

Where he is not known, he will be beforehand with thee.

28 And if for want of power he be hindered from sinning,

If he find opportunity, he will do mischief.

29 A man shall be known by his look,

And one that hath understanding shall be known by his face, when thou meetest him.

30 A man's attire, and [5]grinning laughter,

And gait, shew what he is.

20 There is a reproof that is not comely;

And there is a man that keepeth silence, and he is wise.

2 How good is it to reprove, rather than to be wroth;

And he that maketh confession shall be kept back from hurt.[6]

4 As is the lust of an eunuch to deflower a virgin;

So is he that executeth judgements with violence.

5 There is one that keepeth silence, and is found wise;

And there is one that is hated for his much talk.

6 There is one that keepeth silence, for he hath no answer to make;

And there is that keepeth silence, as knowing his time.

7 A wise man will be silent till his time come;

But the braggart and fool will overpass his time.

8 He that useth many words shall be abhorred;

And he that taketh to himself authority therein shall be hated.

9 There is a prosperity that a man findeth in misfortunes;

And there is a gain that turneth to loss.

10 There is a gift that shall not profit thee;

And there is a gift whose recompense is double.

11 There is an abasement because of glory;

And there is that hath lifted up his head from a low estate.

12 There is that buyeth much for a little,

And payeth for it again sevenfold.

13 He that is wise in words shall make himself beloved;

But the pleasantries of fools shall be wasted.

14 The gift of a fool shall not profit thee [7];

For his eyes are many instead of one.

15 He will give little, and upbraid much;

And he will open his mouth like a crier:

To-day he will lend, and to-morrow he will ask it again:

Such an one is a hateful man.

16 The fool will say, I have no friend,

And I have no thanks for my good deeds;

They that eat my bread are of evil tongue.

17 How oft, and of how many, shall he be laughed to scorn![8]

18 A slip on a pavement is better than a slip with the tongue;

So the fall of the wicked shall come speedily.

19 A man without grace is as a tale out of season:

It will be continually in the mouth of the ignorant.

20 A [9] wise sentence from a fool's mouth will be rejected;

For he will not speak it in its season.

21 There is that is hindered from sinning through want;

And when he taketh rest, he shall not be troubled.

22 There is that destroyeth his soul through bashfulness;

And by a foolish countenance he will destroy it.

Margin notes:

[1] Verses 18 and 19 are omitted by the best authorities.

[2] The remainder of verse 20, and verse 21, are omitted by the best authorities.

[3] Gr. to bring to light.

[4] The remainder of this verse is omitted by the best authorities.

[5] Gr. laughter of the teeth.

[6] Verse 3 is omitted by the best authorities.

[7] A line of this verse is here omitted by the best authorities.

[8] The latter part of verse 17 is omitted by the best authorities.

[9] Gr. parable.

23 There is that for bashfulness promis-
eth to his friend;
And he maketh him his enemy for
nothing.

24 A lie is a foul blot in a man:
It will be continually in the mouth of
the ignorant.
25 A thief is better than a man that is
continually lying:
But they both shall inherit destruction.
26 The disposition of a liar is dishonour;
And his shame is with him continually.

27 He that is wise in words shall advance himself;
And one that is prudent will please
great men.
28 He that tilleth his land shall raise his
heap high;
And he that pleaseth great men shall
get pardon for iniquity.
29 Presents and gifts blind the eyes of
the wise,
And as a muzzle on the mouth, turn
away reproofs.
30 Wisdom that is hid, and treasure
that is out of sight,
What profit is in them both?
31 Better is a man that hideth his folly
Than a man that hideth his wisdom.[1]

21 My son, hast thou sinned? add no
more thereto;
And make supplication for thy former
sins.
2 Flee from sin as from the face of a
serpent;
For if thou draw nigh it will bite
thee:
The teeth thereof are the teeth of a
lion,
Slaying the souls of men.
3 All iniquity is as a two-edged sword;
Its stroke hath no healing.

4 Terror and violence will lay waste
riches;
So the house of a haughty man shall
be laid waste.
5 Supplication from a poor man's mouth
reacheth to the ears of [2] God,
And his judgement cometh speedily.
6 One that hateth reproof is in the path
of the sinner;
And he that feareth the Lord will turn
again in his heart.
7 He that is mighty in tongue is known
afar off:
But the man of understanding knoweth when he slippeth.

8 He that buildeth his house with other
men's money
Is like one that gathereth himself
stones against winter.
9 The congregation of wicked men is as
tow wrapped together;

And the end of them is a flame of
fire.
10 The way of sinners is made smooth
with stones;
And at the last end thereof is the pit
of Hades.

11 He that keepeth the law becometh
master of the intent thereof;
And the end of the fear of the Lord is
wisdom.
12 He that is not clever will not be instructed;
And there is a cleverness which maketh bitterness to abound.
13 The knowledge of a wise man shall be
made to abound as a flood;
And his counsel as a fountain of life.
14 The inward parts of a fool are like a
broken vessel;
And he will hold no knowledge.

15 If a man of knowledge hear a wise
word,
He will commend it, and add unto
it:
The dissolute man heareth it, and it
displeaseth him,
And he putteth it away behind his
back.
16 The discourse of a fool is like a burden
in the way;
But grace shall be found on the lips of
the wise.
17 The mouth of the prudent man shall
be sought for in the congregation;
And they will ponder his words in
their heart.

18 As a house that is destroyed, so is wisdom to a fool;
And the knowledge of an unwise man
is *as* [3] talk without sense.
19 Instruction is *as* fetters on the feet of
an unwise man,
And as manacles on the right hand.
20 A fool lifteth up his voice with laughter;
But a clever man will scarce smile
quietly.
21 Instruction is to a prudent man as an
ornament of gold,
And as a bracelet upon his right arm.
22 The foot of a fool is soon in *another
man's* house;
But a man of experience will be
ashamed of entering.
23 A foolish man peepeth in from the
door of *another man's* house;
But a man that is instructed will
stand without.
24 It is a want of instruction in a man to
listen at the door;
But the prudent man will be grieved
with the disgrace.
25 [4] The lips of strangers will be grieved
at these things;
But the words of prudent men will be
weighed in the balance.

26 The heart of fools is in their mouth;
  But the mouth of wise men is their heart.
27 When the ungodly curseth Satan,
  He curseth his own soul.
28 A whisperer defileth his own soul,
  And shall be hated wheresoever he sojourneth.

22 A slothful man is compared to a stone that is defiled;
  And every one will hiss him out in his disgrace.
2 A slothful man is compared to the filth of a dunghill:
  Every man that taketh it up will shake out his hand.
3 A father hath shame in having begotten an uninstructed *son*;
  And a *foolish* daughter is born to his loss.
4 A prudent daughter shall inherit a husband of her own;
  And she that bringeth shame is the grief of him that begat her.
5 She that is bold bringeth shame upon father and husband;
  And she shall be despised of them both.
6 Unseasonable discourse is *as* music in mourning;
  But stripes and correction are wisdom at every season.

7 He that teacheth a fool is *as* one that glueth a potsherd together;
  Even as one that waketh a sleeper out of a deep sleep.
8 He that discourseth to a fool is *as* one discoursing to a man that slumbereth;
  And at the end he will say, What is it?[1]
11 Weep for the dead, for light hath failed *him*;
  And weep for a fool, for understanding hath failed *him*:
  Weep more sweetly for the dead, because he hath found rest;
  But the life of the fool is worse than death.
12 Seven days are *the days of* mourning for the dead;
  But for a fool and an ungodly man, all the days of his life.

13 Talk not much with a foolish man,
  And go not to one that hath no understanding:
  Beware of him, lest thou have trouble;
  And *so* thou shalt not be [2]defiled in his onslaught:
  Turn aside from him, and thou shalt find rest;
  And *so* thou shalt not be wearied in his madness.
14 What shall be heavier than lead?

And what is the name thereof, but a fool?
15 Sand, and salt, and a mass of iron, is easier to bear,
  Than a man without understanding.

16 Timber girt and bound into a building shall not be loosed with shaking:
  So a heart established in due season on well advised counsel shall not be afraid.
17 A heart settled upon a thoughtful understanding
  Is as an ornament of plaister on a polished wall.
18 Pales set on a high place will not stand against the wind:
  So a fearful heart in the imagination of a fool will not stand against any fear.

19 He that pricketh the eye will make tears to fall;
  And he that pricketh the heart maketh it to shew feeling.
20 Whoso casteth a stone at birds frayeth them away;
  And he that upbraideth a friend will dissolve friendship.
21 If thou hast drawn a sword against a friend, despair not;
  For there may be a returning.
22 If thou hast opened thy mouth against a friend, fear not;
  For there may be a reconciling;
  Except it be for upbraiding, and arrogance, and disclosing of a secret, and a treacherous blow;
  For these things every friend will flee.

23 Gain trust with thy neighbour in his poverty,
  That in his prosperity thou mayest have gladness:
  Abide stedfast unto him in the time of his affliction,
  That thou mayest be heir with him in his inheritance.[3]
24 Before fire is the vapour and smoke of a furnace;
  So revilings before bloodshed.
25 I will not be ashamed to shelter a friend;
  And I will not hide myself from his face:
26 And if any evil happen unto me because of him,
  Every one that heareth it will beware of him.

27 Who shall set a watch over my mouth,
  And a seal of shrewdness upon my lips,
  That I fall not from it, and that my tongue destroy me not?
23 O Lord, Father and Master of my life,
  Abandon me not to their counsel:
  Suffer me not to fall by them.

[1] Verses 9 and 10 are omitted by the best authorities.

[2] Or, *defiled: in his onslaught turn*

[3] The remainder of this verse is omitted by the best authorities.

2 Who will set scourges over my thought,
And a discipline of wisdom over mine heart?
That they spare me not for mine ignorances,
And *my heart* pass not by their sins :
3 That mine ignorances be not multiplied,
And my sins abound not;
And I shall fall before mine adversaries,
And mine enemy rejoice over me.[1]
4 O Lord, Father and God of my life,
Give me not a [2] proud look,[1]
5 And turn away concupiscence from me.[1]
6 Let not [3] greediness and chambering overtake me;
And give me not over to a shameless mind.

7 Hear ye, my children, the discipline of the mouth;
And he that keepeth it shall not be taken.
8 The sinner shall be [4] overtaken in his lips ;
And the reviler and the proud man shall stumble therein.
9 Accustom not thy mouth to an oath;
And be not accustomed to the naming of the Holy One.
10 For as a servant that is continually scourged shall not lack a bruise,
So he also that sweareth and nameth *God* continually shall not be cleansed from sin.
11 A man of many oaths shall be filled with iniquity ;
And the scourge shall not depart from his house :
If he shall offend, his sin shall be upon him;
And if he disregard it, he hath sinned doubly ;
And if he hath sworn in vain, he shall not be justified ;
For his house shall be filled with calamities.
12 There is a manner of speech that is clothed about with death :
Let it not be found in the heritage of Jacob ;
For all these things shall be far from the godly,
And they shall not wallow in sins.
13 Accustom not thy mouth to gross rudeness,
For therein is the word of sin.
14 Remember thy father and thy mother,
For thou sittest in the midst of great men ;
That thou be not forgetful before them,
And become a fool by thy custom ;
So shalt thou wish that thou hadst not been born,
And curse the day of thy nativity.

15 A man that is accustomed to words of reproach
Will not be corrected all the days of his life.

16 Two sorts *of men* multiply sins,
And the third will bring wrath :
A hot mind, as a burning fire, will not be quenched till it be consumed :
A fornicator in the body of his flesh will never cease till he hath [5] burned out the fire.
17 All bread is sweet to a fornicator :
He will not leave off till he die.
18 A man that goeth astray from his own bed,
Saying in his heart, Who seeth me ?
Darkness is round about me, and the walls hide me,
And no man seeth me; of whom am I afraid ?
The Most High will not remember my sins ;
19 — And the eyes of men are his terror,
And he knoweth not that the eyes of the Lord are ten thousand times brighter than the sun,
Beholding all the ways of men,
And looking into secret places.
20 All things were known unto him or ever they were created ;
And in like manner also after they were perfected.
21 This man shall be punished in the streets of the city ;
And where he suspected not he shall be taken.
22 So also a wife that leaveth her husband,
And bringeth in an heir by a stranger.
23 For first, she was disobedient in the law of the Most High ;
And secondly, she trespassed against her own husband ;
And thirdly, she played the adulteress in whoredom,
And brought in children by a stranger.
24 She shall be brought out into the congregation ;
And upon her children shall there be visitation.
25 Her children shall not spread into roots,
And her branches shall bear no fruit.
26 She shall leave her memory for a curse ;
And her reproach shall not be blotted out.
27 And they that are left behind shall know that there is nothing better than the fear of the Lord,
And nothing sweeter than to take heed unto the commandments of the Lord.[6]

24 Wisdom shall praise [7]herself,
And shall glory in the midst of her people.
2 In the congregation of the Most High shall she open her mouth,

---

Side notes:

[1] The remainder of this verse is omitted by the best authorities.

[2] Gr. *lifting up of eyes.*

[3] Gr. *appetite or the belly.*

[4] Most authorities read *left.*

[5] Or, *made a fire blaze up*

[6] Verse 28 is omitted by the best authorities

[7] Gr. *her own soul.*

And glory in the presence of his power.

3 I came forth from the mouth of the Most High,
And covered the earth as a mist.

4 I dwelt in high places,
And my throne is in the pillar of the cloud.

5 Alone I compassed the circuit of heaven,
And walked in the depth of the abyss.

6 In the waves of the sea, and in all the earth,
And in every people and nation, I got a possession.

7 With all these I sought rest;
And in whose inheritance shall I lodge?

8 Then the Creator of all things gave me a commandment;
And he that created me made my tabernacle to rest,
And said, Let thy tabernacle be in Jacob,
And thine inheritance in Israel.

9 He created me from the beginning before the world;
And to the end I shall not fail.

10 In the holy tabernacle I ministered before him;
And so was I established in Sion. .

11 In the beloved city likewise he gave me rest;
And in Jerusalem was my authority.

12 And I took root in a people that was glorified,
Even in the portion of the Lord's own inheritance.

13 I was exalted like a cedar in Libanus,
And as a cypress tree on the mountains of Hermon.

14 I was exalted like a palm tree on the sea shore,
And as rose plants in Jericho,
And as a fair olive tree in the plain;
And I was exalted as a plane tree.

15 As cinnamon and aspalathus, I have given a scent of perfumes;
And as choice myrrh, I spread abroad a pleasant odour;
As ¹ galbanum, and onyx, and stacte,
And as the fume of frankincense in the tabernacle.

16 As the terebinth I stretched out my branches;
And my branches are branches of glory and grace.

17 As the vine I put forth grace;
And my flowers are the fruit of glory and riches.²

19 Come unto me, ye that are desirous of me,
And be ye filled with my produce.

20 For my memorial is sweeter than honey,
And mine inheritance than the honeycomb.

21 They that eat me shall yet be hungry;
And they that drink me shall yet be thirsty.

22 He that obeyeth me shall not be ashamed;
And they that work in me shall not do amiss.

23 All these things are the book of the covenant of the Most High God,
Even the law which Moses commanded us for a heritage unto the assemblies of Jacob.³

25 It is he that maketh wisdom abundant, as Pishon,
And as Tigris in the days of new *fruits*;

26 That maketh understanding full as Euphrates,
And as Jordan in the days of harvest;

27 That maketh instruction to shine forth as the light,
As Gihon in the days of vintage.

28 The first man knew her not perfectly;
And in like manner the last hath not traced her out.

29 For her thoughts are filled from the sea,
And her counsels from the great deep.

30 And I came out as a ⁴ stream from a river,
And as a conduit into a garden.

31 I said, I will water my garden,
And will water abundantly my garden bed;
And, lo, my stream became a river,
And my river became a sea.

32 I will yet bring instruction to light as the morning,
And will make ⁵ these things to shine forth afar off.

33 I will yet pour out doctrine as prophecy,
And leave it unto generations of ages.

34 Behold that I have not laboured for myself only,
But for all them that diligently seek her.

25 In three things I was beautified,
And stood up beautiful before the Lord and men:
The concord of brethren, and friendship of neighbours,
And a woman and her husband that walk together in agreement.

2 But three sorts *of men* my soul hateth,
And I am greatly offended at their life:
A poor man that is haughty, and a rich man that is a liar,
And an old man that is an adulterer lacking understanding.

3 In *thy* youth thou hast not gathered,
And how shouldest thou find in thine old age?

4 How beautiful a thing is judgement for gray hairs,
And for elders to know counsel!

See Exodus xxx. 34.

² Verse 18 is omitted by the best authorities.

³ Verse 24 is omitted by the best authorities

⁴ Gr. *canal.*

⁵ Gr. *them.*

5 How beautiful is the wisdom of old men,
And thought and counsel to men that are in honour!
6 Much experience is the crown of old men;
And their glorying is the fear of the Lord.

7 There be nine things that I have thought of, and in mine heart counted happy;
And the tenth I will utter with my tongue:
A man that hath joy of his children;
A man that liveth and looketh upon the fall of his enemies:
8 Happy is he that dwelleth with a wife of understanding;
And he that hath not slipped with his tongue;
And he that hath not served a man that is unworthy of him:
9 Happy is he that hath found prudence;
And he that discourseth in the ears of them that listen.
10 How great is he that hath found wisdom!
Yet is there none above him that feareth the Lord.
11 The fear of the Lord passeth all things:
He that holdeth it, to whom shall he be likened?[1]

13 *Give me* any plague but the plague of the heart;
And any wickedness but the wickedness of a woman;
14 Any calamity, but a calamity from them that hate me;
And any vengeance, but the vengeance of enemies.
15 There is no head above the head of a serpent;
And there is no wrath above the wrath of an enemy.

16 I will rather dwell with a lion and a dragon,
Than keep house with a wicked woman.
17 The wickedness of a woman changeth her look,
And darkeneth her countenance as a bear doth.
18 Her husband shall sit at meat among his neighbours,
And when he heareth it he sigheth bitterly.
19 All malice is but little to the malice of a woman:
Let the portion of a sinner fall on her.
20 *As* the going up a sandy way *is* to the feet of the aged,
So is a wife full of words to a quiet man.
21 Throw not thyself upon the beauty of a woman;

And desire not a woman for her beauty.
22 There is anger, and impudence, and great reproach,
If a woman maintain her husband.
23 A wicked woman is abasement of heart,
And sadness of countenance, and a wounded heart:
A woman that will not make her husband happy
Is *as* hands that hang down, and palsied knees.
24 From a woman *was* the beginning of sin;
And because of her we all die.
25 Give not water an outlet;
Neither to a wicked woman freedom of speech.
26 If she go not [2] as thou wouldest have her,
Cut her off from thy flesh.[3]

26 Happy is the husband of a good wife;
And the number of his days shall be twofold.
2 A brave woman rejoiceth her husband;
And he shall fulfil his years in peace.
3 A good wife is a good portion:
She shall be given in the portion of such as fear the Lord.
4 Whether a man be rich or poor,
A good heart *maketh* at all times a cheerful countenance.

5 Of three things my heart was afraid;
And concerning the fourth [4] kind I made supplication:
The slander of a city, and the assembly of a multitude, and a false accusation:
All these are more grievous than death.
6 A grief of heart and sorrow is a woman that is jealous of *another* woman,
And the scourge of a tongue communicating to all.
7 A wicked woman is *as* a yoke of oxen shaken to and fro:
He that taketh hold of her is as one that graspeth a scorpion.
8 A drunken woman *causeth* great wrath;
And she will not cover her own shame.
9 The whoredom of a woman is in the lifting up of her eyes;
And it shall be known by her eyelids.
10 Keep strict watch on a headstrong daughter,
Lest she find liberty for herself, and use it.
11 Look well after an impudent eye;
And marvel not if it trespass against thee.
12 She will open her mouth, as a thirsty traveller,

97

And drink of every water that is near:
At every post will she sit down,
And open her quiver against *any*
arrow.

13 The grace of a wife will delight her
husband;
And her knowledge will fatten his
bones.
14 A silent woman is a gift of the Lord;
And there is nothing so much worth
as a well-instructed soul.
15 A shamefast woman is grace upon
grace;
And there is no [1] price worthy of a
continent soul.
16 As the sun when it ariseth in the
highest places of the Lord,
So is the beauty of a good wife in the
ordering of [2] a man's house.
17 As the lamp that shineth upon the
holy candlestick,
So is the beauty of the face in ripe age.
18 As the golden pillars are upon a base
of silver,
So are beautiful feet with the breasts
of one that is stedfast.[3]

28 For two things my heart is grieved;
And for the third anger cometh upon
me:
A man of war that suffereth for
poverty;
And men of understanding that are
counted as refuse:
One that turneth back from righteousness to sin;
The Lord shall prepare him for the
sword.

29 A merchant shall hardly keep himself from wrong doing;
And a huckster shall not be acquitted
of sin.

27 Many have sinned for a thing indifferent;
And he that seeketh to multiply *gain*
will turn his eye away.
2 A nail will stick fast between the
joinings of stones;
And sin will [4] thrust itself in between
buying and selling.
3 Unless *a man* hold on diligently in
the fear of the Lord,
His house shall soon be overthrown.

4 In the shaking of a sieve, the refuse
remaineth;
So the filth of man in his reasoning.
5 The furnace will prove the potter's
vessels;
And the trial of a man is in his
reasoning.
6 The fruit of a tree declareth the husbandry thereof;
So is the utterance of the thought of
the heart of a man.
7 Praise no man before *thou hearest*
him reason;
For this is the trial of men.

[1] Gr.
weight.

[2] Gr. *his.*

[3] Verses
19-27 are
omitted
by the
best au-
thorities.

[4] Gr.
rub.

8 If thou followest righteousness, thou
shalt obtain her,
And put her on, as a long robe of
glory.
9 Birds will resort unto their like;
And truth will return unto them that
practise her.
10 The lion lieth in wait for prey;
So doth sin for them that work iniquity.
11 The discourse of a godly man is always wisdom:
But the foolish man changeth as the
moon.
12 Among men void of understanding
observe the opportunity;
But stay continually among the
thoughtful.
13 The discourse of fools is an offence;
And their laughter is in the wantonness of sin.
14 The talk of a man of many oaths will
make the hair stand upright;
And their strife maketh one stop his
ears.
15 The strife of the proud is a shedding
of blood;
And their reviling of each other is a
grievous thing to hear.

16 He that revealeth secrets destroyeth
credit,
And shall not find a friend to his
mind.
17 Love a friend, and keep faith with
him:
But if thou reveal his secrets,
Thou shalt not pursue after him;
18 For as a man hath destroyed his
enemy,
So hast thou destroyed the friendship
of thy neighbour.
19 And as a bird which thou hast loosed
out of thy hand,
So hast thou let thy neighbour go, and
thou wilt not catch him again:
20 Pursue him not, for he is gone far
away,
And hath escaped as a gazelle out of
the snare.
21 For a wound may be bound up, and
after reviling there may be a reconcilement;
But he that revealeth secrets hath
lost hope.

22 One that winketh with the eye contriveth evil things;
And no man will remove him from it.
23 When thou art present, he will speak
sweetly,
And will admire thy words;
But afterward he will writhe his
mouth,
And set a trap *for thee* in thy words.
24 I have hated many things, but nothing like him;
And the Lord will hate him.

25 One that casteth a stone on high casteth it on his own head;
And a deceitful stroke will open wounds.
26 He that diggeth a pit shall fall into it;
And he that setteth a snare shall be taken therein.
27 He that doeth evil things, they shall roll upon him,
And he shall not know whence they have come to him.
28 Mockery and reproach are from the haughty;
And vengeance, as a lion, shall lie in wait for him.
29 They that rejoice at the fall of the godly shall be taken in a snare;
And anguish shall consume them before they die.

30 Wrath and anger, these also are abominations;
And a sinful man shall possess them.
28 He that taketh vengeance shall find vengeance from the Lord;
And he will surely make firm his sins.
2 Forgive thy neighbour the hurt that he hath done *thee*;
And then thy sins shall be pardoned when thou prayest.
3 Man cherisheth anger against man;
And doth he seek healing from the Lord?
4 Upon a man like himself he hath no mercy;
And doth he make supplication for his own sins?
5 He being himself flesh nourisheth wrath:
Who shall make atonement for his sins?
6 Remember thy last end, and cease from enmity:
Remember corruption and death, and abide in the commandments.
7 Remember the commandments, and be not wroth with thy neighbour;
And *remember* the covenant of the Highest, and wink at ignorance.

8 Abstain from strife, and thou shalt diminish thy sins:
For a passionate man will kindle strife;
9 And a man that is a sinner will trouble friends,
And will make debate among them that be at peace.
10 ¹ As is the fuel of the fire, so will it burn;
And as the stoutness of the strife is, *so* will it burn:
As is the strength of the man, *so* will be his wrath;
And as is his wealth, *so* will he exalt his anger.
11 A contention begun in haste kindleth a fire;

¹ The order of the lines in this verse is uncertain.

And a hasty fighting sheddeth blood.
12 If thou blow a spark, it shall burn;
And if thou spit upon it, it shall be quenched:
And both these shall come out of thy mouth.

13 Curse the whisperer and double-tongued:
For he hath destroyed many that were at peace.
14 A third person's tongue hath shaken many,
And dispersed them from nation to nation;
And it hath pulled down strong cities,
And overthrown the houses of great men.
15 A third person's tongue hath cast out brave women,
And deprived them of their labours.
16 He that hearkeneth unto it shall not find rest,
Nor shall he dwell quietly.
17 The stroke of a whip maketh a mark in the flesh;
But the stroke of a tongue will break bones. .
18 Many have fallen by the edge of the sword:
Yet not so many as they that have fallen because of the tongue.
19 Happy is he that is sheltered from it,
That hath not passed through the wrath thereof;
That hath not drawn its yoke,
And hath not been bound with its bands.
20 For the yoke thereof is a yoke of iron,
And the bands thereof are bands of brass.
21 The death thereof is an evil death;
And Hades were better than it.
22 It shall not have rule over godly men;
And they shall not be burned in its flame.
23 They that forsake the Lord shall fall into it;
And it shall burn among them, and shall not be quenched:
It shall be sent forth upon them as a lion;
And as a leopard it shall destroy them.
24 Look that thou hedge thy possession about with thorns;
Bind up thy silver and thy gold;
25 And make a balance and a weight for thy words;
And make a door and a bar for thy mouth.
26 Take heed lest thou slip therein;
Lest thou fall before one that lieth in wait.

29 He that sheweth mercy will lend unto his neighbour;
And he that strengtheneth him with

his hand keepeth the commandments.

2 Lend to thy neighbour in time of his need;
And pay thou thy neighbour again in due season.

3 Confirm thy word, and keep faith with him;
And at all seasons thou shalt find what thou needest.

4 Many have reckoned a loan as a windfall,
And have given trouble to those that helped them.

5 Till he hath received, he will kiss a man's hands;
And for his neighbour's money he will speak submissly:
And when payment is due, he will prolong the time,
And return words of heaviness, and complain of [1] the times.

6 If he prevail, he shall hardly receive the half;
And he will count it as a windfall:
If not, he hath deprived him of his money,
And he hath gotten him for an enemy without cause:
He will pay him with cursings and railings;
And for honour he will pay him disgrace.

7 [2] Many on account of *men's* ill-dealing have turned away;
They have feared to be defrauded for nought.

8 Howbeit with a man in poor estate be longsuffering;
And let him not wait for *thine* alms.

9 Help a poor man for the commandment's sake;
And according to his need send him not empty away.

10 Lose *thy* money for a brother and a friend;
And let it not rust under the stone to be lost.

11 Bestow thy treasure according to the commandments of the Most High;
And it shall profit thee more than gold.

12 Shut up alms in thy store-chambers;
And it shall deliver thee out of all affliction:

13 It shall fight for thee against thine enemy
Better than a mighty shield and a ponderous spear.

14 A good man will be surety for his neighbour;
And he that hath lost shame will fail him.

15 Forget not the good offices of thy surety;
For he hath given his life for thee.

16 A sinner will overthrow the good estate of his surety;

17 And he that is of an unthankful mind will fail him that delivered him.

18 Suretiship hath undone many that were prospering,
And shaken them as a wave of the sea:
Mighty men hath it driven from their homes;
And they wandered among strange nations.

19 A sinner that falleth into suretiship,
And undertaketh contracts for work, shall fall into lawsuits.

20 Help thy neighbour according to thy power,
And take heed to thyself that thou fall not *to the same.*

21 The chief thing for life is water, and bread,
And a garment, and a house to cover shame.

22 Better is the life of a poor man under a shelter of logs,
Than sumptuous fare in another man's house.

23 With little or with much, be well satisfied.[3]

24 It is a miserable life to go from house to house:
And where thou art a sojourner, thou shalt not *dare to* open thy mouth.

25 Thou shalt entertain, and give to drink, and have no thanks:
And besides this thou shalt hear bitter words.

26 Come hither, thou sojourner, furnish a table,
And if thou hast aught in thy hand, feed me with it.

27 Go forth, thou sojourner, from the face of honour;
My brother is come to be my guest; I have need of my house.

28 These things are grievous to a man of understanding;
The upbraiding of house-room, and the reproaching of the moneylender.

30 He that loveth his son will continue to lay stripes upon him,
That he may have joy of him in the end.

2 He that chastiseth his son shall have profit of him,
And shall glory of him among his acquaintance.

3 He that teacheth his son shall provoke his enemy to jealousy;
And before friends he shall rejoice of him.

4 His father dieth, and is as though he had not died;
For he hath left one behind him like himself.

5 In his life, he saw and rejoiced *in him*;
And when he died, he sorrowed not:

6 He left behind him an avenger against his enemies,
And one to requite kindness to his friends.

Side notes:

[1] Gr. the season.

[2] Some ancient authorities read *Many therefore.*

[3] The remainder of this verse is omitted by the best authorities.

7 He that maketh too much of his son shall bind up his wounds;
And his heart will be troubled at every cry.

8 An unbroken horse becometh stubborn;
And a son left at large becometh headstrong.

9 Cocker thy child, and he shall make thee afraid:
Play with him, and he will grieve thee.

10 Laugh not with him, lest thou have sorrow with him;
And thou shalt gnash thy teeth in the end.

11 Give him no liberty in his youth,
¹ And wink not at his follies.

12 ¹ Bow down his neck in his youth,
And beat him on the sides while he is a child,
Lest he wax stubborn, and be disobedient unto thee;
¹ And there shall be sorrow to thy soul.

13 Chastise thy son, and take pains with him,
Lest his shameless behaviour be an offence unto thee.

14 Better is a poor man, being sound and strong of constitution,
Than a rich man that is plagued in his body.

15 Health and a good constitution are better than all gold;
And a strong body than wealth without measure.

16 There is no riches better than health of body;
And there is no gladness above the joy of the heart.

17 Death is better than a bitter life,
² And ³ eternal rest than a continual sickness.

18 Good things poured out upon a mouth that is closed
Are as messes of meat laid upon a grave.

19 What doth an offering profit an idol?
For neither shall it eat nor smell:
So is he that is afflicted of the Lord,

20 Seeing with his eyes and groaning,
As an eunuch embracing a virgin and groaning.

21 Give not over thy soul to sorrow;
And afflict not thyself in thine own counsel.

22 Gladness of heart is the life of a man;
And the joyfulness of a man is length of days.

23 Love thine own soul, and comfort thy heart:
And remove sorrow far from thee;
For sorrow hath destroyed many,
And there is no profit therein.

24 Envy and wrath shorten a man's days;
And care bringeth old age before the time.

25 A cheerful and good heart
Will have a care of his meat and diet.

31 Wakefulness that cometh of riches consumeth the flesh,
And the anxiety thereof putteth away sleep.

2 Wakeful anxiety will crave slumber;
And ⁴ in a sore disease sleep will be broken.

3 A rich man toileth in gathering money together;
And when he resteth, he is filled with his good things.

4 A poor man toileth in lack of substance;
And when he resteth, he becometh needy.

5 He that loveth gold shall not be justified;
And he that followeth destruction shall himself have his fill of it.

6 Many have been given over to ruin for the sake of gold;
And their perdition ⁵ meeteth them face to face.

7 It is a stumblingblock unto them that sacrifice unto it;
And every fool shall be taken therewith.

8 Blessed is the rich that is found without blemish,
And that goeth not after gold.

9 Who is he? and we will call him blessed:
For wonderful things hath he done among his people.

10 Who hath been tried thereby, and found perfect?
Then let him glory.
Who hath had the power to transgress, and hath not transgressed?
And to do evil, and hath not done it?

11 His goods shall be made sure,
And the congregation shall declare his alms.

12 Sittest thou at a great table? ⁶ be not greedy upon it,
And say not, Many are the things upon it.

13 Remember that an evil eye is a wicked thing:
What hath been created more evil than an eye?
Therefore it sheddeth tears from every face.

14 Stretch not thine hand whithersoever it looketh,
And thrust not thyself with it into the dish.

15 Consider thy neighbour's liking by thine own;
And be discreet in every point.

16 Eat, as becometh a man, those things which are set before thee;
And eat not greedily, lest thou be hated.

17 Be first to leave off for manners' sake;
And be not insatiable, lest thou offend.

Margin notes (left column):

¹ These three lines are absent from the oldest MSS.

² The oldest MSS. omit And eternal rest.
³ Gr. age-long rest.

Margin notes (right column):

⁴ This appears to be the meaning; but the Greek text here is probably corrupt.

⁵ Or, cometh to pass in their faces

⁶ Gr. open not thy throat upon it

18 And if thou sittest among many,
Reach not out thy hand before them.

19 How sufficient to a well-mannered
man is a very little,
And he doth not breathe hard upon
his bed.
20 Healthy sleep cometh of moderate
eating;
He riseth early, and his wits are with
him:
The pain of wakefulness, and colic,
And griping, are with an insatiable
man.
21 And if thou hast been forced to eat,
Rise up in the midst thereof, and thou
shalt have rest.
22 Hear me, my son, and despise me not,
And at the last thou shalt find my
words *true*:
In all thy works be quick,
And no disease shall come unto thee.

23 Him that is liberal of his meat the
lips shall bless;
And the testimony of his excellence
shall be believed.
24 Him that is a niggard of his meat the
city shall murmur at;
And the testimony of his niggardness
shall be sure.

25 Shew not thyself valiant in wine;
For wine hath destroyed many.
26 The furnace proveth the temper *of
steel* by dipping;
So doth wine *prove* hearts in the quar-
relling of the proud.
27 Wine is as good as life to men,
If thou drink it in its measure:
What life is there to a man that is
without wine?
And it hath been created to make
men glad.
28 Wine drunk in season *and* to satisfy
Is joy of heart, and gladness of soul:
29 Wine drunk largely is bitterness of
soul,
With provocation and conflict.
30 Drunkenness increaseth the rage of a
fool unto his hurt;
It diminisheth strength, and addeth
wounds.

31 Rebuke not thy neighbour at a banquet of wine,
Neither set him at nought in his
mirth:
Speak not unto him a word of reproach,
And press not upon him by asking
back *a debt.*
32 Have they made thee ruler *of a
feast*?
Be not lifted up,
Be thou among them as one of them;
Take thought for them, and so sit
down.
2 And when thou hast done all thy
office, take thy place,

That thou mayest be gladdened on
their account,
And receive a crown for thy well ordering.

3 Speak, thou that art the elder, for it
becometh thee, *but* with sound
knowledge;
And hinder not music.
4 Pour not out talk where there is a
performance of music,
And display not thy wisdom out of
season.
5 *As* a signet of carbuncle in a setting
of gold,
So is a concert of music in a banquet
of wine.
6 *As* a signet of emerald in a work of
gold,
So is a strain of music with pleasant
wine.

7 Speak, young man, if there be need of
thee;
Yet scarcely if thou be twice asked.
8 Sum up thy speech, many things in
few words;
Be as one that knoweth and yet holdeth his tongue.
9 *If thou be* among great men, behave
not as their equal;
And when another is speaking, make
not much babbling.
10 Before thunder speedeth lightning;
And before a shamefast man favour
shall go forth.
11 Rise up betimes, and be not the last;
Get thee home quickly and loiter
not:
12 There take thy pastime, and do what
is in thy heart;
And sin not by proud speech:
13 And for these things bless him that
made thee,
And giveth thee to drink freely of his
good things.

14 He that feareth the Lord will receive
his discipline;
And they that seek *him* early shall
find favour.
15 He that seeketh the law shall be filled
therewith:
But the hypocrite shall stumble
thereat.
16 They that fear the Lord shall find
judgement,
And shall kindle righteous acts as a
light.
17 A sinful man shunneth reproof,
And will find a judgement according
to his will.

18 A man of counsel will not neglect a
thought;
A strange and proud man will not
crouch in fear,
Even after he hath done a thing by
himself without counsel.
19 Do nothing without counsel;

And when thou hast once done, repent not.

20 Go not in a way of conflict;
And stumble not in stony places.

21 Be not confident in a [1] smooth way.

22 And beware of thine own children.

23 In every work trust thine own soul;
For this is the keeping of the commandments.

24 He that believeth the law giveth heed
to the commandment;
And he that trusteth in the Lord shall
suffer no loss.

33 There shall no evil happen unto him
that feareth the Lord;
But in temptation once and again will
he deliver him.

2 A wise man will not hate the law;
But he that is a hypocrite therein is
as a ship in a storm.

3 A man of understanding will put his
trust in the law;
And the law is faithful unto him, as
when one asketh at the oracle.

4 Prepare *thy* speech, and so shalt thou
be heard;
Bind up instruction, and make thine
answer.

5 The heart of a fool is *as* a cartwheel;
And his thoughts like a rolling axletree.

6 A stallion horse is as a mocking
friend;
He neigheth under every one that
sitteth upon him.

7 Why doth one day excel another,
When all the light of every day in the
year is of the sun?

8 By the knowledge of the Lord they
were distinguished;
And he varied seasons and feasts:

9 Some of them he exalted and hallowed,
And some of them hath he made ordinary days.

10 And all men are from the ground,
And Adam was created of earth.

11 In the abundance of his knowledge
the Lord distinguished them,
And made their ways various:

12 Some of them he blessed and exalted,
And some of them he hallowed and
brought nigh to himself:
Some of them he cursed and brought
low,
And overthrew them from their place.

13 As the clay of the potter in his hand,
All his ways are according to his good
pleasure;
So men are in the hand of him that
made them,
To render unto them according to his
judgement.

14 Good is set over against evil,
And life over against death:
So is [2] the sinner over against the
godly.

15 And thus look upon all the works of
the Most High;
Two and two, one against another.

16 And I awaked up last,
As one that gleaneth after the grapegatherers:
By the blessing of the Lord I got
before them,
And filled my winepress as one that
gathereth grapes.

17 Consider that I laboured not for myself alone,
But for all them that seek instruction.

18 Hear me, ye great men of the people,
And hearken with your ears, ye rulers
of the congregation.

19 To son and wife, to brother and
friend,
Give not power over thee while thou
livest;
And give not thy goods to another,
Lest thou repent and make supplication for them *again*.

20 Whilst thou yet livest, and breath is
in thee,
Give not thyself over to anybody.

21 For better it is that thy children
should supplicate thee,
Than that thou shouldest look to the
hand of thy sons.

22 In all thy works keep the upper
hand;
Bring not a stain on thine honour.

23 In the day that thou endest the days
of thy life,
And in the time of death, distribute
thine inheritance.

24 Fodder, a stick, and burdens, for an
ass;
Bread, and discipline, and work, for a
servant.

25 Set thy servant to work, and thou
shalt find rest:
Leave his hands idle, and he will seek
liberty.

26 Yoke and thong will bow the neck:
And for an evil servant there are
racks and tortures.

27 Send him to labour, that he be not
idle;
For idleness teacheth much mischief.

28 Set him to work, as is fit for him;
And if he obey not, make his fetters
heavy.

29 And be not excessive toward any;
And without judgement do nothing.

30 If thou hast a servant, let him be as
thyself,
Because thou hast bought him with
blood.

31 If thou hast a servant, treat him as
thyself;
[3] For as thine own soul wilt thou have
need of him:

[2] A line
of this
verse is
here
omitted
by the
best authorities.

[3] The
Greek
text of
this line
is probably
corrupt.

103

If thou treat him ill, and he depart and run away,
Which way wilt thou go to seek him?

34 Vain and false hopes are for a man void of understanding;
And dreams give wings to fools.

2 As one that catcheth at a shadow, and followeth after the wind,
So is he that setteth his mind on dreams.

3 The vision of dreams is *as* this thing against that,
The likeness of a face over against a face.

4 Of an unclean thing what shall be cleansed?
And of that which is false what shall be true?

5 Divinations, and soothsayings, and dreams, are vain:
And the heart fancieth, as a woman's in travail.

6 If they be not sent from the Most High in *thy* visitation,
Give not thy heart unto them.

7 For dreams have led many astray:
And they have failed by putting their hope in them.

8 Without lying shall the law be accomplished;
And wisdom is perfection to a faithful mouth.

9 A well-instructed man knoweth many things;
And he that hath much experience will declare understanding.

10 He that hath no experience knoweth few things:
But he that hath wandered shall increase *his* skill.

11 In my wandering I have seen many things;
And more than my words is my understanding.

12 Ofttimes was I in danger even unto death;
And I was preserved because of these things.

13 The spirit of those that fear the Lord shall live;
For their hope is upon him that saveth them.

14 Whoso feareth the Lord shall not be afraid, and shall not play the coward;
For he is his hope.

15 Blessed is the soul of him that feareth the Lord:
To whom doth he give heed? and who is his stay?

16 The eyes of the Lord are upon them that love him,
A mighty protection and strong stay,
A cover from the hot blast, and a cover from the noonday,
A guard from stumbling, and a succour from falling.

17 He raiseth up the soul, and enlighteneth the eyes:

He giveth healing, life, and blessing.

18 He that sacrificeth of a thing wrongfully gotten, his offering is made in mockery;
And the mockeries of wicked men are not well-pleasing.

19 The Most High hath no pleasure in the offerings of the ungodly;
Neither is he pacified for sins by the multitude of sacrifices.

20 *As* one that killeth the son before his father's eyes
Is he that bringeth a sacrifice from the goods of the poor.

21 The bread of the needy is the life of the poor:
He that depriveth him thereof is a man of blood.

22 *As* one that slayeth his neighbour is he that taketh away his living;
And *as* a shedder of blood is he that depriveth a hireling of his hire.

23 One building, and another pulling down,
What profit have they had but toil?

24 One praying, and another cursing,
Whose voice will the Lord listen to?

25 He that washeth himself after *touching* a dead body, and toucheth it again,
What profit hath he in his washing?

26 Even so a man fasting for his sins,
And going again, and doing the same;
Who will listen to his prayer?
And what profit hath he in his humiliation?

35 He that keepeth the law multiplieth offerings;
He that taketh heed to the commandments sacrificeth a peace offering.

2 He that requiteth a good turn offereth fine flour;
And he that giveth alms sacrificeth a thank offering.

3 To depart from wickedness is a thing pleasing to the Lord;
And to depart from unrighteousness is a propitiation.

4 See that thou appear not in the presence of the Lord empty.

5 For all these things *are to be done* because of the commandment.

6 The offering of the righteous maketh the altar fat;
And the sweet savour thereof *is* before the Most High.

7 The sacrifice of a righteous man is acceptable;
And the memorial thereof shall not be forgotten.

8 Glorify the Lord with a good eye,
And stint not the firstfruits of thine hands.

9 In every gift shew a cheerful countenance,
And dedicate thy tithe with gladness.

10 Give unto the Most High according as he hath given;
And as thy hand hath found, *give* with a good eye.
11 For the Lord recompenseth,
And he will recompense thee sevenfold.

12 Think not to corrupt with gifts; for he will not receive them:
And set not thy mind on an unrighteous sacrifice;
For the Lord is judge,
And with him is no respect of persons.
13 He will not accept any person against a poor man;
And he will listen to the prayer of him that is wronged.
14 He will in no wise despise the supplication of the fatherless;

Nor the widow, ¹ when she poureth out her tale.
15 Do not the tears of the widow run down her cheek?
And is not her cry against him that hath caused them to fall?
16 He that serveth *God* according to his good pleasure shall be accepted,
And his supplication shall reach unto the clouds.
17 The prayer of the humble pierceth the clouds;
And till it come nigh, he will not be comforted;
And he will not depart, till the Most High shall visit;

And he shall judge ² righteously, and execute judgement.
18 And the Lord will not be slack, neither will he be longsuffering toward them,
Till he have crushed the loins of the unmerciful;
And he shall repay vengeance to the heathen;
Till he have taken away the multitude of the haughty,
And broken in pieces the sceptres of the unrighteous;
19 Till he have rendered to *every* man according to his doings,
And *to* the works of men according to their devices;
Till he have judged the cause of his people;
And he shall make them to rejoice in his mercy.
20 Mercy is seasonable in the time of his afflicting *them*,
As clouds of rain in the time of drought.

36 Have mercy upon us, O Lord the God of all, and behold;
2 And send thy fear upon all the nations: ³
3 Lift up thy hand against the strange nations;
And let them see thy mighty power.

4 As thou wast sanctified in us before them,
So be thou magnified in them before us.
5 And let them know thee, as we also have known thee,
That there is no God but only thou, O God.
6 Shew new signs, and work divers wonders;
Glorify thy hand and thy right arm.
7 Raise up indignation, and pour out wrath;
Take away the adversary, and destroy the enemy.
8 Hasten the time, and remember the oath;
And let them declare thy mighty works.
9 Let him that escapeth be devoured by the rage of fire;
And may they that harm thy people find destruction.
10 Crush the heads of the rulers of the enemies,
That say, There is none but we.
11 Gather all the tribes of Jacob together,

And ⁴ take them for thine inheritance, as from the beginning.
12 O Lord, have mercy upon the people that is called by thy name,
And upon Israel, whom thou didst liken unto a firstborn.
13 Have compassion upon the city of thy sanctuary,
Jerusalem, the place of thy rest.
14 Fill Sion; exalt thine oracles,
And *fill* thy people with thy glory.
15 Give testimony unto those that were thy creatures in the beginning,
And raise up the prophecies that have been in thy name.
16 Give reward unto them that wait for thee:
And men shall put their trust in thy prophets.
17 Hearken, O Lord, to the prayer of thy suppliants,
According to the blessing of Aaron concerning thy people;
And all they that are on the earth shall know

That thou art the Lord, the ⁵ eternal God.

18 The belly will eat any meat;
Yet is one meat better than another.
19 The ⁶ mouth tasteth meats taken in hunting:

So doth an understanding heart false speeches.
20 A froward heart will cause heaviness:
And a man of experience will recompense him.
21 A woman will receive any man;
But one daughter is better than another.
22 The beauty of a woman cheereth the countenance;
And a man desireth nothing so much.

23 If there is on her tongue mercy and
meekness,
Her husband is not like the sons of
men.
24 He that getteth a wife entereth upon
a possession;
A help meet for him, and a pillar of
rest.
25 Where no hedge is, the possession will
be laid waste:
And he that hath no wife will mourn
as he wandereth up and down.
26 For who will trust a nimble robber,
that skippeth from city to city?
Even so *who shall trust* a man that
hath no nest, and lodgeth wheresoever he findeth himself at night-
fall?

37 Every friend will say, I also am his
friend;
But there is a friend, which is only a
friend in name.
2 Is there not a grief in it even unto
death,
When a companion and friend is
turned to enmity?
3 O wicked imagination, whence camest
thou rolling in
To cover the dry land with deceitful-
ness?
4 There is a companion, which rejoiceth
in the gladness of a friend,
But in time of affliction will be against
him.
5 There is a companion, which for the
belly's sake laboureth with his
friend,
In the face of battle will take up the
buckler.
6 Forget not a friend in thy soul;
And be not unmindful of him in thy
riches.

7 Every counsellor extolleth counsel;
But there is that counselleth for himself.
8 Let thy soul beware of a counsellor,
And know thou before what is his
interest
(For he will take counsel for himself);
Lest he cast the lot upon thee,
9 And say unto thee, Thy way is good:
And he will stand over against thee,
to see what shall befall thee.
10 Take not counsel with one that looketh askance at thee;
And hide thy counsel from such as are
jealous of thee.
11 *Take not counsel* with a woman about
her rival;
Neither with a coward about war;
Nor with a merchant about exchange;
Nor with a buyer about selling;
Nor with an envious man about thankfulness;
Nor with an unmerciful man about
kindliness;
Nor with a sluggard about any kind
of work;

Nor with a hireling in thy house about
finishing *his work*;
Nor with an idle servant about much
business:
Give not heed to these in any matter
of counsel.
12 But rather be continually with a godly
man,
Whom thou shalt have known to be a
keeper of the commandments,
Who in his soul is as thine own soul,
And who will grieve with thee, if thou
shalt miscarry.
13 And make the counsel of thy heart to
stand;
For there is none more faithful unto
thee than it.
14 For a man's soul is sometime wont
to bring him tidings,
More than seven watchmen that sit
on high on a watch-tower.
15 And above all this intreat the Most
High,
That he may direct thy way in truth.

16 Let reason be the beginning of every
work,
And let counsel go before every action.
17 As a token of the changing of the heart,
18   four manner of things do rise up,
Good and evil, life and death;
And that which ruleth over them continually is the tongue.
19 There is one that is shrewd *and* the
instructor of many,
And yet is unprofitable to his own
soul.
20 There is *one* that is subtil in words,
and is hated;
He shall be destitute of all food:
21 For grace was not given him from the
Lord;
Because he is deprived of all wisdom.
22 There is one that is wise to his own
soul;
And the fruits of his understanding
are trustworthy in the mouth.
23 A wise man will instruct his own
people;
And the fruits of his understanding
are trustworthy.
24 A wise man shall be filled with blessing;
And all they that see him shall call
him happy.
25 The life of man is numbered by days;
And the days of Israel are innumerable.
26 The wise man shall inherit confidence
among his people,
And his name shall live for ever.

27 My son, prove thy soul in thy life,
And see what is evil for it, and give
not that unto it.
28 For all things are not profitable for
all men,
Neither hath every soul pleasure in
every thing.
29 Be not insatiable in any luxury,

And be not greedy on the things that thou eatest.

30 For in multitude of meats there shall be disease,
And surfeiting shall come nigh unto colic.

31 Because of surfeiting have many perished;
But he that taketh heed shall prolong his life.

38 Honour a physician according to thy need *of him* with the honours due unto him:
For verily the Lord hath created him.

2 For from the Most High cometh healing;
And from the king he shall receive a gift.

3 The skill of the physician shall lift up his head;
And in the sight of great men he shall be admired.

4 The Lord created medicines out of the earth;
And a prudent man will have no disgust at them.

5 Was not water made sweet with wood,
That the virtue thereof might be known?

6 And he gave men skill,
That [1] they might be glorified in his marvellous works.

7 With them doth he heal *a man*,
And taketh away his pain.

8 With these will the apothecary make a confection;
And his works shall not be brought to an end;
And from him is peace upon the face of the earth.

9 My son, in thy sickness be not negligent;
But pray unto the Lord, and he shall heal thee.

10 Put away wrong doing, and order thine hands aright,
And cleanse thy heart from all manner of sin.

11 Give a sweet savour, and a memorial of fine flour;
And make fat thine offering, as one that is not.

12 Then give place to the physician, for verily the Lord hath created him;
And let him not go from thee, for thou hast need of him.

13 There is a time when in their very hands is the issue for good.

14 For they also shall beseech the Lord,
That he may prosper them in *giving* relief and in healing for the maintenance of life.

15 He that sinneth before his Maker,
Let him fall into the hands of the physician.

16 My son, let thy tears fall over the dead,

And as one that suffereth grievously begin lamentation;
And wind up his body according to his due,
And neglect not his burial.

17 Make bitter weeping, and make passionate wailing,
And let thy mourning be according to his desert,
For one day or two, lest thou be evil spoken of:
And so be comforted for thy sorrow.

18 For of sorrow cometh death,
And sorrow of heart will bow down the strength.

19 In calamity sorrow also remaineth:
And the poor man's life is [2]grievous to the heart.

20 Give not thy heart unto sorrow:
Put it away, remembering the last end:

21 Forget it not, for there is no returning again:
Him thou shalt not profit, and thou wilt hurt thyself.

22 Remember the sentence upon him;
for so also shall thine be;
Yesterday for me, and to-day for thee.

23 When the dead is at rest, let his remembrance rest;
And be comforted for him, when his spirit departeth from him.

24 The wisdom of the scribe cometh by opportunity of leisure;
And [3] he that hath little business shall become wise.

25 How shall he become wise that holdeth the plough,
That glorieth in the shaft of the goad,
That driveth oxen, and is occupied in their labours,
And whose discourse is of the stock of bulls?

26 He will set his heart upon turning his furrows;
And his wakefulness is to give his heifers their fodder.

27 So is every artificer and workmaster,
That passeth his time by night as by day;
They that cut gravings of signets,
And his diligence is to make great variety;
He will set his heart to preserve likeness in his portraiture,
And will be wakeful to finish his work.

28 So is the smith sitting by the anvil,
And considering the unwrought iron:
The vapour of the fire will waste his flesh;
And in the heat of the furnace will he wrestle *with his work*:
The noise of the hammer will [4] be ever in his ear,
And his eyes are upon the pattern of the vessel;
He will set his heart upon perfecting his works,

---

[1] Or, *he*

[2] Gr. *against the heart.*

[3] Gr. *he that is lessened in his business.*

[4] Gr. *renew.*

And he will be wakeful to adorn them
perfectly.

29 So is the potter sitting at his work,
And turning the wheel about with his
feet,
Who is alway anxiously set at his
work,
And all his handywork is by number;

30 He will fashion the clay with his
arm,
And will bend its strength in front of
his feet;
He will apply his heart to finish the
glazing;
And he will be wakeful to make clean
the furnace.

31 All these put their trust in their
hands;
And each becometh wise in his own
work.

32 Without these shall not a city be inhabited,
And men shall not sojourn nor walk
up and down *therein.*

33 [1] They shall not be sought for in the
council of the people,
And in the assembly they shall not
mount on high;
They shall not sit on the seat of the
judge,
And they shall not understand the
covenant of judgement:
Neither shall they declare instruction
and judgement;
And where parables are they shall
not be found.

34 But they will maintain the fabric of
the [2] world;
And in the handywork of their craft
is their prayer.

39 [3] Not so he that hath applied his
soul,
And meditateth in the law of the
Most High;
He will seek out the wisdom of all
the ancients,
And will be occupied in prophecies.

2 He will keep the discourse of the men
of renown,
And will enter in amidst the subtilties
of parables.

3 He will seek out the hidden meaning
of proverbs,
And be conversant in the dark sayings of parables.

4 He will serve among great men,
And appear before him that ruleth:
He will travel through the land of
strange nations;
For he hath tried good things and
evil among men.

5 He will apply his heart to resort early
to the Lord that made him,
And will make supplication before
the Most High,
And will open his mouth in prayer,
And will make supplication for his
sins.

6 If the great Lord will,
He shall be filled with the spirit of
understanding:
He shall pour forth the words of his
wisdom,
And in prayer give thanks unto the
Lord.

7 He shall direct his counsel and knowledge,
And in his secrets shall he meditate.

8 He shall shew forth the instruction
which he hath been taught,
And shall glory in the law of the covenant of the Lord.

9 Many shall commend his understanding;
And so long as the world endureth, it
shall not be blotted out:
His memorial shall not depart,
And his name shall live from generation to generation.

10 Nations shall declare his wisdom,
And the congregation shall tell out
his praise.

11 If he continue, he shall leave a greater
name than a thousand:
And if he [4] die, he addeth thereto.

12 Yet more will I utter, which 1 have
thought upon;
And I am filled as the moon at the
full.

13 Hearken unto me, ye holy children,
And bud forth as a rose growing by a
brook of water:

14 And give ye a sweet savour as frank-
incense,
And put forth flowers as a lily,
Spread abroad a sweet smell, and
sing a song of praise;
Bless ye the Lord for all his works.

15 Magnify his name,
And give utterance to his praise
With the songs of your lips, and with
harps;
And thus shall ye say when ye utter
his praise:

16 All the works of the Lord are exceeding good,
And every command shall be *accomplished* in his season.

17 None can say, What is this? wherefore is that?
For in his season they shall all be
sought out.
At his word the waters stood as a
heap,
And the receptacles of waters at the
word of his mouth.

18 At his command is all his good pleasure *done*;
And there is none that shall hinder
his salvation.

19 The works of all flesh are before him;
And it is not possible to be hid from
his eyes.

20 He beholdeth from everlasting to
everlasting;

[1] This
line is
absent
from the
oldest
MSS.

[2] Gr.
age.

[3] Gr.
*Except
him that.*

[4] Gr.
cease.

And there is nothing wonderful before him.

21 None can say, What is this? wherefore is that?
For all things are created for their uses.

22 His blessing covered the dry land as a river,
And saturated it as a flood.

23 As he hath turned the waters into saltness;
So shall the heathen inherit his wrath.

24 His ways are plain unto the holy;
So are they stumblingblocks unto the wicked.

25 Good things are created from the beginning for the good;
So are evil things for sinners.

26 The chief of all things necessary for the life of man
Are water, and fire, and iron, and salt,
And flour of wheat, and honey, and milk,
The blood of the grape, and oil, and clothing.

27 All these things are for good to the godly;
So to the sinners they shall be turned into evil.

28 There be winds that are created for vengeance,
And in their fury lay on their scourges heavily;
In the time of consummation they pour out their strength,
And shall appease the wrath of him that made them.

29 Fire, and hail, and famine, and death,
All these are created for vengeance;

30 Teeth of wild beasts, and scorpions and adders,
And a sword punishing the ungodly unto destruction.

31 They shall rejoice in his commandment,
And shall be made ready upon earth, when need is;
And in their seasons they shall not transgress *his* word.

32 Therefore from the beginning I was resolved,
And I thought *this*, and left it in writing;

33 All the works of the Lord are good:
And he will supply every need in its season.

34 And none can say, This is worse than that:
For they shall all be well approved in their season.

35 And now with all your heart and mouth sing ye praises,
And bless the name of the Lord.

40 Great travail is created for every man,

And a heavy yoke is upon the sons of Adam,
From the day of their coming forth from their mother's womb,
Until the day for their burial in the mother of all things.

2 The expectation of things to come, and the day of death,
[1] *Trouble* their thoughts, and *cause* fear of heart;

3 From him that sitteth on a throne of glory,
Even unto him that is humbled in earth and ashes;

4 From him that weareth purple and a crown,
Even unto him that is clothed with a hempen frock.

5 *There is* wrath, and jealousy, and trouble, and disquiet,
And fear of death, and anger, and strife;
And in the time of rest upon his bed
His night sleep doth change his knowledge.

6 A little or nothing is his resting,
And afterward in his sleep, as in a day of keeping watch,
He is troubled in the vision of his heart,
As one that hath escaped from the front of battle.

7 In the very time of his deliverance he awaketh,
And marvelleth that the fear is nought.

8 *It is thus* with all flesh, from man to beast,
And upon sinners sevenfold more.

9 Death, and bloodshed, and strife, and sword,
Calamities, famine, tribulation, and the scourge;

10 All these things were created for the wicked,
And because of them came the flood.

11 All things that are of the earth turn to the earth again:
And *all things that are* of the waters return into the sea.

12 All bribery and injustice shall be blotted out;
And good faith shall stand for ever.

13 The goods of the unjust shall be dried up like a river,
And like a great thunder in rain shall go off in noise.

14 In opening his hands *a man* shall be made glad:
So shall transgressors utterly fail.

15 The children of the ungodly shall not put forth many branches;
And *are as* unclean roots upon a sheer rock.

16 The sedge *that groweth* upon every water and bank of a river
Shall be plucked up before all grass.

[1] The Greek text of this line is probably corrupt.

17 Bounty is as a garden ¹ of blessings,
And almsgiving endureth for ever.

18 The life of one that laboureth, and is
contented, shall be made sweet;
And he that findeth a treasure is
above both.

19 Children and the building of a city
establish a *man's* name;
And a blameless wife is counted above
both.

20 Wine and music rejoice the heart;
And the love of wisdom is above
both.

21 The pipe and the psaltery make
pleasant melody;
And a pleasant tongue is above both.

22 Thine eye shall desire grace and
beauty;
And above both the green blade of
corn.

23 A friend and a companion never meet
amiss;
And a wife with her husband is above
both.

24 Brethren and succour are for a time
of affliction;
And almsgiving is a deliverer above
both.

25 Gold and silver will make the foot
stand sure;
And counsel is esteemed above them
both.

26 Riches and strength will lift up the
heart;
And the fear of the Lord is above both:
There is nothing wanting in the fear
of the Lord,
And there is no need to seek help
therein.

27 The fear of the Lord is as a garden
of blessing,
And covereth ² a man above all glory.

28 My son, lead not a beggar's life;
Better it is to die than to beg.

29 A man that looketh unto the table of
another,
His life is not to be counted for a
life;
He will pollute his soul with another
man's meats:
But a man wise and well-instructed
will beware thereof.

30 In the mouth of the shameless begging
will be sweet;
And in his belly a fire shall be kindled.

41 O death, how bitter is the remembrance of thee to a man that is at
peace in his possessions,
Unto the man that hath nothing to
distract him, and hath prosperity in
all things,
And that still hath strength to receive
meat!

2 O death, acceptable is thy sentence
unto a man that is needy, and that
faileth in strength,

That is in extreme old age, and is distracted about all things,
And is perverse, and hath lost patience!

3 Fear not the sentence of death;
Remember them that have been before thee, and that come after:
This is the sentence from the Lord
over all flesh.

4 And why dost thou refuse, when it
is the good pleasure of the Most
High?
Whether it be ten, or a hundred, or a
thousand years,
There is no inquisition of life in ³ the
grave.

5 The children of sinners are abominable children,
And they frequent the dwellings of
the ungodly.

6 The inheritance of sinners' children
shall perish,
And with their posterity shall be a
perpetual reproach.

7 Children will complain of an ungodly
father,
Because they shall be reproached for
his sake.

8 Woe unto you, ungodly men,
Which have forsaken the law of the
Most High God!⁴

9 If ye be born, ye shall be born to a
curse;
If ye die, a curse shall be your portion.

10 All things that are of the earth shall
go back to the earth:
So the ungodly shall go from a curse
unto perdition.

⁴ The
remain-
der of
this
verse is
omitted
by the
best au-
thorities.

11 The mourning of men is about their
bodies:
But the name of sinners being evil
shall be blotted out.

12 Have regard to thy name;
For it continueth with thee longer
than a thousand great treasures of
gold.

13 A good life hath its number of days;
And a good name continueth for ever.

14 My children, keep instruction in
peace:
But wisdom that is hid, and a treasure
that is not seen,
What profit is in them both?

15 Better is a man that hideth his foolishness
Than a man that hideth his wisdom.

16 Wherefore shew reverence to my
word:
For it is not good to retain every kind
of shame;
And not all things are approved by
all in good faith.

17 Be ashamed of whoredom before father and mother:
And of a lie before a prince and a
mighty man;

18 Of an offence before a judge and ruler;

Of iniquity before the congregation and the people ;

Of unjust dealing before a partner and friend ;

19 And of theft in regard of the place where thou sojournest,

And in regard of the truth of God and his covenant;

And of leaning with thine elbow at meat ;

And of scurrility in the matter of giving and taking ;

20 And of silence before them that salute thee ;

And of looking upon a woman that is a harlot;

21 And of turning away [1] thy face from a kinsman ;

Of taking away a portion or a gift ;

And of gazing upon a woman that hath a husband ;

22 Of being over busy with his maid ; and come not near her bed ;

Of upbraiding speeches before friends;

And after thou hast given, upbraid not;

23 Of repeating and speaking what thou hast heard ;

And of revealing of secrets.

24 So shalt thou be truly shamefast,

And find favour in the sight of every man.

42 Of these things be not ashamed,

And accept no man's person to sin *thereby* :

2 Of the law of the Most High, and his covenant;

And of judgement to do justice to the ungodly ;

3 Of reckoning with a partner and with travellers ;

And of a gift from the heritage of friends ;

4 Of exactness of balance and weights ;

And of getting much or little ;

5 Of indifferent selling of merchants ;

And of much correction of children ;

And of making the side of an evil servant to bleed.

6 [2] Sure keeping is good, where an evil wife is ;

And where many hands are, shut thou close.

7 Whatsoever thou handest over, let it be by number and weight ;

And in giving and receiving let all be in writing.

8 *Be not ashamed* to instruct the unwise and foolish,

And one of extreme old age that contendeth with those that are young ;

And so shalt thou be well instructed indeed,

And approved in the sight of every man living.

9 A daughter is a secret cause of wakefulness to a father ;

And the care for her putteth away sleep ;

In her youth, lest she pass the flower of her age ;

And when she is married, lest she should be hated :

10 In her virginity, lest she should be defiled

And be with child in her father's house ;

And when she hath a husband, lest she should transgress ;

And when she is married, lest she should be barren.

11 Keep a strict watch over a headstrong daughter,

Lest she make thee [3] a laughingstock to thine enemies,

A byword in the city and [4] notorious among the people,

And shame thee before the multitude.

12 Look not upon every body in regard of beauty,

And sit not in the midst of women ;

13 For from garments cometh a moth,

And from a woman a woman's wickedness.

14 Better is the wickedness of a man than a pleasant-dealing woman,

And a woman which putteth thee to shameful reproach.

15 I will make mention now of the works of the Lord,

And will declare the things that I have seen :

In the words of the Lord are his works.

16 The sun that giveth light looketh upon all things ;

And the work of the Lord is full of his glory.

17 The Lord hath not given power to the saints to declare all his marvellous works ;

Which the Almighty Lord firmly settled,

That whatsoever is might be established in his glory.

18 He searcheth out the deep, and the heart,

And he hath understanding of their cunning devices :

For the Most High knoweth all knowledge,

And he looketh into the [5] signs of the world,

19 Declaring the things that are past, and the things that shall be,

And revealing the traces of hidden things.

20 No thought escapeth him ;

There is not a word hid from him.

21 The mighty works of his wisdom he hath ordered,

Who is from everlasting to everlasting :

Nothing hath been added unto them, nor diminished from them ;

And he had no need of any counsellor.

[1] Or, *the face of a kinsman*

[2] Or, *A seal*

[3] Or, *a rejoicing*

[4] Gr. *called forth.*

[5] Gr. *sign.*

22 How desirable are all his works!
One may behold *this* even unto a
spark.
23 All these things live and remain for
ever in all manner of uses,
And they are all obedient.
24 All things are double one against
another:
And he hath made nothing imperfect.
25 One thing establisheth the good things
of another:
And who shall be filled with beholding his glory?

43 The pride of the height is the firmament [1] in its clearness,
The appearance of heaven, in the
spectacle of its glory.
2 The sun when he appeareth, bringing
tidings as he goeth forth,
Is a marvellous instrument, the work
of the Most High:
3 At his noon he drieth up the country,
And who shall stand against his burning heat?
4 A man blowing a furnace is in works
of heat,
But the sun three times more, burning
up the mountains:
Breathing out fiery vapours,
And sending forth bright beams, he
dimmeth the eyes.
5 Great is the Lord that made him;
And at his word he hasteneth his
course.

6 The moon also is in all things for her
season,
For a declaration of times, and a sign
of the world.
7 From the moon is the sign of the
feast day;
A light that waneth when she is come
to the full.
8 The month is called after her name,
Increasing wonderfully in her changing;
An instrument of the hosts on high,
Shining forth in the firmament of
heaven;
9 The beauty of heaven, the glory of the
stars,
An ornament giving light in the highest places of the Lord.
10 At the word of the Holy One they will
stand in [2] due order,
And they will not faint in their
watches.
11 Look upon the rainbow, and praise
him that made it;
Exceeding beautiful in the brightness
thereof.
12 It compasseth the heaven round about
with a circle of glory;
The hands of the Most High have
stretched it.

13 By his commandment he maketh the
snow to fall apace,
And sendeth swiftly the lightnings of
his judgement.
14 By reason thereof the treasure-houses
are opened;
And clouds fly forth as fowls.
15 By his mighty power he maketh
strong the clouds,
And the hailstones are broken small:
16 And at his appearing the mountains
will be shaken,
And at his will the south wind will
blow.
17 The voice of his thunder maketh the
earth to travail;
So doth the northern storm and the
whirlwind:
As birds flying down he sprinkleth the
snow;
And as the lighting of the locust is
the falling down thereof:
18 The eye will marvel at the beauty of
its whiteness,
And the heart will be astonished at
the raining of it.
19 The hoar frost also he poureth on the
earth as salt;
And when it is congealed, it is *as*
points of thorns.

20 The cold north wind shall blow,
And the ice shall be congealed on the
water:
It shall lodge upon every gathering
together of water,
And the water shall put on as it were
a breastplate.
21 It shall devour the mountains, and
burn up the wilderness,
And consume the green herb as fire.
22 A mist coming speedily is the healing
of all things;
A dew coming after heat shall bring
cheerfulness.
23 By his counsel he hath stilled the
deep,
And [3] planted islands therein.
24 They that sail on the sea tell of the
danger thereof;
And when we hear it with our ears,
we marvel.
25 Therein be also those strange and
wondrous works,
Variety of all that hath life, the [4] race
of sea-monsters.
26 By reason of him his end hath success,
And by his word all things consist.
27 We may say many things, yet shall
we not attain;
And the sum of our words is, He is all.
28 How shall we have strength to glorify
him?
For he is himself the great one above
all his works.
29 The Lord is terrible and exceeding
great;
And marvellous is his power.
30 When ye glorify the Lord, exalt him
as much as ye can;

[1] Gr. *of clearness.*

[2] Gr. *judgement.*

[3] The most ancient authorities read *Jesus planted it.*

[4] Gr. *creation.* Several ancient authorities read *possession of cattle.*

For even yet will he exceed:
And when ye exalt him, put forth your full strength:
Be not weary; for ye will never attain.
31 Who hath seen him, that he may declare him?
And who shall magnify him as he is?
32 Many things are hidden greater than these;
For we have seen but a few of his works.
33 For the Lord made all things;
And to the godly gave he wisdom.

44 Let us now praise famous men,
And our fathers that begat us.
2 The Lord [1] manifested *in them* great glory,
Even his mighty power from the beginning.
3 Such as did bear rule in their kingdoms,
And were men renowned for their power,
[2] Giving counsel by their understanding,
Such as have brought tidings in prophecies:
4 Leaders of the people by their counsels,
And by their understanding [3] *men of* learning for the people;
Wise *were* their words in their instruction:
5 Such as sought out musical tunes,
And set forth verses in writing:
6 Rich men furnished with ability,
Living peaceably in their habitations:
7 All these were honoured in their generations,
And were a glory in their days.
8 There be of them, that have left a name behind them,
To declare their praises.
9 And some there be, which have no memorial;
Who are perished as though they had not been,
And are become as though they had not been born;
And their children after them.
10 But these were men of mercy,
Whose righteous deeds have not been forgotten.
11 With their seed shall remain continually a good inheritance;
Their children *are* [4] within the covenants.
12 Their seed standeth fast,
And their children for their sakes.
13 Their seed shall remain for ever,
And their glory shall not be blotted out.
14 Their bodies were buried in peace,
And their name liveth to all generations.
15 Peoples will declare their wisdom,
And the congregation telleth out their praise.

[1] Gr. *created.*

[2] Most authorities read *They shall take counsel.*

[3] The Greek text is here corrupt.

[4] Or, *in their testaments*

16 Enoch pleased the Lord, and was translated,
Being an example of repentance to all generations.
17 Noah was found perfect *and* righteous;
In the season of wrath he was taken in exchange *for the world*;
Therefore was there left a remnant unto the earth,
When the flood came.
18 Everlasting covenants were made with him,
That all flesh should no more be blotted out by a flood.
19 Abraham was a great father of a multitude of nations;
And there was none found like him in glory;
20 Who kept the law of the Most High,
And was taken into covenant with him:
In his flesh he established the covenant;
And when he was proved, he was found faithful.
21 Therefore he assured him by an oath,
That the nations should be blessed in his seed;
That he would multiply him as the dust of the earth,
And exalt his seed as the stars,
And cause them to inherit from sea to sea,
And from the River unto the utmost part of the earth.
22 In Isaac also did he establish likewise, for Abraham his father's sake,
The blessing of all men, and the covenant:
23 And he made it rest upon the head of Jacob;
He acknowledged him in his blessings,
And gave to him by inheritance,
And divided his portions;
Among twelve tribes did he part them.

45 And he brought out of him a man of mercy,
Which found favour in the sight of all flesh;
A man beloved of God and men, even Moses,
Whose memorial is blessed.
2 He made him like to the glory of the saints,
And magnified him in the fears of his enemies.
3 By his words he caused the wonders to cease;
He glorified him in the sight of kings;
He gave him commandment for his people,
And shewed him part of his glory.

4 He sanctified him in his faithfulness
and meekness;
He chose him out of all flesh.
5 He made him to hear his voice,
And led him into the thick darkness,
And gave him commandments face to
face,
Even the law of life and knowledge,
That he might teach Jacob the cove-
nant,
And Israel his judgements.

6 He exalted Aaron, a holy man like
unto him,
Even his brother, of the tribe of Levi.
7 He established for him an everlasting
covenant,
And gave him the priesthood of the
people;

¹ Gr.
blessed.

He ¹ beautified him with comely ornaments,
And girded him about with a robe of
glory.
8 He clothed him with the perfection of
exultation;
And strengthened him with apparel

² Gr.
strength.

of ² honour,
The linen breeches, the long robe,
and the ephod.
9 And he compassed him with pome-
granates of gold,
And with many bells round about,
To send forth a sound as he went,
To make a sound that might be heard
in the temple,
For a memorial to the children of his
people;
10 With a holy garment, with gold and
blue and purple, the work of the
embroiderer,
With an oracle of judgement, *even*
with the Urim and Thummim;
11 With twisted scarlet, the work of the
craftsman;
With precious stones graven like a
signet, in a setting of gold, the work
of the jeweller,
For a memorial engraved in writing,
after the number of the tribes of
Israel;
12 With a crown of gold upon the mitre,

³ Gr. an
engrav-
ing of a
signet of
holiness.

³ having graven on it, as on a signet,
HOLINESS,
An ornament of honour, a work of
might,
The desires of the eyes, goodly and
beautiful.
13 Before him there never have been
any such;
No stranger put them on, but his sons
only, and his offspring perpetually.
14 His sacrifices shall be wholly consumed
Every day twice continually.

⁴ Gr.
filled his
hands.

15 Moses ⁴ consecrated him,
And anointed him with holy oil:
It was unto him for an everlasting
covenant,
And to his seed, all the days of hea-
ven,

To minister unto him, and to execute
also the priest's office,
And bless his people in his name.
16 He chose him out of all living
To offer sacrifice to the Lord,
Incense, and a sweet savour, for a
memorial,
To make reconciliation for thy people.
17 He gave unto him in his commandments,
Yea, authority in the covenants of
judgements,
To teach Jacob the testimonies,
And to enlighten Israel in his law.
18 Strangers gathered themselves together against him,
And envied him in the wilderness,
Even Dathan and Abiram with their
company,
And the congregation of Korah, with
wrath and anger.
19 The Lord saw it, and it displeased
him;
And in the wrath of his anger they
were destroyed:
He did wonders upon them,
To consume them with flaming fire.
20 And he added glory to Aaron,
And gave him a heritage:
He divided unto him the firstfruits of
the increase;
And first did he prepare bread in
abundance:
21 For they shall eat the sacrifices of the
Lord,
Which he gave unto him and to his
seed.
22 Howbeit in the land of the people he
shall have no inheritance,
And he hath no portion among the
people:
For he himself is thy portion *and* inheritance.

23 And Phinehas the son of Eleazar is
the third in glory,
In that he was zealous in the fear of
the Lord,
And stood fast in the good forward-
ness of his soul when the people
turned away,
And he made reconciliation for Israel.
24 Therefore was there a covenant of
peace established for him,
That he should be leader of the

⁵ Or,
sanc-
tuary

⁵ saints and of his people;
That he and his seed
Should have the dignity of the priesthood for ever.
25 Also *he made* a covenant with David
the son of Jesse, of the tribe of
Judah;
The inheritance of the king is his
alone from son to son;
So the inheritance of Aaron is also
unto his seed.
26 *God* give you wisdom in your heart
To judge his people in righteousness,

That their good things be not abolished,
And *that* their glory *endure* for all
their generations.

¹ Gr. *Nave.*

46 Joshua the son of ¹ Nun was valiant
in war,
And was the successor of Moses in
prophecies:
Who according to his name was made
great

² Gr. *his.*

For the saving of ² God's elect,
To take vengeance of the enemies
that rose up against them,
That he might give Israel their inheritance.
2 How was he glorified in the lifting
up his hands,
And in stretching out his sword
against the cities!
3 Who before him so stood fast?
For the Lord himself brought his
enemies unto him.
4 Did not the sun go back by his hand?
And did not one day become as two?
5 He called upon the Most High *and*
Mighty One,
When his foes pressed him round
about;
And the great Lord heard him.
6 With hailstones of mighty power
He caused war to break violently upon the nation,

³ See
Joshua
x. 11.

And ³ in the going down he destroyed
them that resisted;
That the nations might know his

⁴ Gr. *panoply.*

⁴ armour,
How that he fought in the sight of
the Lord;
For he followed after the Mighty
One.
7 Also in the time of Moses he did a
work of mercy,
He and Caleb the son of Jephunneh,
In that they withstood the adversary,
Hindered the people from sin,
And stilled the murmuring of wickedness.
8 And of six hundred thousand people
on foot, they two alone were preserved
To bring them into the heritage,
Even into a land flowing with milk
and honey.
9 Also the Lord gave strength unto
Caleb,
And it remained with him unto his
old age;
So that he entered upon the height of
the land,
And his seed obtained it for a heritage:
10 That all the children of Israel might
see
That it is good to walk after the
Lord.

11 Also the judges, every one by his
name,
All whose hearts went not a whoring,

And who turned not away from the
Lord,
May their memorial be blessed.
12 May their bones flourish again out of
their place,
And may the name of them that have
been honoured be renewed upon
their children.
13 Samuel, the prophet of the Lord, beloved of his Lord,
Established a kingdom, and anointed
princes over his people.
14 By the law of the Lord he judged the
congregation,
And the Lord visited Jacob.
15 By his faithfulness he was proved to
be a prophet,
And by his words he was known to
be faithful in vision.
16 Also when his enemies pressed him
round about
He called upon the Lord, the Mighty
One,
With the offering of the sucking lamb.
17 And the Lord thundered from heaven,
And with a mighty sound made his
voice to be heard.
18 And he utterly destroyed the rulers of
the Tyrians,
And all the princes of the Philistines.
19 Also before the time of his ⁵ long sleep
He made protestations in the sight of
the Lord and *his* anointed,
I have not taken any man's goods, so
much as a shoe:
And no man did accuse him.
20 And after he fell asleep he prophesied,
And shewed the king his end,
And lifted up his voice from the earth
in prophecy,
To blot out the wickedness of the
people.

⁵ Gr.
*age-long
sleep.*

47 And after him rose up Nathan
To prophesy in the days of David.
2 As is the fat when it is separated
from the peace offering,
So was David *separated* from the children of Israel.
3 He played with lions as with kids,
And with bears as with lambs of the
flock.
4 In his youth did he not slay a giant,
And take away reproach from the
people,
When he lifted up his hand with a
sling stone,
And beat down the boasting of Goliath?
5 For he called upon the Most High
Lord;
And he gave him strength in his right
hand,
To slay a man mighty in war,
To exalt the horn of his people.
6 So they glorified him for *his* ten thousands,
And praised him for the blessings of
the Lord,

In that there was given him a diadem
of glory.
7 For he destroyed the enemies on every
side,
And brought to nought the Philistines
his adversaries,
Brake their horn in pieces unto this
day.
8 In every work of his he gave thanks
to the Holy One Most High with
words of glory;
With his whole heart he sang praise,
And loved him that made him.
9 Also he set singers before the altar,
And to make sweet melody by their
music.[1]
10 He gave comeliness to the feasts,
And set in order the seasons to perfection,
While they praised his holy name,
And the sanctuary sounded from early
morning.
11 The Lord took away his sins,
And exalted his horn for ever;
And gave him a covenant of kings,
And a throne of glory in Israel.

12 After him rose up a son, a man of
understanding;
And for his sake he dwelt at large.
13 Solomon reigned in days of peace;
And to him God gave rest round about,
That he might set up a house for his
name,
And prepare a sanctuary for ever.
14 How wise wast thou made in thy
youth,
And filled as a river with understanding!
15 Thy soul covered the earth,
And thou filledst it with [2] dark parables.
16 Thy name reached unto the isles afar
off;
And for thy peace thou wast beloved.
17 For thy songs and proverbs and parables,
And for thine interpretations, the
countries marvelled at thee.
18 By the name of the Lord God,
Which is called the God of Israel,
Thou didst gather gold as tin,
And didst multiply silver as lead.
19 Thou didst bow thy loins unto women,
And in thy body thou wast brought
into subjection.
20 Thou didst blemish thine honour,
And profane thy seed,
To bring wrath upon thy children;
And I was grieved for thy folly:
21 So that the sovereignty was divided,
And out of Ephraim ruled a disobedient kingdom.
22 But the Lord will never forsake his
mercy;
And he will not destroy any of his
works,
Nor blot out the posterity of his elect;
And the seed of him that loved him he
will not take away;
And he gave a remnant unto Jacob,
And unto David a root out of him.

23 And *so* rested Solomon with his fathers;
And of his seed he left behind him
Rehoboam,
Even the foolishness of the people,
and one that lacked understanding,
Who made the people to revolt by his
counsel.
Also Jeroboam the son of Nebat,
Who made Israel to sin,
And gave unto Ephraim a way of sin.
24 And their sins were multiplied exceedingly,
To remove them from their land.
25 For they sought out all manner of
wickedness,
Till vengeance should come upon
them.

48 Also there arose Elijah the prophet
as fire,
And his word burned like a torch:
2 Who brought a famine upon them,
And by his zeal made them few in
number.
3 By the word of the Lord he shut up
the heaven:
Thrice did he thus bring down fire.
4 How wast thou glorified, O Elijah, in
thy wondrous deeds!
And who shall glory like unto thee?
5 Who did raise up a dead man from
death,
And from [3] the place of the dead, by
the word of the Most High:
6 Who brought down kings to destruction,
And honourable men from their bed:
7 Who heard rebuke in Sinai,
And judgements of vengeance in
Horeb:
8 Who anointed kings for retribution,
And prophets to succeed after him:
9 Who was taken up in a tempest of fire,
In a chariot of fiery horses:
10 Who was recorded for reproofs in
their seasons,
To pacify anger, before it brake forth
into wrath;
To turn the heart of the father unto
the son,
And to restore the tribes of Jacob.
11 Blessed are they that saw thee,
And they that have been beautified
with love;
For we also shall surely live.

12 Elijah *it was*, who was wrapped in a
tempest:
And Elisha was filled with his spirit;
And in *all* his days he was not moved
by *the fear of* any ruler,
And no one brought him into subjection.
13 [4] Nothing was too high for him;
And when he was laid on sleep his
body prophesied.

[1] The remainder of this verse is omitted by the best authorities.

[2] Gr. *parables of riddles.*

[3] Gr. *Hades.*

[4] Or, *No man's word overcame him*

14 As in his life he did wonders,
So in death were his works marvellous.
15 For all this the people repented not,
And they departed not from their sins,
Till they were carried away as a spoil from their land,
And were scattered through all the earth;
And the people was left very few in number,
And a ruler *was left* in the house of David.
16 Some of them did that which was pleasing *to God*,
And some multiplied sins.

17 Hezekiah fortified his city,
And brought in [1] water into the midst of them:
He digged the sheer rock with iron,
And builded up wells for waters.
18 In his days Sennacherib came up,
And sent Rabshakeh, and departed;
And he lifted up his hand against Sion,
And boasted great things in his arrogancy.
19 Then were their hearts and their hands shaken,
And they were in pain, as women in travail;
20 And they called upon the Lord which is merciful,
Spreading forth their hands unto him:
And the Holy One heard them speedily out of heaven,
And delivered them by the hand of Isaiah.
21 He smote the camp of the Assyrians,
And his angel utterly destroyed them.
22 For Hezekiah did that which was pleasing to the Lord,
And was strong in the ways of David his father,
Which Isaiah the prophet commanded,
Who was great and faithful in his vision.
23 In his days the sun went backward;
And he added life to the king.
24 He saw by an excellent spirit what should come to pass at the last;
And he comforted them that mourned in Sion.
25 He shewed the things that should be to the end of time,
And the hidden things or ever they came.

49 The memorial of Josiah is like the composition of incense
Prepared by the work of the apothecary:
It shall be sweet as honey in every mouth,
And as music at a banquet of wine.
2 He behaved himself uprightly in the conversion of the people,

And took away the abominations of iniquity.
3 He set his heart right toward the Lord;
In the days of wicked men he made godliness to prevail.

4 Except David and Hezekiah and Josiah,
All committed trespass:
For they forsook the law of the Most High;
The kings of Judah failed.
5 For they gave their [2] power unto others,
And their glory to a strange nation.
6 They set on fire the chosen city of the sanctuary,
And made her streets desolate, *as it was written* by the hand of Jeremiah.
7 For they entreated him evil;
And yet he was sanctified in the womb to be a prophet,
To root out, and to afflict, and to destroy;
And in like manner to build and to plant.
8 *It was* Ezekiel who saw the vision of glory,
Which *God* shewed him upon the chariot of the cherubim.
9 For verily he remembered the enemies in [3] storm,
And to do good to them that directed their ways aright.
10 Also of the twelve prophets [4]
May the bones flourish again out of their place.
And he comforted Jacob,
And delivered them by confidence of hope.

11 How shall we magnify Zerubbabel?
And he was as a signet on the right hand:
12 So was Jesus the son of Josedek:
Who in their days builded the house,
And exalted a [5] people holy to the Lord,
Prepared for everlasting glory.
13 Also of Nehemiah the memorial is great;
Who raised up for us the walls that were fallen,
And set up the gates and bars,
And raised up our homes again.

14 No man was created upon the earth such as was Enoch;
For he was taken up from the earth.
15 Neither was there a man born like unto Joseph,
A governor of his brethren, a stay of the people:
Yea, his bones were visited.
16 Shem and Seth were glorified among men;
And above every living thing in the creation is Adam.

[1] Some ancient authorities, apparently by a confusion, read *Gog*.

[2] Gr. *horn*.

[3] Gr. *rain*.

[4] The remainder of this line is omitted by the best authorities.

[5] Some ancient authorities read *temple*.

50 It was Simon, the son of Onias, the ¹great priest,

¹ Or, high

Who in his life repaired the house,
And in his days strengthened the temple:

2 And by him was built from the foundation the height of the double *wall*,
The lofty underworks of the inclosure of the temple :

3 In his days the cistern of waters was ²diminished,

² The text here seems to be corrupt.

The brasen vessel in compass as the sea.

4 It was he that took thought for his people that they should not fall,
And fortified the city ³against besieging :

³ Gr. to besiege : that is, as to besieging it.

5 How glorious was he when the people gathered round him
At his coming forth out of the ⁴sanctuary !

⁴ Gr. house of the veil.

6 As the morning star in the midst of a cloud,
As the moon at the full :

7 As the sun shining forth upon the temple of the Most High,
And as the rainbow giving light in clouds of glory :

8 As the flower of roses in the days of new *fruits*,
As lilies at the waterspring,
As the shoot of the frankincense tree in the time of summer :

9 As fire and incense in the censer,
As a vessel all of beaten gold
Adorned with all manner of precious stones :

10 As an olive tree budding forth fruits,
And as a cypress growing high among the clouds.

11 When he took up the robe of glory,
And put on the perfection of exultation,
In the ascent of the holy altar,
He made glorious the precinct of the sanctuary.

12 And when he received the portions out of the priests' hands,
Himself also standing by the hearth of the altar,
His brethren as a garland round about him,
He was as a young cedar in Libanus ;
And as stems of palm trees compassed they him round about,

13 And all the sons of Aaron in their glory,
And the Lord's offering in their hands, before all the congregation of Israel.

14 And finishing the service at the altars,
That he might adorn the offering of the Most High, the Almighty,

15 He stretched out his hand to the ⁵cup,
And poured of the blood of the grape ;
He poured out at the foot of the altar

⁵ Gr. cup of libation.

A sweet-smelling savour unto the Most High, the King of all.

16 Then shouted the sons of Aaron,
They sounded the trumpets of beaten work,
They made a great noise to be heard,
For a remembrance before the Most High.

17 Then all the people together hasted,
And fell down upon the earth on their faces
To worship their Lord, the Almighty, God Most High.

18 The singers also praised him with their voices ;
In the whole house was there made sweet melody.

19 And the people besought the Lord Most High,
In prayer before him that is merciful,
Till the ⁶worship of the Lord should be ended ;

⁶ Gr. adornment.

And so they accomplished his service.

20 Then he went down, and lifted up his hands
Over the whole congregation of the children of Israel,
To give blessing unto the Lord with his lips,
And to glory in his name.

21 And he bowed himself down in worship the second time,
To declare the blessing from the Most High.

22 And now bless ye the God of all,
Which everywhere doeth great things,
Which exalteth our days from the womb,
And dealeth with us according to his mercy.

23 May he grant us joyfulness of heart,
And that peace may be in our days in Israel for the days of eternity :

24 To intrust his mercy with us ;
And let him deliver us in his time !

25 With two nations is my soul vexed,
And the third is no nation :

26 They that sit upon the mountain of ⁷Samaria, *and* the Philistines,
And that foolish people that dwelleth in Sichem.

⁷ According to some ancient versions Seir.

27 I have ⁸written in this book the instruction of understanding and knowledge,
I Jesus, the son of Sirach Eleazar, of Jerusalem,
Who out of his heart poured forth wisdom.

⁸ Gr. graven.

28 Blessed is he that shall be exercised in these things ;
And he that layeth them up in his heart shall become wise.

29 For if he do them, he shall be strong to all things :
For the light of the Lord is his ⁹guide.¹⁰

⁹ Gr. footstep.
¹⁰ The remainder of this verse is omitted by the best authorities.

A Prayer of Jesus the son of Sirach.

51 I will give thanks unto thee, O Lord,
O King.
And will praise thee, God my Saviour:
I do give thanks unto thy name:
2 For thou wast my protector and
helper,
And didst deliver my body out of
destruction,
And out of the snare of a slanderous
tongue,
From lips that forge lies,
And wast my helper before them that
stood by;
3 And didst deliver me, according to
the abundance of thy mercy, and
greatness of thy name,
From the gnashings *of teeth* ready to
devour,
Out of the hand of such as sought my
life,
Out of the manifold afflictions which
I had;
4 From the choking of a fire on every
side,
And out of the midst of fire which I
kindled not;
5 Out of the depth of the belly of ¹the
grave,
And from an unclean tongue,
And from lying words,
6 The slander of an unrighteous tongue
unto the king.
My soul drew near even unto death,
And my life was near to ¹ the grave
beneath.
7 They compassed me on every side,
And there was none to help *me*.
I was looking for the succour of men,
And it was not.
8 And I remembered thy mercy, O
Lord,
And thy working which hath been
from everlasting,
How thou deliverest them that wait
for thee,
And savest them out of the hand of
the enemies.
9 And I lifted up my supplication from
the earth,
And prayed for deliverance from
death.
10 I called upon the Lord, the Father of
my Lord,
That he would not forsake me in the
days of affliction,
In the time when there was no help
against the proud.
11 I will praise thy name continually,
And will sing praise with thanksgiving;
And my supplication was heard:
12 For thou savedst me from destruction,
And deliveredst me from the evil
time:

¹ Gr.
Hades.

Therefore will I give thanks and
praise unto thee,
And bless the name of the Lord.
13 When I was yet young,
Or ever I went abroad,
I sought wisdom openly in my prayer.
14 Before the temple I asked for her,
And I will seek her out even to the
end.
15 From *her* flower as from the ripening
grape my heart delighted in her:
My foot trod in uprightness,
From my youth I tracked her out.
16 I bowed down mine ear a little, and
received her,
And found for myself much instruction.
17 I profited in her:
Unto him that giveth me wisdom I
will give glory.
18 For I purposed to practise her,
And I was zealous for that which is
good;
And I shall never be put to shame.
19 My soul hath wrestled in her,
And in my doing I was exact:
I spread forth my hands to the heaven
above,
And bewailed my ignorances of her.
20 I set my soul aright unto her,
And in pureness I found her.
I gat me a heart *joined* with her from
the beginning:
Therefore shall I not be forsaken.
21 My inward part also was troubled to
seek her:
Therefore have I gotten a good possession.
22 The Lord gave me a tongue for my
reward;
And I will praise him therewith.

23 Draw near unto me, ye unlearned,
And lodge in the house of instruction.
24 Say, wherefore are ye lacking in these
things,
And your souls are very thirsty?
25 I opened my mouth, and spake,
Get her for yourselves without money.
26 Put your neck under the yoke,
And let your soul receive instruction:
She is hard at hand to find.
27 Behold with your eyes,
How that I laboured but a little,
And found for myself much rest.
28 Get you instruction with a great sum
of silver,
And gain much gold by her.
29 May your soul rejoice in his mercy,
And may ye not be put to shame in
praising him.
30 Work your work before the time
cometh,
And in his time he will give you your
reward.

BARUCH.

1 AND these are the words of the book, which Baruch the son of Nerias, the son of Maaseas, the son of Sedekias, the son of Asadias, the son of Helkias, 2 wrote in Babylon, in the fifth year, *and* in the seventh day of the month, what time as the Chaldeans took Je-3 rusalem, and burnt it with fire. And Baruch did read the words of this book in the hearing of Jechonias the son of Joakim king of Judah, and in the hearing of all the people that 4 came to *hear* the book, and in the hearing of the mighty men, and of the kings' sons, and in the hearing of the elders, and in the hearing of all the people, from the least unto the greatest, even of all them that dwelt at 5 Babylon by the river Sud. And they wept, and fasted, [1] and prayed before 6 the Lord; they made also a collection of money according to every man's 7 power: and they sent *it* to Jerusalem unto Joakim the *high* priest, the son of Helkias, the son of Salom, and to the priests, and to all the people which were found with him at Jeru-8 salem, at the same time when he took the vessels of the house of the Lord, that had been carried out of the temple, to return *them* into the land of Judah, the tenth day of *the month* Sivan, *namely,* silver vessels, which Sedekias the son of Josias king of Ju-9 dah had made, after that Nabucho-donosor king of Babylon had carried away Jechonias, and the princes, and the captives, and the mighty men, and the people of the land, from Jerusa-lem, and brought them unto Babylon. 10 And they said, Behold, we have sent you money; buy you therefore with the money burnt offerings, and sin of-ferings, and incense, and prepare an oblation, and offer upon the altar of 11 the Lord our God; and pray for the life of Nabuchodonosor king of Baby-lon, and for the life of Baltasar his son, that their days may be [2] as the 12 days of heaven above the earth: and the Lord will give us strength, and lighten our eyes, and we shall live under the shadow of Nabuchodonosor king of Babylon, and under the sha-dow of Baltasar his son, and we shall serve them many days, and find fa-13 vour in their sight. Pray for us also unto the Lord our God, for we have sinned against the Lord our God; and unto this day the wrath of the Lord and his indignation is not turned from 14 us. And ye shall read this book which we have sent unto you, to make confession in the house of the Lord, upon the day of the feast and on the days of the solemn assembly. 15 And ye shall say, To the Lord our God *belongeth* righteousness, but un-to us confusion of face, as at this day, unto the men of Judah, and to the in-16 habitants of Jerusalem, and to our kings, and to our princes, and to our priests, and to our prophets, and to 17 our fathers: for that we have sinned 18 before the Lord, and disobeyed him, and have not hearkened unto the voice of the Lord our God, to walk in the commandments of the Lord that 19 he hath set before us: since the day that the Lord brought our fathers out of the land of Egypt, unto this pre-sent day, we have been disobedient unto the Lord our God, and we have dealt unadvisedly in not hearkening 20 unto his voice. Wherefore the plagues clave unto us, and the curse, which the Lord commanded Moses his ser-vant *to pronounce* in the day that he brought our fathers out of the land of Egypt, to give us a land that floweth with milk and honey, as at this day. 21 Nevertheless we hearkened not unto the voice of the Lord our God, accord-ing unto all the words of the prophets, 22 whom he sent unto us: but we walked every man in the imagination of his own wicked heart, to serve strange gods, and to do that which is evil in 2 the sight of the Lord our God. There-fore the Lord hath made good his word, which he pronounced against us, and against our judges that judged Israel, and against our kings, and against our princes, and against the 2 men of Israel and Judah, to bring upon us great plagues, such as never happened under the whole heaven, [3] as it came to pass in Jerusalem, according to the things that are writ-3 ten in the law of Moses; that we should eat every man the flesh of his own son, and every man the flesh of his own 4 daughter. Moreover he hath given them to be in subjection to all the kingdoms that are round about us, to be a reproach and a desolation among all the people round about, where the 5 Lord hath scattered them. Thus were they cast down, and not exalted, be-cause we sinned against the Lord our God, in not hearkening unto his voice. 6 To the Lord our God *belongeth* right-eousness: but unto us and to our fa-thers confusion of face, as at this day.

[1] An-
other
reading
is, *and
vowed
vows.*

[2] See
Deut. xi.
21.

[3] An-
other
reading
is, *even
as he
hath
done.*

7 *For* all these plagues are come upon us, which the Lord hath pronounced 8 against us. Yet have we not intreated the favour of the Lord, in turning every one from the thoughts of his 9 wicked heart. Therefore hath the Lord kept watch over the plagues, and the Lord hath brought *them* upon us; for the Lord is righteous in all his works which he hath commanded us. 10 Yet we have not hearkened unto his voice, to walk in the commandments of the Lord that he hath set before us. 11 And now, O Lord, thou God of Israel, that hast brought thy people out of the land of Egypt with a mighty hand, and with signs, and with wonders, and with great power, and with a high arm, and hast gotten thyself a name, 12 as at this day : O Lord our God, we have sinned, we have done ungodly, we have dealt unrighteously in all 13 thine ordinances. Let thy wrath turn from us : for we are but a few left among the heathen, where thou hast 14 scattered us. Hear our prayer, O Lord, and our petition, and deliver us for thine own sake, and give us favour in the sight of them which have led us 15 away captive : that all the earth may know that thou art the Lord our God, because Israel and his posterity is 16 called by thy name. O Lord, look down from thine holy house, and consider us : incline thine ear, O Lord, 17 and hear : open thine eyes, and behold : for the dead that are in ¹ the grave, whose breath is taken from their bodies, will give unto the Lord 18 neither glory nor righteousness : but the soul that is greatly vexed, which goeth stooping and feeble, and the eyes that fail, and the hungry soul, will give thee glory and righteousness, 19 O Lord. For we do not present our supplication before thee, O Lord our God, for the righteousness of our 20 fathers, and of our kings. For thou hast sent thy wrath and thine indignation upon us, as thou hast spoken by thy servants the prophets, *saying,* 21 Thus saith the Lord, Bow your shoulders to serve the king of Babylon, and remain in the land that I gave unto 22 your fathers. But if ye will not hear the voice of the Lord, to serve the 23 king of Babylon, I will cause to cease out of the cities of Judah, and from without Jerusalem, the voice of mirth, and the voice of gladness, the voice of the bridegroom, and the voice of the bride : and the whole land shall be 24 desolate without inhabitant. But we would not hearken unto thy voice, to serve the king of Babylon : therefore hast thou made good thy words that thou spakest by thy servants the prophets, *namely,* that the bones of our kings, and the bones of our fathers,

should be taken out of their places. 25 And, lo, they are cast out to the heat by day, and to the frost by night, and they died in great miseries by famine, 26 by sword, and by ² pestilence. And the house which is called by thy name hast thou laid *waste,* as at this day, for the wickedness of the house of 27 Israel and the house of Judah. Yet, O Lord our God, thou hast dealt with us after all thy kindness, and accord-28 ing to all that great mercy of thine, as thou spakest by thy servant Moses in the day when thou didst command him to write thy law before the children of 29 Israel, saying, If ye will not hear my voice, surely this very great multitude shall be turned into a small *number* among the nations, where I will scat-30 ter them. For I know that they will not hear me, because it is a stiffnecked people : but in the land of their cap-31 tivity they shall lay it to heart, and shall know that I am the Lord their God : and I will give them a heart, 32 and ears to hear : and they shall praise me in the land of their captivity, and 33 think upon my name, and shall return from their stiff neck, and from their wicked deeds : for they shall remember the way of their fathers, which 34 sinned before the Lord. And I will bring them again into the land which I sware unto their fathers, to Abraham, to Isaac, and to Jacob, and they shall be lords of it : and I will increase them, and they shall not be dimin-35 ished. And I will make an everlasting covenant with them to be their God, and they shall be my people : and I will no more remove my people of Israel out of the land that I have given them.

3 O Lord Almighty, thou God of Israel, the soul in anguish, the troubled 2 spirit, crieth unto thee. Hear, O Lord, and have mercy ; for thou art a merciful God : yea, have mercy upon us, because we have sinned before 3 thee. For thou sittest *as king* for 4 ever, and we perish evermore. O Lord Almighty, thou God of Israel, hear now the prayer of ³ the dead Israelites, and of the children of them which were sinners before thee, that hearkened not unto the voice of 5 their God : for the which cause these plagues clave unto us. Remember not the iniquities of our fathers : but remember thy power and thy name 6 *now* at this time. For thou art the Lord our God, and thee, O Lord, will 7 we praise. For for this cause thou hast put thy fear in our hearts, ⁴ to the intent that we should call upon thy name : and we will praise thee in our captivity, for we have ⁵ called to mind all the iniquity of our fathers, that 8 sinned before thee. Behold, we are yet this day in our captivity, where thou

¹ Gr.
Hades.

² See
Jer.
xxxii. 36

³ Probably a mistake for *the men of Israel.*

⁴ Another reading is, *and made us to call.*

⁵ Another reading is, *put away from our heart all &c.*

hast scattered us, for a reproach and a curse, and to be subject to penalty, according to all the iniquities of our fathers, which departed from the Lord our God.

9 Hear, O Israel, the commandments of life: give ear to understand wisdom.
10 How happeneth it, O Israel, that thou art in thine enemies' land, that thou art waxen old in a strange country, that thou art defiled with the dead,
11 that thou art counted with them that
12 *go down* into [1] the grave? Thou hast
13 forsaken the fountain of wisdom. *For* if thou hadst walked in the way of God, thou shouldest have dwelled in
14 peace for ever. Learn where is [2] wisdom, where is strength, where is understanding; that thou mayest know also where is length of days, and life, where is the light of the eyes, and peace.
15 Who hath found out her place? and who hath come into her treasuries?
16 Where are the princes of the heathen, and such as ruled the beasts that are
17 upon the earth; they that had their pastime with the fowls of the air, and they that hoarded up silver and gold, wherein men trust; and of whose get-
18 ting there is no end? For they that [3] wrought in silver, and were so careful, and whose works are past finding
19 out, they are vanished and gone down to [1] the grave, and others are come up
20 in their steads. Younger men have seen the light, and dwelt upon the earth: but the way of knowledge have
21 they not known, neither understood they the paths thereof: neither have their children laid hold of it: they are
22 far off from [4] their way. It hath not been heard of in Canaan, neither hath it
23 been seen in Teman. The sons also of Agar that seek understanding, which are in the land, the merchants of Merran and Teman, and the authors of fables, and the searchers out of understanding; none of these have known the way of wisdom, or remembered
24 her paths. O Israel, how great is the house of God! and how large is the
25 place of his possession! great, and hath none end; high, and unmeasur-
26 able. There were the giants born that were famous of old, great of stature,
27 *and* expert in war. These did not God choose, neither gave he the way of
28 knowledge unto them: so they perished, because they had no [2] wisdom,
29 they perished through their own foolishness. Who hath gone up into heaven, and taken her, and brought
30 her down from the clouds? Who hath gone over the sea, and found her, and
31 will bring her for choice gold? There is none that knoweth her way, nor any that comprehendeth her path.
32 But he that knoweth all things knoweth her, he found her out with his understanding: he that prepared the

earth for evermore hath filled it with
33 fourfooted beasts: he that sendeth forth the light, and it goeth; he called
34 it, and it obeyed him with fear: and the stars shined in their watches, and were glad: when he called them, they said, Here we be; they shined with gladness unto him that made them.
35 This is our God, *and* there shall none other be accounted of in comparison
36 of him. He hath found out all the way of knowledge, and hath given it unto Jacob his servant, and to Israel
37 that is beloved of him. Afterward did she appear upon earth, and was conversant with men.

4 This is the book of the commandments of God, and the law that endureth for ever: all they that hold it fast *are appointed* to life; but such
2 as leave it shall die. Turn thee, O Jacob, and take hold of it: walk towards her shining in the presence of the light
3 thereof. Give not thy glory to another, nor the things that are profitable unto thee to a strange nation.
4 O Israel, happy are we: for the things that are pleasing to God are made
5 known unto us. Be of good cheer, my people, the memorial of Israel.
6 Ye were sold to the nations, *but* not for destruction: because ye moved God to wrath, ye were delivered unto
7 your adversaries. For ye provoked him that made you by sacrificing unto
8 demons, and not to God. Ye forgat the everlasting God, that brought you up; ye grieved also Jerusalem, that
9 nursed you. For she saw the wrath that is come upon you from God, and said, Hearken, ye *women* that dwelt about Sion: for God hath brought
10 upon me great mourning; for I have seen the captivity of my sons and daughters, which the Everlasting hath
11 brought upon them. For with joy did I nourish them; but sent them away
12 with weeping and mourning. Let no man rejoice over me, a widow, and forsaken of many: for the sins of my children am I left desolate; because they turned aside from the law of
13 God, and had no regard to his statutes, neither walked they in the ways of God's commandments, nor trod in the paths of discipline in his righteous-
14 ness. Let them that dwell about Sion come, and remember ye the captivity of my sons and daughters, which the Everlasting hath brought upon them.
15 For he hath brought a nation upon them from far, a shameless nation, and of a strange language, [5] who neither reverenced old man, nor pitied
16 child. And they have carried away the dear beloved sons of the widow, and left her that was alone desolate
17 of her daughters. But I, what can I
18 help you? For he that brought these plagues upon you will deliver you

[1] Gr. *Hades.*

[2] Or, *prudence*

[3] Or, *diligently sought after:* Prov. xi. 27 (Sept.).

[4] Another reading is, *the way thereof.*

[5] Another reading is, *for they.*

122

19 from the hand of your enemies. Go your way, O my children, go your way: 20 for I am left desolate. I have put off the garment of peace, and put upon me the sackcloth of my petition: I will cry unto the Everlasting as long 21 as I live. Be of good cheer, O my children, cry unto God, and he shall deliver you from the power and hand 22 of the enemies. For I have trusted in the Everlasting, that he will save you; and joy is come unto me from the Holy One, because of the mercy which shall soon come unto you [1] from 23 the Everlasting your Saviour. For I sent you out with mourning and weeping: but God will give you to me again with joy and gladness for ever. 24 For like as now they that dwell about Sion have seen your captivity: so shall they see shortly your salvation from [2] our God, which shall come upon you with great glory, and brightness 25 of the Everlasting. My children, suffer patiently the wrath that is come upon you from God: for thine enemy hath persecuted thee; but shortly thou shalt see his destruction, and 26 shalt tread upon their necks. My delicate ones have gone rough ways; they were taken away as a flock 27 carried off by the enemies. Be of good cheer, O my children, and cry unto God: for ye shall be remembered of him that hath brought *these* 28 *things* upon you. For as it was your mind to go astray from God: so, return and seek him ten times more. 29 For he that brought these plagues upon you shall bring you everlasting 30 joy again with your salvation. Be of good cheer, O Jerusalem: for he that called thee by name will comfort thee. 31 Miserable are they that afflicted thee, 32 and rejoiced at thy fall. Miserable are the cities which thy children served: miserable is she that received 33 thy sons. For as she rejoiced at thy fall, and was glad of thy ruin: so shall she be grieved for her own desolation. 34 And I will take away her exultation in her great multitude, and her boasting shall be turned into mourning. 35 For fire shall come upon her from the Everlasting, long to endure; and she shall be inhabited of [3] devils for a great time. 36 O Jerusalem, look about thee toward the east, and behold the joy that 37 cometh unto thee from God. Lo, thy sons come, whom thou sentest away, they come gathered together from the east to the west at the word of the Holy One, rejoicing in the glory of 5 God. Put off, O Jerusalem, the garment of thy mourning and affliction, and put on the comeliness of the glory 2 that *cometh* from God for ever. Cast about thee the robe of the righteousness which *cometh* from God; set a

[2] Another reading is, *your*.

[3] Gr. *demons*.

diadem on thine head of the glory of 3 the Everlasting. For God will shew thy brightness unto every *region* un-4 der heaven. For thy name shall be called of God for ever The peace of righteousness, and The glory of godli-5 ness. Arise, O Jerusalem, and stand upon the height, and look about thee toward the east, and behold thy children gathered from the going down of the sun unto the rising thereof at the word of the Holy One, rejoicing that 6 God hath remembered them. For they went from thee on foot, being led away of their enemies: but God bringeth them in unto thee borne on high with glory, [4] as *on* a royal throne. 7 For God hath appointed that every high mountain, and the everlasting hills, should be made low, and the valleys filled up, to make plain the ground, that Israel may go safely in 8 the glory of God. Moreover the woods and every sweet-smelling tree have overshadowed Israel by the command-9 ment of God. For God shall lead Israel with joy in the light of his glory with the mercy and righteousness that cometh from him.

[4] Another reading is, as *children of the kingdom*.

THE EPISTLE OF JEREMY.

6 A copy of an epistle, which Jeremy sent unto them which were to be led captives into Babylon by the king of the Babylonians, to certify them, as it was commanded him of God. 2 Because of the sins which ye have committed before God, ye shall be led away captives into Babylon by Nabuchodonosor king of the Babylonians. 3 So when ye be come unto Babylon, ye shall remain there many years, and for a long season, even for seven generations: and after that I will bring you out peaceably from thence. 4 But now shall ye see in Babylon gods of silver, and of gold, and of wood, borne upon shoulders, which cause the 5 nations to fear. Beware therefore that ye in no wise become like unto the strangers, neither let fear take hold upon you because of them, when ye see the multitude before them and 6 behind them, worshipping them. But say ye in your hearts, O Lord, we 7 must worship thee. For mine angel is with you, [5] and I myself do care 8 for your [6] souls. For their tongue is polished by the workman, and they themselves are overlaid with gold and 9 with silver; yet are they but false, and cannot speak. And taking gold, as it were for a virgin that loveth to go gay, they make crowns for the heads 10 of their gods: and sometimes also the priests convey from their gods gold and silver, and bestow it upon them-11 selves; and will even give thereof to

[5] Or, *and he careth*
[6] Or, *lives*

the common harlots: and they deck them as men with garments, *even* the gods of silver, and gods of gold, and of 12 wood. Yet cannot these gods save themselves from rust and moths, though they be covered with purple 13 raiment. They wipe their faces because of the dust of the temple, which 14 is thick upon them. And he that cannot put to death one that offendeth against him holdeth a sceptre, as though he were judge of a country. 15 He hath also a dagger in his right hand, and an axe: but cannot deliver 16 himself from war and robbers. Whereby they are known not to be gods: 17 therefore fear them not. For like as a vessel that a man useth is nothing worth when it is broken; even so it is with their gods: when they be set up in the temples their eyes be full of dust through the feet of them that 18 come in. And as the courts are made sure on every side upon him that offendeth the king, as being committed to suffer death; *even so* the priests make fast their temples with doors, with locks, and bars, lest they be 19 carried off by robbers. They light them candles, yea, more than for themselves, whereof they cannot see 20 one. They are as one of the beams of the temple; and men say their hearts are eaten out, when things creeping out of the earth devour both them and their raiment: they feel 21 it not when their faces are blacked through the smoke that cometh out 22 of the temple: upon their bodies and heads alight bats, swallows, and birds; and in like manner the cats also. 23 Whereby ye may know that they are no gods: therefore fear them not. 24 Notwithstanding the gold wherewith they are beset to make them beautiful, except one wipe off the rust, they will not shine: for not even when they 25 were molten did they feel it. Things wherein there is no breath are bought 26 at any cost. Having no feet, they are borne upon shoulders, whereby they declare unto men that they be nothing 27 worth. They also that serve them are ashamed: for if they fall to the ground at any time, they cannot rise up again of themselves: neither, if one set them upright, can they move of themselves: neither, if they be set awry, can they make themselves straight: but the offerings are set before them, as if they were dead 28 men. And the things that are sacrificed unto them, their priests sell and spend; and in like manner their wives also lay up part thereof in salt; but unto the poor and to the impotent will 29 they give nothing thereof. The menstruous woman and the woman in childbed touch their sacrifices: knowing therefore by these things that they

30 are no gods, fear them not. For how can they be called gods? because women set meat before the gods of 31 silver, gold, and wood. And in their temples the priests [1] sit on seats, having their clothes rent, and their heads and beards shaven, and nothing 32 upon their heads. They roar and cry before their gods, as men do at the 33 feast when one is dead. The priests also take off garments from them, and clothe their wives and children withal. 34 Whether it be evil that one doeth unto them, or good, they are not able to recompense it: they can neither set 35 up a king, nor put him down. In like manner, they can neither give riches nor money: though a man make a vow unto them, and keep it not, they 36 will never exact it. They can save no man from death, neither deliver the 37 weak from the mighty. They cannot restore a blind man to his sight, nor 38 deliver any that is in distress. They can shew no mercy to the widow, nor 39 do good to the fatherless. They are like the stones that be *hewn* out of the mountain, *these gods* of wood, and that are overlaid with gold and with silver: they that minister unto them 40 shall be confounded. How should a man then think or say that they are gods, when even the Chaldeans them-41 selves dishonour them? Who if they shall see one dumb that cannot speak, they bring him, and intreat him to call upon Bel, as though he were able 42 to understand. Yet they cannot perceive this themselves, and forsake them: for they have no understand-43 ing. The women also with cords about them sit in the ways, burning bran for incense: but if any of them, drawn by some that passeth by, lie with him, she reproacheth her fellow, that she was not thought as worthy as herself, 44 nor her cord broken. Whatsoever is done among them is false: how should a man then think or say that they 45 are gods? They are fashioned by carpenters and goldsmiths: they can be nothing else than the workmen 46 will have them to be. And they themselves that fashioned them can never continue long: how then should the things that are fashioned by them? 47 For they have left lies and reproaches 48 to them that come after. For when there cometh any war or plague upon them, the priests consult with themselves, where they may be hidden with 49 them. How then cannot men understand that they be no gods, which can neither save themselves from war, 50 nor from plague? For seeing they be but of wood, and overlaid with gold and with silver, it shall be known 51 hereafter that they are false: and it shall be manifest to all nations and kings that they are no gods, but the

[1] Or, *bear the litter*

works of men's hands, and that there 52 is no work of God in them. Who then may not know that they are 53 no gods? For neither can they set up a king in a land, nor give rain 54 unto men. Neither can they judge their own cause, nor [1] redress a wrong, being unable: for they are as crows 55 between heaven and earth. For even when fire falleth upon the house of gods of wood, or overlaid with gold or with silver, their priests will flee away, and escape, but they themselves shall 56 be burnt asunder like beams. Moreover they cannot withstand any king or enemies: how should a man then allow or think that they be gods? 57 Neither are those gods of wood, and overlaid with silver or with gold, able to escape either from thieves or rob- 58 bers. Whose gold, and silver, and garments wherewith they are clothed, they that are strong will take from them, and go away withal: neither shall they be able to help themselves. 59 Therefore it is better to be a king that sheweth his manhood, or else a vessel in a house profitable for that whereof the owner shall have need, than such false gods; or even a door in a house, to keep the things safe that be therein, than such false gods; or a pillar of wood in a palace, than 60 such false gods. For sun, and moon, and stars, being bright and sent to do 61 their offices, are obedient. Likewise also the lightning when it glittereth is fair to see; and after the same manner the wind also bloweth in 62 every country. And when God commandeth the clouds to go over the whole world, they do as they are 63 bidden. And the fire sent from above to consume mountains and woods doeth as it is commanded: but these are to be likened unto them neither in 64 shew nor power. Wherefore a man should neither think nor say that they are gods, seeing they are able neither to judge causes, nor to do good unto 65 men. Knowing therefore that they 66 are no gods, fear them not. For they can neither curse nor bless kings: 67 neither can they shew signs in the heavens among the nations, nor shine as the sun, nor give light as the moon. 68 The beasts are better than they: for they can get under a covert, and help 69 themselves. In no wise then is it manifest unto us that they are gods: 70 therefore fear them not. For as a scarecrow in a garden of cucumbers that keepeth nothing, so are their gods of wood, and overlaid with gold 71 and with silver. Likewise also their gods of wood, and overlaid with gold and with silver, are like to a white thorn in an orchard, that every bird sitteth upon; as also to a dead body, 72 that is cast forth into the dark. And ye shall know them to be no gods by the [2] bright purple that rotteth upon them: and they themselves afterward shall be consumed, and shall be a re- 73 proach in the country. Better therefore is the just man that hath none idols: for he shall be far from reproach.

THE SONG OF THE

THREE HOLY CHILDREN,

Which followeth in the third Chapter of DANIEL after this place, — *fell down bound into the midst of the burning fiery furnace.* — Verse 23. That which followeth is not in the Hebrew, to wit, *And they walked* — unto these words, *Then Nebuchadnezzar* — verse 24.

1 AND they walked in the midst of the fire, praising God, and blessing the 2 Lord. Then Azarias stood, and prayed on this manner; and opening his mouth in the midst of the fire said, 3 Blessed art thou, O Lord, thou God of our fathers, [1] and worthy to be praised; and thy name is glorified for evermore: 4 for thou art righteous in all the things that thou hast done: yea, true are all thy works, and thy ways are right, 5 and all thy judgements truth. In all the things that thou hast brought upon us, and upon the holy city of our fathers, *even* Jerusalem, thou hast executed true judgements: for according to truth and justice hast thou brought all these things upon us be- 6 cause of our sins. For we have sinned and committed iniquity, in departing 7 from thee. In all things have we trespassed, and not obeyed thy commandments, nor kept them, neither done as thou hast commanded us, that 8 it might go well with us. Wherefore all that thou hast brought upon us, and everything that thou hast done to us, thou hast done in true judge-

9 ment. And thou didst deliver us into the hands of lawless enemies, and most hateful forsakers *of God*, and to an unjust king, and the most wicked
10 in all the world. And now we cannot open our mouth ; shame and reproach have befallen thy servants, and them
11 that worship thee. Deliver us not up utterly, for thy name's sake, neither
12 disannul thou thy covenant: and cause not thy mercy to depart from us, for the sake of Abraham that is beloved of thee, and for the sake of Isaac thy
13 servant, and Israel thy holy one; to whom thou didst promise, that thou wouldest multiply their seed as the stars of heaven, and as the sand that
14 is upon the sea shore. For we, O Lord, are become less than any nation, and be kept under this day in all the world
15 because of our sins. Neither is there at this time prince, or prophet, or leader, or burnt offering, or sacrifice, or oblation, or incense, or place to offer before thee, and to find mercy.
16 Nevertheless in a contrite heart and a humble spirit let us be accepted;
17 like as in the burnt offerings of rams and bullocks, and like as in ten thousands of fat lambs; so let our sacrifice be in thy sight this day, and *grant* that we may wholly go after thee, for they shall not be ashamed that put
18 their trust in thee. And now we follow thee with all our heart, we fear
19 thee, and seek thy face. Put us not to shame : but deal with us after thy kindness, and according to the multi-
20 tude of thy mercy. Deliver us also according to thy marvellous works, and give glory to thy name, O Lord : and let all them that do thy servants
21 hurt be confounded; and let them be ashamed of all their [1]power and might, and let their strength be bro-
22 ken ; and let them know that thou art the Lord, the only God, and glorious over the whole world.
23 And the king's servants, that put them in, ceased not to make the furnace hot with naphtha, pitch, tow, and
24 small wood ; so that the flame streamed forth above the furnace forty and
25 nine cubits. And it spread, and burned those Chaldeans whom it
26 found about the furnace. But the angel of the Lord came down into the furnace together with Azarias and his fellows, and he smote the flame of the fire out of the furnace;
27 and made the midst of the furnace as it had been a moist whistling wind, so that the fire touched them not at all, neither hurt nor troubled them.
28 Then the three, as out of one mouth, praised, and glorified, and blessed God
29 in the furnace, saying, Blessed art thou, O Lord, thou God of our fathers : and to be praised and exalted above

30 all for ever. And blessed is thy glorious and holy name : and to be praised and exalted above all for
31 ever. Blessed art thou in the temple of thine holy glory : and to be praised and glorified above all for ever.
32 Blessed art thou that beholdest the depths, and sittest upon the cherubim : and to be praised and exalted above
33 all for ever. Blessed art thou on the throne of thy kingdom : and to be praised and [2]extolled above all for
34 ever. Blessed art thou in the firmament of heaven: and to be praised and glorified for ever.
35 O all ye works of the Lord, bless ye the Lord : praise and exalt him above
36 all for ever. O ye heavens, bless ye the Lord : praise and exalt him above
37 all for ever. O ye angels of the Lord, bless ye the Lord : praise and exalt
38 him above all for ever. O all ye waters that be above the heaven, bless ye the Lord : praise and exalt him above
39 all for ever. O all [3]ye powers of the Lord, bless ye the Lord : praise and
40 exalt him above all for ever. O ye sun and moon, bless ye the Lord : praise and exalt him above all for ever.
41 O ye stars of heaven, bless ye the Lord : praise and exalt him above
42 all for ever. O every shower and dew, bless ye the Lord : praise and
43 exalt him above all for ever. O all ye winds, bless ye the Lord : praise and
44 exalt him above all for ever. O ye fire and heat, bless ye the Lord : praise
47 and exalt him above all for ever.[4] [5]O ye nights and days, bless ye the Lord : praise and exalt him above all for ever.
48 O ye light and darkness, bless ye the Lord : praise and exalt him above all for ever. O ye cold and heat, bless ye
50 the Lord : praise and exalt him above all for ever. [6]O ye frost and snow, bless ye the Lord : praise and exalt
51 him above all for ever. O ye lightnings and clouds, bless ye the Lord : praise
52 and exalt him above all for ever. O let the earth bless the Lord : let it praise
53 and exalt him above all for ever. O ye mountains and hills, bless ye the Lord : praise and exalt him above all for ever.
54 O ye things that grow on the earth, bless ye the Lord : praise and exalt
56 him above all for ever. [7]O sea and rivers, bless ye the Lord : praise and
55 exalt him above all for ever. O ye fountains, bless ye the Lord : praise
57 and exalt him above all for ever. O ye whales, and all that move in the waters, bless ye the Lord : praise and
58 exalt him above all for ever. O all ye fowls of the air, bless ye the Lord : praise and exalt him above all for
59 ever. O all ye beasts and cattle, bless ye the Lord : praise and exalt
60 him above all for ever. O ye children of men, bless ye the Lord : praise and
61 exalt him above all for ever. [8]O let

[1] Some MSS. omit *power and.*

[2] Another reading is, *exalted.*

[3] Another reading is. *the host.*

[4] Verse 45 is omitted by the best authorities.

[5] Before this verse some authorities insert verse 46, *O ye dews and storms of snow, bless ye* &c.

[6] Before this verse some authorities insert verse 49, *O ye ice and cold, bless ye* &c.

[7] Some authorities transpose verses 56 and 55.

[8] Some MSS. read *O Israel, bless ye.*

1 Some MSS. omit *of the Lord.*

Israel bless the Lord: praise and 62 exalt him above all for ever. O ye priests [1] of the Lord, bless ye the Lord: praise and exalt him above all 63 for ever. O ye servants [1] of the Lord, bless ye the Lord: praise and exalt 64 him above all for ever. O ye spirits and souls of the righteous, bless ye the Lord: praise and exalt him above all 65 for ever. O ye that are holy and humble of heart, bless ye the Lord: praise and exalt him above all for ever. 66 O Ananias, Azarias, and Misael, bless ye the Lord: praise and exalt him above all for ever: for he hath rescued us from [2] hell, and saved us from the hand of death: he hath delivered us out of the midst of the furnace *and* burning flame, even out of the midst 67 of the fire hath he delivered us. O give thanks unto the Lord, for he is good: for his mercy *endureth* for ever. 68 O all ye that worship the Lord, bless the God of gods, praise him, and give him thanks: for his mercy *endureth* for ever.

2 Or, *th grave* Gr. *Hades.*

THE

HISTORY OF SUSANNA,

Set apart from the beginning of DANIEL, because it is not in the Hebrew, as neither the Narration of *Bel and the Dragon.*

1 THERE dwelt a man in Babylon, and 2 his name was Joakim: and he took a wife, whose name was Susanna, the daughter of Helkias, a very fair woman, and one that feared the Lord. 3 Her parents also were righteous, and taught their daughter according to the 4 law of Moses. Now Joakim was a great rich man, and had a fair garden joining unto his house: and to him resorted the Jews; because he was 5 more honourable than all others. And the same year there were appointed two of the ancients of the people to be judges, such as the Lord spake of, that wickedness came from Babylon from ancient judges, who were ac- 6 counted to govern the people. These kept much at Joakim's house: and all that had any suits in law came unto 7 them. Now when the people departed away at noon, Susanna went into her 8 husband's garden to walk. And the two elders beheld her going in every day, and walking; and they were in- 9 flamed with love for her: And they perverted their own mind, and turned away their eyes, that they might not look unto heaven, nor remember just 10 judgements. And albeit they both were wounded with her love, yet durst not one shew another his grief. 11 For they were ashamed to declare their lust, that they desired to have to 12 do with her. Yet they watched jealously from day to day to see her. 13 And the one said to the other, Let us 14 now go home: for it is dinner time. So when they were gone out, they parted the one from the other, and turning back again they came to the same place; and after that they had asked one another the cause, they acknowledged their lust: and then appointed they a time both together, when they 15 might find her alone. And it fell out, as they watched a fit day, she went in as aforetime with two maids only, and she was desirous to wash herself in 16 the garden: for it was hot. And there was nobody there save the two elders, that had hid themselves, and watched 17 her. Then she said to her maids, Bring me oil and washing balls, and shut the garden doors, that I may wash me. 18 And they did as she bade them, and shut the garden doors, and went out themselves at the side doors to fetch the things that she had commanded them: and they saw not the elders, 19 because they were hid. Now when the maids were gone forth, the two elders 20 rose up, and ran unto her, saying, Behold, the garden doors are shut, that no man can see us, and we are in love with thee; therefore consent unto us, 21 and lie with us. If thou wilt not, we will bear witness against thee, that a young man was with thee: and therefore thou didst send away thy maids 22 from thee. Then Susanna sighed, and said, I am straitened on every side: for if I do this thing, it is death unto me: and if I do it not, I cannot escape 23 your hands. It is better for me to fall into your hands, and not do it, than 24 to sin in the sight of the Lord. With that Susanna cried with a loud voice: and the two elders cried out against 25 her. Then ran the one, and opened the 26 garden doors. So when the servants of the house heard the cry in the garden, they rushed in at the side door, to 27 see what had befallen her. But when

the elders had told their tale, the servants were greatly ashamed: for there was never such a report made of 28 Susanna. And it came to pass on the morrow, when the people assembled to her husband Joakim, the two elders came full of their wicked intent against 29 Susanna to put her to death; and said before the people, Send for Susanna, the daughter of Helkias, Joakim's 30 wife. So they sent; and she came with her father and mother, her children, 31 and all her kindred. Now Susanna was a very delicate woman, and 32 beauteous to behold. And these wicked men commanded her to be unveiled, (for she was veiled) that they 33 might be filled with her beauty. Therefore her friends and all that saw her 34 wept. Then the two elders stood up in the midst of the people, and laid their 35 hands upon her head. And she weeping looked up toward heaven: for her 36 heart trusted in the Lord. And the elders said, As we walked in the garden alone, this *woman* came in with two maids, and shut the garden doors, and 37 sent the maids away. Then a young man, who there was hid, came unto 38 her, and lay with her. And we, being in a corner of the garden, saw this 39 wickedness, and ran unto them. And when we saw them together, the man we could not hold: for he was stronger than we, and opened the doors, and 40 leaped out. But having taken this *woman*, we asked who the young man was, but she would not tell us: these 41 things do we testify. Then the assembly believed them, as those that were elders of the people and judges: 42 so they condemned her to death. Then Susanna cried out with a loud voice, and said, O everlasting God, that knowest the secrets, that knowest all 43 things before they be: thou knowest that they have borne false witness against me, and, behold, I must die; whereas I never did such things as these men have maliciously invented 44 against me. And the Lord heard her 45 voice. Therefore when she was led away to be put to death, God raised up the holy spirit of a young youth, 46 whose name was Daniel: and he cried with a loud voice, I am clear from the 47 blood of this woman. Then all the people turned them toward him, and said, What mean these words that 48 thou hast spoken? So he standing in the midst of them said, Are ye such fools, ye sons of Israel, that without examination or knowledge of the truth ye have condemned a daughter of

49 Israel? Return again to the place of judgement: for these have borne false 50 witness against her. Wherefore all the people turned again in haste, and the elders said unto him, Come, sit down among us, and shew it us, seeing God hath given thee the honour of an 51 elder. Then said Daniel unto them, Put them asunder one far from an- 52 other, and I will examine them. So when they were put asunder one from another, he called one of them, and said unto him, O thou that art waxen old in wickedness, now are thy sins come *home to thee* which thou hast 53 committed aforetime, in pronouncing unjust judgement, and condemning the innocent, and letting the guilty go free; albeit the Lord saith, The innocent and righteous shalt thou not slay. 54 Now then, if thou sawest her, tell me, Under what tree sawest thou them companying together? Who answered, 55 Under a mastick tree. And Daniel said, Right well hast thou lied against thine own head; for even now the angel of God hath received the sentence of God and shall cut thee in 56 two. So he put him aside, and commanded to bring the other, and said unto him, O thou seed of Canaan, and not of Judah, beauty hath deceived thee, and lust hath perverted thine 57 heart. Thus have ye dealt with the daughters of Israel, and they for fear companied with you: but the daughter of Judah would not abide your wicked- 58 ness. Now therefore tell me, Under what tree didst thou take them companying together? Who answered, 59 Under a holm tree. Then said Daniel unto him, Right well hast thou also lied against thine own head: for the angel of God waiteth with the sword to cut thee in two, that he may de- 60 stroy you. With that all the assembly cried out with a loud voice, and blessed God, who saveth them that hope in 61 him. And they arose against the two elders, for Daniel had convicted them of false witness out of their own 62 mouth: and according to the law of Moses they did unto them in such sort as they maliciously intended to do to their neighbour: and they put them to death, and the innocent blood 63 was saved the same day. Therefore Helkias and his wife praised God for their daughter Susanna, with Joakim her husband, and all the kindred, because there was no dishonesty found 64 in her. And from that day forth was Daniel had in great reputation in the sight of the people.

BEL AND THE DRAGON.

1 AND king Astyages was gathered to his fathers, and Cyrus the Persian 2 received his kingdom. And Daniel lived with the king, and was honoured 3 above all his friends. Now the Babylonians had an idol, called Bel, and there were spent upon him every day twelve great measures of fine flour, and forty sheep, and six firkins of 4 wine. And the king did honour to it, and went daily to worship it: but Daniel worshipped his own God. And the king said unto him, Why 5 dost thou not worship Bel? And he said, Because I may not do honour to idols made with hands, but to the living God, who hath created the heaven and the earth, and hath sov-6 ereignty over all flesh. Then said the king unto him, Thinkest thou not that Bel is a living god? or seest thou not how much he eateth and drinketh 7 every day? Then Daniel laughed, and said, O king, be not deceived: for this is but clay within, and brass without, and did never eat or drink anything. 8 So the king was wroth, and called for his priests, and said unto them, If ye tell me not who this is that devoureth 9 these expenses, ye shall die. But if ye can shew me that Bel devoureth them, then Daniel shall die: for he hath spoken blasphemy against Bel. And Daniel said unto the king, Let it 10 be according to thy word. Now the priests of Bel were threescore and ten, beside their wives and children. And the king went with Daniel into the 11 temple of Bel. So Bel's priests said, Lo, we will get us out: but thou, O king, set on the meat, and mingle the wine and set it forth, and shut the door fast, and seal it with thine own 12 signet; and when thou comest in the morning, if thou find not that Bel hath eaten up all, we will suffer death: or else Daniel, that speaketh falsely 13 against us. And they little regarded it: for under the table they had made a privy entrance, whereby they entered in continually, and consumed 14 those things. And it came to pass, when they were gone forth, the king set the meat before Bel. Now Daniel had commanded his servants to bring ashes, and they strewed all the temple *with them* in the presence of the king alone: then went they out, and shut the door, and sealed it with the king's 15 signet, and so departed. Now in the night came the priests with their wives and children, as they were wont

16 to do, and did eat and drink up all. In the morning betime the king arose, 17 and Daniel with him. And the king said, Daniel, are the seals whole? And he said, Yea, O king, they be 18 whole. And as soon as he had opened the door, the king looked upon the table, and cried with a loud voice, Great art thou, O Bel, and with thee 19 is no deceit at all. Then laughed Daniel, and held the king that he should not go in, and said, Behold now the pavement, and mark well 20 whose footsteps are these. And the king said, I see the footsteps of men, women, and children. And then the 21 king was angry, and took the priests with their wives and children, who shewed him the privy doors, where they came in, and consumed such 22 things as were upon the table. Therefore the king slew them, and delivered Bel into Daniel's power, who overthrew him and his temple.

23 And in that same place there was a great ¹dragon, which they of Babylon 24 worshipped. And the king said unto Daniel, Wilt thou also say that this is of brass? lo, he liveth, and eateth and drinketh; thou canst not say that he is no living god: therefore worship 25 him. Then said Daniel, I will worship the Lord my God: for he is a 26 living God. But give me leave, O king, and I shall slay this dragon without sword or staff. The king 27 said, I give thee leave. Then Daniel took pitch, and fat, and hair, and did seethe them together, and made lumps thereof: this he put in the dragon's mouth, so the dragon did eat and burst in sunder: and *Daniel* said, Lo, 28 these are the gods ye worship. When they of Babylon heard that, they took great indignation, and conspired against the king, saying, The king is become a Jew, and he hath pulled down Bel, and slain the dragon, and 29 put the priests to the sword. So they came to the king, and said, Deliver us Daniel, or else we will destroy thee 30 and thine house. Now when the king saw that they pressed him sore, being constrained, the king delivered Dan-31 iel unto them: who cast him into the lions' den: where he was six days. 32 And in the den there were seven lions, and they had given them every day two carcases, and two sheep: which then were not given to them, to the intent they might devour Daniel. 33 Now there was in Jewry the prophet

¹ Or, *serpent*

[1] Habakkuk, who had made pottage, and had broken bread into a bowl, and was going into the field, for to 34 bring it to the reapers. But the angel of the Lord said unto Habakkuk, Go carry the dinner that thou hast into Babylon unto Daniel, in the lions' den. 35 And Habakkuk said, Lord, I never saw Babylon; neither do I know 36 where the den is. Then the angel of the Lord took him by the crown, and lifted him up by the hair of his head, and with the blast of his breath set 37 him in Babylon over the den. And Habakkuk cried, saying, O Daniel, Daniel, take the dinner which God 38 hath sent thee. And Daniel said,

Thou hast remembered me, O God: neither hast thou forsaken them that 39 love thee. So Daniel arose, and did eat: and the angel of God set Habakkuk in his own place again immedi-40 ately. Upon the seventh day the king came to bewail Daniel: and when he came to the den, he looked in, and, behold, Daniel was sitting. 41 Then cried the king with a loud voice, saying, Great art thou. O Lord, thou God of Daniel, and there is none other 42 beside thee. And he drew him out, and cast those that were the cause of his destruction into the den: and they were devoured in a moment before his face.

THE

PRAYER OF MANASSES

KING OF JUDAH,

WHEN HE WAS HOLDEN CAPTIVE IN BABYLON.

O LORD Almighty, that art in heaven, thou God of our fathers, of Abraham, and Isaac, and Jacob, and of their righteous seed; who hast made heaven and earth, with all the [1] ornament thereof; who hast bound the sea by the word of thy commandment; who hast shut up the deep, and sealed it by thy terrible and glorious name; whom all things fear, yea, tremble before thy power; for the majesty of thy glory cannot be borne, and the anger of thy threatening toward sinners is importable: thy merciful promise is unmeasurable and unsearchable; for thou art the Lord Most High, of great compassion, longsuffering and abundant in mercy, and repentest [2] of bringing evils upon men. [3] Thou, O Lord, according to thy great goodness hast promised repentance and forgiveness to them that have sinned against thee: and of thine infinite mercies hast appointed repentance unto sinners, that they may be saved. Thou therefore, O Lord, that art the God of the just, hast not appointed repentance to the just, to Abraham, and Isaac, and Jacob, which have not sinned against thee; but thou hast appointed repentance unto me that am a sinner: for I have sinned above the number of the sands of the sea. My transgressions are multiplied, [4] O Lord: my transgressions are multiplied, and I am not worthy to behold and see the height of heaven for the multitude of mine iniquities. I am bowed down with many iron bands, that I cannot lift up mine head [5] by reason of my sins, neither have I any respite: for I have provoked thy wrath, and done that which is evil before thee: [6] I did not thy will, neither kept I thy commandments: I have set up abominations, and have multiplied [7] detestable things. Now therefore I bow the knee of mine heart, beseeching thee of grace. I have sinned, O Lord, I have sinned, and I acknowledge mine iniquities: but, I humbly beseech thee, forgive me, O Lord, forgive me, and destroy me not with mine iniquities. Be not angry with me for ever, by reserving evil for me; neither condemn me into the lower parts of the earth. For thou, [8] O Lord, art the God of them that repent; and in me thou wilt shew all thy goodness: for thou wilt save me, that am unworthy, according to thy great mercy. And I will praise thee for ever all the days of my life: for all the host of heaven doth sing thy praise, and thine is the glory for ever and ever. Amen.

THE FIRST BOOK OF THE

MACCABEES.

1 That is, the Greek Empire. Compare ver. 10 and ch. vi. 2.

2 circa B. C. 176.

3 Or, nations: and so throughout this book.

4 See 2 Macc. iv. 9, 12.

1 AND it came to pass, after that Alexander the Macedonian, the son of Philip, who came out of the land of Chittim, and smote Darius king of the Persians and Medes, *it came to pass*, after he had smitten him, that he reigned in his stead, in former time, 2 over ¹ Greece. And he fought many battles, and won many strongholds, 3 and slew the kings of the earth, and went through to the ends of the earth, and took spoils of a multitude of nations. And the earth was quiet before him, and he was exalted, and his heart 4 was lifted up, and he gathered together an exceeding strong host, and ruled over countries and nations and principalities, and they became tribu-5 tary unto him. And after these things he fell sick, and perceived that he 6 should die. And he called his servants, which were honourable, which had been brought up with him from his youth, and he divided unto them his 7 kingdom, while he was yet alive. And Alexander reigned twelve years, and 8 he died. And his servants bare rule, 9 each one in his place. And they did all put diadems upon themselves after that he was dead, and so did their sons after them many years : and they multiplied evils in the earth.

10 And there came forth out of them a sinful root, Antiochus Epiphanes, son of Antiochus the king, who had been a hostage at Rome, and he reigned in ² the hundred and thirty and seventh year of the kingdom of the Greeks. 11 In those days came there forth out of Israel transgressors of the law, and persuaded many, saying, Let us go and make a covenant with the ³ Gentiles that are round about us ; for 12 since we were parted from them many evils have befallen us. And the saying 13 was good in their eyes. And certain of the people were forward *herein* and went to the king, and he gave them licence to do after the ordinances of 14 the ³ Gentiles. And ⁴ they built a place of exercise in Jerusalem according to 15 the laws of the ³ Gentiles ; and they made themselves uncircumcised, and forsook the holy covenant, and joined themselves to the ³ Gentiles, and sold themselves to do evil. 16 And the kingdom was well ordered in the sight of Antiochus, and he thought to reign over Egypt, that he might reign over the two kingdoms.

17 And he entered into Egypt with a ⁵ great multitude, with chariots, and with elephants, and with horsemen, 18 and with a great ⁶ navy ; and he made war against Ptolemy king of Egypt ; and Ptolemy was put to shame before him, and fled ; and many fell wounded 19 to death. And they got possession of the strong cities in the land of Egypt ; and he took the spoils of Egypt. 20 And Antiochus, after that he had smitten Egypt, returned in ⁷ the hundred and forty and third year, and went up against Israel and Jerusalem 21 with a ⁵ great multitude, and entered presumptuously into the sanctuary, and took the golden altar, and the candlestick of the light, and all that 22 pertained thereto, and the table of the shewbread, and the cups to pour withal, and the bowls, and the golden censers, and the veil, and the crowns, and the adorning of gold which was on the face of the temple, and he scaled 23 it all off. And he took the silver and the gold and the precious vessels ; and he took the hidden treasures 24 which he found. And when he had taken all, he went away into his own land, and he made a great slaughter, 25 and spake very presumptuously. And there came great mourning upon Is-26 rael, in every place where they were ; and the rulers and elders groaned, the virgins and young men were made feeble, and the beauty of the women 27 was changed. Every bridegroom took up lamentation, she that sat in the marriage chamber was in heaviness. 28 And the land was moved for the inhabitants thereof, and all the house of Jacob was clothed with shame.

29 And ⁸ after ⁹ two full years the king sent a chief collector of tribute unto the cities of Judah, and he came unto Jerusalem with a ⁵ great multitude. 30 And spake words of peace unto them in subtilty, and they gave him credence : and he fell upon the city suddenly, and smote it very sore, and destroyed much people out of Israel. 31 And he took the spoils of the city, and set it on fire, and pulled down the houses thereof and the walls thereof 32 on every side. And they led captive the women and the children, and the 33 cattle they took in possession. And they builded the city of David with a great and strong wall, with strong towers, and it became unto them a

5 Gr. heavy.

6 Or, armament

7 circa B. C. 170. See 2 Macc. v. 11-16.

8 See 2 Macc. v. 24.

9 Gr. two years of days.

34 citadel. And they put there a sinful
nation, transgressors of the law, and
they strengthened themselves therein.
35 And they stored up arms and victuals,
and gathering together the spoils of
Jerusalem, they laid them up there,
36 and they became a sore snare : and it
became a place to lie in wait in against
the sanctuary, and an evil adversary
37 to Israel continually. And they shed
innocent blood on every side of the
sanctuary, and defiled the sanctuary.
38 And the inhabitants of Jerusalem fled
because of them ; and she became a
habitation of strangers, and she became strange to them that were born
in her, and her children forsook her.

39 Her sanctuary was laid waste like a
wilderness, ¹ her feasts were turned
into mourning, her sabbaths into reproach, her honour into contempt.
40 According to her glory, so was her
dishonour multiplied, and her high
estate was turned into mourning.
41 And king Antiochus wrote to his
whole kingdom, that all should be
42 one people, and that each should forsake his own laws. And all the nations agreed according to the word of
43 the king ; and many of Israel consented to his worship, and sacrificed
to the idols, and profaned the sabbath.
44 And the king sent letters by the hand
of messengers unto Jerusalem and
the cities of Judah, that they should
45 follow laws strange to the land, and
should forbid whole burnt offerings
and sacrifice and drink offerings in
the sanctuary ; and should profane
46 the sabbaths and feasts, and pollute
the sanctuary and them that were
47 holy ; that they should build altars,
and temples, and shrines for idols,
and should sacrifice swine's flesh and
48 unclean beasts: and that they should
leave their sons uncircumcised, that
they should make their souls abominable with all manner of uncleanness
49 and profanation ; so that they might
forget the law, and change all the or-
50 dinances. And whosoever shall not
do according to the word of the king,
51 he shall die. According to all these
words wrote he to his whole kingdom ;
and he appointed overseers over all the
people, and he commanded the cities
of Judah to sacrifice, city by city.
52 And from the people were gathered
together unto them many, every one

that had forsaken the law ; and they
53 did evil things in the land ; and they
made Israel to hide themselves in
every place of refuge which they
had.
54 And on the fifteenth day of Chislev,
in ² the hundred and forty and fifth
year, they builded an abomination of
desolation upon the ³ altar, and in the
cities of Judah on every side they
55 builded idol ³ altars. And at the

doors of the houses and in the streets
56 they burnt incense. And they rent
in pieces the books of the law which
57 they found, and set them on fire. And
wheresoever was found with any a
book of the covenant, and if any consented to the law, the king's sentence
58 delivered him to death. Thus did
they in their might unto Israel, to
those that were found month by
59 month in the cities. And on the five
and twentieth day of the month they
sacrificed upon the idol ³ altar, which
60 was upon the ³ altar of God. And
⁴ the women that had circumcised
their children they put to death ac-
61 cording to the commandment. And
they hanged their babes about their
necks, and destroyed their houses,
and them that had circumcised them.
62 And many in Israel were fully resolved and confirmed in themselves
63 not to eat unclean things. And ⁵ they
chose to die, that they might not be
defiled with the meats, and that they
might not profane the holy covenant :
64 and they died. And there came exceeding great wrath upon Israel.

2 In those days rose up Mattathias the
son of John, the son of Simeon, a priest
of the sons of Joarib, from Jerusalem ;
2 and he dwelt at Modin. And he had
five sons, ⁶ John, who was surnamed
3 Gaddis ; Simon, who was called
4 Thassi ; Judas, who was called Mac-
5 cabæus ; Eleazar, who was called
Avaran ; Jonathan, who was called
Apphus.
6 And he saw the blasphemies that
were committed in Judah and in Jeru-
7 salem, and he said,
Woe is me ! wherefore was I born to
see the destruction of my people, and
the destruction of the holy city, and
to dwell there, when it was given into
the hand of the enemy, the sanctuary
8 into the hand of aliens ? Her temple
is become as a man ⁷ that was glori-
9 ous : her vessels of glory are carried
away into captivity, her infants are
slain in her streets, her young men
10 with the sword of the enemy. What
nation hath not inherited her palaces,
and gotten possession of her spoils ?
11 her adorning is all taken away ; instead of a free woman she is become
12 a bond woman : and, behold, our holy
things and our beauty and our glory
are laid waste, and the Gentiles have
13 profaned them. Wherefore should
we live any longer ?
14 And Mattathias and his sons rent
their clothes, and put on sackcloth,
and mourned exceedingly.
15 And the king's officers, that were
enforcing the apostasy, came into the
16 city Modin to sacrifice. And many of
Israel came unto them, and Mattathias
and his sons were gathered together.
17 And the king's officers answered and

spake to Mattathias, saying, Thou art a ruler and an honourable and great man in this city, and strengthened 18 with sons and brethren: now therefore come thou first and do the commandment of the king, as all the nations have done, and the men of Judah, and they that remain in Jerusalem: and thou and thy house shall be in the number of the king's 19 Friends, and thou and thy sons shall be honoured with silver and gold and many gifts. And Mattathias answered and said with a loud voice, If all the nations that are in the house of the king's dominion hearken unto him, to fall away each one from the worship of his fathers, and have made choice 20 to follow his commandments, yet will I and my sons and my brethren walk 21 in the covenant of our fathers. [2] Heaven forbid that we should forsake the 22 law and the ordinances. We will not hearken to the king's words, to go aside from our worship, on the right hand, or on the left.

23 And when he had left speaking these words, there came a Jew in the sight of all to sacrifice on the altar which was at Modin, according to the king's 24 commandment. And Mattathias saw it, and his zeal was kindled, and his reins trembled, and he shewed forth his wrath according to judgement, and 25 ran, and slew him upon the altar. And the king's officer, who compelled men to sacrifice, he killed at that time, and 26 pulled down the altar. And he was zealous for the law, even as Phinehas 27 did unto Zimri the son of Salu. And Mattathias cried out in the city with a loud voice, saying, Whosoever is zealous for the law, and maintaineth the covenant, let him come forth after 28 me. And he and his sons fled unto the mountains, and forsook all that they had in the city.

29 Then many that sought after justice and judgement went down into the 30 wilderness, to dwell there, they, and their sons, and their wives, and their cattle; because evils were multiplied 31 upon them. And it was told the king's officers, and the forces that were in Jerusalem, the city of David, that certain men, who had broken the king's commandment, were gone down into the secret places in the wilder-32 ness; and many pursued after them, and having overtaken them, they encamped against them, and set the battle in array against them on the 33 sabbath day. And they said unto them, Thus far. Come forth, and do according to the word of the king, and 34 ye shall live. And they said, We will not come forth, neither will we do the word of the king, to profane the sab-35 bath day. And they hasted to give 36 them battle. And they answered them

not, neither cast they a stone at them, 37 nor stopped up the secret places, saying, Let us die all in our innocency: heaven and earth witness over us, that 38 ye put us to death without trial. And they rose up against them in battle on the sabbath, and they died, they and their wives and their children, and their cattle, unto the number of a thousand [3] souls.

39 And Mattathias and his friends knew 40 it, and they mourned over them exceedingly. And one said to another, If we all do as our brethren have done, and fight not against the Gentiles for our lives and our ordinances, they will now quickly destroy us from off the 41 earth. And they took counsel on that day, saying, Whosoever shall come against us to battle on the sabbath day, let us fight against him, and we shall in no wise all die, as our brethren 42 died in the secret places. Then were gathered together unto them a company of [4] Hasidæans, mighty men of Israel, every one that offered himself 43 willingly for the law. And all they that fled from the evils were added to them, and became a stay unto them. 44 And they mustered a host, and smote sinners in their anger, and lawless men in their wrath: and the rest fled to the 45 Gentiles for safety. And Mattathias and his friends went round about, and 46 pulled down the altars; and they circumcised by force the children that were uncircumcised, as many as they 47 found in the coasts of Israel. And they pursued after the sons of pride, and 48 the work prospered in their hand. And they rescued the law out of the hand of the Gentiles, and out of the hand of the kings, neither [5] suffered they the sinner to triumph.

49 And the days of Mattathias drew near that he should die, and he said unto his sons,

Now have pride and rebuke gotten strength, and a season of overthrow, 50 and wrath of indignation. And now, my children, be ye zealous for the law, and give your lives for the covenant 51 of your fathers. And call to remembrance the deeds of our fathers which they did in their generations; and receive great glory and an everlasting 52 name. Was not Abraham found faithful in temptation, and it was reckoned 53 unto him for righteousness? Joseph in the time of his distress kept the commandment, and became lord of 54 Egypt. Phinehas our father, for that he was zealous exceedingly, obtained the covenant of an everlasting priest-55 hood. Joshua for fulfilling the word 56 became a judge in Israel. Caleb for bearing witness in the congregation 57 inherited a heritage in the land. David for being merciful inherited the throne 58 of a kingdom for ever and ever. Elijah,

[1] See ch. iii. 38; vi. 10, &c. Compare ch. x. 65; xi. 27; 2 Macc. viii. 9.

[2] Gr. *May he be propitious.* Compare 2 Sam. xxiii. 17 (Sept.).

[3] Gr. *souls of men.*

[4] That is *Chasidim.*

[5] Gr. *gave they a horn to the sinner.*

for that he was exceeding zealous for the law, was taken up into heaven.

59 Hananiah, Azariah, Mishael, believed, and were saved out of the flame.

60 Daniel for his innocency was delivered 61 from the mouth of lions. And thus consider ye from generation to generation, that none that put their trust in 62 him shall want for strength. And be not afraid of the words of a sinful man; for his glory shall be dung and 63 worms. To-day he shall be lifted up, and to-morrow he shall in no wise be found, because he is returned unto his dust, and his thought is perished. 64 And ye, my children, be strong, and shew yourselves men in behalf of the law; for therein shall ye obtain glory. 65 And, behold, Simon your brother, I know that he is a man of counsel; give ear unto him alway: he shall 66 be a father unto you. And Judas Maccabæus, he hath been strong and mighty from his youth: he shall be your captain, and ¹shall fight the 67 battle of the people. And take ye unto you all the doers of the law, and avenge 68 the wrong of your people. Render a recompense to the Gentiles, and take heed to the commandments of the law.

69 And he blessed them, and was gather-70 ed to his fathers. And he died in ²the hundred and forty and sixth year, and his sons buried him in the sepulchres of his fathers at Modin, and all Israel made great lamentation for him.

3 And his son Judas, who was called 2 Maccabæus, rose up in his stead. And all his brethren helped him, and so did all they that clave unto his father, and they fought with gladness the battle of 3 Israel. And he gat his people great glory, and put on a breastplate as a giant, and girt his warlike harness about him, and set battles in array, protecting the army with his sword. 4 And he was like a lion in his deeds, and as a lion's whelp roaring for prey. 5 And he pursued the lawless, seeking them out, and he burnt up those that 6 troubled his people. And the lawless shrunk for fear of him, and all the workers of lawlessness were sore troubled, and salvation prospered in his 7 hand. And he angered many kings, and made Jacob glad with his acts, and 8 his memorial is blessed for ever. And he went about among the cities of Judah, and destroyed the ungodly ³out of the land, and turned away wrath 9 from Israel: and he was renowned unto the utmost part of the earth, and he gathered together such as were ready to perish.

10 And Apollonius gathered the Gentiles together, and a great host from Sa-11 maria, to fight against Israel. And Judas perceived it, and he went forth to meet him, and smote him, and slew him: and many fell wounded to death,

12 and the rest fled. And they took their spoils, and Judas took the sword of Apollonius, and therewith he fought all his days.

13 And Seron, the commander of the host of Syria, heard say that Judas had gathered a gathering and a con-14 gregation of faithful men with him, and of such as went out to war; and he said, I will make myself a name and get me glory in the kingdom; and I will fight against Judas and them that are with him, that set at nought 15 the word of the king. And there went up with him also a mighty army of the ungodly to help him, to take vengeance on the children of Israel.

16 And he came near unto the going up of Bethhoron, and Judas went forth to 17 meet him with a small company. But when they saw the army coming to meet them, they said unto Judas, What? shall we be able, being a small company, to fight against so great and strong a multitude? and we for our part are faint, having tasted no food 18 this day. And Judas said, It is an easy thing for many to be shut up in the hands of a few; and with ⁴heaven 19 it is all one, to save by many or by few: for victory in battle standeth not in the multitude of a host; but 20 strength is from heaven. They come unto us in fulness of insolence and lawlessness, to destroy us and our wives and our children, for to spoil 21 us: but we fight for our lives and our 22 laws. And he himself will discomfit them before our face: but as for you, be ye not afraid of them.

23 Now when he had left off speaking, he leapt suddenly upon them, and Seron and his army were discomfited 24 before him. And they pursued them in the going down of Bethhoron unto the plain, and there fell of them about eight hundred men; but the residue fled into the land of the Philistines. 25 And the fear of Judas and his brethren, and the dread of them, began to fall upon the nations round about 26 them: and his name came near even unto the king, and every nation told of the battles of Judas.

27 But when king Antiochus heard these words, he was full of indignation: and he sent and gathered together all the forces of his realm, an 28 exceeding strong army. And he opened his treasury, and gave his forces pay for a year, and commanded them 29 to be ready for every need. And he saw that the money failed from his treasures, and that the tributes of the country were small, because of the dissension and plague which he had brought upon the land, to the end that he might take away the laws which 30 had been from the first days; and he feared that he should not have enough

¹ Some ancient authorities read *ye shall fight.*

² circa B. C. 167.

³ Gr. *out of it.*

⁴ Some ancient authorities read *the God of heaven.*

as at other times for the charges and the gifts which he gave aforetime with a liberal hand, and he abounded above the kings that were before him.
31 And he was exceedingly perplexed in his mind, and he determined to go into Persia, and to take the tributes of the countries, and to gather much
32 money. And he left Lysias, an honourable man, and one of the seed royal, to be over the affairs of the king from the river Euphrates unto
33 the borders of Egypt, and to bring up his son Antiochus, until he came
34 again. And he delivered unto him the half of his forces, and the elephants, and gave him charge of all the things that he would have done, and concerning them that dwelt in Judæa and
35 in Jerusalem, that he should send a host against them, to root out and destroy the strength of Israel, and the remnant of Jerusalem, and to take away their memorial from the place;
36 and that he should make strangers to dwell in all their coasts, and should
37 divide their land to them by lot. And the king took the half that remained of the forces, and removed from Antioch, from his royal city, [1] the hundred and forty and seventh year; and he passed over the river Euphrates, and went through the upper countries.
38 And Lysias chose Ptolemy the son of Dorymenes, and Nicanor, and Gorgias, mighty men of the king's [2] Friends;
39 and with them he sent forty thousand footmen, and seven thousand horse, to go into the land of Judah, and to destroy it, according to the word of the
40 king. And they removed with all their host, and came and pitched near unto Emmaus in the plain country.
41 And the merchants of the country heard the fame of them, and took silver and gold exceeding much, with [3] fetters, and came into the camp to take the children of Israel for servants: and there were added unto them the forces of Syria and of the land of the [4] Philistines.
42 And Judas and his brethren saw that evils were multiplied, and that the forces were encamping in their borders; and they took knowledge of the king's words which he had commanded, to destroy the people and make an
43 end of them; and they said each man to his neighbour, Let us raise up the ruin of our people, and let us fight for
44 our people and the holy place. And the congregation was gathered together, that they might be ready for battle, and that they might pray, and
45 ask for mercy and compassion. And Jerusalem was without inhabitant as a wilderness, there was none of her offspring that went in or went out; and the sanctuary was trodden down, and the sons of strangers were in the

citadel, the Gentiles lodged therein; and joy was taken away from Jacob, and the pipe and the harp ceased.
46 And they gathered themselves together, and came to Mizpeh, over against Jerusalem; for in Mizpeh was there a place of prayer aforetime for
47 Israel. And they fasted that day, and put on sackcloth, and *put* ashes upon
48 their heads, and rent their clothes, and laid open the book of the law, concerning which the Gentiles were wont to inquire, seeking the likenesses of
49 their idols. And they brought the priests' garments, and the firstfruits, and the tithes: and they stirred up the Nazirites, who had accomplished their
50 days. And they cried aloud toward heaven, saying, What shall we do with these men, and whither shall we carry
51 them away? And thy holy place is trodden down and profaned, and thy priests are in heaviness and brought
52 low. And, behold, the Gentiles are assembled together against us to destroy us: thou knowest what things
53 they imagine against us. How shall we be able to stand before them,
54 except thou be our help? And they sounded with the trumpets, and cried with a loud voice.
55 And after this Judas appointed leaders of the people, captains of thousands, and captains of hundreds, and captains of fifties, and captains of
56 tens. And he said to them that were building houses, and were betrothing wives, and were planting vineyards, and were fearful, that they should
57 return, each man to his own house, according to the law. And the army
58 removed, and encamped upon the south side of Emmaus. And Judas said, Gird yourselves, and be valiant men, and be in readiness against the morning, that ye may fight with these Gentiles, that are assembled together against us to destroy us, and our holy
59 place: for it is better for us to die in battle, than to look upon the evils of
60 our nation and the holy place. Nevertheless, as may be the will in heaven, so shall he do.
4 And Gorgias took five thousand footmen, and a thousand chosen horse,
2 and the army removed by night, that it might fall upon the army of the Jews and smite them suddenly: and the men of the citadel were his guides.
3 And Judas heard thereof, and removed, he and the valiant men, that he might smite the king's host which was
4 at Emmaus, while as yet the forces
5 were dispersed from the camp. And Gorgias came into the camp of Judas by night, and found no man; and he sought them in the mountains; for he
6 said, These men flee from us. And as soon as it was day, Judas appeared in the plain with three thousand men:

[1] circa B. C. 166.

[2] See ch. ii. 18.

[3] Most of the authorities read *servants*.

[4] Gr. *strangers*.

howbeit they had not armour nor 7 swords to their minds. And they saw the camp of the Gentiles strong *and* fortified, and horsemen compassing it round about; and these were expert in 8 war. And Judas said to the men that were with him, Fear ye not their multitude, neither be ye afraid of their 9 onset. Remember how our fathers were saved in the Red sea, when Pha- 10 raoh pursued them with a host. And now let us cry unto heaven, if he will have us, and will remember the covenant of our fathers, and destroy this 11 army before our face to-day: and all the Gentiles shall know that there is one who redeemeth and saveth Is- 12 rael. And the strangers lifted up their eyes, and saw them coming over 13 against them: and they went out of the camp to battle. And they that were with Judas sounded their trum- 14 pets, and joined battle, and the Gentiles were discomfited, and fled into 15 the plain. But all the hindmost fell by the sword: and they pursued them

1 Gr. *Gazera.*

unto [1] Gazara, and unto the plains of Idumæa and Azotus and Jamnia, and there fell of them about three thou- 16 sand men. And Judas and his host returned from pursuing after them, 17 and he said unto the people, Be not greedy of the spoils, inasmuch as 18 there is a battle before us; and Gorgias and his host are nigh unto us in the mountain. But stand ye now against our enemies, and fight against them, and afterwards take the spoils 19 with boldness. While Judas was yet making an end of these words, there appeared a part of them looking out 20 from the mountain: and they saw that their host had been put to flight, and that the Jews were burning the camp: for the smoke that was seen declared 21 what was done. But when they perceived these things, they were sore afraid; and perceiving also the army of Judas in the plain ready for battle, 22 they fled all of them into the land of

2 Gr. *strangers.*

23 the [2] Philistines. And Judas returned to spoil the camp, and they got much gold, and silver, and blue, and sea 24 purple, and great riches. And they returned home, and sang a song of thanksgiving, and gave praise [3] unto

3 Or, looking up *unto heaven*

heaven; because *his mercy* is good, because his mercy endureth for ever. 25 And Israel had a great deliverance that day. 26 But the strangers, as many as had escaped, came and told Lysias all the 27 things that had happened: but when he heard thereof, he was confounded and discouraged, because neither had such things as he would been done unto Israel, nor had such things as the king commanded him come to pass. 28 And in the next year he gathered

together threescore thousand chosen footmen, and five thousand horse, that 29 he might subdue them. And they came into Idumæa, and encamped at Bethsura; and Judas met them with 30 ten thousand men. And he saw that the army was strong, and he prayed and said, Blessed art thou, O Saviour of Israel, who didst quell the onset of the mighty man by the hand of thy servant David, and didst deliver the army of the [2] Philistines into the hands of Jonathan the son of Saul, and of his 31 armourbearer: shut up this army in the hand of thy people Israel, and let them be ashamed for their host and 32 their horsemen: give them faintness of heart, and cause the boldness of their strength to melt away, and let 33 them quake at their destruction: cast them down with the sword of them that love thee, and let all that know thy name praise thee with thanksgiving. 34 And they joined battle; and there fell of the army of Lysias about five thousand men, and they fell down over 35 against them. But when Lysias saw that his array was put to flight, and the boldness that had come upon them that were with Judas, and how they were ready either to live or to die nobly, he removed to Antioch, and gathered together hired soldiers, that he might come again into Judæa with even a greater company. 36 But Judas and his brethren said, Behold, our enemies are discomfited: let us go up to cleanse the holy place, 37 and to dedicate it afresh. And all the army was gathered together, and they 38 went up unto mount Sion. And they saw the sanctuary laid desolate, and the altar profaned, and the gates burned up, and shrubs growing in the courts as in a forest or as on one of the mountains, and the priests' cham- 39 bers pulled down; and they rent their clothes, and made great lamentation, 40 and put ashes upon their heads, and fell on their faces to the ground, and [4] blew with the [5] solemn trumpets, and 41 cried toward heaven. Then Judas appointed certain men to fight against those that were in the citadel, until he should have cleansed the holy place. 42 And he chose blameless priests, such 43 as had pleasure in the law: and they cleansed the holy place, and bare out the stones of defilement into an un- 44 clean place. And they took counsel concerning the altar of burnt offerings, which had been profaned, what they 45 should do with it: and there came into their mind a good counsel, that they should pull it down, lest it should be a reproach to them, because the Gentiles had defiled it: and they pulled 46 down the altar, and laid up the stones

4 Compare Num. xxxi. 6
5 Gr. *trumpets of signals.*

in the mountain of the house in a convenient place, until there should come a prophet to give an answer con-
47 cerning them. And they took whole stones according to the law, and built a new altar after the fashion of the
48 former ; and they built the holy place, and the inner parts of the house ; and
49 they hallowed the courts. And they made the holy vessels new, and they brought the candlestick, and the altar of burnt offerings and of incense, and
50 the table, into the temple. And they burned incense upon the altar, and they lighted the lamps that were upon the candlestick, and they gave light
51 in the temple. And they set loaves upon the table, and spread out the veils, and finished all the works which they made.
52 And they rose up early in the morning, on the five and twentieth day of the ninth month, which is the month

¹ circa B. C. 165.

Chislev, in ¹ the hundred and forty
53 and eighth year, and offered sacrifice according to the law upon the new altar of burnt offerings which they
54 had made. At what time and on what day the Gentiles had profaned it, even on that *day* was it dedicated afresh, with songs and harps and lutes, and
55 with cymbals. And all the people fell upon their faces, and worshipped, and

² Or, *gave praise,* looking up *unto heaven, to him which*

² gave praise unto heaven, which had
56 given them good success. And they kept the dedication of the altar eight days, and offered burnt offerings with gladness, and sacrificed a sacrifice of
57 deliverance and praise. And they decked the forefront of the temple with crowns of gold and small shields, and dedicated afresh the gates and the priests' chambers, and made doors for
58 them. And there was exceeding great gladness among the people, and the reproach of the Gentiles was turned
59 away. And Judas and his brethren and the whole congregation of Israel ordained, that the days of the dedication of the altar should be kept in their seasons from year to year by the space of eight days, from the five and twentieth day of the month Chislev,
60 with gladness and joy. And at that season they builded up the mount Sion with high walls and strong towers round about, lest haply the Gentiles should come and tread them down, as
61 they had done aforetime. And he set there a force to keep it, and they fortified Bethsura to keep it ; that the people might have a stronghold over against Idumæa.

.5 And it came to pass, when the Gentiles round about heard that the altar was built, and the sanctuary dedicated as aforetime, they were exceeding
2 wroth. And they took counsel to destroy the race of Jacob that was in the midst of them, and they began to slay and destroy among the people.
3 And Judas fought against the children of Esau in Idumæa at Akrabattine, because they besieged Israel : and he smote them with a great slaughter, and brought down their pride, and
4 took their spoils. And he remembered the wickedness of the children of
³ Bæan, who were unto the people a snare and a stumblingblock, lying in
5 wait for them in the ways. And they were shut up by him in the towers ; and he encamped against them, and destroyed them utterly, and burned with fire the towers of the place, with
6 all that were therein. And he passed over to the children of Ammon, and found a mighty band, and much people, with Timotheus for their
7 leader. And he fought many battles with them, and they were discomfited before his face : and he smote them,
8 and gat possession of Jazer, and the ⁴ villages thereof, and returned again into Judæa.
9 And the Gentiles that were in Gilead gathered themselves together against the Israelites that were on their borders, to destroy them. And they fled
10 to the stronghold of Dathema, and sent letters unto Judas and his brethren, saying, The Gentiles that are round about us are gathered together
11 against us to destroy us : and they are preparing to come and get possession of the stronghold whereunto we are fled for refuge, and Timotheus is the
12 leader of their host. Now therefore come and deliver us from their hand,
13 for many of us are fallen. And all our brethren that were in the land of
⁵ Tubias have been put to death ; and they have carried into captivity their wives and their children and their stuff ; and they destroyed there about
14 a thousand men. While the letters were yet reading, behold, there came other messengers from Galilee with their clothes rent, bringing a report
15 after this wise, saying, That there were gathered together against them those of Ptolemais, and of Tyre, and of Sidon, and all Galilee of the ⁶ Gentiles, to consume them.
16 Now when Judas and the people heard these words, there assembled together a great congregation, to consult what they should do for their brethren, that were in tribulation, and
17 were assaulted of them. And Judas said unto Simon his brother, Choose thee out men, and go and deliver thy brethren that are in Galilee, but I and Jonathan my brother will go into the
18 land of Gilead. And he left Joseph the son of Zacharias, and Azarias, as leaders of the people, with the remnant of the host, in Judæa, for to keep
19 it. And he gave commandment unto them, saying, Take ye the charge of

³ Compare 2 Macc. x. 18-23.

⁴ Gr. *daughters.* Compare Num. xxi. 25.

⁵ Compare 2 Macc. xii. 17.

⁶ Gr. *strangers.*

this people, and fight no battle with the Gentiles until that we come again.

20 And unto Simon were divided three thousand men to go into Galilee, but unto Judas eight thousand men *to go* into the land of Gilead.

21 And Simon went into Galilee, and fought many battles with the Gentiles, and the Gentiles were discomfited

22 before him. And he pursued them unto the gate of Ptolemais; and there fell of the Gentiles about three thousand men, and he took their spoils.

23 And they took to them those that were in Galilee, and in Arbatta, with their wives and their children, and all that they had, and brought them into Judæa with great gladness.

24 And Judas Maccabæus and his brother Jonathan passed over Jordan, and went three days' journey in the

25 wilderness; and they met with the Nabathæans, and these met them in a peaceable manner, and told them all things that had befallen their brethren

26 in the land of Gilead: and how that many of them were shut up in Bosora, and Bosor, and Alema, [1] Casphor, Maked, and [2] Carnaim; all these cities

27 are strong and great: and how that they were shut up in the rest of the cities of the land of Gilead, and that to-morrow they have appointed to encamp against the strongholds, and to take them, and to destroy all these

28 men in one day. And Judas and his army turned suddenly by the way of the wilderness unto Bosora; and he took the city, and slew all the males with the edge of the sword, and took all their spoils, and burned the city

29 with fire. And he removed from thence by night, and went till he came

30 to the stronghold. And the morning came, and they lifted up their eyes, and, behold, much people which could not be numbered, bearing ladders and engines of war, to take the stronghold; and they were fighting against them.

31 And Judas saw that the battle was begun, and that the cry of the city went up to heaven, with trumpets and

32 a great sound, and he said unto the men of his host, Fight this day for

33 your brethren. And he went forth behind them in three companies, and they sounded with their trumpets, and

34 cried out in prayer. And the army of Timotheus perceived that it was Maccabæus, and they fled from before him: and he smote them with a great slaughter; and there fell of them on that day about eight thousand men.

35 And he turned aside to Mizpeh and fought against it, and took it, and slew all the males thereof, and took the spoils thereof, and burned it with

36 fire. From thence he removed, and took [3] Casphor, Maked, Bosor, and the other cities of the land of Gilead.

37 Now after these things Timotheus gathered another army, and encamped over against Raphon beyond the

38 brook. And Judas sent men to espy the army; and they brought him word, saying, All the Gentiles that be round about us are gathered together unto

39 them, an exceeding great host. And they have hired Arabians to help them, and are encamping beyond the brook, ready to come against thee to battle. And Judas went to meet them.

40 And Timotheus said unto the captains of his host, when Judas and his army drew nigh unto the brook of water, If he pass over first unto us, we shall not be able to withstand him; for he

41 will mightily prevail against us: but if he be afraid, and encamp beyond the river, we will cross over unto him,

42 and prevail against him. Now when Judas came nigh unto the brook of water, he caused the scribes of the people to remain by the brook, and gave commandment unto them, saying, Suffer no man to encamp, but let

43 all come to the battle. And he crossed over the first against them, and all the people after him: and all the Gentiles were discomfited before his face, and cast away their arms, and fled unto

44 the temple at [3] Carnaim. And they took the city, and burned the temple with fire, together with all that were therein. And Carnaim was subdued, neither could they stand any longer before the face of Judas.

45 And Judas gathered together all Israel, them that were in the land of Gilead, from the least unto the greatest, and their wives, and their children, and their stuff. an exceeding great army, that they might come into

46 the land of Judah. And they came as far as Ephron, and this same city was great, *and it was* in the way as they should go, exceeding strong: they could not turn aside from it on the right hand or on the left, but must needs pass through the midst of it.

47 And they of the city shut them out, and stopped up the gates with stones.

48 And Judas sent unto them with words of peace, saying, We will pass through thy land to go into our own land, and none shall do you any hurt, we will only pass by on our feet. And they

49 would not open unto him. And Judas commanded proclamation to be made in the army, that each man should encamp in the place where he was.

50 And the men of the host encamped, and fought against the city all that day and all that night, and the city

51 was delivered into his hands; and he destroyed all the males with the edge of the sword, and rased the city, and took the spoils thereof, and passed through the city over them that were

52 slain. And they went over Jordan

[1] Compare 2 Macc. xii. 13.
[2] Compare 2 Macc. xii. 21.
[3] See ver. 26.

into the great plain over against Beth-
53 shan. And Judas gathered together
those that lagged behind, and encouraged the people all the way through,
until he came into the land of Judah.
54 And they went up to mount Sion with
gladness and joy, and offered whole
burnt offerings, because not so much
as one of them was slain until they
returned in peace.
55 And in the days when Judas and
Jonathan were in the land of Gilead,
and Simon his brother in Galilee be-
56 fore Ptolemais, Joseph the son of
Zacharias, and Azarias, rulers of the
host, heard of their exploits and of the
57 war, what things they had done; and
they said, Let us also get us a name,
and let us go fight against the Gentiles
58 that are round about us. And they
gave charge unto the men of the host
that was with them, and went toward
59 Jamnia. And Gorgias and his men
came out of the city to meet them in
60 battle. And Joseph and Azarias were
put to flight, and were pursued unto
the borders of Judæa; and there fell
on that day of the people of Israel
61 about two thousand men. And there
was a great overthrow among the people, because they hearkened not unto
Judas and his brethren, thinking to do
62 some exploit. But they were not of the
seed of those men, by whose hand
deliverance was given unto Israel.
63 And the man Judas and his brethren
were glorified exceedingly in the sight
of all Israel, and of all the Gentiles,
wheresoever their name was heard of;
64 and men gathered together unto them,
acclaiming them.
65 And Judas and his brethren went
forth, and fought against the children
of Esau in the land toward the south;
and he smote Hebron and the [1] villages
thereof, and pulled down the strongholds thereof, and burned the towers
66 thereof round about. And he removed
to go into the land of the [2] Philistines,
67 and he went through [3] Samaria. In
that day certain priests, desiring to
do exploits there, were slain in battle,
when as [4] he went out to battle unad-
68 visedly. And Judas turned aside to
Azotus, to the land of the [2] Philistines,
and pulled down their altars, and
burned the carved images of their
gods with fire, and took the spoil of
their cities, and returned into the
land of Judah.
6 And king Antiochus was journeying
through the upper countries; and he
heard say, that in Elymais in Persia
there was a city renowned for riches,
2 for silver and gold; and that the temple which was in it was rich exceedingly, and that therein were golden
shields, and breastplates, and arms,
which Alexander, son of Philip, the
Macedonian king, who reigned first

among the Greeks, left behind there.
3 And he came and sought to take the
city, and to pillage it; and he was not
able, because the thing was known to
4 them of the city, and they rose up
against him to battle: and he fled,
and removed thence with great heaviness, to return unto Babylon.
5 And there came one bringing him
tidings into Persia, that the armies,
which went against the land of Ju-
6 dah, had been put to flight; and that
Lysias went first with a strong host,
and was put to shame before them;
and that they had waxed strong by
reason of arms and power, and with
store of spoils, which they took from
7 the armies that they had cut off; and
that they had pulled down the abomination which he had built upon the
altar that was in Jerusalem; and that
they had compassed about the sanctuary with high walls, as before, and
8 Bethsura, his city. And it came to
pass, when the king heard these
words, he was astonished and moved
exceedingly: and he laid him down
upon his bed, and fell sick for grief,
because it had not befallen him as he
9 looked for. And he was there many
days, because great grief was renewed
upon him, and he made account that
10 he should die. And he called for all
his [5] Friends, and said unto them,
Sleep departeth from mine eyes, and
11 my heart faileth for care. And I said
in my heart, Unto what tribulation
am I come, and how great a flood is
it, wherein I now am! for I was gra-
12 cious and beloved in my power. But
now I remember the evils which I did
at Jerusalem, and that I took all the
vessels of silver and gold that were
therein, and sent forth to destroy the
inhabitants of Judah without a cause.
13 I perceive that on this account these
evils are come upon me, and, behold,
I perish through great grief in a
14 strange land. And he called for
Philip, one of his [5] Friends, and gave
15 him over all his kingdom, and gave
him his diadem, and his robe, and his
signet-ring, to the end he should bring
Antiochus his son, and nourish him
16 up that he might be king. And king
Antiochus died there in [6] the hundred
17 and forty and ninth year. And Lysias
knew that the king was dead, and he
set up Antiochus his son to reign,
whom he had nourished up being
young, and he called his name Eu-
18 pator. And they that were in the citadel
shut up Israel round about the sanctuary, and sought always their hurt,
and the strengthening of the Gentiles.
19 And Judas thought to destroy them,
and called all the people together to
20 besiege them. And they were gathered together, and besieged them

---

Margin notes (left):

[1] Gr. *daugh-
ters.*
Compare
Num.
xxi. 25.
[2] Gr.
*stran-
gers.*
[3] Or,
Marisa
See Jo-
sephus,
Antiq.
xii. 8. 6,
and
2 Macc.
xii. 35.
[4] Some
ancient
authori-
ties read
they.

Margin notes (right):

[5] See ch.
ii. 18.

[6] circa
B. C. 164

1 circa B. C. 163.

in [1] the hundred and fiftieth year, and he made mounds to shoot from, and 21 engines of war. And there came forth some of them that were shut up, and there were joined unto them certain 22 ungodly men of Israel. And they went unto the king, and said, How long wilt thou not execute judgement, 23 and avenge our brethren? We were willing to serve thy father, and to walk after his words, and to follow 24 his commandments; and for this cause the children of our people besieged [2] the citadel, and were alienated from us: but as many of us as they could light on they slew, and 25 spoiled our inheritances. And not against us only did they stretch out their hand, but also against all their 26 borders. And, behold, they are encamped this day against the citadel at Jerusalem, to take it: and the sanctuary and Bethsura have they fortified. 27 And if ye are not beforehand with them quickly, they will do greater things than these, and thou shalt not be able to control them. 28 And when the king heard this, he was angry, and gathered together all his [3] Friends, *even the* rulers of his 29 host, and them that were over the horse. And there came unto him from other kingdoms, and from isles of the sea, bands of hired soldiers. 30 And the number of his forces was a hundred thousand footmen, and twenty thousand horsemen, and two and thirty elephants trained for war. 31 And they went through Idumæa, and encamped against Bethsura, and fought against it many days, and made engines of war; and they *of Bethsura* came out, and burned them with fire, 32 and fought valiantly. And Judas removed from the citadel, and encamped at Bethzacharias, over against the 33 king's camp. And the king rose early in the morning, and removed his army [4] at full speed along the road to Bethzacharias, and his forces made them ready to battle, and sounded with the 34 trumpets. And they shewed the elephants the blood of grapes and mulberries, that they might prepare them 35 for the battle. And they divided the beasts among the phalanxes, and they set by each elephant a thousand men armed with coats of mail, and helmets of brass on their heads; and for each beast were appointed five 36 hundred chosen horsemen. These were ready beforehand, wheresoever the beast was; and whithersoever the beast went, they went with him; 37 they departed not from him. And towers of wood were upon them, strong *and* covered, one upon each beast, girt fast upon him with cunning contrivances; and upon each *beast* were two and thirty valiant men that fought

38 upon them, beside his Indian (and the residue of the horsemen he set on this side and that side at the two parts of the army), striking terror *into the enemy*, and protected by the 39 phalanxes. Now when the sun shone upon the shields of gold and brass, the mountains shone therewith, and 40 blazed like torches of fire. And a part of the king's army was spread upon the high mountains, and some on the low ground, and they went on 41 firmly and in order. And all that heard the noise of their multitude, and the marching of the multitude, and the rattling of the arms, did quake: for the army was exceeding 42 great and strong. And Judas and his army drew near for battle, and there fell of the king's army six hundred 43 men. And Eleazar, who was *called* Avaran, saw one of the beasts armed with royal breastplates, and he was higher than all the beasts, and the 44 king seemed to be upon him; and he gave himself to deliver his people, and to get him an everlasting name; 45 and he ran upon him courageously into the midst of the phalanx, and slew on the right hand and on the left, and they parted asunder from 46 him on this side and on that. And he crept under the elephant, and thrust him from beneath, and slew him; and *the elephant* fell to the earth upon 47 him, and he died there. And they saw the strength of the kingdom, and the fierce onset of the hosts, and turned away from them.

48 But they of the king's army went up to Jerusalem to meet them, and the king encamped toward Judæa, and 49 toward mount Sion. And he made peace with them of Bethsura; and he came out of the city, because they had no food there to endure the siege, because it was a sabbath to the land. 50 And the king took Bethsura, and appointed a garrison there to keep it. 51 And he encamped against the sanctuary many days; and set there mounds to shoot from, and engines of war, and instruments for casting fire and stones, and pieces to cast darts, 52 and slings. And they also made engines against their engines, and 53 fought for many days. But there were no victuals in the sanctuary, because it was the seventh year, and they that fled for safety into Judæa from among the Gentiles had eaten 54 up the residue of the store; and there were but a few left in the sanctuary, because the famine prevailed against them, and they were scattered, each man to his own place. 55 And Lysias heard say, that Philip, whom Antiochus the king, whiles he was yet alive, appointed to nourish up his son Antiochus, that he might be

2 Gr. *it.*

3 See ch. ii. 18.

4 Or, *itself eager for the fight*

56 king, was returned from Persia and Media, and with him the forces that went with the king, and that he was seeking to take unto him the govern-
57 ment. And he made haste, and gave consent to depart; and he said to the king and the leaders of the host and to the men, We decay daily, and our food is scant, and the place where we encamp is strong, and the affairs of
58 the kingdom lie upon us : now therefore let us give the right hand to these men, and make peace with them and
59 with all their nation, and covenant with them, that they shall walk after their own laws, as aforetime : for because of their laws which we abolished they were angered, and did all
60 these things. And the saying pleased the king and the princes, and he sent unto them to make peace ; and they
61 accepted thereof. And the king and the princes sware unto them : thereupon they came forth from the strong-
62 hold. And the king entered into mount Sion ; and he saw the strength of the place, and set at nought the oath which he had sworn, and gave commandment to pull down the wall
63 round about. And he removed in haste, and returned unto Antioch, and found Philip master of the city ; and he fought against him, and took the city by force.

^{1 circa B. C. 162.}

7 In [1] the hundred and one and fiftieth year Demetrius the son of Seleucus came forth from Rome, and went up with a few men unto a city by the sea,
2 and reigned there. And it came to pass, when he would go into the house of the kingdom of his fathers, that the army laid hands on Antiochus and
3 Lysias, to bring them unto him. And the thing was known to him, and he said, Shew me not their faces.
4 And the army slew them. And Demetrius sat upon the throne of his
5 kingdom. And there came unto him all the lawless and ungodly men of Israel ; and Alcimus was their leader,
6 desiring to be high priest ; and they accused the people to the king, saying, Judas and his brethren have destroyed all thy friends, and have
7 scattered us from our own land. Now therefore send a man whom thou trustest, and let him go and see all the havock which he hath made of us, and of the king's country, and how he hath punished them and all that
8 helped them. And the king chose

^{2 See ch. ii. 18.}

Bacchides, one of the king's [2] Friends, who was ruler in the country beyond the river, and was a great man in the kingdom, and faithful to the king.
9 And he sent him, and that ungodly Alcimus, and made sure to him the high priesthood, and he commanded him to take vengeance upon the children of Israel.

10 And they removed, and came with a great host into the land of Judah, and he sent messengers to Judas and his brethren with words of peace
11 deceitfully. And they gave no heed to their words ; for they saw that they
12 were come with a great host. And there were gathered together unto Alcimus and Bacchides a company of
13 scribes, to seek for justice. And the [3] Hasidæans were the first among the children of Israel that sought peace
14 of them ; for they said, One that is a priest of the seed of Aaron is come with the forces, and he will do us no
15 wrong. And he spake with them words of peace, and sware unto them, saying, We will seek the hurt neither
16 of you nor your friends. And they gave him credence : and he laid hands on threescore men of them, and slew them in one day, according to the word which the psalmist wrote,
17 [4] 'The flesh of thy saints did they cast out,
And their blood did they shed round about Jerusalem ;
And there was no man to bury them.
18 And the fear and the dread of them fell upon all the people, for they said, There is neither truth nor judgement in them ; for they have broken the covenant and the oath which they
19 sware. And Bacchides removed from Jerusalem, and encamped in Bezeth ; and he sent and took many of the deserters that were with him, and certain of the people, and he slew them,
20 and cast them into the great pit. And he made sure the country to Alcimus, and left with him a force to aid him ; and Bacchides went away unto the
21 king. And Alcimus strove for his high
22 priesthood. And there were gathered unto him all they that troubled their people, and they got the mastery of the land of Judah, and did great hurt
23 in Israel. And Judas saw all the mischief that Alcimus and his company had done among the children of Israel,
24 even above the Gentiles, and he went out into all the coasts of Judæa round about, and took vengeance on the men that had deserted from him, and they were restrained from going forth into
25 the country. But when Alcimus saw that Judas and his company waxed strong, and knew that he was not able to withstand them, he returned to the king, and brought evil accusations against them.
26 [5] And the king sent Nicanor, one of his honourable princes, a man that hated Israel and was their enemy, and commanded him to destroy the people.
27 And Nicanor came to Jerusalem with a great host ; and he sent unto Judas and his brethren deceitfully with
28 words of peace, saying, Let there be

^{3 That is, Chasidim.}

^{4 Ps. lxxix. 2, 3.}

^{5 See 2 Macc. xiv. 12.}

no battle between me and you; I will come with a few men, that I may see 29 your faces in peace. And he came to Judas, and they saluted one another peaceably. And the enemies were ready to take away Judas by vio-30 lence. And the thing was known to Judas, *to wit,* that he came unto him with deceit, and he was sore afraid of him, and would see his face no more. 31 And Nicanor knew that his counsel was discovered; and he went out to meet Judas in battle beside Capharsa-32 lama; and there fell of Nicanor's side about [1] five hundred men, and they fled into the city of David.

33 And after these things Nicanor went up to mount Sion: and there came some of the priests out of the sanctuary, and some of the elders of the people, to salute him peaceably, and to shew him the whole burnt sacrifice that was being offered for the king. 34 And he mocked them, and laughed at them, and [2] entreated them shamefully, 35 and spake haughtily, and sware in a rage, saying, Unless Judas and his army be now delivered into my hands, it shall be that, if I come again in peace, I will burn up this house: and 36 he went out in a great rage. And the priests entered in, and stood before the altar and the temple; and they 37 wept, and said, Thou didst choose this house to be called by thy name, to be a house of prayer and supplication 38 for thy people: take vengeance on this man and his army, and let them fall by the sword: remember their blasphemies, and suffer them not to live any longer.

39 And Nicanor went forth from Jerusalem, and encamped in Bethhoron, and there met him the host of Syria. 40 And Judas encamped in Adasa with three thousand men: and Judas pray-41 ed and said, When they that came from the king blasphemed, thine angel went out, and smote among them a hundred and fourscore and five 42 thousand. Even so discomfit thou this army before us to-day, and let all the rest know that he hath spoken wickedly against thy sanctuary, and judge thou him according to his wick-43 edness. And on the thirteenth day of the month Adar the armies joined battle: and Nicanor's army was discomfited, and he himself was the first 44 to fall in the battle. Now when his army saw that Nicanor was fallen, they 45 cast away their arms, and fled. And they pursued after them a day's journey from Adasa until thou comest to [3] Gazara, and they sounded an alarm after them with the [4] solemn trumpets. 46 And they came forth out of all the villages of Judæa round about, and [5] closed them in; and these turned them back on those, and they all fell

by the sword, and there was not one 47 of them left. And they took the spoils, and the booty, and they smote off Nicanor's head, and his right hand, which he stretched out so haughtily, and brought them, and [6] hanged them 48 up beside Jerusalem. And the people was exceeding glad, and they kept that day as a day of great gladness. 49 And [7] they ordained to keep this day year by year, *to wit,* the thirteenth 50 day of Adar. And the land of Judah had rest [8] a little while.

8 And Judas heard of the fame of the Romans, that they are valiant men, and have pleasure in all that join themselves unto them, and make amity with all such as come unto 2 them, and that they are valiant men. And they told him of their wars and exploits which they do among the Gauls, and how that they conquered them, and brought them under tri-3 bute; and what things they did in the land of Spain, that they might become masters of the mines of silver 4 and gold which were there; and how that by their policy and persistence they conquered all the place (and the place was exceeding far from them), and the kings that came against them from the uttermost part of the earth, until they had discomfited them, and smitten them very sore; and how the rest give them tribute year by year: 5 and Philip, and Perseus, king of Chittim, and them that lifted up themselves against them, did they discomfit in battle, and conquered them: 6 Antiochus also, the great king of Asia, who came against them to battle, having a hundred and twenty elephants, with horse, and chariots, and an exceeding great host, and he 7 was discomfited by them, and they took him alive, and appointed that both he and such as reigned after him should give them a great tribute, and should give hostages, and a parcel *of* 8 *land, to wit,* the country of India, and Media, and Lydia, and of the goodliest of their countries; and they took them from him, and gave them to king 9 Eumenes: and how they of Greece took counsel to come and destroy 10 them; and the thing was known to them, and they sent against them a captain, and fought against them, and many of them fell down wounded to death, and they made captive their wives and their children, and spoiled them, and conquered their land, and pulled down their strongholds, and spoiled them. and brought them into 11 bondage unto this day: and the residue of the kingdoms and of the isles, as many as rose up against them at any time, they destroyed and made 12 them to be their servants; but with their friends and such as relied upon

[1] Some ancient authorities read *five thousand.*

[2] Gr. *polluted them.*

[3] Gr. *Gazara.*
[4] Gr. *trumpets of signals.*
[5] Gr. *outflanked them.*

[6] Gr. *stretched them out.*

[7] See 2 Macc. xv. 36.

[8] Gr. *a few days*

142

them they kept amity ; and they conquered the kingdoms that were nigh and those that were far off, and all that heard of their fame were afraid
13 of them : moreover, whomsoever they will to succour and to make kings, these do they make kings ; and whomsoever they will, do they depose ; and
14 they are exalted exceedingly : and for all this none of them did ever put on a diadem, neither did they clothe themselves with purple, to be
15 magnified thereby : and how they had made for themselves a senate house, and day by day three hundred and twenty men sat in council, consulting alway for the people, to the end
16 they might be well ordered : and how they commit their government to one man year by year, that he should rule over them, and be lord over all their country, and all are obedient to that one, and there is neither envy nor emulation among them.
17 And Judas chose Eupolemus the son of John, the son of Accos, and Jason the son of Eleazar, and sent them to Rome, to make a league of amity and
18 confederacy with them, and that they should take the yoke from them ; for they saw that the kingdom of the Greeks did keep Israel in bondage.
19 And they went to Rome (and the way was exceeding long), and they entered into the senate house, and answered
20 and said, Judas, who is also *called* Maccabæus, and his brethren, and the people of the Jews, have sent us unto you, to make a confederacy and peace with you, and that we might be registered your confederates and friends.
21 And the thing was well-pleasing in
22 their sight. And this is the copy of the writing which they wrote back again on tables of brass, and sent to Jerusalem, that it might be with them there for a memorial of peace and confederacy :
23 Good success be to the Romans, and to the nation of the Jews, by sea and by land for ever : the sword also and
24 the enemy be far from them. But if war arise for Rome first, or any of their confederates in all their domin-
25 ion, the nation of the Jews shall help them as confederates, as the occasion shall prescribe to them, with all their
26 heart : and unto them that make war upon them they shall not give, neither supply, food, arms, money, or ships, as it hath seemed good unto Rome, and they shall keep their ordinances with-
27 out taking anything therefore. In the same manner, moreover, if war come first upon the nation of the Jews, the Romans shall help them as confederates with all their soul, as the occasion
28 shall prescribe to them : and to them that are confederates *with their foes*

there shall not be given food, arms, money, or ships, as it hath seemed good unto Rome ; and they shall keep these ordinances, and that without de-
29 ceit. According to these words have the Romans made a covenant thus
30 with the people of the Jews. But if hereafter the one party and the other shall take counsel to add or diminish anything, they shall do it at their pleasure, and whatsoever they shall add or take away shall be established.
31 And as touching the evils which king Demetrius doeth unto them, we have written to him, saying, Wherefore hast thou made thy yoke heavy upon our friends and confederates the
32 Jews? If therefore they plead any more against thee, we will do them justice, and fight with thee by sea and by land.

9 And Demetrius heard that Nicanor was fallen with his forces in battle, and he sent Bacchides and Alcimus again into the land of Judah a second time, and the right wing *of his army* with
2 them : and they went by the way that leadeth to Gilgal, and encamped against Mesaloth, which is in Arbela, and gat possession of it, and destroy-
3 ed much people. And the first month of [1] the hundred and fifty and second year they encamped against Jerusa-
4 lem : and they removed, and went to Berea, with twenty thousand footmen
5 and two thousand horse. And Judas was encamped at Elasa, and three
6 thousand chosen men with him : and they saw the multitude of the forces, that they were many, and they feared exceedingly : and many slipped away out of the army ; there were not left of them more than eight hundred men.
7 And Judas saw that his army slipped away, and that the battle pressed upon him, and he was sore troubled in heart, for that he had no time to gather them together, and he waxed
8 faint. And he said to them that were left, Let us arise and go up against our adversaries, if peradventure we
9 may be able to fight with them. And they would have dissuaded him, saying, We shall in no wise be able : but let us rather save our lives now : let us return again, *we* and our brethren, and fight against them : but we are
10 few. And Judas said, Let it not be so that I should do this thing, to flee from them : and if our time is come, let us die manfully for our brethren's sake, and not leave a cause of re-
11 proach against our glory. And the host removed from the camp, and stood to encounter them, and the horse was parted into two companies, and the slingers and the archers went before the host, and all the mighty men that fought in the front of the
12 battle. But Bacchides was in the

1 circa
B. C. 161

right wing; and the phalanx drew
13 near on the two parts, and they blew
with their trumpets. And the men
of Judas' side, even they sounded
with their trumpets, and the earth
shook with the shout of the armies,
and the battle was joined, and continued from morning until evening.
14 And Judas saw that Bacchides and
the strength of his army were on the
right side, and there went with him all
15 that were brave in heart, and the right
wing was discomfited by them, and he
pursued after them unto the mount
16 Azotus. And they that were on the
left wing saw that the right wing was
discomfited, and they turned and followed upon the footsteps of Judas and
17 of those that were with him: and the
battle waxed sore, and many on both
18 parts fell wounded to death. And
19 Judas fell, and the rest fled. And
Jonathan and Simon took Judas their
brother, and buried him in the sepul-
20 chre of his fathers at Modin. And
they bewailed him, and all Israel
made great lamentation for him, and
21 mourned many days, and said, How
is the mighty fallen, the saviour of
22 Israel! And the rest of the acts of
Judas, and his wars, and the valiant
deeds which he did, and his greatness,
they are not written; for they were
exceeding many.
23 And it came to pass after the death
of Judas, that the lawless put forth
their heads in all the coasts of Israel,
and all they that wrought iniquity
24 rose up (in those days was there an
exceeding great famine), and the coun-
25 try went over with them. And Bacchides chose out the ungodly men,
and made them lords of the country.
26 And they sought out and searched
for the friends of Judas, and brought
them unto Bacchides, and he took
vengeance on them, and used them
27 despitefully. And there was great
tribulation in Israel, such as was not
since the time that no prophet ap-
28 peared unto them. And all the
friends of Judas were gathered together, and they said unto Jonathan,
29 Since thy brother Judas hath died, we
have no man like him to go forth
against our enemies and Bacchides,
and among them of our nation that
30 hate us. Now therefore we have
chosen thee this day to be our prince
and leader in his stead, that thou
31 mayest fight our battles. And Jonathan took the governance upon him
at that time, and rose up in the stead
of his brother Judas.
32 And Bacchides knew it, and he
33 sought to slay him. And Jonathan,
and Simon his brother, and all that
were with him, knew it; and they fled
into the wilderness of Tekoah, and
encamped by the water of the pool

34 Asphar. And Bacchides knew it on
the sabbath day, and came, he and
35 all his army, over Jordan. And Jonathan sent his brother, a leader of the
multitude, and besought his friends
the Nabathæans, that they might
leave with them their baggage, which
36 was much. And the children of Jambri came out of Medaba, and took
John, and all that he had, and went
their way with it.
37 But after these things they brought
word to Jonathan and Simon his brother, that the children of Jambri were
making a great marriage, and were
bringing the bride from Nadabath
with a great train, a daughter of one
38 of the great nobles of Canaan. And
they remembered John their brother,
and went up, and hid themselves un-
39 der the covert of the mountain: and
they lifted up their eyes, and saw, and,
behold, a great ado and much baggage:
and the bridegroom came forth, and
his friends and his brethren, to meet
them with timbrels, and minstrels, and
40 many weapons. And they rose up
against them from their ambush, and
slew them, and many fell wounded to
death, and the remnant fled into the
mountain, and they took all their
41 spoils. And the marriage was turned
into mourning, and the voice of their
42 minstrels into lamentation. And they
avenged fully the blood of their brother, and turned back to the marsh of
Jordan.
43 And Bacchides heard it, and he came
on the sabbath day unto the banks of
44 Jordan with a great host. And Jonathan said to his company, Let us stand
up now and fight for our lives, for it is
not *with us* to-day, as yesterday and
45 the day before. For, behold, the battle
is before us and behind us; moreover
the water of the Jordan is on this side
and on that side, and marsh and wood;
and there is no place to turn aside.
46 Now therefore cry unto heaven, that
ye may be delivered out of the hand
47 of your enemies. And the battle was
joined, and Jonathan stretched forth
his hand to smite Bacchides, and he
48 turned away back from him. And
Jonathan and they that were with him
leapt into the Jordan, and swam over
to the other side: and they did not
49 pass over Jordan against them. And
there fell of Bacchides' company that
50 day about a thousand men; and he returned to Jerusalem. And they builded
strong cities in Judæa, the stronghold
that was in Jericho, and Emmaus, and
Bethhoron, and Bethel, and Timnath,
Pharathon, and Tephon, with high
51 walls and gates and bars. And in
them he set a garrison, to vex Israel.
52 And he fortified the city Bethsura, and
Gazara, and the citadel, and put forces
53 in them, and store of victuals. And

1 circa
B. C. 160.

he took the sons of the chief men of the country for hostages, and put them in ward in the citadel at Jerusalem.

54 And in [1] the hundred and fifty and third year, in the second month, Alcimus commanded to pull down the wall of the inner court of the sanctuary; he pulled down also the works 55 of the prophets; and he began to pull down. At that time was Alcimus stricken, and his works were hindered; and his mouth was stopped, and he was taken with a palsy, and he could no more speak anything and give 56 order concerning his house. And Alcimus died at that time with great 57 torment. And Bacchides saw that Alcimus was dead, and he returned to the king: and the land of Judah had rest two years.

58 And all the lawless men took counsel, saying, Behold, Jonathan and they of his part are dwelling at ease, and in security: now therefore we will bring Bacchides, and he shall lay hands on 59 them all in one night. And they went 60 and consulted with him. And he removed, and came with a great host, and sent letters privily to all his confederates that were in Judæa, that they should lay hands on Jonathan and those that were with him: and they could not, because their counsel 61 was known unto them. And *they that were of Jonathan's part* laid hands on about fifty of the men of the country, that were authors of the wickedness, 62 and he slew them. And Jonathan, and Simon, and they that were with him, gat them away to Bethbasi, which is in the wilderness, and he built up that which had been pulled down 63 thereof, and they made it strong. And Bacchides knew it, and he gathered together all his multitude, and sent word to them that were of Judæa. 64 And he went and encamped against Bethbasi, and fought against it many 65 days, and made engines of war. And Jonathan left his brother Simon in the city, and went forth into the coun-66 try, and he went with a few men. And he smote Odomera and his brethren, and the children of Phasiron in their 67 tent. And they began to smite them, and to go up with their forces. And Simon and they that were with him went out of the city, and set on fire 68 the engines of war, and fought against Bacchides, and he was discomfited by them, and they afflicted him sore; for his counsel was in vain, and his in-69 road. And they were very wroth with the lawless men that gave him counsel to come into the country, and they slew many of them. And he took coun-70 sel to depart into his own land. And Jonathan had knowledge thereof, and sent ambassadors unto him, to the

end that they should make peace with him, and that he should restore unto 71 them the captives. And he accepted the thing, and did according to his words, and sware unto him that he would not seek his hurt all the days 72 of his life. And he restored unto him the captives which he had taken aforetime out of the land of Judah, and he returned and departed into his own land, and came not any more 73 into their borders. And the sword ceased from Israel. And Jonathan dwelt at Michmash; and Jonathan began to judge the people; and he destroyed the ungodly out of Israel.

10 And in [2] the hundred and sixtieth year Alexander Epiphanes, the son of Antiochus, went up and took possession of Ptolemais: and they received 2 him, and he reigned there. And king Demetrius heard thereof, and he gathered together exceeding great forces, and went forth to meet him in battle.
3 And Demetrius sent letters unto Jonathan with words of peace, so as 4 to magnify him. For he said, Let us be beforehand to make peace with them, ere he make peace with Alex-5 ander against us: for he will remember all the evils that we have done against him, and unto his brethren 6 and unto his nation. And he gave him authority to gather together forces, and to provide arms, and that he should be his confederate: and he commanded that they should deliver up to him the hostages that were in the citadel.
7 And Jonathan came to Jerusalem, and read the letters in the audience of all the people, and of them that were 8 in the citadel: and they were sore afraid, when they heard that the king had given him authority to gather 9 together a host. And they of the citadel delivered up the hostages unto Jonathan, and he restored them unto 10 their parents. And Jonathan dwelt in Jerusalem, and began to build and 11 renew the city. And he commanded them that did the work to build the walls and the mount Sion round about with [3] square stones for defence; and 12 they did so. And the strangers, that were in the strongholds which Bacchi-13 des had built, fled away; and each man left his place, and departed into 14 his own land. Only at Bethsura were there left certain of those that had forsaken the law and the commandments; for it was a place of refuge unto them.
15 And king Alexander heard all the promises which Demetrius had sent unto Jonathan: and they told him of the battles and the valiant deeds which he and his brethren had done, and of 16 the toils which they had endured; and he said, Shall we find such another

2 circa
B. C. 153

3 So the versions and Josephus. Gr. *four foot stones.*

1 See ch.
ii. 18.
Compare
ver. 65.

man? and now we will make him our
17 ¹Friend and confederate. And he
wrote letters, and sent them unto
him, according to these words, saying,

18 King Alexander to his brother Jona-
19 than, greeting: We have heard of thee,
that thou art a mighty man of valour,
20 and meet to be our ¹Friend. And
now we have appointed thee this day
to be high priest of thy nation, and to
be called the king's ¹Friend (and he
sent unto him a purple robe and a
crown of gold), and to take our part,
and to keep friendship with us.

21 And Jonathan put on the holy garments in the seventh month of ²the
hundred and sixtieth year, at the
feast of tabernacles, and he gathered
together forces, and provided arms in
abundance.

² circa
B. C. 153.

22 And Demetrius heard these things,
23 and he was grieved, and said, What is
this that we have done, that Alexander
hath been beforehand with us in estab-
lishing friendship with the Jews, to
24 strengthen himself? I also will write
unto them words of encouragement
and of honour and of gifts, that they
25 may be with me to aid me. And he
sent unto them according to these
words:

King Demetrius unto the nation of
26 the Jews, greeting: Forasmuch as ye
have kept your covenants with us,
and continued in our friendship, and
have not joined yourselves to our
enemies, we have heard hereof, and
27 are glad. And now continue ye still to
keep faith with us, and we will recompense unto you good things in return
28 for your dealings with us, and will
grant you many immunities, and give
29 you gifts. And now do I free you, and
release all the Jews, from the tributes,
and from the customs of salt, and from
30 the crowns. And instead of the third
part of the seed, and instead of the
half of the fruit of the trees, which
falleth to me to receive. I release it
from this day and henceforth, so that
I will not take it from the land of
Judah, and from the three governments which are added thereunto from
the country of Samaria and Galilee,
from this day forth and for all time.
31 And let Jerusalem be holy and free,
and her borders; the tenths and the
32 tolls *also*. I yield up also my authority over the citadel which is at Jerusalem, and give it to the high priest,
that he may appoint in it such men as
33 he shall choose to keep it. And every
soul of the Jews. that hath been carried captive from the land of Judah
into any part of my kingdom, I set at
liberty without price; and let all remit
34 the tributes of their cattle also. And
all the feasts, and the sabbaths, and
new moons, and appointed days, and

three days before a feast, and three
days after a feast, let them all be
days of immunity and release for all
the Jews that are in my kingdom.
35 And no man shall have authority to
exact from any of them, or to trouble
36 them concerning any matter. And let
there be enrolled among the king's
forces about thirty thousand men of
the Jews, and pay shall be given unto
them, as belongeth to all the king's
37 forces. And of them some shall be
placed in the king's great strongholds,
and some of them shall be placed over
the affairs of the kingdom, which are
of trust: and let those that are over
them, and their rulers, be of themselves. and let them walk after their
own laws, even as the king hath com-
38 manded in the land of Judah. And the
three governments that have been
added to Judæa from the country of
Samaria, let them be added to Judæa,
that they may be reckoned to be under one, that they may not obey other
39 authority than the high priest's. As
for Ptolemais. and the land pertaining
thereto, I have given it as a gift to
the sanctuary that is at Jerusalem,
for the expenses that befit the sanc-
40 tuary. And I give every year fifteen
thousand shekels of silver from the
king's revenues from the places that
41 are convenient. And all the overplus,
which they that manage the king's
affairs paid not in as in the first years,
they shall give from henceforth to-
42 ward the works of the house. And
beside this, the five thousand shekels
of silver, which they received from
the uses of the sanctuary from the
revenue year by year, this also is released, because it appertaineth to the
43 priests that minister. And whosoever shall flee unto the temple that
is at Jerusalem, and *be found* within
all the borders thereof, whether one
owe moneys to the king, or any other
matter, let them go free, and all that
44 they have in my kingdom. And for
the building and renewing of the
works of the sanctuary the expense
shall be given also out of the king's
45 revenue. And for the building of the
walls of Jerusalem, and the fortifying
thereof round about, shall the expense
be given also out of the king's revenue. and for the building of the walls
in Judæa.
46 Now when Jonathan and the people
heard these words, they gave no credence unto them, nor received them,
because they remembered the great
evil which he had done in Israel, and
that he had afflicted them very sore.
47 And they were well pleased with
Alexander, because he was the first
that spake words of peace unto them,
and they were confederate with him
48 always. And king Alexander ga-

49 thered together great forces, and en-camped over against Demetrius. And the two kings joined battle, and the army of Alexander fled; and Deme-trius followed after him, and prevailed
50 against them. And he strengthened the battle exceedingly until the sun went down: and Demetrius fell that day.

51 And Alexander sent ambassadors to Ptolemy king of Egypt according to
52 these words, saying, Forasmuch as I am returned to my kingdom, and am set on the throne of my fathers, and have gotten the dominion, and have overthrown Demetrius, and have got-
53 ten possession of our country; yea, I joined battle with him, and he and his army were discomfited by us, and we sat upon the throne of his
54 kingdom: now also let us establish amity one with the other, and give me now thy daughter to wife: and I will make affinity with thee, and will give both thee and her gifts worthy of thee.
55 And Ptolemy the king answered, say-ing, Happy is the day wherein thou didst return into the land of thy fathers, and didst sit on the throne
56 of their kingdom. And now will I do to thee, as thou hast written: but meet me at Ptolemais, that we may see one another; and I will make affinity with thee, even as thou hast
57 said. And Ptolemy went out of Egypt, himself and Cleopatra his daughter, and came unto Ptolemais in ¹ the hundred and threescore and
58 second year: and king Alexander met him, and he bestowed on him his daughter Cleopatra, and celebrated her marriage at Ptolemais with great pomp, as the manner of kings is.
59 And king Alexander wrote unto Jo-nathan, that he should come to meet
60 him. And he went with pomp to Ptolemais, and met the two kings, and gave them and their ² Friends silver and gold, and many gifts, and found
61 favour in their sight. And there were gathered together against him certain pestilent fellows out of Israel, men that were transgressors of the law, to complain against him: and the king
62 gave no heed to them. And the king commanded, and they took off Jona-than's garments, and clothed him in
63 purple: and thus they did. And the king made him sit with him, and said unto his princes, Go forth with him into the midst of the city, and make proclamation, that no man complain against him of any matter, and let no man trouble him for any manner of
64 cause. And it came to pass, when they that complained against him saw his glory according as *the herald* made proclamation, and *saw* him clothed in purple, they all fled away.
65 And the king gave him honour, and

wrote him among his ³ Chief Friends, and made him a captain, and gover-
66 nor of a province. And Jonathan returned to Jerusalem with peace and gladness.
67 And in ⁴ the hundred and threescore and fifth year came Demetrius, son of Demetrius, out of Crete into the land
68 of his fathers: and king Alexander heard thereof, and he was grieved ex-ceedingly, and returned unto Antioch.
69 And Demetrius appointed Apollonius, who was over Cœlesyria, and he gathered together a great host, and encamped in Jamnia, and sent unto Jonathan the high priest, saying,
70 Thou alone liftest up thyself against us, but I am had in derision and in re-proach because of thee. And why dost thou vaunt thy power against us in the
71 mountains? Now therefore, if thou trustest in thy forces, come down to us into the plain, and there let us try the matter together; for with me is the
72 power of the cities. Ask and learn who I am, and the rest that help us; and they say, Your foot cannot stand before our face; for thy fathers have been twice put to flight in their own
73 land. And now thou shalt not be able to abide the horse and such a host as this in the plain, where is neither stone nor flint, nor place to flee unto.
74 Now when Jonathan heard the words of Apollonius, he was moved in his mind, and he chose out ten thousand men, and went forth from Jerusalem, and Simon his brother met him for to
75 help him. And he encamped against Joppa: and they of the city shut him out, because Apollonius had a garrison
76 in Joppa: and they fought against it. And they of the city were afraid, and opened unto him: and Jonathan be-
77 came master of Joppa. And Apollo-nius heard, and he gathered an army of three thousand horse, and a great host, and went to Azotus as though he were on a journey, and therewithal drew onward into the plain, because he had a multitude of horse, and
78 trusted therein. And he pursued after him to Azotus, and the armies joined
79 battle ⁵. And Apollonius had left a thousand horse behind them privily.
80 And Jonathan knew that there was an ambushment behind him. And they compassed round his army, and cast their darts at the people, from morn-
81 ing until evening: but the people stood still, as Jonathan commanded them:
82 and their horses were wearied. And Simon drew forth his host, and joined battle with the phalanx (for the horse-men were spent), and they were dis-
83 comfited by him, and fled. And the horsemen were scattered in the plain, and they fled to Azotus, and entered into Beth-dagon, their idol's temple,
84 to save themselves. And Jonathan

¹ circa B. C. 151.

² See ch. ii. 18. Compare ver. 65.

³ See ch. xi. 27 ; 2 Macc. viii. 9. Compare ch. ii. 18 ; ver. 16, &c.

⁴ circa B. C. 143.

⁵ Most of the authori-ties here repeat *after him.*

burned Azotus, and the cities round about it, and took their spoils; and the temple of Dagon, and them that 85 fled into it, he burned with fire. And they that had fallen by the sword, with them that were burned, were 86 about eight thousand men. And from thence Jonathan removed, and encamped against Ascalon, and they of the city came forth to meet him with 87 great pomp. And Jonathan, with them that were on his side, returned unto 88 Jerusalem, having many spoils. And it came to pass, when king Alexander heard these things, he honoured Jona-89 than yet more; and he sent unto him a buckle of gold, as the use is to give to such as are of the kindred of the kings: and he gave him Ekron and all the coasts thereof for a possession.

11 And the king of Egypt gathered together great forces, as the sand which is by the sea shore, and many ships, and sought to make himself master of Alexander's kingdom by deceit, and 2 to add it to his own kingdom. And he went forth into Syria with words of peace, and they of the cities opened unto him, and met him; for king Alexander's commandment was that they should meet him, because he was 3 his father in law. Now as he entered into the cities of Ptolemais, he set his forces for a garrison in each city. 4 But when he came near to Azotus, they shewed him the temple of Dagon burned with fire, and Azotus and the suburbs thereof pulled down, and the bodies cast abroad, and them that had been burned, whom he burned in the war, for they had made heaps of them 5 in his way. And they told the king what things Jonathan had done, that they might cast blame on him: and 6 the king held his peace. And Jonathan met the king with pomp at Joppa, and they saluted one another, and 7 they slept there. And Jonathan went with the king as far as the river that is called Eleutherus, and returned to 8 Jerusalem. But king Ptolemy became master of the cities upon the sea coast, unto Seleucia which is by the sea, and he devised evil devices concerning 9 Alexander. And he sent ambassadors unto king Demetrius, saying, Come, let us make a covenant with one another, and I will give thee my daughter whom Alexander hath, and thou shalt 10 reign over thy father's kingdom; for I have repented that I gave my daughter unto him, for he sought to 11 slay me. And he cast blame on him, 12 because he coveted his kingdom. And taking his daughter from him, he gave her to Demetrius, and was estranged from Alexander, and their enmity was 13 openly seen. And Ptolemy entered into Antioch, and put on himself the diadem of Asia; and he put two dia-

dems upon his head, the diadem of 14 Egypt and that of Asia. But king Alexander was in Cilicia at that season, because they of those parts were 15 in revolt. And Alexander heard of it, and he came against him in war: and Ptolemy led forth his host, and met him with a strong force, and put him 16 to flight. And Alexander fled into Arabia, that he might be sheltered there; but king Ptolemy was exalted. 17 And Zabdiel the Arabian took off Alexander's head, and sent it to Ptol-18 emy. And king Ptolemy died the third day after, and they that were in his strongholds were slain by them 19 that were in the strongholds. And Demetrius reigned in [1] the hundred and threescore and seventh year.

20 In those days Jonathan gathered together them of Judæa, to take the citadel that was at Jerusalem: and he made many engines of war against it. 21 And certain that hated their own nation, men that transgressed the law, went unto the king, and reported to him that Jonathan was besieging the 22 citadel. And he heard, and was angered; but when he heard it, he set forth immediately, and came to Ptolemais, and wrote unto Jonathan, that he should not besiege it, and that he should meet him and speak with him 23 at Ptolemais with all speed. But when Jonathan heard this, he commanded to besiege it still: and he chose certain of the elders of Israel and of the priests, and put himself 24 in peril, and taking silver and gold and raiment and divers presents besides, went to Ptolemais unto the king. And he found favour in his 25 sight. And certain lawless men of them that were of the nation made 26 complaints against him, and the king did unto him even as his predecessors had done unto him, and exalted him 27 in the sight of all his [2] Friends, and confirmed to him the high priesthood, and all the other honours that he had before, and gave him preeminence among his [3] Chief Friends. 28 And Jonathan requested of the king, that he would make Judæa free from tribute, and the three [4] provinces, and the country of Samaria; and pro-29 mised him three hundred talents. And the king consented, and wrote letters unto Jonathan concerning all these things after this manner:

30 King Demetrius unto his brother Jonathan, and unto the nation of the 31 Jews, greeting: The copy of the letter which we wrote unto Lasthenes our kinsman concerning you, we have written also unto you, that ye may see 32 it. King Demetrius unto Lasthenes 33 his father, greeting: We have determined to do good to the nation of the Jews, who are our friends, and ob-

[1] circa B. C. 146

[2] See ch ii. 18.

[3] See ch. x. 65.

[4] Gr. toparchies.

serve what is just toward us, because 34 of their good will toward us. We have confirmed therefore unto them the borders of Judæa, and also the three governments of Aphærema and Lydda and Ramathaim (*these* were added unto Judæa from the country of Samaria), and all things appertaining unto them, for all such as do sacrifice in Jerusalem, instead of the king's dues which the king received of them yearly aforetime from the produce of the earth and the fruits of trees. 35 And as for the other things that pertain unto us from henceforth, of the tenths and the tolls that pertain unto us, and the saltpits, and the crowns that pertain unto us, all these we will 36 bestow upon them. And not one of these things shall be annulled from 37 this time forth and for ever. Now therefore be careful to make a copy of these things, and let it be given unto Jonathan, and let it be set up on the holy mount in a meet and conspicuous place.

38 And king Demetrius saw that the land was quiet before him, and that no resistance was made to him, and he sent away all his forces, each man to his own place, except the foreign forces, which he had raised from the isles of the Gentiles: and all the forces 39 of his fathers hated him. Now Tryphon was of those who aforetime had been of Alexander's part, and he saw that all the forces murmured against Demetrius, and he went to Imalcue the Arabian, who was nourishing up Antiochus the young child 40 of Alexander, and pressed sore upon him that he should deliver him unto him, that he might reign in his father's stead: and he told him all that Demetrius had done, and the hatred wherewith his forces hated him; and he abode there many days.

41 And Jonathan sent unto king Demetrius, that he should cast out of Jerusalem them of the citadel, and them that were in the strongholds; for they fought against Israel con-42 tinually. And Demetrius sent unto Jonathan, saying, I will not only do this for thee and thy nation, but I will greatly honour thee and thy na-43 tion, if I find fair occasion. Now therefore thou shalt do well, if thou send me men who shall fight for me; for all 44 my forces are revolted. And Jonathan sent him three thousand valiant men unto Antioch: and they came to the king, and the king was glad at 45 their coming. And they of the city gathered themselves together into the midst of the city, to the number of a hundred and twenty thousand men, and they were minded to slay the 46 king. And the king fled into the court of the palace, and they of the city

seized the passages of the city, and 47 began to fight. And the king called the Jews to help him, and they were gathered together unto him all at once, and they dispersed themselves in the city, and slew that day to the number 48 of a hundred thousand. And they set the city on fire, and gat many spoils 49 that day, and saved the king. And they of the city saw that the Jews had made themselves masters of the city as they would, and they waxed faint in their hearts, and they cried out to the king with supplication, saying, 50 Give us thy right hand, and let the Jews cease from fighting against us 51 and the city. And they cast away their arms, and made peace; and the Jews were glorified in the sight of the king, and before all that were in his kingdom; and they returned to Je-52 rusalem, having many spoils. And king Demetrius sat on the throne of his kingdom, and the land was quiet 53 before him. And he lied in all that he spake, and estranged himself from Jonathan, and recompensed him not according to the benefits with which he had recompensed him, and afflicted him exceedingly.

54 Now after this Tryphon returned, and with him the young child Antiochus; and he reigned, and put on a 55 diadem. And there were gathered unto him all the forces which Demetrius had sent away with disgrace, and they fought against him, and he fled 56 and was put to the rout. And Tryphon took the elephants, and became mas-57 ter of Antioch. And the young Antiochus wrote unto Jonathan, saying, I confirm unto thee the high priesthood, and appoint thee over the four governments, and to be one of the king's 58 [1] Friends. And he sent unto him golden vessels and furniture for the table, and gave him leave to drink in golden vessels, and to be clothed in purple, and to have a golden buckle. 59 And his brother Simon he made captain from the Ladder of Tyre unto the 60 borders of Egypt. And Jonathan went forth, and took his journey beyond the river and through the cities; and all the forces of Syria gathered themselves unto him for to be his confederates. And he came to Ascalon, and they of the city met him honourably. 61 And he departed thence to Gaza, and they of Gaza shut him out; and he laid siege unto it, and burned the suburbs thereof with fire, and spoiled 62 them. And they of Gaza made request unto Jonathan, and he gave them his right hand, and took the sons of their princes for hostages, and sent them away to Jerusalem; and he passed through the country as far as Damascus.

63 And Jonathan heard that Demetrius'

[1] See ch ii. 18.

princes were come to Kedesh, which is in Galilee, with a great host, purposing
64 to remove him from his office; and he went to meet them, but Simon his
65 brother he left in the country. And Simon encamped against Bethsura, and fought against it many days, and shut
66 it up: and they made request to him that he would give them his right hand, and he gave it to them; and he put them out from thence, and took possession of the city, and set a gar-
67 rison over it. And Jonathan and his army encamped at the water of Gennesareth, and early in the morning they gat them to the plain of Hazor.
68 And, behold, an army of strangers met him in the plain, and they laid an ambush for him in the mountains, but
69 themselves met him face to face. But they that lay in ambush rose out of their places, and joined battle; and all they that were of Jonathan's side
70 fled: not one of them was left, except Mattathias the son of Absalom, and Judas the son of Chalphi, captains of
71 the forces. And Jonathan rent his clothes, and put earth upon his head,
72 and prayed. And he turned again unto them in battle, and put them to the
73 rout, and they fled. And they of his side that fled saw it, and returned unto him, and pursued with him unto Kedesh unto their camp, and they
74 encamped there. And there fell of the strangers on that day about three thousand men: and Jonathan returned to Jerusalem.

12 And Jonathan saw that the time served him, and he chose men, and sent them to Rome, to confirm and renew the friendship that they had
2 with them. And to the Spartans, and to other places, he sent letters after
3 the same manner. And they went unto Rome, and entered into the senate house, and said, Jonathan the high priest, and the nation of the Jews, have sent us, to renew for them the friendship and the confederacy, as in
4 former time. And they gave them letters unto the men in every place, that they should bring them on their way to the land of Judah in peace.
5 And this is the copy of the letters which Jonathan wrote to the Spartans:
6 Jonathan the high priest, and the senate of the nation, and the priests, and the rest of the people of the Jews, unto their brethren the Spartans,
7 greeting: Even before this time were letters sent unto Onias the high priest from [1] Arius, who was reigning among you, to signify that ye are our brethren, as the copy here underwritten
8 sheweth. And Onias entreated honourably the man that was sent, and received the letters, wherein declaration was made of confederacy and

9 friendship. Therefore we also, albeit we need none of these things, having for our encouragement the holy books
10 which are in our hands, have assayed to send that we might renew our brotherhood and friendship with you, to the end that we should not become estranged from you altogether: for long time is passed since ye sent unto
11 us. We therefore at all times without ceasing, both in our feasts, and on the other convenient days, do remember you in the sacrifices which we offer, and in our prayers, as it is right and meet to be mindful of brethren:
12 and moreover are glad for your glory.
13 But as for ourselves, many afflictions and many wars have encompassed us, and the kings that are round about us
14 have fought against us. We were not minded therefore to be troublesome unto you, and to the rest of our confederates and friends, in these wars;
15 for we have the help which is from heaven to help us, and we have been delivered from our enemies, and our
16 enemies have been brought low. We chose therefore Numenius the son of Antiochus, and Antipater the son of Jason, and have sent them unto the Romans, to renew the friendship that we had with them, and the former con-
17 federacy. We commanded them therefore to go also unto you, and to salute you, and to deliver you our letters concerning the renewing of
18 friendship and our brotherhood. And now ye shall do well if ye give us an answer thereto.
19 And this is the copy of the letters which they sent to Onias:
20 Arius king of the Spartans to Onias
21 the chief priest, greeting: It hath been found in writing, concerning the Spartans and the Jews, that they are brethren, and that they are of the
22 stock of Abraham: and now, since this is come to our knowledge, ye shall do well to write unto us of your
23 [2] prosperity. And we moreover do write on our part to you, that your cattle and goods are ours, and ours are yours. We do command therefore that they make report unto you on this wise.
24 And Jonathan heard that Demetrius' princes were returned to fight against him with a greater host than afore,
25 and he removed from Jerusalem, and met them in the country of Hamath; for he gave them no respite to set foot
26 in his country. And he sent spies into his camp, and they came again, and reported to him that they were appointed in such and such a way to fall upon them in the night season.
27 But so soon as the sun was down, Jonathan commanded his men to watch, and to be in arms, that all the night long they might be ready for

[1] So the old Latin versions and Josephus: compare ver. 20. All the other authorities read *Darius* in this place.

[2] Gr. *peace*

battle: and he put forth sentinels
28 round about the camp. And the adversaries heard that Jonathan and his men were ready for battle, and they feared, and trembled in their hearts, and they kindled fires in their camp¹.
29 But Jonathan and his men knew it not till the morning; for they saw the
30 lights burning. And Jonathan pursued after them, and overtook them not; for they were gone over the river
31 Eleutherus. And Jonathan turned aside to the Arabians, who are called Zabadæans, and smote them, and took
32 their spoils. And he set out from thence, and came to Damascus, and took his journey through all the coun-
33 try. And Simon went forth, and took his journey as far as Ascalon, and the strongholds that were near unto it. And he turned aside to Joppa, and
34 took possession of it; for he had heard that they were minded to deliver the stronghold unto the men of Demetrius; and he set a garrison there to keep it.
35 And Jonathan returned, and called the elders of the people together; and he took counsel with them to build
36 strongholds in Judæa, and to make the walls of Jerusalem higher, and to raise a great mound between the citadel and the city, for to separate it from the city, that so it might be all alone, that men might neither
37 buy nor sell. And they were gathered together to build the city, and there fell down part of the wall of the brook that is on the east side, and he repaired that which is called Chaphenatha.
38 And Simon also built Adida in the ² plain country, and made it strong, and set up gates and bars.
39 And Tryphon sought to reign over Asia and to put on himself the diadem, and to stretch forth his hand against
40 Antiochus the king. And he was afraid lest haply Jonathan should not suffer him, and lest he should fight against him; and he sought a way how to take him, that he might destroy him. And he removed, and came to Bethshan.
41 And Jonathan came forth to meet him with forty thousand men chosen for
42 battle, and came to Bethshan. And Tryphon saw that he came with a great host, and he was afraid to stretch
43 forth his hand against him: and he received him honourably, and commended him unto all his ³ Friends, and gave him gifts, and commanded his forces to be obedient unto him, as unto
44 himself. And he said unto Jonathan, Why hast thou put all this people to trouble, seeing there is no war
45 betwixt us? And now send them away to their homes, but choose for thyself a few men who shall be with thee, and come thou with me to Ptolemais, and I will give it up to thee,

and the rest of the strongholds and the rest of the forces, and all the king's officers: and I will return and depart; for this is the cause of my
46 coming. And he put trust in him, and did even as he said, and sent away his forces, and they departed in-
47 to the land of Judah. But he reserved to himself three thousand men, of whom he left two thousand in Galilee, but one thousand went with him.
48 Now as soon as Jonathan entered into Ptolemais, they of Ptolemais shut the gates, and laid hands on him; and all them that came in with him they
49 slew with the sword. And Tryphon sent forces and horsemen into Galilee, and into the great plain, to destroy all
50 Jonathan's men. And they perceived that he was taken and had perished, and they that were with him; and they encouraged one another, and went on their way close together,
51 prepared to fight. And they that followed upon them saw that they were ready to fight for their lives, and
52 turned back again. And they all came in peace into the land of Judah, and they mourned for Jonathan, and them that were with him, and they were sore afraid: and all Israel mourned with
53 a great mourning. And all the Gentiles that were round about them sought to destroy them utterly: for they said, They have no ruler, nor any to help them: now therefore let us fight against them, and take away their memorial from among men.
13 And Simon heard that Tryphon had gathered together a mighty host to come into the land of Judah, and
2 destroy it utterly. And he saw that the people trembled and was in great fear; and he went up to Jerusalem,
3 and gathered the people together; and he encouraged them, and said unto them, Ye yourselves know all the things that I, and my brethren, and my father's house, have done for the laws and the sanctuary, and the battles and the distresses which we have seen:
4 by reason hereof all my brethren have perished for Israel's sake, and I am
5 left alone. And now be it far from me, that I should spare mine own life in any time of affliction; for I am not
6 better than my brethren. Howbeit I will take vengeance for my nation, and for the sanctuary, and for our wives and children; because all the Gentiles are gathered to destroy us of very
7 hatred. And the spirit of the people revived, as soon as they heard these
8 words. And they answered with a loud voice, saying, Thou art our leader instead of Judas and Jonathan thy
9 brother. Fight thou our battles, and all that thou shalt say unto us, that
10 will we do. And he gathered together all the men of war, and made haste

to finish the walls of Jerusalem, and
11 he fortified it round about. And he
sent Jonathan the son of Absalom,
and with him a great host, to Joppa:
and he cast out them that were therein, and abode there in it.
12 And Tryphon removed from Ptolemais with a mighty host to enter into
the land of Judah, and Jonathan was
13 with him in ward. But Simon encamped at Adida, over against the
14 plain. And Tryphon knew that Simon
was risen up instead of his brother
Jonathan, and meant to join battle
with him, and he sent ambassadors
15 unto him, saying, It is for money
which Jonathan thy brother owed unto
the king's treasure, by reason of the
offices which he had, that we hold
16 him fast. And now send a hundred
talents of silver, and two of his sons
for hostages, that when he is set at
liberty he may not revolt from us,
17 and we will set him at liberty. And
Simon knew that they spake unto him
deceitfully; and he sendeth the money
and the children, lest peradventure he
should procure to himself great hatred
18 of the people, and they should say,
Because I sent him not the money and
19 the children, he perished. And he
sent the children and the hundred
talents. And he dealt falsely, and did
20 not set Jonathan at liberty. And after
this Tryphon came to invade the land,
and destroy it, and he went round
about by the way that leadeth unto
Adora: and Simon and his army
marched over against him to every
21 place, wheresoever he went. Now
they of the citadel sent unto Tryphon
ambassadors, hastening him to come
unto them through the wilderness, and
22 to send them victuals. And Tryphon
made ready all his horse to come: and
on that night there fell a very great
snow, and he came not by reason of
the snow. And he removed, and came
23 into the country of Gilead. But when
he came near to Bascama, he slew
Jonathan, and he was buried there.
24 And Tryphon returned, and went
away into his own land.
25 And Simon sent, and took the bones
of Jonathan his brother, and buried
him at Modin, the city of his fathers.
26 And all Israel made great lamentation
over him, and mourned for him many
27 days. And Simon built a *monument*
upon the sepulchre of his father and
his brethren, and raised it aloft to the
sight, with polished stone behind and
28 before. And he set up seven pyra-
mids, one over against another, for
his father, and his mother, and his
29 four brethren. And for these he made
cunning devices, setting about them
great pillars, and upon the pillars he
fashioned [1] all manner of arms for a
perpetual memory, and beside the

[1] Gr.
pan-
oplies.

[1] arms ships carved, that they should
be seen of all that sail on the sea.
30 This is the sepulchre which he made
at Modin, *and it is there* unto this day.
31 Now Tryphon dealt deceitfully with
the young king Antiochus, and slew
32 him, and reigned in his stead, and put
on himself the diadem of Asia, and
brought a great calamity upon the
33 land. And Simon built the strongholds of Judæa, and fenced them
about with high towers, and great
walls, and gates, and bars; and he
laid up victuals in the strongholds.
34 And Simon chose men, and sent to
king Demetrius, to the end he should
give the country an immunity, because
all that Tryphon did was to plunder.
35 And king Demetrius sent unto him
according to these words, and answered him, and wrote a letter unto
him, after this manner:
36 King Demetrius unto Simon the high
priest and [2] Friend of kings, and unto
the elders and nation of the Jews,
37 greeting: The golden crown, and the
palm branch, which ye sent, we have
received: and we are ready to make a
[3] stedfast peace with you, yea, and to
write unto our officers, to grant im-
38 munities unto you. And whatsoever
things we confirmed unto you, they
are confirmed; and the strongholds,
which ye have builded, let them be
39 your own. As for any oversights and
faults committed unto this day, we
forgive them, and the crown which ye
owed us: and if there were any other
toll exacted in Jerusalem, let it be
40 exacted no longer. And if there be
any among you meet to be enrolled
in our court, let them be enrolled, and
let there be peace betwixt us.
41 In [4] the hundred and seventieth year
was the yoke of the heathen taken
42 away from Israel. And the people
began to write in their instruments
and contracts, In the first year of
Simon the great high priest and captain and leader of the Jews.
43 In those days he encamped against
[5] Gazara, and compassed it round
about with armies; and he made an
engine of siege, and brought it up to
the city, and smote a tower, and took
44 it. And they that were in the engine
leaped forth into the city; and there
45 was a great uproar in the city: and
they of the city rent their clothes, and
went up on the walls with their wives
and children, and cried with a loud
voice, making request to Simon to give
46 them [6] his right hand. And they said,
Deal not with us according to our
wickednesses, but according to thy
47 mercy. And Simon was reconciled
unto them, and did not fight against
them: and he put them out of the
city, and cleansed the houses wherein
the idols were, and so entered into it

[2] See ch.
ii. 18.

[3] Gr.
great.

[4] circa
B. C. 143.

[5] See
ver. 53
(com-
pare ver.
48) : ch.
xiv. 7, 34;
xvi. 1 :
also Jo-
sephus.
All the
authori-
ties read
Gaza
in this
verse.
[6] Gr.
*right
hands.*

48 with singing and giving praise. And he put all uncleanness out of it, and placed in it such men as would keep the law, and made it stronger than it was before, and built therein a dwelling place for himself.

49 But they of the citadel in Jerusalem were hindered from going forth, and from going into the country, and from buying and selling; and they hungered exceedingly, and a great number of

50 them perished through famine. And they cried out to Simon, that he should give them his right hand; and he gave it to them: and he put them out from thence, and he cleansed the citadel

51 from its pollutions. And he entered into it on the three and twentieth day of the second month, in ¹ the hundred and seventy and first year, with praise and palm branches, and with harps, and with cymbals, and with viols, and with hymns, and with songs: because a great enemy was destroyed out of

52 Israel. And he ordained that they should keep that day every year with gladness. And the hill of the temple that was by the citadel he made stronger than before, and there he

53 dwelt, himself and his men. And Simon saw that John his son was a *valiant* man, and he made him leader of all his forces: and he dwelt in Gazara.

14 And in ² the hundred and seventy and second year king Demetrius gathered his forces together, and went into Media, to get him help, that he

2 might fight against Tryphon. And Arsaces, the king of Persia and Media, heard that Demetrius was come into his borders, and he sent one of his

3 princes to take him alive: and he went and smote the army of Demetrius, and took him, and brought him to Arsaces; and he put him in ward.

4 And the land had rest all the days of Simon: and he sought the good of his nation; and his authority and his glory was well-pleasing to them all his days.

5 And amid all his glory he took Joppa for a haven, and made it an entrance

6 for the isles of the sea; and he enlarged the borders of his nation, and

7 gat possession of the country; and he gathered together a great number of captives, and gat the dominion of Gazara, and Bethsura, and the citadel, and he took away from it its uncleannesses; and there was none that re-

8 sisted him. And they tilled their land in peace, and the land gave her increase, and the trees of the plains

9 their fruit. The ancient men sat in the streets, they communed all of them together of good things, and the young men put on glorious and warlike ap-

10 parel. He provided victuals for the cities, and furnished them with ³ all manner of munition, until the name of

his glory was named unto the end of

11 the earth. He made peace in the land, and Israel rejoiced with great

12 joy: and they sat each man under his vine and his fig tree, and there was

13 none to make them afraid: and there ceased in the land any that fought against them: and the kings were

14 discomfited in those days. And he strengthened all those of his people that were brought low: the law he searched out, and every lawless and

15 wicked person he took away. He glorified the sanctuary, and the vessels of the temple he multiplied.

16 And it was heard at Rome that Jonathan was dead, and even unto Sparta,

17 and they were exceeding sorry. But as soon as they heard that his brother Simon was made high priest in his stead, and ruled the country, and the

18 cities therein, they wrote unto him on tables of brass, to renew with him the friendship and the confederacy which they had confirmed with Judas and

19 Jonathan his brethren; and they were read before the congregation at

20 Jerusalem. And this is the copy of the letters which the Spartans sent:

The rulers of the Spartans, and the city, unto Simon the high priest, and unto the elders, and the priests, and the residue of the people of the Jews,

21 our brethren, greeting: The ambassadors that were sent unto our people made report to us of your glory and honour: and we were glad for their

22 coming, and we did register the things that were spoken by them in the ⁴ public records after this manner: Numenius son of Antiochus, and Antipater son of Jason, the Jews' ambassadors, came unto us to renew the

23 friendship they had with us. And it pleased the people to entertain the men honourably, and to put the copy of their words in the ⁵ public records, to the end that the people of the Spartans might have a memorial thereof: moreover they wrote a copy of these things unto Simon the high priest.

24 After this Simon sent Numenius to Rome with a great shield of gold of a thousand pound weight, in order to confirm the confederacy with them.

25 But when the people heard these things, they said, What thanks shall

26 we give to Simon and his sons? for he and his brethren and the house of his father have made themselves strong, and have chased away in fight the enemies of Israel from them, and

27 confirmed liberty to ⁶ Israel. And they wrote on tables of brass, and set them upon pillars in mount Sion: and this is the copy of the writing:

On the eighteenth day of Elul, in ² the hundred and seventy and second year, and this is the third year of

¹ circa B. C. 142.

² circa B. C. 141.

³ Gr. *implements of munition.*

⁴ Gr. *counsels of the people.*

⁵ Gr. *books that are appointed for the people.*

⁶ Gr. *him.*

28 Simon the high priest, [1] in Asaramel, in a great congregation of priests and people and princes of the nation, and of the elders of the country, [2] was it 29 notified unto us: Forasmuch as oftentimes there have been wars in the country, but Simon the son of Mattathias, the son of the sons of Joarib, and his brethren, put themselves in jeopardy, and withstood the enemies of their nation, that their sanctuary and the law might be established, and glorified their nation with great glory: 30 and Jonathan assembled their nation together, and became their high priest, and was gathered to his peo- 31 ple: and their enemies purposed to invade their country, that they might destroy their country utterly, and stretch forth their hands against their 32 sanctuary: then rose up Simon, and fought for his nation, and spent much of his own substance, and armed the valiant men of his nation, and gave 33 them wages: and he fortified the cities of Judæa, and Bethsura that lieth upon the borders of Judæa, where the arms of the enemies were aforetime, and set there a garrison of 34 Jews: and he fortified Joppa which is upon the sea, and Gazara which is upon the borders of Azotus, wherein the enemies dwelt aforetime, and placed Jews there, and set therein all things convenient for the reparation 35 thereof: and the people saw the [3] faith of Simon, and the glory which he thought to bring unto his nation, and they made him their leader and high priest, because he had done all these things, and for the justice and the faith which he kept to his nation, and for that he sought by all means 36 to exalt his people: and in his days things prospered in his hands, so that the Gentiles were taken away out of their country, and they also that were in the city of David, they that were in Jerusalem, who had made themselves a citadel, out of which they issued, and polluted all things round about the sanctuary, and did great hurt 37 unto its purity; and he placed Jews therein, and fortified it for the safety of the country and the city, and made 38 high the walls of Jerusalem: and king Demetrius confirmed to him the high priesthood according to these things, 39 and made him one of his [4] Friends, and honoured him with great honour; 40 for he had heard say, that the Jews had been called by the Romans friends and confederates and brethren, and that they had met the ambassadors of 41 Simon honourably; and that the Jews and the priests were well pleased that Simon should be their leader and high priest for ever, until there should 42 arise a faithful prophet; and that he should be captain over them, and

should take charge of the sanctuary, to set them over their works, and over the country, and over the arms, and over the strongholds; and that he should take charge of the sanctuary, 43 and that he should be obeyed by all, and that all instruments in the country should be written in his name, and that he should be clothed in purple, 44 and wear gold; and that it should not be lawful for any of the people or of the priests to set at nought any of these things, or to gainsay the words that he should speak, or to gather an assembly in the country without him, or to be clothed in purple, or wear a 45 buckle of gold; but whosoever should do otherwise, or set at nought any of these things, he should be liable to 46 punishment. All the people consented to ordain for Simon that he should 47 do according to these words; and Simon accepted hereof, and consented to be high priest, and to be captain and [5] governor of the Jews and of the priests, and to be protector of all. 48 And they commanded to put this writing on tables of brass, and to set them up within the precinct of the sanctuary in a conspicuous place; 49 and moreover to put the copies thereof in the treasury, to the end that Simon and his sons might have them. 15 And Antiochus son of Demetrius the king sent letters from the isles of the sea unto Simon the priest and [5] governor of the Jews, and to all the 2 nation; and the contents thereof were after this manner:

King Antiochus to Simon the chief priest and [5] governor, and to the 3 nation of the Jews, greeting: Forasmuch as certain pestilent fellows have made themselves masters of the kingdom of our fathers, but my purpose is to claim the kingdom, that I may restore it as it was before; and moreover I have raised a multitude of foreign soldiers, and have prepared 4 ships of war; moreover I am minded to land in the country, that I may punish them that have destroyed our country, and them that have made many cities in the kingdom desolate: 5 Now therefore I confirm unto thee all the exactions which the kings that were before me remitted unto thee, and whatsoever gifts besides they 6 remitted unto thee: and I give thee leave to coin money for thy country 7 with thine own stamp, but that Jerusalem and the sanctuary should be free: and all the arms that thou hast prepared, and the strongholds that thou hast built, which thou hast in thy possession, let them remain unto 8 thee: and everything owing to the king, and the things that shall be owing to the king from henceforth and for evermore, let them be remit-

---

Margin notes:

[1] Perhaps a Hebrew title of Simon underlies these words.
[2] Gr. he made known.
[3] Some authorities read acts.
[4] See ch. x. 18.
[5] Gr. ethnarch.

9 ted unto thee: moreover, when we shall have established our kingdom, we will glorify thee and thy nation and the temple with great glory, so that your glory shall be made manifest in all the earth.

1 circa B. C. 139.

10 In [1] the hundred and seventy and fourth year went Antiochus forth into the land of his fathers; and all the forces came together unto him, so that there were few men with Tryphon.

11 And king Antiochus pursued him, and [2] he came, as he fled, unto Dor,

2 Or, he came unto Dor, fleeing by the way which is by the sea

12 which is by the sea: for he knew that troubles were come upon him all at once, and that his forces had for-

13 saken him. And Antiochus encamped against Dor, and with him a hundred and twenty thousand men of war, and

14 eight thousand horse. And he compassed the city round about, and the ships joined in the attack from the sea; and he vexed the city by land and sea, and suffered no man to go out or in.

15 And Numenius and his company came from Rome, having letters to the kings and to the countries, wherein were written these things:

16 Lucius, consul of the Romans, unto

17 king Ptolemy, greeting: The Jews' ambassadors came unto us as our friends and confederates, to renew the old friendship and confederacy, being sent from Simon the high priest, and from the people of the Jews:

18 moreover they brought a shield of

19 gold of a thousand pound. It pleased us therefore to write unto the kings and unto the countries, that they should not seek their hurt, nor fight against them, and their cities, and their country, nor be confederates with such as fight against them.

20 Moreover it seemed good to us to

21 receive the shield of them. If therefore any pestilent fellows have fled from their country unto you, deliver them unto Simon the high priest, that he may take vengeance on them according to their law.

22 And the same things wrote he to Demetrius the king, and to Attalus, and

23 to Arathes, and to Arsaces, and unto all the countries, and to [3] Sampsames, and to the Spartans, and unto Delos, and unto Myndos, and unto Sicyon, and unto Caria, and unto Samos, and unto Pamphylia, and unto Lycia, and unto Halicarnassus, and unto Rhodes, and unto Phaselis, and unto Cos, and unto Side, and unto Aradus, and Gortyna, and Cnidus, and

24 Cyprus, and Cyrene. But the copy hereof they wrote to Simon the high priest.

3 Some authorities read Sampsaces: the Latin versions have Lampsacus.

25 But Antiochus the king encamped against Dor the second day, bringing his forces up to it continually, and making engines of war, and he shut up

26 Tryphon from going in or out. And Simon sent him two thousand chosen men to fight on his side; and silver, and gold, and instruments of war in

27 abundance. And he would not receive them, but set at nought all the covenants which he had made with him aforetime, and was estranged from

28 him. And he sent unto him Athenobius, one of his [4] Friends, to commune with him, saying,

4 See ch ii. 18.

Ye hold possession of Joppa and Gazara, and the citadel that is in Jerusalem, cities of my kingdom.

29 The borders thereof ye have wasted, and done great hurt in the land, and got the dominion of many places in

30 my kingdom. Now therefore deliver up the cities which ye have taken, and the tributes of the places whereof ye have gotten dominion without the

31 borders of Judæa: or else give me for them five hundred talents of silver; and for the harm that ye have done, and the tributes of the cities, other five hundred talents: or else we will come and subdue you.

32 And Athenobius the king's [4] Friend came to Jerusalem; and he saw the glory of Simon, and the cupboard of gold and silver vessels, and his great attendance, and he was amazed; and he reported to him the king's words.

33 And Simon answered, and said unto him,

We have neither taken other men's land, nor have we possession of that which appertaineth to others, but of the inheritance of our fathers; howbeit, it was had in possession of our enemies wrongfully for a certain time.

34 But we, having opportunity, hold fast

35 the inheritance of our fathers. But as touching Joppa and Gazara, which thou demandest, they did great harm among the people throughout our country, we will give a hundred talents for them.

And he answered him not a word,

36 but returned in a rage to the king, and reported unto him these words, and the glory of Simon, and all that he had seen: and the king was ex-

37 ceeding wroth. But Tryphon embarked on board a ship, and fled to Orthosia.

38 And the king appointed Cendebæus chief captain of the sea coast, and gave him forces of foot and horse:

39 and he commanded him to encamp before Judæa, and he commanded him to build up Kidron, and to fortify the gates, and that he should fight against the people: but the king pursued Try-

40 phon. And Cendebæus came to Jamnia, and began to provoke the people, and to invade Judæa, and to take the

41 people captive, and to slay them. And he built Kidron, and set horsemen there, and forces of foot, to the end

that issuing out they might make out-roads upon the ways of Judæa, according as the king commanded him.

16 And John went up from Gazara, and told Simon his father what Cendebæus 2 was doing. And Simon called his two eldest sons, Judas and John, and said unto them, I and my brethren and my father's house have fought the battles of Israel from our youth, even unto this day; and things have prospered in our hands, that we should deliver 3 Israel oftentimes. But now I am old, and ye moreover, by *his* mercy, are of a sufficient age: be ye instead of me and my brother, and go forth and fight for our nation; but let the help which is from heaven be with you. 4 And he chose out of the country twenty thousand men of war and horsemen, and they went against 5 Cendebæus, and slept at Modin. And rising up in the morning, they went into the plain, and, behold, a great host came to meet them, of footmen and horsemen: and there was a brook 6 betwixt them. And he encamped over against them, he and his people: and he saw that the people were afraid to pass over the brook, and he passed over first, and the men saw 7 him, and passed over after him. And he divided the people, and *set* the horsemen in the midst of the footmen: but the enemies' horsemen were ex-8 ceeding many. And they sounded with the trumpets; and Cendebæus and his army were put to the rout, and there fell of them many wounded to death, but they that were left fled 9 to the stronghold: at that time was Judas John's brother wounded: but John pursued after them, till he came unto Kidron, which *Cendebæus* had 10 built; and they fled unto the towers that are in the fields of Azotus; and he burned it with fire: and there fell of them about two thousand men. And he returned into Judæa in peace.

11 And Ptolemy the son of Abubus had been appointed captain for the plain of Jericho, and he had much silver and 12 gold; for he was the high priest's son

13 in law. And his heart was lifted up, and he was minded to make himself master of the country, and he took counsel deceitfully against Simon and his sons, to make away with them. 14 Now Simon was visiting the cities that were in the country, and taking care for the good ordering of them; and he went down to Jericho, himself and Mattathias and Judas his sons, in [1] the hundred and seventy and seventh year, in the eleventh month, 15 the same is the month Sebat: and the son of Abubus received them deceitfully into the little stronghold that is called Dok, which he had built, and made them a great banquet, and hid 16 men there. And when Simon and his sons had drunk freely, Ptolemy and his men rose up, and took their arms, and came in upon Simon into the banqueting place, and slew him, and his two sons, and certain of his 17 servants. And he committed a great iniquity, and recompensed evil for 18 good. And Ptolemy wrote these things, and sent to the king, that he should send him forces to aid him, and should deliver him their country and 19 the cities. And he sent others to Gazara to make away with John: and unto the captains of thousands he sent letters to come unto him, that he might give them silver and gold and 20 gifts. And others he sent to take possession of Jerusalem, and the mount 21 of the temple. And one ran before to Gazara, and told John that his father and brethren were perished, and 22 he hath sent to slay thee also. And when he heard, he was sore amazed; and he laid hands on the men that came to destroy him, and slew them; for he perceived that they were seeking to destroy him.

23 And the rest of the acts of John, and of his wars, and of his valiant deeds which he did, and of the building of the walls which he built, and of his 24 doings, behold, they are written in the [2] chronicles of his high priesthood, from the time that he was made high priest after his father.

[1] circa B. C. 136.

[2] Gr. *book of days.*

156

THE SECOND BOOK OF THE

MACCABEES.

1 THE brethren, the Jews that are in Jerusalem and they that are in the country of Judæa, send greeting to the brethren, the Jews that are throughout Egypt, *and wish them good*
2 peace: and may God do good unto you, and remember his covenant with Abraham and Isaac and Jacob, his
3 faithful servants; and give you all a heart to worship him and do his [1]pleasure with a great heart and a
4 willing soul; and open your heart in his law and in his statutes, and make
5 peace, and hearken to your supplications, and be reconciled with you, and
6 not forsake you in an evil time. And
7 now we here are praying for you. In the reign of Demetrius, in the hundred threescore and ninth year, we the Jews have *already* written unto you in the tribulation and in the extremity that hath come upon us in these years, from the time that Jason and his company revolted from the holy
8 land and the kingdom, and set the [2]gate on fire, and shed innocent blood: and we besought the Lord, and were heard; and we offered sacrifice and meal *offering*, and we lighted the
9 lamps, and we set forth the [3]shew-bread. And now *see* that ye keep the days of the feast of tabernacles of
10 the month Chislev. *Written* in the hundred fourscore and eighth year.

THEY that are in Jerusalem and they that are in Judæa and the senate and Judas, unto Aristobulus, king Ptolemy's teacher, who is also of the stock of the anointed priests, and unto the Jews that are in Egypt, send
11 greeting and health. Having been saved by God out of great perils, as men arrayed against a king, we thank
12 him greatly. For himself cast forth into Persia them that arrayed themselves [4]*against us* in the holy city.
13 For when the prince was come *there*, and the army with him that seemed irresistible, they were cut to pieces in the temple of Nanæa by the treach-
14 ery of Nanæa's priests. For Antiochus, on the pretence that he would marry her, came into the place, he and his [5]Friends that were with him, that they might take a great part of the treasures in name of a dowry.
15 And when the priests of Nanæa's temple had set [6]the treasures forth, and he was come there with a small company within the wall of the precincts, they shut to the temple when
16 Antiochus was come in: and opening the secret door of the panelled cieling, they threw stones and [7]struck down the prince, and they hewed [8]*him and his company* in pieces, and smote off their heads, and cast them to those
17 that were without. Blessed *be* our God in all things, who gave *for a prey* them that had committed impiety.
18 Whereas we are now about to keep the purification of the temple in the *month* Chislev, on the five and twentieth day, we thought it necessary to certify you thereof, that [9]ye also may keep a feast of tabernacles, and *a memorial* of the fire *which was given* when Nehemiah offered sacrifices, after that he had builded both the
19 temple and the altar. For indeed when our fathers were about to be led into the land of Persia, the godly priests of that time took of the fire of the altar, and hid it privily in the hollow of a well that was without water, wherein they made *it* sure, so that the place was unknown to all
20 men. Now after many years, when it pleased God, Nehemiah, having received a charge from the king of Persia, sent in quest of the fire the descendants of the priests that hid it. When they declared to us that they
21 had found no fire, but thick water, he commanded them to draw out thereof and bring *to him*: and when [10]the sacrifices had been offered *on the altar*, Nehemiah commanded the priests to sprinkle with the water both the wood
22 and the things laid thereupon. And when it was done, and some time had passed, and the sun shone out, which before was hid with clouds, there was kindled a great blaze, so that all men
23 marvelled. And the priests made a prayer while the sacrifice was consuming, both the priests and all *others*, Jonathan leading and the rest answer-
24 ing, as Nehemiah did. And the prayer was after this manner:

O Lord, Lord God, the Creator of all things, who art terrible and strong
25 and righteous and merciful, who alone art King and gracious, who alone suppliest *every need*, who alone art righteous and almighty and eternal, thou that savest Israel out of all evil, who madest the fathers *thy* chosen, and

[1] Gr. wills.

[2] Or, porch

[3] Gr. loaves.

[4] Or, against the holy city

[5] See ch. viii. 9.

[6] Gr. them.

[7] Gr. struck down as with a thunderbolt.
[8] Or, his company

[9] The Greek text here is corrupt.

[10] Gr. the things of the sacrifices. Similarly in verses 31, 32, and ch. ii. 10.

26 didst sanctify them: accept the sacrifice for all thy people Israel, and guard thine own portion, and consecrate it. 27 Gather together our Dispersion, set at liberty them that are in bondage among the heathen, look upon them that are despised and abhorred, and let the heathen know that thou art our 28 God. Torment them that oppress us and in arrogancy shamefully entreat 29 us. Plant thy people in thy holy place, even as Moses said. 30 And thereupon the priests sang the 31 hymns. And as soon as the sacrifice was consumed, then Nehemiah commanded [1] to pour on great stones the 32 water that was left. And when this was done, a flame was kindled; [2] but when the light from the altar [3] shone over against it, all was consumed. 33 And when the matter became known, and it was told the king of the Persians, that, in the place where the priests that were led away had hid the fire, there appeared the water, wherewith also Nehemiah and they that were with him purified the sacri-34 fice, then the king, inclosing the place, made it sacred, after he had proved 35 the matter. And when the king would shew favour to any, he would take from them many presents and give 36 them some of this water. And Nehemiah and they that were with him called this thing Nephthar, which is by interpretation, Cleansing; but most men call it Nephthai.

2 It is also found in the records, that Jeremiah the prophet commanded them that were carried away to take of the fire, as hath been signified above: 2 and how that the prophet charged them that were carried away, having given them the law, that they should not forget the statutes of the Lord, neither be led astray in their minds, when they saw images of gold and silver, and the adornment thereof. 3 And with other such words exhorted he them, that the law should not de-4 part from their heart. And it was contained in the writing, that the prophet, being warned of God, commanded that the tabernacle and the ark should follow with him, [4] when he went forth into the mountain where Moses went up and beheld the herit-5 age of God. And Jeremiah came and found [5] a chamber in the rock, and there he brought in the tabernacle, and the ark, and the altar of incense; 6 and he made fast the door. And some of those that followed with him came there that they might mark the way, 7 and could not find it. But when Jeremiah perceived it, he blamed them, saying, Yea and the place shall be unknown until God [6] gather the people 8 again together, and mercy come: and then shall the Lord disclose these

things, and the glory of the Lord shall be seen, and the [7] cloud.

As also it was shewed with Moses; as also Solomon besought that the place might be consecrated greatly, 9 and it was also declared that he, having wisdom, offered a sacrifice of dedication, and of the finishing of the temple; so we would have it now. 10 As Moses prayed unto the Lord, and fire came down out of heaven and consumed the sacrifice, even so prayed Solomon also, and the fire came down and consumed the burnt offerings; 11 ([8] and Moses said, Because the sin offering had not been eaten, it was consumed in like manner with the 12 rest;) and Solomon kept the eight days. 13 And the same things were related [9] both in the public archives and in [10] the records that concern Nehemiah; and how he, founding a library, gathered together the books about the kings and prophets, and the books of David, and letters of kings about sa-14 cred gifts. And in like manner Judas also gathered together for us all those writings that had been scattered by reason of the war that befell, and they 15 are still with us. If therefore ye have need thereof, send some to fetch them unto you. 16 Seeing then that we are about to keep the purification, we write unto you; ye will therefore do well if ye 17 keep the days. Now God, who saved all his people, and restored the heritage to all, and the kingdom, and the 18 priesthood, and the hallowing, even as he promised through the law, — in God have we hope, that he will quickly have mercy upon us, and gather us together out of [11] all the earth into the holy place: for he delivered us out of great evils, and purified the place.

19 Now the things concerning Judas Maccabæus and his brethren, and the purification of the [12] great temple, and 20 the dedication of the altar, and further the wars against Antiochus Epipha-21 nes, and Eupator his son, and the manifestations that came from heaven unto those that vied with one another in manful deeds for the religion of the Jews; so that, being but a few, they [13] rescued the whole country, and chas-22 ed the barbarous multitudes, and

---

Left margin notes:

[1] Some authorities read that great stones should inclose the water that was left. Both the Greek text and the meaning of this verse and the next are uncertain.
[2] Or, but it spent itself, whereas the ... shone still.
[3] Or, shone back

[4] Gr. and when. The Greek text here is probably corrupt.
[5] Gr. a cavernous chamber.

[6] Gr. gather together a gathering of the people.

Right margin notes:

[7] Or, cloud, as ... temple. As Moses

[8] See Lev. x. 16 and ix. 24.

[9] Or, also
[10] Or, Nehemiah's records

[11] Gr. the earth under heaven.

[12] Gr. greatest.

[13] Gr. took for a prey.

recovered again the temple renowned all the world over, and freed the city, and restored the laws which were like to be overthrown, seeing the Lord became [1] gracious unto them with all
23 forbearance: *these things, I say,* which have been declared by Jason of Cyrene in five books, we will assay to abridge
24 in one work. For having in view the confused mass of the numbers, and the [2] difficulty which awaiteth them that would enter into the narratives of the history, by reason of the abun-
25 dance of the matter, we were careful that they who choose to read may be attracted, and that they who wish well *to our cause* may find it easy to recall
[3] *what we have written,* and that all
26 readers may have profit. And although to us, who have taken upon us the painful labour of the abridgement, the task is not easy, but *a matter* of
27 sweat and watching (even as it is no light thing unto him that prepareth a banquet, and seeketh the benefit of others); yet for the sake of the gratitude of the many we will gladly en-
28 dure the painful labour, leaving to the historian the exact handling of every particular, and again [4] having no strength to [5] fill in the outlines of our
29 abridgement. For as the master-builder of a new house must care for the whole [6] structure, and again he that undertaketh to [7] decorate and paint it must seek out the things fit for the adorning thereof; even so I
30 think it is also with us. To occupy the ground, and to [8] indulge in long discussions, and to be curious in particulars, becometh the first author of
31 the history : but to strive after brevity of expression, and to avoid a laboured fulness in the treatment, is to be granted to him that would bring a
32 writing into a new form. Here then let us begin the narration, only adding thus much to that which hath been already [9] said ; for it is a foolish thing to make a long prologue to the history, and to abridge the history *itself.*

3 WHEN the holy city was inhabited with all peace, and the laws were kept very well, because of the godliness of Onias the high priest, and his hatred
2 of wickedness, it came to pass that even the kings themselves did honour the place, and glorify the temple with
3 the noblest presents ; insomuch that even Seleucus the king of Asia of his own revenues bare all the costs belonging to the services of the sacrifices.
4 But one Simon of the tribe of Benjamin, having been made guardian of the temple, fell out with the high priest about the [10] ruling of the market in the
5 city. And when he could not over-

come Onias, he gat him to Apollonius *the son* of [11] Thrasæus, who at that time was governor of Cœlesyria and
6 Phœnicia : and he brought him word how that the treasury in Jerusalem was full of untold sums of money, so that the multitude of the funds was innumerable, and that they did not per-tain to the account of the sacrifices, but that it was possible that these should fall under the king's power.
7 And when Apollonius met the king, he informed him of the money whereof he had been told ; and the *king* appointed Heliodorus, who was his chancellor, and sent him with a commandment to accomplish the removal
8 of the aforesaid money. So forthwith Heliodorus took his journey, under a colour of visiting the cities of Cœlesyria and Phœnicia, but in fact to exe-
9 cute the king's purpose. And when he was come to Jerusalem, and had been courteously received by the high priest [12] of the city, he laid before [13] *them* an account of the information which had been given *him,* and declared wherefore he was come ; and
10 he inquired if in truth these things were so. And the high priest explained to him that there were *in the treasury* deposits of widows and orphans,
11 and moreover some *money* belonging to Hyrcanus the *son* of Tobias, a man in very high place, [14] *and that the case was* not as that impious Simon falsely alleged ; and that in all there were four hundred talents of silver and two
12 hundred of gold ; and that it was altogether impossible that wrong should be done unto them that had put trust in the holiness of the place, and in the majesty and inviolable sanctity of the temple. honoured over all the world.
13 But [15] Heliodorus, because of the king's commandments given him, said that in any case this *money* must be confiscated for the king's treasury.
14 So having appointed a day, he entered in to direct the inquiry concerning these matters ; and there was no small distress throughout the whole city.
15 And the priests, prostrating themselves before the altar in their priestly garments, and *looking* toward heaven, called upon him that gave the law concerning deposits, that he should preserve these *treasures* safe for those
16 that had deposited them. And whosoever saw the mien of the high priest was wounded in mind ; for his countenance and the change of his colour
17 betrayed the distress of his soul. For a terror and a shuddering of the body had come over the man, whereby the pain that was in his heart was plainly shewn to them that looked upon him.
18 And they that were in the houses rushed flocking out to make a universal supplication, because the place

[1] Gr. *propitious.*

[2] Or, *weariness*

[3] Or, *the past*

[4] Or, *making no effort*
[5] Or, *enlarge on*
[6] Gr. *foundation.*
[7] Gr. *decorate in encaustic.*
[8] Or, *provide a place for discussions*

[9] Or, *spoken of*

[10] Or, *charge of the buildings* Gr. *office of ædile.*

[11] Or, *Thraseas* The Greek text is probably corrupt. Perhaps the true reading is *Apollonius of Tarsus.*

[12] Some authorities read *and of the city.*
[13] Or, *him*

[14] Or, *and not such a man as that impious Simon slanderously alleged*

[15] Some authorities read *the other.*

19 was like to come into contempt. And the women, girt with sackcloth under their breasts, thronged the streets, and the virgins that were kept in ward ran together, some to the [1]gates, others to the walls, and some looked out 20 through the windows. And all, stretching forth their hands toward heaven, 21 made their solemn supplication. Then it would have pitied a man to see the multitude prostrating themselves all mingled together, and the expectation of the high priest in his sore distress. 22 While therefore they called upon the Almighty Lord to keep the things intrusted to them [2]safe and sure for 23 those that had intrusted them, Heliodorus went on to execute that which 24 had been decreed. But when he was already present there with his guards over against the treasury, the Sovereign of spirits and of all authority caused a great [3]apparition, so that all that had presumed to come in with him, stricken with dismay at the power of God, fainted and were sore afraid. 25 For there was seen by them a horse with a terrible rider upon him, and adorned with beautiful trappings, and he rushed fiercely and smote at Heliodorus with his forefeet, and it seemed that he that sat upon the horse had 26 complete armour of gold. Two other also appeared unto him, young men notable in their strength, and beautiful in their glory, and splendid in their apparel, who stood by him on either side, and scourged him unceasingly, inflicting on him many sore stripes. 27 And when he had fallen suddenly unto the ground, and great darkness had come over him, his guards caught him 28 up and put him into a litter, and carried him, him that had just now entered with a great train and all his guard into the aforesaid treasury, himself now brought to utter helplessness, manifestly made to recog- 29 nise the sovereignty of God. And so, while he, through the working of God, speechless and bereft of all hope and 30 deliverance, lay prostrate, they blessed the Lord, that made marvellous his own place; and the temple, which a little afore was full of terror and alarm, was filled with joy and gladness after the Almighty Lord appeared. 31 But quickly certain of Heliodorus's familiar friends besought Onias to call upon the Most High, and grant life to him who lay quite at the last gasp. 32 And the high priest, secretly fearing lest the king might come to think that some treachery toward Heliodorus had been perpetrated by the Jews, brought a sacrifice for the deliverance 33 of the man. But as the high priest was making the propitiation, the same young men appeared again to Heliodorus, arrayed in the same garments;

and they stood and said, Give Onias the high priest great thanks, for for his sake the Lord hath granted thee 34 life; and do thou, since thou hast been scourged from heaven, publish unto all men the sovereign majesty of God. And when they had spoken these 35 words, they vanished out of sight. So Heliodorus, having offered a sacrifice unto the Lord and vowed [4]great vows unto him that had saved his life, and having graciously received Onias, returned with his host to the king. 36 And he testified to all men the works of the great God which he had beheld with his eyes. 37 And when the king asked Heliodorus, what manner of man was fit to be sent yet once again to Jerusalem, 38 he said, If thou hast any enemy or conspirator against the state, send him thither, and thou shalt receive him back well scourged, if he even escape with his life; because of a truth there is about the place a power 39 of God. For he that hath his dwelling in heaven himself hath his eyes upon that place, and helpeth it; and them that come to hurt it he smiteth and destroyeth. 40 And such was the history of Heliodorus and the keeping of the treasury. 4 But the aforesaid Simon, he who had given information of the money, and had betrayed his country, slandered Onias, saying that it was he who had incited Heliodorus, and made himself 2 the author of these evils. And him that was the benefactor of the city, and the guardian of his fellow-countrymen, and a zealot for the laws, he dared to call a conspirator against 3 the state. But when the growing enmity between them waxed so great, that even murders were perpetrated through one of [5]Simon's trusted fol- 4 lowers, Onias, seeing the [6]danger of the contention, and that [7]Apollonius the son of Menestheus, the governor of Cœlesyria and Phœnicia, was in- 5 creasing Simon's malice, betook himself to the king, not to be an accuser of his fellow-citizens, but looking to the good of all the [8]people, both pub- 6 lic and private; for he saw that without the king's providence it was impossible for the state to obtain peace any more, and that Simon would not cease from his madness. 7 But when Seleucus was deceased, and Antiochus, who was called Epiphanes, succeeded to the kingdom, Jason the brother of Onias supplanted 8 his brother in the high priesthood, having promised unto the king at an audience three hundred and threescore talents of silver, and out of another 9 fund eighty talents; and beside this, he undertook to assign a hundred and fifty more, if it might be allowed him

[1] Or, porches

[2] Gr. safe with all security.

[3] Gr. manifestation.

[4] Gr. greatest

[5] Gr. those that had been approved by Simon.

[6] Or, severity

[7] Compare ver. 21. See also ch. iii. 5. The Greek as commonly read means Apollonius, as being the governor ... Phœnicia, did rage and increase &c.

[8] Gr. multitude.

1 Gr.
through
his.

1 through the king's authority to set him up a *Greek* place of exercise and *form* a body of youths *to be trained therein,* and to register the inhabitants of Jerusalem as *citizens* of Antioch.

10 And when the king had given assent, and he had gotten possession of the office, he forthwith brought over them of his own race to the Greek fashion.

11 And setting aside the royal ordinances of special favour to the Jews, granted by the means of John the father of Eupolemus, who went on the ambassage to the Romans for friendship and alliance, and seeking to overthrow the lawful modes of life, he brought in new

12 customs forbidden by the law : for he eagerly established a *Greek* place of exercise under the citadel itself ; and caused the noblest of the young men

13 to wear the *Greek* cap. And thus there was an extreme of Greek fashions, and an advance of an alien religion, by reason of the exceeding profaneness of Jason, that ungodly man and no high

14 priest ; so that the priests had no more any zeal for the services of the altar: but despising the sanctuary, and neglecting the sacrifices, they hastened to 2 enjoy that which was unlawfully provided in the palæstra, after the

15 summons 3 of the discus ; making of no account the honours of their fathers, and thinking the glories of the

16 Greeks best of all. By reason whereof sore calamity beset them ; and the men whose ways of living they earnestly followed, and unto whom they desired to be made like in all things, these they had to be their enemies and

17 to punish them. For it is not a light thing to do impiously against the laws of God : but 4 these things the time following shall declare.

18 Now when certain games that came every fifth year were kept at Tyre, and

19 the king was present, the vile Jason sent sacred envoys, 5 as being Antiochians of Jerusalem, bearing three hundred drachmas of silver to the sacrifice of Hercules, which even the bearers thereof thought not right to use for *any* sacrifice, because it was not fit, but to 6 expend on another

20 charge. And though in the purpose of the sender this *money was* for the sacrifice of Hercules, yet on account of 7 present circumstances it went to the equipment of the galleys.

21 Now when Apollonius the *son* of Menestheus was sent into Egypt for the 8 enthronement of *Ptolemy* Philometor as king, Antiochus, learning that *Ptolemy* had shewn himself ill affected toward his state, took thought for the security of his realm; wherefore, going *by sea* to Joppa, he trav-

22 elled on to Jerusalem. And being magnificently received by Jason and the city, he was brought in with

2 Or,
take
part in
the un-
lawful
provi-
sion
for the
palæstra
3 Or,
to the
game of
the
discus

4 Or,
this the
due
season of
requital
will
make
plain
5 See
ver. 9.

6 Or,
reserve
for

7 Some
authori-
ties read
the
bearers.
8 The
exact
meaning
of the
Greek
word is
uncer-
tain.

torches and shoutings. This done, he afterward led his army down into Phœnicia.

23 Now after a space of three years Jason sent Menelaus, the aforesaid Simon's brother, to bear the money unto the king, and to 9 make reports concerning some necessary matters.

24 But he being commended to the king, and 10 having glorified 11 himself 12 by the display of his authority, got the high priesthood for himself, outbidding Jason by three hundred talents

25 of silver. And having received the royal mandates he came *to Jerusalem,* bringing nothing worthy the high priesthood, but having the passion of a cruel tyrant, and the rage of a sav-

26 age beast. And whereas Jason, who had supplanted his own brother, was supplanted by another and driven as a fugitive into the country of the Am-

27 monites, Menelaus had possession of the office : but of the money that had been promised to the king nothing 13 was duly paid, and that though

28 Sostratus the governor of the citadel demanded it (for unto him appertained the gathering of the revenues) ; for

29 which cause they were both called by the king to his presence. And Menelaus left his own brother Lysimachus for his 14 deputy in the high priesthood ; and Sostratus *left* Crates, who was over the Cyprians.

30 Now while such was the state of things, it came to pass that they of Tarsus and Mallus made insurrection, because they were to be given as a present to Antiochis, the king's con-

31 cubine. The king therefore came *to Cilicia* in all haste to settle matters, leaving for his 14 deputy Andronicus,

32 a man of high rank. And Menelaus, supposing that he had gotten a favourable opportunity, presented to Andronicus certain vessels of gold belonging to the temple, which he had stolen: other *vessels* also he had already sold

33 into Tyre and the cities round about. And when Onias had sure knowledge *of this,* he sharply reproved him, having withdrawn himself into a sanctuary at Daphne, that lieth by Antioch.

34 Wherefore Menelaus, taking Andronicus apart, prayed him 15 to kill Onias. And coming to Onias, and 16 being persuaded to use treachery, and being received as a friend, *Andronicus* gave him his right hand with oaths of *fidelity,* and, though he was suspected *by him, so* persuaded him to come forth out of the sanctuary ; and forthwith he 17 despatched him without regard of

35 justice. For the which cause not only Jews, but many also of the other nations, had indignation and displeasure at the unjust murder of

36 the man. And when the king was come back again from the places in

9 Or,
convey
to him
reports
10 The
Greek
text of
this
verse
is un-
certain.
11 Or,
him
12 Or,
by flat-
tering
the
dignity
of his au
thority

13 Gr.
was in
due
order.

14 Gr.
suc-
cessor.

15 Or,
to get
Onias
into his
hands
16 The
Greek
text of
this sen-
tence is
probably
corrupt.
17 Or, im-
prisoned
him
Gr. shut
him off.

¹ Or, in the several cities

² Or, rent his

³ Or, growing in

⁴ Gr. established as a.

⁵ Or, charges

⁶ Gr. manifestation.

⁷ Gr. perpetrated.

⁸ The Greek text here is uncertain.

⁹ See 1 Macc. xii. 7.

Cilicia, the Jews that were ¹in the city pleaded before *him against Andronicus* (the Greeks also joining with them in hatred of the wickedness), urging that Onias had been 37 wrongfully slain. Antiochus therefore was heartily sorry, and was moved to pity, and wept, because of the sober and well ordered life of him that was 38 dead; and being inflamed with passion, forthwith he stripped off Andronicus's purple robe, and ²rent off his under garments, and when he had led him round through the whole city unto that very place where he had committed impiety against Onias, there he put the murderer out of the way, the Lord rendering to him the punishment he had deserved.

39 Now when many sacrileges had been committed in the city by Lysimachus with the consent of Menelaus, and when the bruit thereof was spread abroad outside, the people gathered themselves together against Lysima- 40 chus, after many vessels of gold had been already dispersed. And when the multitudes were rising against *him*, and were filled with anger, Lysimachus armed about three thousand men, and with unrighteous violence began *the conflict*, one Hauran, a man far gone in years and no less also in 41 madness, leading *the attack*. But when they perceived the assault of Lysimachus, some caught up stones, others logs of wood, and some took handfuls of the ashes that lay near, and they flung them all pell-mell upon Lysimachus and them that were 42 with him; by reason of which they wounded many of them, and some they struck to the ground, and all *of them* they forced to flee, but the author of the sacrilege himself they killed beside the treasury.

43 But touching these matters there was an accusation laid against Menelaus. 44 And when the king was come to Tyre, the three men that were sent by the senate pleaded the cause before him. 45 But Menelaus, seeing himself now defeated, promised much money to Ptolemy the *son* of Dorymenes, that 46 he might win over the king. Whereupon Ptolemy taking the king aside into a cloister, as it were to take the air, brought him to be of another 47 mind: and him that was the cause of all the evil, Menelaus, he discharged from the accusations; but those hapless men, who, if they had pleaded even before Scythians, would have been discharged uncondemned, them 48 he sentenced to death. Soon then did they that were spokesmen for the city and the families *of Israel* and the holy vessels suffer that unrighteous 49 penalty. For which cause even certain Tyrians, moved with hatred of the

wickedness, provided magnificently 50 for their burial. But Menelaus through the covetous dealings of them that were in power remained still in his office, ³cleaving to wickedness, ⁴as a great conspirator against his fellow-citizens.

5 Now about this time Antiochus made 2 his second inroad into Egypt. And it *so* befell that throughout all the city, for the space of almost forty days, there appeared in the midst of the sky horsemen in swift motion, wearing robes inwrought with gold and *carrying* spears, equipped in troops for battle; and drawing of swords; 3 and *on the other side* squadrons of horse in array; and encounters and ⁵pursuits of both *armies*; and shaking of shields, and multitudes of lances, and casting of darts, and flashing of golden trappings, and gird- 4 ing on of all sorts of armour. Wherefore all men besought that the ⁶vision might have been given for good. 5 But when a false rumour had arisen that Antiochus was deceased, Jason took not less than a thousand men, and suddenly ⁷made an assault upon the city; and they that were upon the wall being routed, and the city being now at length well nigh taken, Mene- 6 laus took refuge in the citadel. But Jason slaughtered his own citizens without mercy, not considering that good success against kinsmen is the greatest ill success, but supposing himself to be setting up trophies over enemies, and not over fellow-country- 7 men. The office *however* he did not get, but, receiving shame as the end of his conspiracy, he passed again a fugitive into the country of the 8 Ammonites. At the last therefore he met with a miserable end: having been ⁸shut up at the court of Aretas the prince of the Arabians, fleeing from city to city, pursued of all men, hated as an apostate from the laws, and held in abomination as the butcher of his country and his fellow-citizens, he was cast forth into Egypt; 9 and he that had driven many from their own country into strange lands perished *himself* in a strange land, having crossed the sea to the Lacedæmonians, as thinking to find shelter *there* because they were ⁹near of kin; 10 and he that had cast out a multitude unburied had none to mourn for him, nor had he any funeral at all, or place in the sepulchre of his fathers. 11 Now when tidings came to the king concerning that which was done, he thought that Judæa was in revolt; whereupon setting out from Egypt in a furious mind, he took the city by 12 force of arms, and commanded his soldiers to cut down without mercy such as came in their way, and to slay

13 such as went up upon the houses ; and there was killing of young and old, making away of boys, women, and children, slaying of virgins and in-
14 fants. And in all the three days *of the slaughter* there were destroyed fourscore thousand, *whereof* forty thousand *were slain* in close combat, and no fewer were sold than slain.
15 But not content with this he presumed to enter into the most holy temple of all the earth, having Menelaus for his guide (him that had proved himself a traitor both to the laws and to his
16 country), even taking the sacred vessels with his polluted hands, and dragging down with his profane hands the offerings that had been dedicated by other kings to the augmentation and glory and honour of the place.
17 And Antiochus was lifted up in mind, not seeing that because of the sins of them that dwelt in the city the Sovereign Lord had been provoked to anger a little while, and therefore his eye was *then* turned away from the
18 place. But had it not so been that they were already holden by many sins, this man, even as Heliodorus who was sent by Seleucus the king to view the treasury, would, so soon as he pressed forward, have been scourged and turned back from his
19 daring deed. Howbeit the Lord did not choose the nation for the place's sake, but the place for the nation's
20 sake. Wherefore also the place itself, having partaken in the calamities that befell the nation, did afterward share in *its* benefits ; and the *place* which was forsaken in the wrath of the Almighty was, at the reconciliation of the great Sovereign, restored again with all glory.
21 As for Antiochus, when he had carried away out of the temple a thousand and eight hundred talents, he departed in all haste unto Antioch, weening in his arrogancy to make the land navigable and the sea passable by foot,
22 because his heart was lifted up. And moreover he left governors to afflict the race : at Jerusalem, Philip, by race a Phrygian, and in character more barbarous than him that set
23 him there ; and at Gerizim, Andronicus ; and besides these, Menelaus, who worse than all the rest exalted himself against his fellow-citizens. And having a malicious mind [1] toward the Jews [2] *whom he had made* his
24 citizens, he sent that [3] lord of pollutions Apollonius with an army of two and twenty thousand, commanding him to slay all those that were of full age, and to sell the women and the
25 younger men. And he coming to Jerusalem, and playing the man of peace, waited till the holy day of the sabbath, and finding the Jews at rest

from work, he commanded his men to
26 parade in arms. And he put to the sword all them that came forth to the spectacle ; and running into the city with the armed men he slew great
27 multitudes. But Judas, who is also *called* Maccabæus, with nine others or thereabout, withdrew himself, and with his company kept himself alive in the mountains after the manner of wild beasts ; and they continued feeding on [4] such poor herbs as grew there, that they might not be partakers of the *threatened* pollution.

6 And not long after this the king sent forth [5] an old man of Athens to compel the Jews to depart from the laws of
2 their fathers, and not to live after the laws of God ; and also to pollute the sanctuary in Jerusalem, and to call it by the name of [6] Jupiter Olympius, and *to call* the *sanctuary* in Gerizim by the name of [6] Jupiter the Protector of
3 strangers, even as they [7] were that dwelt in the place. But sore and
4 utterly grievous was the visitation of this evil. For the temple was filled with riot and revellings by the heathen, who [8] dallied with harlots, and had to do with women within the sacred precincts, and moreover brought
5 inside things that were not befitting ; and [9] the place of sacrifice was filled with those abominable things which
6 had been prohibited by the laws. And a man could neither keep the sabbath, nor observe the feasts of the fathers, nor so much as confess himself to be
7 a Jew. And on the day of the king's birth every month they were led along with bitter constraint to eat of the sacrifices ; and when the [10] feast of Bacchus came, they were compelled to go in procession in honour of [11] Bac-
8 chus, wearing wreaths of ivy. And there went out a decree to the neighbouring Greek cities, by the suggestion of Ptolemy, that they should observe the same conduct against the Jews, and should make them eat of
9 the sacrifices ; and that they should slay such as did not choose to go over to the Greek rites. So the present
10 misery was for all to see : for two women were brought up for having circumcised their children ; and these, when they had led them publicly round about the city, with the babes hung from their breasts, they cast
11 down headlong from the wall. And others, that had run together into the caves near by to keep the seventh day secretly, being betrayed to Philip were all burnt together, because they scrupled to defend themselves, from regard to the honour of that most solemn day.
12 I beseech therefore those that read this book, that they be not discouraged because of the calamities, but

[1] Some authorities read *toward the Jews, he sent.* The Greek text of this sentence is uncertain.
[2] Compare ch. iv. 9, 19 ; ix. 19.
[3] Gr. *mysarch,* which may also mean *ruler of the Mysians.*

[4] Gr. *the grassy food.*
[5] Or, *Geron an Athenian*
[6] Gr. *Zeus.*
[7] Or, *did*
[8] Or, *idled with their fellows*
[9] Or, *the altar*
[10] Gr. *feast of Dionysia.*
[11] Gr. *Dionysus.*

account that these punishments were
not for the destruction, but for the
13 chastening of our race. For indeed
that those who act impiously be not
let alone any long time, but straightway meet with retribution, is a sign
14 of great beneficence. For in the case
of the other nations the Sovereign
Lord doth with longsuffering forbear.
until that he punish them when they
have attained unto the full measure
of *their* sins; but not so judged he as
15 touching us, that he may not take
vengeance on us afterward, [1] when we
be come unto the [2] height of our sins.
16 Wherefore he never withdraweth his
mercy from us; but though he chas-
teneth with calamity, yet doth he not
17 forsake his own people. Howbeit let
this that we have spoken suffice to
put *you* in remembrance; but after
these few words we must come to the
narrative.
18 Eleazar, one of the principal scribes,
a man already well stricken in years,
and of a noble countenance, was compelled to open his mouth to eat swine's
19 flesh. But he, welcoming death with
renown rather than life with pollution,
advanced of his own accord to the
instrument of torture, but first spat
20 forth *the flesh, coming forward* as men
ought to come that are resolute to
repel such things as not *even* for the
natural love of life is it lawful to taste.
21 But they that had the charge of that
forbidden sacrificial feast took the
man aside, for the acquaintance which
of old times they had with him, and
privately besought him to bring flesh
of his own providing, such as was
befitting for him to use, and to make
as if he did eat of the flesh from the
sacrifice, as had been commanded by
22 the king; that by so doing he might
be delivered from death, and for his
ancient friendship with them might be
23 treated kindly. But he, having formed
a high resolve, and one that became
his years, and the dignity of old age,
and the gray hairs [3] which he had
reached with honour, and his excellent
[4] education from a child, [5] or rather
that became the holy [6] laws of God's
ordaining, declared his mind accordingly, bidding them quickly send him
24 unto Hades. For it becometh not our
years to dissemble, *said he*, that
through this many of the young
should suppose that Eleazar, the man
of fourscore years and ten, had gone
25 over unto an alien religion; and *so*
they, by reason of my dissimulation,
and for the sake of this brief and
momentary life, should be led astray
because of me, [7] and *thus* I get to myself a pollution and a stain of mine
26 old age. For even if for the present
time I shall remove from me the punishment of men, yet shall I not escape
the hands of the Almighty, either liv-
27 ing or dead. Wherefore, by manfully
parting with my life now, I will shew
28 myself worthy of mine old age, and
[8] leave behind a noble ensample to
the young to die willingly and nobly a
glorious death for the reverend and
holy laws. And when he had said
these words, he went straightway to
29 the instrument of torture. [9] And
when they changed the good will they
bare him a little before into ill will,
because [10] these words of his were, as
30 they thought, sheer madness, and
when he was at the point to die with
the [11] stripes, he groaned aloud and
said, To the Lord, that hath the holy
knowledge, it is manifest that, whereas I might have been delivered from
death, I endure sore pains in my body
by being scourged; but in soul I
gladly suffer these things for my fear
31 of him. So this man also died after
this manner, leaving his death for an
ensample of nobleness and a memorial of virtue, not only to the young
but also to the great body of his
nation.
7 And it came to pass that seven brethren also with their mother were at
the king's command taken and shamefully handled with scourges and cords,
to compel them to taste of the abomin-
2 able swine's flesh. But one of them
made himself the spokesman and said,
What wouldest thou ask and learn
of us? for we are ready to die rather
than transgress the laws of our fa-
3 thers. And the king fell into a rage,
and commanded to heat pans and
4 caldrons: and when these forthwith
were heated, he commanded to cut
out the tongue of him that had been
their spokesman, and to scalp him,
and to cut off his extremities, the rest
of his brethren and his mother look-
5 ing on. And when he was utterly
[12] maimed, *the king* commanded to
bring him to the fire, being yet alive,
and to fry him in the pan. And as
the vapour of the pan spread far, they
and their mother also exhorted one
another to die nobly, saying thus:
6 The Lord God beholdeth, and in
truth is [13] intreated for us, as Moses
declared in [14] his song, which witnesseth against *the people* to their faces,
saying, And he shall be [13] intreated
for his servants.
7 And when the first had died after
this manner, they brought the second
to the mocking; and they pulled off
the skin of his head with the hair and
asked him, Wilt thou eat, before thy
8 body be punished in every limb? But
he answered in the language of his
fathers and said to them, No. Wherefore he also underwent the next torture in succession, as the first had
9 done. And when he was at the last

[1] Or, *when our sins be come to their height*
[2] Gr. *end.*
[3] The Greek text appears to be corrupt.
[4] Some authorities read *manner of life.*
[5] Or, *but yet more*
[6] Gr. *legislation.*
[7] Or, *while I shall get*
[8] Gr. *one that hath left behind.*
[9] The Greek text of this verse is uncertain.
[10] Gr. *the aforesaid words were.*
[11] Or, *blows*
[12] Gr. *useless.*
[13] Or, *comforted in*
[14] See Deut. xxxi. 21 and xxxii. 36

gasp, he said, Thou, miscreant, dost release us out of this present life, but the King of the world shall raise up us, who have died for his laws, unto an eternal renewal of life. 10 And after him was the third made a mocking-stock. And when he was required, he quickly put out his tongue, and stretched forth his hands cou-11 rageously, and nobly said, From heaven I possess these ; and for his laws' sake I contemn these ; and from him I hope to receive these back again : 12 insomuch that the king himself and they that were with him were astonished at the young man's soul, for that he nothing regarded the pains. 13 And when he too was dead, they shamefully handled and tortured the 14 fourth in like manner. And being come near unto death he said thus : It is good to die at the hands of men and look for the hopes which are *given* by God, that we shall be raised up again by him ; for as for thee, thou shalt have no resurrection unto life. 15 And next after him they brought the fifth, and shamefully handled him. 16 But he looked toward [1] the king and said, Because thou hast authority among men, though thou art *thyself* corruptible, thou doest what thou wilt ; yet think not that our race hath 17 been forsaken of God ; but hold thou on thy way, and behold his sovereign majesty, how it will torture thee and thy seed. 18 And after him they brought the sixth. And when he was at the point to die he said, Be not vainly deceived, for we suffer these things for our own doings, as sinning against our own God : marvellous things are come to 19 pass ; but think not thou that thou shalt be unpunished, having assayed to fight against God. 20 But above all was the mother marvellous and worthy of honourable memory ; for when she looked on seven sons perishing within the space of one day, she bare *the sight* with a good courage for the hopes *that she* 21 *had set* on the Lord. And she exhorted each one of them in the language of their fathers, filled with a noble temper and stirring up her womanish thought with manly passion, saying 22 unto them, I know not how ye came into my womb, neither was it I that bestowed on you your [2] spirit and your life, and it was not I that brought into order the first elements of each one 23 of you. Therefore the Creator of the world, who fashioned the [3] generation of man and devised the [3] generation of all things, in mercy giveth back to you again both your [2] spirit and your life, as ye now contemn your own selves 24 for his laws' sake. But Antiochus, thinking himself to be despised, and

suspecting the reproachful voice, whilst the youngest was yet alive did not only make his appeal *to him* by words, but also at the same time promised with oaths that he would enrich him and [4] raise him to high estate, if he would turn from the *customs* of his fathers, and that he would take him for his [5] Friend and intrust him with 25 affairs. But when the young man would in no wise give heed, the king called unto him his mother, and exhorted her that she would counsel the 26 lad to save himself. And when he had exhorted her with many words, she 27 undertook to persuade her son. But bending toward him, laughing the cruel tyrant to scorn, she spake thus in the language of her fathers : My son, have pity upon me that carried thee nine months in my womb, and gave thee suck three years, and nourished and brought thee up unto this 28 age, and sustained thee. I beseech thee, my child, to lift thine eyes unto the heaven and the earth, and to see all things that are therein, and thus to recognise that God made them not of things that were, and *that* the race of men in this wise cometh into being. 29 Fear not this butcher, but, proving thyself worthy of thy brethren, accept thy death, that in the mercy *of God* I may receive thee again with thy brethren. 30 But before she had yet ended speaking, the young man said, Whom wait ye for ? I obey not the commandment of the king, but I hearken to the commandment of the law that was given 31 to our fathers through Moses. But thou, that hast devised all manner of evil against the Hebrews, shalt in no 32 wise escape the hands of God. For we are suffering because of our own 33 sins ; and if for rebuke and chastening our living Lord hath been angered a little while, yet shall he again be re-34 conciled with his own servants. But thou, O unholy man and of all most vile, be not vainly lifted up in thy wild pride with uncertain hopes, raising thy hand against the heavenly children ; 35 for not yet hast thou escaped the judgement of the Almighty God that seeth 36 *all things.* For these our brethren, having endured a [6] short pain that bringeth everlasting life, have now [7] died under God's covenant ; but thou, through the judgement of God, shalt receive in just measure the penalties 37 of thine arrogancy. But I, as my brethren, give up both body and soul for the laws of our fathers, calling upon God that he may speedily become [8] gracious to the nation ; and that thou amidst trials and plagues mayest con-38 fess that he alone is God ; and that in me and my brethren [9] thou mayest stay the wrath of the Almighty, which

Margin notes:

[1] Gr. *him.*

[2] Or, *breath*

[3] Or, *first origin*

[4] Gr. *make him one that is counted happy.*

[5] See ch viii. 9.

[6] Gr. *short pain of ever-flowing life.*

[7] Gr. *fallen.* By the omission of one Greek letter the words would signify *having endured a short pain, have now drunk of ever-flowing life under God's covenant.*

[8] Gr. *propitious.*

[9] Some authorities read *may be stayed.*

hath been justly brought upon our 39 whole race. But the king, falling into a rage, handled him worse than all the rest, being exasperated at his mock-40 ing. So he also died pure *from pollution*, putting his whole trust in the Lord.

41 And last of all after her sons the mother died.

42 Let it then suffice to have said thus much concerning the *enforcement of* sacrificial feasts and the *king's* exceeding barbarities.

8 But Judas, who is also *called* Maccabæus, and they that were with him, making their way privily into the villages, called unto them their kinsfolk; and taking unto them such as had continued in the Jews' religion, gathered 2 together as many as six thousand. And they called upon the Lord, *beseeching him* to look upon the people that was oppressed by all; and to have compassion on the sanctuary also that had been profaned by the ungod-3 ly men; and to have pity on the city also that was suffering ruin and ready to be made even with the ground; and to hearken to the blood 4 that cried unto him; and to remember also the lawless [1] slaughter of the innocent infants, and [2] the blasphemies that had been committed against his name; and to shew his hatred of 5 wickedness. And when Maccabæus had trained his men for service, the heathen at once found him irresistible, for that the wrath of the Lord 6 was turned into pity. [3] And coming unawares he set fire to cities and villages. And in winning back the most important positions, putting to flight 7 no small number of the enemies, he specially took advantage of the nights for such assaults. And his courage was loudly talked of everywhere.

8 But when Philip saw the man gaining ground by little and little, and increasing more and more in his prosperity, he wrote unto Ptolemy, the governor of Cœlesyria and Phœnicia, that he should support the king's 9 cause. And *Ptolemy* quickly appointed Nicanor the *son of* Patroclus, one of the *king's* [4] Chief Friends, and sent him, in command of no fewer than twenty thousand of all nations, to destroy the whole race of Judæa; and with him he joined Gorgias also, a captain and one that had experience 10 in matters of war. And Nicanor [5] undertook by *the sale of* the captive Jews to make up for the king the tribute of two thousand talents which he 11 was to pay to the Romans. And immediately he sent unto the cities upon the sea coast, inviting them to buy Jewish [6] slaves, promising to allow fourscore and ten [6] slaves for a talent, not expecting the judgement

that was to follow upon him from the Almighty.

12 But tidings came to Judas concerning the inroad of Nicanor; and when he communicated to them that were with him the presence of the army, 13 they that were cowardly and distrustful of the judgement of God [7] ran 14 away and left the country. And others sold all that was left over to them, and withal besought the Lord to deliver them that had been sold *as slaves* by the impious Nicanor or ever 15 he met them; and *this*, if not for their own sakes, yet for the covenants made with their fathers, and because he had called them by his reverend and 16 glorious name. And Maccabæus gathered his men together, six thousand in number, and exhorted them not to be stricken with dismay at the enemy, nor to fear the great multitude of the heathen who came wrongfully against 17 them; but to contend nobly, setting before their eyes the outrage that had been lawlessly perpetrated upon the holy place, and the shameful handling of the city that had been turned to mockery, and further the overthrow of the mode of life received 18 from their ancestors. For they, said he, trust to arms, and withal to deeds of daring; but we trust on the Almighty God, since he is able at a beck to cast down them that are coming against us, and even the whole 19 world. And moreover he recounted unto them the help given from time to time in the days of their ancestors, both the *help given* in the days of Sennacherib, how that a hundred four-20 score and five thousand perished, and the *help given* in the land of Babylon, even the battle that was fought against the [8] Gauls, how that they came to the engagement eight thousand in all, with four thousand Macedonians, *and how that*, the Macedonians being hard pressed, the [9] six thousand destroyed the hundred and twenty thousand, because of the succour which they had from heaven, 21 and took great booty. And when he had with these words made them of good courage, and ready to die for the laws and their country, he divided 22 his army into four parts; [10] appointing his brethren to be with himself leaders of the several bands, *to wit*, Simon and Joseph and Jonathan, giving each the command of fifteen hundred 23 men, and moreover Eleazar also: *then*, having read aloud the sacred book, and having given as watchword, THE HELP OF GOD, leading the first band himself, he joined battle 24 with Nicanor. And, since the Almighty fought on their side, they slew of the enemy above nine thousand, and wounded and [11] disabled the more

[1] Gr. *destruction.*
[2] Gr. *concerning the blasphemies.*

[3] The Greek text of verses 6 and 7 is uncertain.

[4] See 1 Macc. x. 65. Compare ch. i. 14; vii. 24; x. 13; xiv. 11; 1 Macc. ii. 18.
[5] Or, *resolved*

[6] Gr. *bodies.*

[7] The Greek text here is uncertain.

[8] Gr. *Galatians.*

[9] Some authorities read *eight.*

[10] Gr. *appointing his brethren also leaders.*

[11] Gr. *disabled in their limbs.*

part of Nicanor's army, and compelled
25 all to flee; and they took the money
of those that had come there to buy
them. And after they had pursued
them for some ¹ distance, they returned, being constrained by the time
26 of the day; for it was the day before
the sabbath, and for this cause they
made no effort to chase them far.
27 ²And when they had gathered ³the
arms of the enemy together, and had
stripped off their spoils, they occupied
themselves about the sabbath, blessing and thanking the Lord exceedingly, who had saved them unto this
day, for that he had caused a beginning of mercy to distil upon them.
28 And after the sabbath, when they
had given of the spoils to the ⁴maimed,
and to the widows and orphans, the
residue they distributed among them-
29 selves and their children. And when
they had accomplished these things,
and had made a common supplication, they besought the merciful Lord
to be wholly reconciled with his servants.
30 And having had an encounter with
the forces of Timotheus and Bacchides, they killed above twenty
thousand of them, and made themselves masters of strongholds exceeding high, and divided very much plunder, giving the ⁴maimed and orphans
and widows, and moreover the aged
also, an equal share with themselves.
31 ²And when they had gathered the
arms ⁵of the enemy together, they
stored them all up carefully in the
most important positions, and the
residue of the spoils they carried to
32 Jerusalem. And they killed the
⁶phylarch of Timotheus's forces, a
most unholy man, and one who had
33 done the Jews much hurt. ⁷And as
they kept the feast of victory in the
⁸city of their fathers, they burned
those that had set the sacred ⁹gates
on fire, *and among them* Callisthenes,
who had fled into ¹⁰an outhouse; and
so they received the meet reward of
their impiety.
34 And the thrice-accursed Nicanor,
who had brought the thousand mer-
35 chants to buy the Jews *for slaves*, being through the help of the Lord
humbled by them who in his eyes
were held to be of least account, put
off his glorious apparel, and *passing*
through the midland, ¹¹shunning all
company like a fugitive slave, arrived
at Antioch, ¹²having, *as he thought*,
had the greatest possible good for-
tune, though his host was destroyed.
36 And he that had taken upon him to
make tribute sure for the Romans by
the captivity of the men of Jerusalem
published abroad that the Jews had
One who fought for them, and that
¹³because this was so the Jews were

invulnerable, because they followed
the laws ordained by him.
9 Now about that time it befell that
Antiochus had returned ¹⁴in disorder
2 from the region of Persia. For he
had entered into the city called Per-
sepolis, and he assayed to rob ¹⁵a
temple and to hold down the city.
Whereupon there was an onset of the
multitudes, and ¹⁶*Antiochus and his
men* turned to make defence with
arms; and it came to pass that Antiochus was put to flight by the people
of the country and broke up his camp
3 with disgrace. And while he was at
Ecbatana, news was brought him
what had happened unto Nicanor and
4 the forces of Timotheus. And being
lifted up ¹⁷by his passion he thought
to make the Jews suffer even for the
evil-doing of those that had put him
to rout. Wherefore, the judgement
from heaven even now accompanying
him, he gave order to his charioteer
to drive without ceasing and despatch
the journey; for thus he arrogantly
spake: I will make Jerusalem a com-
5 mon graveyard of Jews, when I come
there. But the All-seeing Lord, the
God of Israel, smote him with a ¹⁸fatal
and invisible stroke; and as soon as
he had ceased speaking this word, an
incurable pain of the bowels seized
6 him, and bitter torments of the inner
parts; and that most justly, for he
had tormented other men's bowels
with many and strange sufferings.
7 But he in no wise ceased from his
rude insolence; nay, still more was
he filled with arrogancy, breathing
fire in his passion against the Jews,
and commanding to haste the journey. But it came to pass moreover
that he fell from his chariot as it
rushed along, and having a grievous
8 fall was racked in all the members of
his body. And he that but now supposed himself to have the waves of
the sea at his bidding, so vainglorious
was he beyond the condition of a man,
and that thought to weigh the heights
of the mountains in a balance, was
now brought to the ground and carried in a litter, ¹⁹shewing unto all that
9 the power was manifestly God's; so
that out of the body of the impious
man worms swarmed, and while he
was still living in anguish and pains,
his flesh fell off, and by reason of the
stench all the army turned with loath-
10 ing from his corruption. And the man
that a little afore supposed himself
to touch the stars of heaven, no one
could endure to carry for his intoler-
11 able stench. Hereupon therefore he
began in great part to cease from his
arrogancy, being broken *in spirit*,
and to come to knowledge under the
scourge of God, his pains increasing
12 every moment. And when he himself

Left margin notes:

¹ Or, *while*

² The exact meaning of this clause is uncertain.
³ Gr. *their arms . . . the spoils of the enemy.*
⁴ Or, *wounded* Gr. *shamefully handled.*

⁵ Gr. *of them.*
⁶ That is, probably, the captain of an irregular auxiliary force. Some write *Phylarches,* as a proper name.
⁷ The Greek text here is perhaps corrupt.
⁸ Or, *country*
⁹ Or, *porches*
¹⁰ Or, *a solitary hut*
¹¹ Gr. *having made himself solitary.*
¹² Or, *having won the greatest possible favour by reason of the destruction of his host*
¹³ Or, *because of this their way of life* Gr. *because of this manner.*

Right margin notes:

¹⁴ Or, *with dishonour*
¹⁵ Or, *temples*
¹⁶ Or, *the people of the country turned*

¹⁷ Or, *in his spirit*

¹⁸ Gr. *remediless.*

¹⁹ Or, *shewing manifestly unto all the power of God*

could not abide his own smell, he said these words : It is right to be subject unto God, and that one who is mortal should not [1] be minded arrogantly.

13 And the vile man vowed unto the Sovereign Lord, who now no more would have pity upon him, saying on this 14 wise: that the holy city, to the which he was going in haste, to lay it even with the ground and to [2] make it a common 15 graveyard, he would declare free; and as touching the Jews, whom he had decided not even to count worthy of burial, but to cast them out to the beasts with their infants, for the birds to devour, he would make them all 16 equal to citizens of Athens; and the holy sanctuary, which before he had spoiled, he would adorn with goodliest offerings, and would restore all the sacred vessels many times multiplied, and out of his own revenues would defray the charges that were required 17 for the sacrifices; and, beside all this, that he would become a Jew, and would visit every inhabited place, pub-18 lishing abroad the might of God. But when his sufferings did in no wise cease, for the judgement of God had come upon him in righteousness, having given up all hope of himself, he wrote unto the Jews the letter written below, having the nature of a supplication, to this effect:

19 To the worthy Jews, his fellow-citizens, Antiochus, king and general, wisheth much joy and health and pro-20 sperity. [3] May ye and your children fare well; and your affairs shall be to your mind. Having my hope in 21 heaven, I remembered with affection your honour and good will *toward me*. Returning out of the region of Persia, and being taken with a noisome sickness, I deemed it necessary to take thought for the common safety of all, 22 not despairing of myself, but having great hope to escape from the sick-23 ness. But considering that my father also, at what time he led an army into the upper country, appointed his suc-24 cessor, to the end that, if anything fell out contrary to expectation, or if any unwelcome tidings were brought, they *that remained* in the country, knowing to whom the state had been left, 25 might not be troubled; and, beside all this, observing how that the princes that are borderers and neighbours unto my kingdom watch opportunities, and look for the future event, I have appointed my son Antiochus *to be* king, whom I often committed and commended to most of you, when I was hastening unto the upper provinces; and I have written to him what 26 is written below. I exhort you therefore and beseech you, having in your remembrance the benefits done to you in common and severally, to preserve

each of you your present good will 27 toward me and my son. For I am persuaded that he in gentleness and kindness will follow my purpose and treat you with indulgence.

28 So the murderer and blasphemer, having endured the sorest sufferings, even as he had dealt with other men, ended his life among the mountains by a most piteous fate in a strange 29 land. And Philip his foster-brother conveyed the body *home*; and then, fearing the son of Antiochus, he betook himself to Ptolemy Philometor in Egypt.

10 And Maccabæus and they that were with him, the Lord leading them on, recovered the temple and the city; 2 and they pulled down the altars that had been built in the marketplace by the aliens, and also *the walls of* sacred 3 inclosures. And having cleansed the sanctuary they made another altar of sacrifice; and [4] striking stones and taking fire out of them, they offered sacrifices, after *they had ceased for* two years, and *burned* incense, and *lighted* lamps, and set forth the shew-4 bread. And when they had done these things, they fell prostrate and besought the Lord that they might fall no more into such evils; but that, if ever they should sin, they might be chastened by him with forbearance, and not be delivered unto blasphem-5 ing and barbarous heathen. Now on the same day that the sanctuary was profaned by aliens, upon that very day did it come to pass that the cleansing of the sanctuary was made, even on the five and twentieth day of the 6 same month, which is Chislev. And they kept eight days with gladness in the manner *of the feast* of tabernacles, remembering how that [5] not long afore, during the feast of tabernacles, they were wandering in the mountains and in the caves after the manner 7 of wild beasts. Wherefore bearing wands wreathed with leaves, and fair boughs, and palms also, they offered up hymns of thanksgiving to him that had prosperously brought to pass the 8 cleansing of his own place. They ordained also with a common statute and decree, for all the nation of the Jews, that they should keep these days every year.

9 And [6] such was the end of Antiochus 10 who was called Epiphanes. But now will we declare what came to pass under Antiochus *named* [7] Eupator, who proved himself a *true* son of that ungodly man, and will gather up briefly the [8] successive evils of the 11 wars. For this man, when he succeeded to the kingdom, appointed one Lysias *to be* chancellor, and supreme governor of Cœlesyria and Phœnicia. 12 For Ptolemy that was called Macron,

setting an example of observing justice toward the Jews because of the wrong that had been done unto them, endeavoured to ¹ conduct his dealings 13 with them on peaceful terms. Whereupon being accused by the *king's* ² Friends before Eupator, and hearing himself called traitor at every turn, because he had abandoned Cyprus which Philometor had intrusted to him, and had withdrawn himself unto Antiochus *called* Epiphanes, and ³ failing to uphold the honour of his office, he took poison and made away with himself.

14 But Gorgias, when he was made governor of the district, maintained a force of mercenaries, and at every 15 turn kept up war with the Jews. And together with him the Idumæans also, being masters of important strongholds, harassed the Jews; and receiving unto them those that had taken refuge *there* from Jerusalem, they as-16 sayed to keep up war. But Maccabæus and his men, having made solemn supplication and besought God to fight on their side, rushed upon the strong-17 holds of the Idumæans; and assaulting them vigorously they made themselves masters of the positions, and kept off all that fought upon the wall, and slew those that fell in their way, and killed no fewer than twenty thou-18 sand. And because no less than nine thousand were fled into two towers exceeding strong and having all things 19 *needed* for a siege, Maccabæus, having left Simon and Joseph, and Zacchæus besides and them that were with him, a force sufficient to besiege them, departed himself unto places where he 20 was most needed. But Simon and they that were with him, yielding to covetousness, were bribed by certain of those that were in the towers, and receiving seventy thousand drachmas 21 let some of them slip away. But when word was brought to Maccabæus of what was done, he gathered the leaders of the people together, and accused *those men* of having sold their brethren for money, by setting their enemies free *to fight* against 22 them. So he slew these men for having turned traitors, and forthwith took 23 possession of the two towers. And prospering with his arms in all things he took, and destroyed in the two strongholds more than twenty thousand.

24 Now Timotheus, who had been before defeated by the Jews, having gathered together foreign forces in great multitudes, and having collected the ⁴ horsemen which belonged to Asia, not a few, came as though he would take Judæa 25 by force of arms. But as he drew near, Maccabæus and his men sprinkled earth upon their heads and girded

their loins with sackcloth, in suppli-26 cation to God, and falling down upon the step in front of the altar, besought him to become ⁵ gracious to them, and ⁶ be an enemy to their enemies and an adversary to their adver-27 saries, as the law declareth. And rising from their prayer they took up their arms, and advanced some distance from the city; and when they had come near to their enemies they 28 ⁷ halted. And when the dawn was now spreading, the two *armies* joined battle; the one part having this, beside *their* virtue, for a pledge of success and victory, that they had fled unto the Lord for refuge, the others making their passion their leader in 29 the strife. But when the battle waxed strong, there appeared out of heaven unto their adversaries five men on horses with bridles of gold, *in* splendid *array*; ⁸ and two of them, leading on 30 the Jews, and taking Maccabæus in the midst of them, and covering him with their own armour, guarded him from wounds, while on the adversaries they shot forth arrows and thunderbolts; by reason whereof they were blinded and thrown into confusion, and were cut to pieces, filled with be-31 wilderment. And there were slain twenty thousand and five hundred, beside six hundred horsemen.

32 But Timotheus himself fled into a stronghold called Gazara, a fortress of exceeding strength. ⁹ Chæreas being 33 in command there. But Maccabæus and his men were glad and laid siege to the fortress four and twenty days. 34 And they that were within, trusting to the strength of the place, blasphemed exceedingly, and hurled forth impious 35 words. But at dawn of the five and twentieth day certain young men of the company of Maccabæus, inflamed with passion because of the blasphemies, assaulted the wall with masculine force and with ¹⁰ furious passion, and cut down whosoever came in their 36 way. And others climbing up in like manner, while *the besieged* were distracted with them *that had made their way* within, set fire to the towers, and kindling fires burned the blasphemers alive; while others broke open the gates, and, having given entrance to the rest of the band, occupied 37 the city. And they slew Timotheus, who was hidden in a cistern, and his brother Chæreas, and Apollophanes. 38 And when they had accomplished these things, they blessed the Lord with hymns and thanksgivings, him who doeth great benefits unto Israel, and giveth them the victory.

11 Now after a very little time Lysias, the king's guardian and kinsman and chancellor, being sore displeased for 2 the things that had come to pass, col-

¹ Or, *settle his relations with*

² See ch. viii. 9.

³ The Greek text here is corrupt.

⁴ Or, *horses*

⁵ Gr. *propitious.*

⁶ See Ex. xxiii. 22

⁷ Gr. *were by themselves.*

⁸ Some authorities read *and leading on the Jews; who also taking.*

⁹ See ver. 37.

¹⁰ Gr. *passion as of wild beasts.*

1 Or, on all the sacred places of the heathen

2 The Greek text here is uncertain.

3 Gr. a panoply.

4 Gr. wound.

5 The Greek text here is corrupt.

6 Gr. multitude.
7 Or, document

lected about fourscore thousand *footmen* and all his horsemen and came against the Jews, thinking to make the city a place for Greeks to dwell 3 in, and to levy tribute on the temple, as [1] on the other sacred places of the nations, and to put up the high priest-4 hood to sale every year; holding in no account the might of God, but puffed up with his ten thousands of footmen, and his thousands of horsemen, and 5 his fourscore elephants. And coming into Judæa and drawing near to Beth-suron, which was a strong place and distant from Jerusalem about [2] five 6 leagues, he pressed it hard. But when Maccabæus and his men learned that he was besieging the strongholds, they and all the people with lamentations and tears made supplication unto the Lord to send a good angel to save 7 Israel. And Maccabæus himself took up arms first, and exhorted the others to jeopard themselves together with him and succour their brethren; and they sallied forth with him right will-8 ingly. And as they were there, close to Jerusalem, there appeared at their head one on horseback in white apparel, brandishing [3] weapons of gold. 9 And they all together praised the merciful God, and were yet more strengthened in heart: being ready to [4] assail not men only but the wildest 10 beasts, and walls of iron, they advanced in array, having him that is in heaven to fight on their side, for the 11 Lord had mercy on them. And hurling *themselves* like lions upon the enemy, they slew of them eleven thousand *footmen* and sixteen hundred horse-12 men, and forced all *the rest* to flee. But the more part of them escaped wounded *and* naked; and Lysias also him-13 self escaped by shameful flight. But as he was a man not void of understanding, weighing with himself the defeat which had befallen him, and considering that the Hebrews could not be overcome, because the Almighty God fought on their side, he sent again 14 *unto them*, and persuaded them to come to terms on condition that all their rights were acknowledged, and [5] *promised* that he would also persuade the king to become their friend. 15 And Maccabæus gave consent upon all the conditions which Lysias proposed to him, being careful of the *common* good; for whatsoever *requests* Maccabæus delivered in writing unto Lysias concerning the Jews the 16 king allowed. For the letters written unto the Jews from Lysias were to this effect:

Lysias unto the [6] people of the Jews, 17 greeting. John and Absalom, who were sent from you, having delivered the [7] petition written below, made request concerning the things signified 18 therein. What things soever therefore had need to be brought before the king I declared *to him*, and what 19 things were possible he allowed. If then ye will preserve your good will toward the state, henceforward also will I endeavour to contribute to *your* 20 good. [8] And on this behalf I have given order in detail, both to these men and to those *that are sent* from 21 me, to confer with you. Fare ye well. *Written* in the hundred forty and eighth year, on the four and twentieth day of *the month* [9] Dioscorinthius. 22 And the king's letter was in these words:

King Antiochus unto his brother Ly-23 sias, greeting. Seeing that our father passed unto the gods having the wish that the subjects of his kingdom [10] should be undisturbed and give themselves to the care of their own 24 affairs, we, having heard that the Jews do not consent to our father's purpose to turn them unto the *customs* of the Greeks, but choose rather their own manner of living, and make request that the *customs* of their law be 25 allowed unto them, — choosing therefore that this nation also should be free from [11] disturbance, we determine that their temple be restored to them, and that they live according to the customs that were in the days of their 26 ancestors. Thou wilt therefore do well to send *messengers* unto them and give them the right hand *of friendship*, that they, knowing our mind, may be of good heart, and gladly occupy themselves with the conduct of their own affairs.

27 And unto the nation the king's letter was after this manner:

King Antiochus to the senate of the Jews and to the other Jews, greeting. 28 If ye fare well, we have our desire: we ourselves also are in good health. 29 Menelaus informed us that your desire was to return home and follow your 30 own business. They therefore that depart home up to the thirtieth day of Xanthicus shall have our [12] friend-31 ship, with full permission that the Jews use their own *proper* meats and *observe their own* laws, even as heretofore; and none of them shall be in 32 any way molested for the things that have been ignorantly done. Moreover I have sent Menelaus also, that he 33 may encourage you. Fare ye well. *Written* in the hundred forty and eighth year, on the fifteenth day of Xanthicus. 34 And the Romans also sent unto them a letter in these words:

Quintus Memmius *and* Titus Mani-35 us, ambassadors of the Romans, unto the people of the Jews, greeting. In regard to the things which Lysias the king's kinsman granted you, we also

8 Or, But as to this

9 This name is not found elsewhere, and is perhaps corrupt

10 Or, should not be disquieted but

11 Or, disquiet

12 Gr. right hand.

36 give consent. But as for the things which he judged should be referred to the king, send one forthwith, after ye have advised thereof, that we may publish such *decrees* as befit your case; for we are on our way to An-
37 tioch. Wherefore send some with speed, that we also may learn what is
38 your mind. [1] Farewell. *Written* in the hundred forty and eighth year, on the fifteenth day of Xanthicus.

12 So when these covenants had been made, Lysias departed unto the king, and the Jews went about their husbandry.
2 But *certain* of the governors of districts, Timotheus and Apollonius the *son* of Gennæus, and Hieronymus also and Demophon, and beside them Nicanor the governor of Cyprus, would not suffer them to enjoy tranquillity
3 and live in peace. And men of Joppa perpetrated this great impiety: they invited the Jews that dwelt among them to go with their wives and children into the boats which they had provided, as though they had no ill
4 will towards them; and when [2] the Jews, [3] relying on the common decree of the city, accepted *the invitation*, as men desiring to live in peace and suspecting nothing, they took them out to sea and drowned them, *in number* not less than two hundred.
5 But when Judas heard of the cruelty done unto his fellow-countrymen, giving command to the men that were
6 with him and calling upon God the righteous Judge, he came against the murderers of his brethren, and set the haven on fire by night, and burned the boats, and put to the sword those
7 that had fled thither. But when the town was closed *against him*, he withdrew, intending to come again to root out the whole community of the men
8 of Joppa. But learning that the men of Jamnia were minded to do in like manner unto the Jews that sojourned
9 among them, he fell upon the Jamnites also by night, and set fire to the haven together with the fleet, so that the glare of the light was seen at Jerusalem, two hundred and forty furlongs distant.
10 Now when they had drawn off nine furlongs from thence, as they marched against Timotheus, *a host of* Arabians attacked him, no fewer than five thousand *footmen* and five hun-
11 dred horsemen. And when a sore battle had been fought, and Judas and his company by the help of God had good success, the nomads being overcome besought Judas to grant them friendship, promising to give *him* cattle, and to help [4] his people in
12 all other ways. So Judas, thinking that they would indeed be profitable in many things, agreed to live in

peace with them; and receiving pledges of friendship they departed
13 to their tents. And he also fell upon a certain city [5] Gephyrun, strong and fenced about with walls, and inhabited by a mixed multitude of divers nations; and it was named Caspin.
14 But they that were within, trusting to the strength of the walls and to their store of provisions, behaved themselves rudely toward Judas and them that were with him, railing, and furthermore blaspheming and speak-
15 ing impious words. But Judas and his company, calling upon the great Sovereign of the world, who without rams and cunning engines of war hurled down Jericho in the times of Joshua, rushed wildly against the
16 wall; and having taken the city by the will of God, they made unspeakable slaughter, insomuch that the adjoining lake, which was two furlongs broad, appeared to be filled with the deluge of blood.
17 And when they had drawn off seven hundred and fifty furlongs from thence, they made their way to Charax, unto the Jews that are called
18 [6] Tubieni. And Timotheus they found not in occupation of that district, for he had then departed from the district without accomplishing anything, but had left behind a garrison, and that a very strong one, in a certain post.
19 But Dositheus and Sosipater, who were of Maccabæus's captains, sallied forth and destroyed those that had been left by Timotheus in the strong-
20 hold, above ten thousand men. And Maccabæus, ranging his own army by bands, set [4] these two over the bands, and marched in haste against Timotheus, who had with him a hundred and twenty thousand footmen and two thousand and five hundred horsemen.
21 But when Timotheus heard of the inroad of Judas, he at once sent away the women and the children and also the baggage into the *fortress* called
22 [7] Carnion; for the place was hard to besiege and difficult of access by reason of the narrowness of the approaches on all sides. But when the band of Judas, who led the van, appeared in sight, and when terror came upon the enemy and fear, because the manifestation of him who beholdeth all things came upon them, they fled amain, carried this way and that, so that they were often hurt of their own men, and pierced with the
23 points of their swords. And Judas continued the pursuit the more hotly, putting the wicked wretches to the sword, and he destroyed as many as
24 thirty thousand men. But Timotheus himself, falling in with the company of Dositheus and Sosipater, besought them with much [8] crafty guile to let

[1] Gr. *Be in good health.*

[2] Gr. *they also.* [3] Gr. *after.*

[4] Gr. *them.*

[5] The relation between the names *Gephyrun* and *Caspin* is unknown, and perhaps the Greek text is corrupt. Compare *Gephyrun*, the name of a city of Gilead mentioned by Polybius, v. 70. 12; and *Casphor*, 1 Macc. v. 26, 36.

[6] That is, *men of Tob*: see Judg. xi. 3, 2 Sam. x. 6, and compare 1 Macc. v. 13.

[7] Compare *Carnain*, 1 Macc. v. 26, 43, 44.

[8] Gr. *jugglery*

him go with his life, because he had *in his power* the parents of many *of them* and the brethren of some: [1]otherwise, *said he*, little regard will [2]be
25 shewn to these. So when he had with many words confirmed the agreement to restore them without hurt, they let him go that they might save their brethren.

26 And *Judas*, marching against [3]Carnion and the temple of Atergatis, slew five and twenty thousand persons.
27 And after he had put these to flight and destroyed them, he marched against Ephron also, a strong city, [4]wherein were multitudes of people of all nations; and stalwart young men placed [5]on the walls made a vigorous defence; and there were great stores of engines and darts
28 there. But calling upon the Sovereign who with might breaketh in pieces the [6]strength of [7]the enemy, they got the city into their hands, and slew as many as twenty and five thousand of them that were within.
29 And setting out from thence they marched in haste against Scythopolis, which is distant from Jerusalem
30 six hundred furlongs. But when the Jews that were settled there testified of the good will that the Scythopolitans had shewn toward them, and of their kindly bearing *toward them* in
31 the times of their misfortune, they gave thanks, and further exhorted them to remain well affected toward the race for the future; and they went up to Jerusalem, the feast of weeks being close at hand.
32 But after the *feast* called Pentecost they marched in haste against Gor-
33 gias the governor of Idumæa: and he came out with three thousand footmen
34 and four hundred horsemen. And when they had set themselves in array, it came to pass that a few of the Jews
35 fell. And a certain Dositheus, one [8]of Bacenor's company, who was on horseback and a strong man, pressed hard on Gorgias, and taking hold of his cloke drew him along by main force; and while he was minded to take the accursed man alive, one of the Thracian horsemen bore down upon him and disabled his shoulder, and so Gorgias escaped unto [9]Marisa.
36 And when they that were with Esdris had been fighting long and were wearied out, Judas called upon the Lord to shew himself, fighting on their side and leading the van of the
37 battle; and *then* in the language of his fathers he raised the battle-cry joined with hymns, and rushing unawares upon the troops of Gorgias put them to flight.
38 And Judas gathering his army came unto the city of [10]Adullam; and as the seventh day was coming on, they

purified themselves according to the custom, and kept the sabbath there.
39 And on the day following, [11]at which time it had become necessary, Judas and his company came to take up the bodies of them that had fallen, [12]and in company with their kinsmen to bring them back unto the sepulchres
40 of their fathers. But under the garments of each one of the dead they found [13]consecrated tokens of the idols of Jamnia, which the law forbids the Jews to have aught to do with; and it became clear to all that it was for this cause that they had fallen.
41 All therefore, blessing the *works* of the Lord, the righteous Judge, who maketh manifest the things that are
42 hid, betook themselves unto supplication, beseeching that the sin committed might be wholly blotted out. And the noble Judas exhorted the multitude to keep themselves from sin, forsomuch as they had seen before their eyes what things had come to pass because of the sin of them that had
43 fallen. And when he had made a collection man by man to the sum of two thousand drachmas of silver, he sent unto Jerusalem to offer a sacrifice for sin, doing therein right well and honourably, in that he took
44 thought for a resurrection. For if he were not expecting that they that had fallen would rise again, it were superfluous and idle to pray for the dead.
45 (And if *he did it* looking unto an honourable memorial of gratitude laid up for them that [14]die [15]in godliness, holy and godly was the thought.) Wherefore he made the propitiation for them that had died, that they might be released from their sin.

13 In the hundred forty and ninth year tidings were brought to Judas and his company that Antiochus Eupator was coming with *great* multitudes against
2 Judæa, and with him Lysias his guardian and chancellor, [16]each having a Greek force, a hundred and ten thousand footmen, and five thousand and three hundred horsemen, and two and twenty elephants, and three hundred chariots armed with scythes.
3 And Menelaus also joined himself with them, and with great dissimulation encouraged Antiochus, not for the saving of his country, but because he thought that he would be set over the
4 government. But the King of kings stirred up the [17]passion of Antiochus against the wicked wretch; and when Lysias informed him that this man was the cause of all the evils, *the king* commanded to bring him unto Berœa, and [4]to put him to death after the
5 manner of that place. Now there is in that place a tower of fifty cubits high, full of ashes, and it had all round it a [18]gallery [19]descending sheer

---

[Left margin footnotes:]

[1] Gr. *and the result will be that these be disregarded.* The Greek text here is perhaps corrupt.

[2] Or, *have been shewn*

[3] Compare *Carnain*, 1 Macc. v. 26, 43, 44.

[4] The Greek text here is perhaps corrupt.

[5] Gr. *in front of.*

[6] Some authorities read *weight.*

[7] Or, *his enemies*

[8] The Greek text is uncertain.

[9] Compare 1 Macc. v. 66.

[10] Gr. *Odollam.*

[Right margin footnotes:]

[11] The Greek text here is uncertain.

[12] Or, *and to bring them back to be with their kinsmen in the sepulchres*

[13] Perhaps these were consecrated images of the idols.

[14] Gr. *fall asleep.*

[15] Or, *on the side of godliness*

[16] The Greek text here is corrupt.

[17] Or, *spirit*

[18] Gr. *contrivance or machine.*

[19] Or, *sloping steeply*

6 on every side into the ashes. Here him that is guilty of sacrilege, or hath attained a preeminence in any other evil deeds, they [1] all push forward 7 into destruction. By such a fate it befell the breaker of the law, Menelaus, to die, without obtaining so much as *a grave in* the earth, and 8 that right justly; for inasmuch as he had perpetrated many sins [2] against the altar, whose fire and whose ashes were holy, in ashes did he receive his death.

9 Now the king, [3] infuriated in spirit, was coming with intent to inflict on the Jews the very worst of the suffer-10 ings that had befallen *them* in his father's time. But when Judas heard of these things, he gave charge to the multitude to call upon the Lord day and night, *beseeching him,* if ever at any other time, so now to succour them that were at the point to be de-prived of the law and their country 11 and the holy temple, and not to suffer the people that had been but now a little while revived to fall into the 12 hands of those profane heathen. So when they had all done the same thing together, [4] beseeching the merciful Lord with weeping and fast-ings and prostration for three days without ceasing, Judas exhorted them and commanded they should join him 13 *for service.* And having gone apart with the elders he resolved that, be-fore the king's army should enter into Judæa and make themselves masters of the city, they should go forth and try the matter *in fight* by 14 the help of [5] God. And committing the decision to the [6] Lord of the world, and exhorting them that were with him to contend nobly even unto death for laws, temple, city, country, [7] commonwealth, he pitched his camp 15 by Modin. And having given out to his men the watchword, VICTORY IS GOD'S, with a chosen body of the bravest young men he fell upon *the camp* by night *and penetrated* to the king's [8] tent, and slew [1] *of* the [9] army as many as two thousand men, and [1] brought down the chiefest elephant with him that was in the [10] tower upon 16 him. And at last they filled the [9] army with terror and alarm, and 17 departed with good success. And this had been accomplished when the day was but now dawning, because of the Lord's protection that gave [11] Judas help.

18 But the king, having had a taste of the exceeding boldness of the Jews, made attempts by stratagem upon 19 their positions, and *upon* a strong fortress of the Jews at Bethsura; he advanced, was turned back, failed, 20 was defeated. And Judas conveyed such things as were necessary unto

21 them that were within. But Rhodo-cus, from the Jewish ranks, made known to the enemy the secrets *of his countrymen.* He was sought out, and 22 taken, and shut up in prison. The king treated with them in Bethsura the second time, gave his hand, took theirs, departed, attacked the forces 23 of Judas, was put to the worse, heard that Philip who had been left as chancellor in Antioch had become reckless, was confounded, made to the Jews an overture *of peace,* submitted himself and sware to acknowledge all their rights, came to terms with them and offered sacrifice, honoured the 24 sanctuary and the place, shewed kind-ness and graciously received Mac-cabæus, left Hegemonides governor from Ptolemais even unto the [12] Ger-25 renians, came to Ptolemais. The men of Ptolemais were displeased at the treaty, for they had exceeding great indignation *against the Jews* : they de-sired to annul the articles of the agree-26 ment. Lysias [13] came forward to speak, made the best defence that was possible, persuaded, pacified, made them well affected, departed unto Antioch. This was the issue of the inroad and departure of the king.

14 Now after a space of three years tidings were brought to Judas and his company that Demetrius the *son of* Seleucus, having sailed into the haven of Tripolis with a mighty host and a 2 fleet, had gotten possession of the country, having made away with An-tiochus and Lysias his guardian.

3 But one Alcimus, who had formerly been high priest, and had wilfully pol-luted himself in the times when there was no mingling *with the Gentiles,* considering that there was no deliver-ance for him in any way, nor any more 4 access unto the holy altar, came to king Demetrius in about the hundred and one and fiftieth year, presenting to him a chaplet of gold and a palm, and beside these *some* of the festal 5 olive boughs of the temple. And for that day he held his peace : but hav-ing gotten opportunity to further his own madness, being called by Deme-trius into a meeting of his council, and asked how the Jews stood affected and what they purposed, he answered 6 thereunto, Those of the Jews that be called [14] Hasidæans, whose leader is Judas Maccabæus, keep up war, and are seditious, not suffering the king-7 dom to find tranquillity. Wherefore, having laid aside mine ancestral glory, I mean the high priesthood, I 8 am now come [15] hither; first for the unfeigned care I have for the things that concern the king, and secondly because I have regard also to mine own fellow-citizens : for, through the unadvised dealing of those of whom

Side notes (left column):

[1] The Greek text here is probably corrupt.

[2] Gr. *about.*

[3] Some authorities read *indignant.*

[4] Gr. *and be-sought.*

[5] Some authorities read *the Lord.*
[6] Some authorities read *Creator.*
[7] Or, *mode of life*

[8] Gr. *court.*
[9] Gr. *camp.*
[10] Gr. *house.*

[11] Gr. *him.*

Side notes (right column):

[12] The form of this word is un-certain. Compare *Girzites* (or *Giz-rites*), 1 Sam. xxvii. 8. One manu-script reads *Gerra-renes.*
[13] Gr. *came forward to the tribune or judge-ment-seat.*

[14] That is, *Chasi-dim.*

[15] Some authori-ties read *a second time.*

I spake before, our whole race is in no 9 small misfortune. But do thou, O king, having informed thyself of these things severally, take thought both for our country and for our race, which 10 ¹ is surrounded *by foes*, according to the gracious kindness with which thou receivest all. For as long as Judas re 11 maineth alive, it is impossible that the state should find peace. And when he had spoken such words as these, at once ² the rest of the *king's* ³ Friends, having ill will against Judas, inflamed 12 Demetrius yet more. And forthwith appointing Nicanor, who had been master of the elephants, and making him governor of Judæa, he sent him 13 forth, giving him written instructions to make away with Judas himself and to scatter them that were with him, and to set up Alcimus as high priest 14 of the ⁴ great temple. And ⁵ those in Judæa that ⁶ had *before* driven Judas into exile thronged to Nicanor in flocks, supposing that the misfortunes and calamities of the Jews would be successes to themselves. 15 But when *the Jews* heard of Nica nor's inroad and the assault of the heathen, they sprinkled earth *upon their heads* and made solemn suppli cation to him who had established his own people for evermore, and who al way, making manifest his presence, upholdeth *them that are* his own por 16 tion. ⁷ And when the leader had given *his* commands, he straightway setteth out from thence, and joineth battle with them at a village *called* Lessau. 17 But Simon, the brother of Judas, had encountered Nicanor, ⁸ yet not till late, having received a check by rea son of the sudden consternation caus ed by his adversaries. 18 Nevertheless Nicanor, hearing of the manliness of them that were with Judas, and their courage in fighting for their country, shrank from bring ing the matter to the decision of the 19 sword. Wherefore he sent Posidonius and Theodotus and Mattathias to give 20 and receive pledges of friendship. So when these proposals had been long considered, and the leader had made the ⁹ troops acquainted therewith, and it appeared that they were all of like mind, they consented to the cove 21 nants. And they appointed a day on which to meet together by themselves. And a litter was borne forward from 22 each *army*; they set chairs of state; Judas stationed ʼarmed men ready in convenient places, lest haply there should suddenly be treachery on the part of the enemy; they held such 23 conference as was meet. Nicanor tarried in Jerusalem, and did nothing to cause disturbance, but dismissed the flocks of people that had gathered 24 together. And he kept Judas always

in his presence; he had gained a 25 hearty affection for the man; he urged him to marry and beget children; he married, settled quietly, took part in common life. 26 But Alcimus, perceiving the good will that was betwixt them, ¹⁰ and having got possession of the cove nants that had been made, came unto Demetrius and told him that Nicanor was ill affected toward the state, for he had appointed that conspirator against his kingdom, Judas, to be his 27 successor. And the king, falling into a rage, and being exasperated by the calumnies of that most wicked man, wrote to Nicanor, signifying that he was displeased at the covenants, and commanding him to send Maccabæus prisoner unto Antioch in all haste. 28 And when this message came to Ni canor, he was confounded, and was sore troubled at the thought of annul ling the articles that had been agreed upon, the man having done no wrong; 29 but because there was no dealing against the king, he watched his time to execute this purpose by strata 30 gem. But Maccabæus, when he per ceived that Nicanor was behaving more harshly in his dealings with him, and that he had become ruder in his customary bearing, understanding that this harshness came not of good, gathered together not a few of his men, and concealed himself from Ni canor. 31 But the other, ¹¹ when he became aware that he had been bravely de feated by the stratagem of ¹² Judas, came to the ⁴ great and holy temple, while the priests were offering the usual sacrifices, and commanded them 32 to deliver up the man. And when they declared with oaths that they had no knowledge where the man was whom 33 he sought, he stretched forth his right hand toward the sanctuary, and sware this oath : If ye will not deliver up to me Judas as a prisoner, I will lay this ¹³ temple of God even with the ground, and will break down the altar, and I will erect here a temple unto ¹⁴ Bacchus 34 for all to see. And having said this he departed. But the priests, stretch ing forth their hands toward heaven, called upon him that ever fighteth for 35 our nation, in these words : Thou, ¹⁵ O Lord of the universe, who in thyself hast need of nothing, wast well pleas ed that a sanctuary of thy ¹⁶ habitation 36 should be set among us; so now, O holy Lord of all hallowing, keep un defiled for ever this house that hath been lately cleansed. 37 Now information was given to Ni canor against one Razis, an elder of Jerusalem, ¹⁷ as being a lover of his countrymen and a man of very good report, and one called Father of the

---

Left margin notes:

¹ Or, *is hardly bestead*

² Or, *the king's Friends likewise*

³ See ch. viii. 9.

⁴ Gr. *greatest.*

⁵ Or, *they that had fled before Judas all over Judæa thronged*

⁶ See ch. v. 27.

⁷ The Greek text of this verse and the next is corrupt.

⁸ Or, *and had received a check, yet not till late by reason of the sudden consternation of his adversaries*

⁹ Or, *people* Gr. *multitudes.*

Right margin notes:

¹⁰ Or, *and the cove nants that had been made, took oc casion and came*

¹¹ Or, *though he was con scious that he had been nobly de feated by*

¹² Gr. *the man.*

¹³ Or, *chapel* Gr. *in closure.*

¹⁴ Gr. *Dio nysus.*

¹⁵ Or, *O Lord, who in thyself hast no need of the uni verse*

¹⁶ Gr. *taber nacling.*

¹⁷ Or, *who was a lover*

Jews for his good will *toward them.*
38 For in the former times when there
was no mingling *with the Gentiles* he
had been accused of *cleaving to* the
Jews' religion, and had jeoparded
body and life with all earnestness for
39 the religion of the Jews. And Nicanor,
wishing to make evident the ill will
that he bare unto the Jews, sent above
40 five hundred soldiers to take him; for
he thought by taking him to inflict a
41 calamity upon them. But when the
[1] troops were on the point of taking
the tower, and were forcing the door
of the court, and bade bring fire and
burn the doors, he being surrounded
on every side fell upon his sword,
42 choosing rather to die nobly than to
fall into the hands of the wicked
wretches, and suffer outrage unworthy
43 of his own nobleness: but since he
missed his stroke through the excite-
ment of the struggle, and the crowds
were now rushing within the door, he
ran bravely up to the wall and cast
himself down manfully among the
44 crowds. But as they quickly gave
back, a space was made, and he fell on
45 the middle of [2] his side. And having
yet breath within him, and being inflamed with passion, he rose up, and
though his blood gushed out in
streams and his wounds were grievous, he ran through the crowds, and
46 standing upon a steep rock, when as
his blood was now well nigh spent,
he drew forth his bowels *through the*
wound, and taking them in both his
hands he shook them at the crowds;
and calling upon him who is Lord of
[3] the life and the [4] spirit to restore
him [5] these again, he thus died.

15 But Nicanor, hearing that Judas and
his company were in the region of
Samaria, resolved to set upon them
with all security on the day of rest.
2 And when the Jews that were compelled to follow him said, O destroy
not so savagely and barbarously, but
give due glory to the day which he
that beholdeth all things hath [6] honoured and hallowed above *other days*;
3 then the thrice-accursed wretch asked
if there were a Sovereign in heaven
that had commanded to keep the sab-
4 bath day. And when they declared,
There is the Lord, living himself a
Sovereign in heaven, who bade *us* ob-
5 serve the seventh day; then saith the
other, I also am a sovereign upon the
earth, [7] who *now* command to take up
arms and execute the king's business.
Nevertheless he prevailed not to execute his [8] cruel purpose.
6 And Nicanor, [9] bearing himself
haughtily in all vaingloriousness, had
determined to set up a monument of
complete victory over Judas and all
7 them that were with him: but Maccabæus still trusted unceasingly, with all

[1] Or, *people* Gr. *multitudes.*
[2] Or, *the void place*
[3] Or, *life and spirit*
[4] Or, *breath*
[5] Some authorities read *the same.*
[6] Or, *honoured above* other days *as a hallowed day*
[7] Or, *that commandeth*
[8] Or, *miserable*
[9] Gr. *carrying his neck high.*

hope that he should obtain help from
8 the Lord. And he exhorted his company not to be fearful at the [10] inroad
of the heathen, but, keeping in mind
the help which of old they had ofttimes received from heaven, so now
also to look for the victory which
would come unto them from the Al-
9 mighty; and comforting them out of
the law and the prophets, and withal
putting them in mind of the conflicts
that they had maintained, he made
10 them more eager *for the battle.* And
when he had roused their [11] spirit, he
gave them *his* commands, at the same
time pointing out the perfidiousness of
the heathen and their breach of their
11 oaths. And arming each one of them,
not so much with the sure defence of
shields and spears as with the encouragement *that lieth* in good words, and
moreover relating to them a dream
[12] worthy to be believed, he made them
12 all exceeding glad. And the vision of
that *dream* was this: *He saw* Onias,
him that was high priest, a noble and
good man, reverend in bearing, yet
gentle in manner and well-spoken, and
exercised from a child in all points
of virtue, with outstretched hands in-
voking *blessings* on the whole body of
13 the Jews: thereupon *he saw* a man
appear, of venerable age and exceeding glory, and wonderful and most
majestic was the dignity around him:
14 and Onias answered and said, This
is the lover of the brethren, he who
prayeth much for the people and the
holy city, Jeremiah the prophet of
15 God: and Jeremiah stretching forth
his right hand delivered to Judas
a sword of gold, and in giving it
16 addressed *him* thus, Take the holy
sword, a gift from God, wherewith
thou shalt smite down the adversaries.
17 And being encouraged by the words
of Judas, which were of a lofty strain,
and able to incite unto virtue and to
stir the souls of the young unto manly
courage, they determined [13] not to
carry on a campaign, but nobly to
bear down upon *the enemy,* and fighting hand to hand with all courage
bring the matter to an issue, because
the city and the sanctuary and the
18 temple were in danger. For their
fear for wives and children, and furthermore for brethren and kinsfolk,
was in less account with them; but
greatest and first was their fear for
19 the consecrated sanctuary. And they
also that were shut up in the city were
in no light distress, being troubled because of the encounter in the open
ground.
20 And when all were now waiting for
the decision of the issue, and the enemy had already joined battle, and the
army had been set in array, and the
[14] elephants [15] brought back to a con-

[10] Or, *assault*
[11] Or, *passion*
[12] Or, *most worthy . . . all glad*
[13] Or, *not to go out to battle, but nobly to engage within* their lines, &c. The Greek text of this passage is uncertain.
[14] Gr. *beasts.*
[15] Or, *stationed for convenient action*

¹ Or,
in line
² Gr.
multi-
tudes.
³ Gr.
beasts.

⁴ Gr.
camp.

⁵ Or, be-
wilder-
ment

venient post, and the horsemen drawn
21 up ¹on the flank, Maccabæus, perceiving the presence of the ²troops,
and the various arms with which they
were equipped, and the savageness of
the ³elephants, holding up his hands
unto heaven called upon the Lord
that worketh wonders, recognising
that *success* cometh not by arms, but
that, according as *the Lord* shall
judge, he gaineth the victory for them
22 that are worthy. And calling upon
God he said after this manner: Thou,
O Sovereign Lord, didst send thine
angel in the time of Hezekiah king of
Judæa, and he slew of the ⁴host of
Sennacherib as many as a hundred
23 fourscore and five thousand; so now
also, O Sovereign of the heavens, send
a good angel before us to bring terror
24 and trembling: through the greatness
of thine arm let them be stricken with
dismay that with blasphemy are come
hither against thy holy people. And
25 as he ended with these words, Nicanor
and his company advanced with trum-
26 pets and pæans; but Judas and his
company joined battle with the enemy
27 with invocation and prayers. And con-
tending with their hands, and praying
unto God with their hearts, they slew
no less than thirty and five thousand
men, being made exceeding glad by
the manifestation of God.
28 And when the engagement was over,
and they were returning again with
joy, they recognised Nicanor lying
29 dead in full armour; and there arose
a shout and ⁵tumult, and *then* they
blessed the Sovereign *Lord* in the
30 language of their fathers. And he
that in all things was in body and soul
the foremost champion of his fellow-
citizens, he that kept through life the
good will of his youth toward his
countrymen, commanded to cut off
Nicanor's head, and his hand with the
shoulder, and bring them to Jerusalem.
31 And when he had arrived there, and
had called his countrymen together

and set the priests before the altar,
he sent for them that were in the
32 citadel; and shewing the head of the
vile Nicanor, and the hand of that
profane man, which with proud brags
he had stretched out against the holy
33 house of the Almighty, and cutting
out the tongue of the impious Nicanor,
he said that he would give ⁶it by pieces
to the birds, and hang up the ⁷rewards
of his madness over against the sanc-
34 tuary. And they all *looking up* unto
heaven blessed ⁸the Lord who had
manifested himself, saying, Blessed be
35 undefiled. And he hanged Nicanor's
head and shoulder from the citadel, a
sign, evident unto all and manifest,
36 of the help of the Lord. And they all
ordained with a common decree in no
wise to let this day pass undistin-
guished, but to mark with honour the
thirteenth day of the twelfth month (it
is called Adar in the Syrian tongue),
the day before the day of Mordecai.

37 THIS then having been the issue of
the attempt of Nicanor, and the city
having from those times been held by
the Hebrews, I also will here make an
38 end of my book. And if *I have written*
well and to the point in my story, this
is what I myself desired; but if meanly
and indifferently, this is all I could at-
39 tain unto. For as it is ⁹distasteful
to drink wine alone and in like manner
again *to drink* water *alone*, ¹⁰while
the mingling of wine with water at
once ¹¹giveth full pleasantness to the
flavour; so also the fashioning of the
language delighteth the ears of them
that read the story.
    And here shall be the end.

⁶ Or,
them
⁷ The
Greek
text hen
is per-
haps
corrupt.
⁸ Or,
the
glorious
Lord

⁹ Or,
hurtful
¹⁰ Gr.
but even
as.
¹¹ Or,
addeth
delight
to the
benefit

THE END OF APOCRYPHA.

Was Jesus Influenced by Buddhism?
A Comparative Study of the Lives and
Thoughts of Gautama and Jesus
by Dwight Goddard.

Christianity as we know it today differs from the eastern religions in many ways. There seems to be a huge gap between east and west when comparing religious traditions. Dwight Goddard manages to bridge that gap, however, with this revealing book. Much of what we find in Christianity today had been added to the faith on top of the original teachings of Jesus. What is interesting is that Buddhism has suffered with the same problems of additions and distortions over the centuries as Christianity did, and has also failed to uphold some of the original teachings of its founder. A powerful religion sprung up based on his teachings and flourished half a millennium before Jesus was ever born. Five hundred years is a long time for a religion to spread and flourish, so Jesus could have easily been influenced by Buddhist teachings as proposed by this book. There were many years in the life of Jesus that remain to this day unaccounted for. Goddard also puts forth evidence that the Essenes, of whom Jesus had contact with and may have been a member himself, had strong Buddhist influences. If either (or both) of these scenarios is true, then the parallels between Jesus and the Buddha are more than just a coincidence.

BT-271 · ISBN 1-58509-027-1 · 252 pages
6 x 9 · trade paper · $19.95

Printed in the United Kingdom
by Lightning Source UK Ltd.
128349UK00002B/155/A

9 781585 090532